The Daily Telegraph

GUIDE TO

BRITAIN'S HISTORIC HOUSES

The Daily Telegraph

GUIDE TO

BRITAIN'S HISTORIC HOUSES

DAMIEN NOONAN

AURUM PRESS

To Teresa and Pete, Roz and Mike,
Al and Ellie, and Abi, with much love

Illustrations:
Cover: Kingston Lacy, Dorset
Frontispiece: Oxburgh Hall, Norfolk
This page: Athelhampton, Dorset
Contents page: Holkham Hall, Norfolk
Page 8: Hardwick Hall, Derbyshire

First published 2004 by Aurum Press Limited,
25 Bedford Avenue, London WC1B 3AT

Maps supplied by Map Creation Ltd, Maidenhead

A catalogue record for this book is available from the British Library.

ISBN 1 85410 963 4 paperback
ISBN 1 84513 034 0 hardback
Printed and bound in Italy

10   9   8   7   6   5   4   3   2   1

2008   2007   2006   2005   2004

Foreword

Welcome to this book.

 First, I hope you have as many enjoyable days out with the help of this book, and make as many fascinating discoveries along the way, as I have while carrying out the research for it.

 There are many hundreds of historic houses open to the public in England, Wales, Scotland and Northern Ireland, but some are open for just a few days each year; so this book concentrates on those that are open regularly, giving the greatest number of people the opportunity to visit. Inevitably this means that some of you will find that a favourite is missing from these pages, especially if it's a house that opens infrequently and doesn't advertize the fact widely, but I hope

that there are no major omissions; and if you do feel I've  missed somewhere that thoroughly deserves to be included, please do write, care of the publisher, and I'll consider your suggestions for a future edition.

 What I have tried to do is give a flavour of what it's like to visit each of the houses covered in this book. I've tried to say a little about when each house was built, and in what style of architecture; to give an impression of any great treasures in the way of art, furniture and

decoration to be found there; to say a little about the people who built the house and lived in it; to decsribe the setting; and to draw your attention to any interesting quirks or outstanding features that you would not want to miss while visiting.

Of course, the limited space in this book means that many stories have to go untold, and often there is much more to discover when you get there. All I can hope is that I have managed to make the most remarkable houses sound as interesting as they are, and that I will draw your attention to at least a few that you might, perhaps, otherwise have missed. And if that happens, and you enjoy your days out exploring Britain's past, all the hard work will have been worthwhile.

Contents

Key map

to the regions of Britain as used in this book

Coming full circle: Penrhyn Castle in North Wales, built in 1820–45, is modelled on the first great secular buildings in Britain – the castles built by the Normans in the 11th and 12th centuries

Introduction, part one: architecture and architects

A brief history of the house

Moats and halls, 1280-1514

From the very earliest times, a British nobleman's home was his castle. It had to be defensible because the country was still largely lawless and there was an ever-present threat from neighbours with dynastic ambitions and a covetous eye on one's cattle. At the same time, a great house was built not just as a place to live, but also as an expression of wealth and prestige – to impress friends, get one up on rivals, make it perfectly clear to the common people who was in charge.

These themes go right back into prehistory, to even before the coming of the Romans. Celtic chiefs in England and Wales built large, round houses defended by ditches and pallisades; their counterparts on the coastal fringes of Scotland went even further, constructing castle-like stone towers known as brochs. With the Roman invasion of AD44 and the eventual subjugation of the British

chieftains, who were banned from carrying weapons and made subject to central law, came the first real stately homes in Britain – the Roman villas, generally built not by Roman incomers but by native grandees adopting Roman ways. Like the medieval manor houses, they were really farmhouses, at the centre of large agricultural estates; but they were also expressions of the artistic taste and social aspirations of their owners.

After the Conquest in 1066, the Norman lords lived in their castles: centres of feudal power more than houses. Not until the 1400s, when the upheavals of the Wars of the Roses and the Peasants' Revolt were over, was there again sufficient peace in the land for the houses of great men to be built without moats and gatehouses, walls and pallisades. The earliest houses to survive in Britain (castles excepted), and among the most beautiful, are the moated or fortified manor houses of the 1200s, 1300s and 1400s. Possibly the oldest in Britain to remain in anything like its original state is

Stokesay Castle in Shropshire, built in the 1280s by Lawrence of Ludlow, the greatest wool merchant in the land at a time when wool was England's largest export and its main source of wealth. Lawrence's house had a moat and battlements – he applied to Edward I for a Licence to Crenellate in 1291 – but in all other respects is really a manor house rather than a castle.

*Stokesay Castle
1280–1300*

Stokesay is typical of the British idea of a house before Elizabethan times in that it has a hall at its heart – indeed, the hall *is* the house. Usually referred to in most houses that have one as the great hall, to reflect its central role in the house, the hall was the main living space for most of the household, most of the time. Meals were taken communally here, with the lord and his family, along with any senior members of the household and honoured guests, sitting at a high table on a slightly raised dais at the end of the hall furthest from the door, and everyone else – servants, estate workers, visitors – seated on benches at the long, 'refectory'-style tables along the walls of the body of the hall. Most of these people would also bed down for the night in the hall, and spend any indoor leisure time during the day here, too.

*Penshurst Place
1341 (hall)*

Chimneys were not yet in widespread use, and the hall was heated by a fire in an open central hearth. Such a hearth survives, and often still has a roaring log fire, at Penshurst Place in Kent, in the superb hall built in 1341 by John de Poultney, four times Lord Mayor of London. Smoke gathered in the eaves and escaped through a vent in the middle of the roof, covered by a louvre – although at Clevedon Court in Somerset, built in the 1320s, ingenious vents at either end of the roof can still be seen.

*Lower Brockhampton
1380–1400*

To reduce draughts from the door, which was set at one end of the hall, there was a separating screen, usually made of wood and often elaborately carved, with doorways cut in it. This created a passageway known as the screens passage separating the hall from doorways leading to service rooms at the end of the hall – a buttery or pantry, in which food could be prepared for the table, and storage rooms for food and drink. The kitchen was usually in a separate building, since a kitchen was the most likely place for a fire to break out.

*Haddon Hall
1370–1500*

The lord and his family had a private apartment, consisting of one or more rooms and usually placed on the first floor, where they could sleep, pass their leisure time and

*Little Moreton Hall
1480s, 1559–80*

receive guests. This private apartment usually had large windows and was known, perhaps because it was designed to get the benefit of the sun, as a 'solar'. Eventually, as fashions changed, a private dining room or parlour became increasingly important; the glorious timber-framed Little Moreton Hall in Cheshire, built in the 1480s, has such a parlour, with a wonderful bay window added in 1559.

Before long, a private dining room and other reception rooms for the exclusive use of the owner of the house, his family and his guests would become more important than the hall itself; yet the hall still remained a key part of the house in Elizabethan times, when its original function had already been superseded – and even in the great Palladian houses of the 1700s, in the form of the entrance hall, it was often the room where most effort was made to impress visitors.

Four other themes that would play a key part in the great houses of Elizabethan times began to emerge in the 1400s. First, the rule of law was stronger and defences were not such a priority. There is a moat at Lower Brockhampton, Herefordshire, a small, pretty timber-framed manor built in 1380–1400 by John Domulton, a local landowner; but its gatehouse was added much later and is a frivolity rather than a necessity. The builders of the even humbler hall-houses of Kent and Sussex, many of them ironmasters of the Weald, clearly had no need to think of defence.

Windows, meanwhile, were getting bigger: glass was more readily available, but still very expensive, so large expanses of glass in a house were a sign of wealth.

Fireplaces and chimneys were being added, to replace smoky old open hearths. And where older houses had been made of timber or stone, brick was now fashionable, having arrived in eastern England from Germany and Holland in the late 1300s: it was used to build Tattershall Castle, Lincolnshire, in the 1430s, and for the remarkable gatehouse at Oxburgh Hall, Norfolk, in the 1480s.

The coming of the Renaissance, 1514–1580

There were no 'architects' in Britain in the 1400s, nor yet in the century that followed (indeed, the first was Inigo Jones, who brought back classical ideas from Italy and applied them to buildings in England in the early 1600s). Instead, houses were built mostly by craftsmen using local materials and traditional techniques, while the greatest buildings – castles, cathedrals and churches – were created by 'master-masons'; either monastic, in which case their names went unrecorded, or military, such as Maurice the Builder, who constructed vast keeps for Henry II in the late 1100s, or the Master of St George, who tried to make Edward I's dream of the perfect castle into reality in the late 1200s.

Both monastic and military masons brought in new ideas from Europe, but castles were largely practical buildings, their function dictating their form; so the only 'aesthetic' in British architecture was that which inspired the soaring arches and lofty pinnacles of cathedrals and churches – a style known as 'gothic'.

Eventually, these two native architectural traditions – the organic, local, practical style of medieval castles and manors, and the gothic of cathedrals – would come to be seen as the true architecture of Britain. But as Renaissance Italy rediscovered the art and philosophy of the classical world, British architecture set out, tentatively at first, on a path that would eventually see the adoption of classical forms as the only truly noble way to build, and would inspire the creation of arguably the greatest British houses, the Palladian and neo-classical villas of the 1700s.

Inevitably, though, Henry VIII must have his say first. With his divorces from both Catherine of Aragon and the Roman Catholic church in 1532–3, Henry ensured

Montacute, Somerset, built in 1601: one of the most pleasing of the later Elizabethan manors

that England was cut off from the direct influence of the new Renaissance ideas that were transforming Italy. Instead, these arrived via intermediaries, mostly French, and were applied superficially to fundamentally traditional English buildings. Henry's palace at Hampton Court, Surrey, begun in 1514 by Cardinal Wolsey and completed by Henry in the 1530s, was still a medieval building, its halls at its heart; but it is adorned with Renaissance decoration, such as the round terracotta plaques depicting Roman emperors on the Anne Boleyn gate, built in 1521. At the same time, the classical idea of symmetry began to make an impact on some houses of the 1520s, with the traditionally offset entrance to the great hall being replaced, rather impractically, by a central doorway.

Scotland was not quite so isolated from European influence. At Falkland Palace, Fife, in 1536–41, King James V built what was then the finest Renaissance building in Britain. The underlying form was still essentially traditional, and Falkland is more a castle than anything else; but inside the courtyard, completed for James by two French master-masons, Moise Martyne and Nicholas Roy, it has an elegant symmetry, with column-like buttresses dividing the face of each wing into regular bays, decorated with sculpted roundels of male and female figures to give a Renaissance flourish.

After Henry VIII's death in 1547, England was ruled for two years by Lord Protector Somerset, whose house in The Strand, London, built in 1547–52, was the first true classical building in Britain. It was demolished in the 1800s, but engravings show an extraordinarily modern building, almost like a Georgian terrace: completely symmetrical, topped with a balustrade that hid the roof, and with the gateway in the centre in the form of a Roman triumphal arch. It had widespread influence in the coming decades, not least on two of Somerset's proteges: his steward, Sir John Thynne, who built Longleat; and his secretary, William Cecil, who built Burghley House (more will be said of both houses shortly). It also influenced his successor as Lord Protector, the Duke of Northumberland, who sent his employee John Shute to Italy in 1550 to study buildings ancient and modern. One result was Shute's book *The First and Chief Groundes of Architecture,* published in 1563, which was the first in Britain to describe and illustrate the classical orders –

Hampton Court
1514–1530s

Falkland Palace
1536–41

Burghley House
1555–87

Kirby Hall
1570–3

Breamore
1583

that is, the different kinds of column (the plain Doric, the scroll-like Ionic and the extravagant, vegetal Corinthian).

The greatest of the first generation of Renaissance-influenced houses in England to survive is Burghley in Lincolnshire, built in 1555–87 by William Cecil, Chief Secretary of State to Queen Elizabeth from 1558 and her Lord Treasurer from 1572. Again, its Renaissance decorative detail is purely superficial, but it is also on an immense scale and unbelievably extravagant. The house takes the form of four ranges around a central courtyard; the interior of the courtyard has Italianate arches running all round and is dominated by a massive three-storey gatehouse, with the classical orders illustrated on each storey. Apparently the gatehouse still wasn't prominent enough for Cecil, however, so he added a clocktower and topped it with a bizarre spire-like obelisk. (Visits to Burghley don't include the courtyard, unfortunately, so it is best glimpsed from the window of the ante-room to the chapel.)

The Elizabethan golden age, 1580–1601

Traditional, Tudor-style fortified manor houses were still built in Elizabeth's reign, but with the peace and prosperity of her later years came a golden age in which the true country house first appeared, and some of the finest houses ever built in England were constructed. They fall into two types: the classic Elizabethan manor house, built to an E-plan; and a number of very large mansions known as 'prodigy houses'.

The typical Elizabethan manor, such as Breamore in Hampshire, built in 1583 by Sir William Dodington, is made of red brick – a practical material, since bricks could be made on-site from local clay, as well as a trendy one. It has large, showy chimney-stacks and big windows – both statements of wealth as well as welcome comforts (natural light had always been at a premium in the small-windowed houses of the past, and good fires must have been essential since Britain was experiencing a miniature ice age, with 'frost fairs' frequently held in winter in London on a frozen River Thames).

The E-plan facade, with two large bays projecting on either side and a smaller one in the middle, is often said to be a tribute to the Queen, referring to the first letter of her name; but its symmetry also shows the classical influence, and it is very practical, with the large bay windows bringing lots of light into the main rooms.

Inside, the hall was now more of an entrance hall, and only the servants took their meals there; but it was still the most important room in the house, and the place where the owner could display his wealth and prestige through bold architectural statements: immense fireplaces, splendid plasterwork ceilings and friezes, and heraldic references to ancestors. The entrance was still offset at one end of the hall, and divided from it by a screens passage; at the beautiful Burton Agnes Hall in Yorkshire, built in 1601–10 by Sir Henry Griffiths, the door was cleverly hidden at the side of one of the bays, so as not to disturb the symmetry of the front; while on the outside, above the door, was a display of the classical orders as well as the coats of arms of the builder and his wife, alongside those of the Queen.

Almost as impressive a public space as the great hall was a new innovation – the long gallery. Usually placed at the top of the house, with excellent views, and often provided with particularly good windows, the long gallery is said to have been used as a place for taking indoor exercise when the weather was bad. It was also an obvious place to hang family portraits, becoming the ancestor of the picture gallery. One of the finest is at Montacute in Somerset, a lovely E-plan manor built in stone in about 1601 by Edward Phelips, a Speaker of the House of Commons under James I; appropriately, its long gallery is now used to display portraits of the era from the National Portrait Gallery's collections.

Throughout the Elizabethan house, walls were decorated with wood panelling or tapestries, or both. The Renaissance influence was often evident in the panelling, which might be in the form of classical arcades; but the plasterwork of the ceilings is frequently in the form of ornate strapwork, influenced by Flemish models (and even more so in Jacobean times). Possibly the finest plaster ceiling in the country is in the Queen's state bedroom at Burton Agnes; it's in the sort of stylized naturalism that inspired the Arts and Crafts movement in the 1800s, with delicately intertwined stems of honeysuckle that actually loop out of the ceiling at points.

With the more dramatically grand 'prodigy houses', we meet the man I have taken the liberty of describing at points in this book as 'the first great English architect', Sir Robert Smythson. He wasn't, of course, exactly an architect, but more a builder, or master mason, in the old tradition; and his clients had as much say in the design of their houses as he did. But he certainly brought an individual style which recurs, and can be recognized by an expert eye, to all the houses he worked on.

LITTLE IS KNOWN about Robert Smythson beyond the facts that he was born in 1535, possibly the son of a master mason from Westmoreland, and died in 1614 at Wollaton, near Nottingham, where he settled after helping to create the extraordinary Wollaton Hall for Sir Francis Willoughby, becoming some kind of general manager and administrator to the Willoughby family while continuing his architectural career as, in effect, a highly respected consultant. His memorial in Wollaton church, incidentally, describes him as an 'Architector and Survayor'.

The earliest house he is known to have worked on is Longleat in Wiltshire, built in 1568–80 by Sir John Thynne, where Smythson worked in tandem with the French stone-mason Allen Maynard to create the wonderfully restrained facades, which blend classical elegance with an almost modern functionality. Longleat still looks much as it did when it was built (on the outside; it has been greatly altered inside) and is still one of the handsomest houses ever created. Smythson also remodelled the castle at Old Wardour in Wiltshire in about 1576–8 before leaving Longleat in 1580 and starting work at Wollaton (probably that same year, although there is no record of him there until 1582).

Wollaton, completed in about 1588, is a little freakish in appearance, thanks largely to the astonishing 'high hall' plonked on the top, which was probably an afterthought. Equally odd, in its own way, is Smythson's other famous creation: Hardwick Hall in Derbyshire, built for the redoubtable Bess of Hardwick in 1590–9. Where Wollaton is lavishly ornamented, perhaps a little too much so, Hardwick is almost excessively plain, its vast expanses of glass and clean, straight lines giving it something of the look of a 1930s factory. Perhaps in each case the wishes of the client were the main driving force.

Where Hardwick introduces something rather new is in the layout of the great hall.

Longleat
1568–80

Sir Robert Smythson,
Allen Maynard

Wollaton Hall
1580–8

Sir Robert Smythson

HardwickHall
1590–9

Sir Robert Smythson

Montacute
1601

Burton Agnes
1601–10

Sir Robert Smythson

Instead of running widthways across the front of the house, with its entrance at one end, it is set lengthways through the middle of the house, with the door in the centre of one of the short sides. It's an intriguing pre-echo of the layout of later, Palladian houses; whether it was Smythson's idea or Bess's, we will never know.

Equally unusual is the arrangement of all the most important state rooms at the top of the house, which seems likely to have been Bess's idea, since the neighbouring Hardwick Old Hall – remodelled just before the new hall was built – has a similar layout. But what makes Hardwick really impressive today is the fact that the interiors are so little changed, with some of the finest plasterwork in England and lots of original panelling and tapestries.

The Jacobeans and Jones, 1603–1687

The richest and most powerful Jacobeans built their own 'prodigy houses' very like those of the Elizabethans, except perhaps that brick was more widely used. The biggest of them all was Audley End in Essex, built in 1603–16 by Lord Suffolk, Lord Treasurer to James I. It was an immense place, but most of it has been demolished; once again, the great hall is on the traditional pattern but making a stab at classical symmetry, with a large oriel window at the centre and two-storey porches at either end, one the real entrance, the other effectively a sham.

Finest of the houses of the era is Hatfield in Hertfordshire, built by Robert Cecil, the son of the builder of Burghley, after his appointment as Lord Treasurer and Chief Secretary of State to King James – and after the king had taken a shine to Cecil's extraordinary house at Theobald's (itself demolished many years ago). It is still on the old pattern, with the hall at its heart, but on its south front – originally the entrance front (the far plainer, uglier north front is now used) – it has a welcoming Renaissance-style open loggia, as well as the usual three-storey entranceway displaying the classical orders.

Equally old-fashioned is another house by the man primarily responsible for Hatfield, Roger Lyminge – Blickling Hall in Norfolk, built in 1619–25 for Sir Henry Hobart, a successful London man of law.

Far more interesting, however, in that it set the pattern for what was to follow was Bolsover Castle, created between 1612 and 1634 by John Smythson, son of the great 'Architector and Survayor' Robert, and Sir Charles Cavendish, son of Bess of Hardwick – and continued after Sir Charles's death in 1617 by his son, William. Bolsover consists, essentially, of two parts, both of which serve as interesting pointers to directions in which houses would go in the future.

The first part is an astonishing pretend-castle, intended apparently as a kind of play-house for a generation of noblemen obsessed with medieval chivalry. In the fan-vaults of its hall, it shows the first flicker of the gothic revival; and at the same time it is the first in a long line of mock-castles that would end in Sir Edwin Lutyens's Castle Drogo in Devon almost exactly 300 years later.

The second part is a range added in 1629–34, containing a huge long gallery. In 1618–19, William sent John Smythson on a trip to London, where he made drawings and took notes of all the latest styles appearing in the city's buildings. Chief among these was a style that was later labelled 'artisan mannerism', imported from the Low Countries and characterized by extravagantly fancy features such as Dutch gables (first recorded in Britain on a house in Holborn drawn by Smythson on his visit to London in 1619) and balcony windows with pediments. Smythson added a few mannerist touches of his own to the outside of the new range at Bolsover, most notably a series of peculiar cannon-like 'rusticated' (rough stone) columns. The style would remain a feature of country houses for many years to come; but it was about to be upstaged, for those in the know, by a completely new way of looking at buildings.

INIGO JONES WAS the first true architect in that he worked in a way that would be imitated by all those that were to follow: the buildings he designed were his own creations, not those of the client who employed him; he was an educated man who travelled in Europe to develop his own ideas about building; and he was equipped with the artistic skills to record those influences and translate his ideas on to paper before setting out on a project.

Little is known about Jones's early life, other than that he was born in London in

1573, the son of a Smithfield clothmaker. Somehow he managed to obtain the patronage of the Earl of Pembroke and was able to spend a number of years in Italy, returning in 1603 with an artistic reputation he may have earned while working as a masque designer in Florence: from 1605 he was employed in exactly that role by James I's queen, Anne of Denmark. His first known architectural designs are from around 1608, and presumably it was his first-hand knowledge of Italian art and architecture that gained him the position of surveyor to the heir to the throne, Prince Henry, in 1610.

The Prince died young in 1612, and in 1613 Jones was chosen by Thomas Howard, Earl of Arundel, one of the most important artistic patrons of his day, to accompany him on a trip first to Heidelberg, where the Earl was to deliver the king's daughter, Princess Elizabeth, to her new husband, and then on to Italy, to spend a year touring the cities. In this time Jones was able to deepen his appreciation of the principles of classical architecture: for what interested him was not Italy's new buildings, but the antique models that had influenced the Venetian architect Andrea Palladio. Jones was the first English Palladian.

BORN IN PADUA in 1508, Palladio had trained first as a mason and then as an architect, earning commissions to build palaces and villas for the aristocracy before turning his hand to religious buildings in the 1560s. He was not only influenced by the great buildings of ancient Rome, but also gave much thought to the principles of 'harmonic proportions' that governed their size and shape. In 1570, the same year that he was appointed architectural consultant to the Venetian Republic, Palladio published his *Four Books of Architecture*, which would have an enormous influence on the coming generations of English architects. Jones's copy, with annotations he made while inspecting the ancient buildings Palladio describes, is in the library of Worcester College, Oxford. Palladio died in 1580, but his ideas would live on.

As for Jones, in 1615 he was appointed Surveyor-General of the King's Works, a post he held until 1642. Too few of his buildings survive, but one, the Banqueting House in Whitehall, London, built in 1619–22, is not only open to the public but serves as a perfect example of the striking contrast his classical style made with the majority of Jacobean architecture. There are

Hatfield House
1607–11

Robert Lyminge,
Simon Basil,
Inigo Jones

Blickling Hall
1619–25

Robert Lyminge

Bolsover Castle
1612–34

John Smythson

Wilton House
(south range)
1636–53

Inigo Jones,
Isaac de Caux

Kingston Lacy
1663

Sir Roger Pratt

The Vyne, Hampshire: the first neoclassical temple portico on any house in Britain, added by John Webb in 1654

English baroque, 1687–1758

While Inigo Jones was picking up antique and Palladian ideas in Italy in 1614, a new architectural movement, which he completely ignored, was flourishing there and elsewhere in Europe. Essentially, the baroque style – which came to influence England chiefly through France – was bolder, more ornate and more theatrical than the sort of classicism admired and practised by Inigo Jones.

Its first and greatest British practitioner was Sir Christopher Wren, who travelled in France in 1665 and there met the greatest European architect of the day, Gianlorenzo Bernini, designer of the Louvre. Appointed Surveyor-General of the King's Works in 1669, Wren oversaw the building of 52 new churches between 1670 and 1686 to replace those lost in the Great Fire of London in 1666, and between 1675 and 1710 built the new St Paul's Cathedral. Wren did not design houses; but he did build new wings at Hampton Court Palace for King William and Queen Mary, and he also employed the great English painter Sir James Thornhill, whose finest works are said to be those in Wren's buildings, including the dome of St Paul's and the painted hall at Greenwich.

The first English baroque architect of country houses was William Talman, who in 1687–96 remodelled the Elizabethan house of Chatsworth in Derbyshire for the Duke of Devonshire. Talman was clearly a highly skilled and imaginative designer, but he was also a thoroughly unpleasant character, which limited his career. In 1702 he lost the post of Comptroller of His Majesty's Works to the man whose work would come to define baroque architecture in Britain, Sir John Vanbrugh.

Vanbrugh was no less flamboyant and theatrical than the buildings he created. Having started out in life as a soldier and quite possibly a spy – he was arrested as such in France in 1688 and spent four years in prison – he then embarked on a highly successful career as a playwright, writing a series of popular and bawdy comedies, including *The Relapse* in 1696 and *The Provok'd Wife* in 1699.

Exactly why Vanbrugh decided to become an architect, and how he managed to do so, is not at all clear, but in 1699 his friend Charles Howard, Earl of Carlisle, engaged him to design his new country seat

no houses designed by Jones, but he did at least oversee the creation of the new south range at Wilton House in Wiltshire, built in 1636–53 for the Earl of Pembroke, a friend of Charles I. The king's architect was too busy to do the job himself, but gave his 'advice and approbation' to his assistant, Isaac de Caux. Inside, the main state rooms are based on a famous Palladian principle: one has the proportions of a cube, 30 feet in each direction; the other a double cube, 30 feet wide, 30 feet high and 60 feet long.

Inevitably, Jones's ideas were to influence a new generation of architects; but these also made their own trips to Italy and France, found their own influences, often in more modern buildings than those that Jones had admired, and introduced their own ideas.

Few houses survive by Hugh May, who spent time in Holland with the future Charles II during his exile and became the king's Comptroller of the Works in 1688. He redesigned much of Windsor Castle in 1675–84, employing the woodcarver Grinling Gibbons and the painter Antonio Verrio to contribute to the castle's highly ornate, French-influenced baroque interiors. Equally little is evident of the work of John Webb, who in 1654 added the first temple portico ever seen on an English country house to The Vyne, in Hampshire; or of Sir Roger Pratt, an educated gentleman lawyer who dabbled rather successfully in architecture. The first of Pratt's highly influential creations was at Coleshill, Berkshire, which burned down in the 1950s; but he almost certainly designed the wonderful Kingston Lacy, Dorset, built in 1663 for Sir Ralph Bankes.

at Castle Howard in Yorkshire. Work started in 1700, Vanbrugh working with Nicholas Hawksmoor, a former assistant to Wren best known for the six churches he designed in London between 1712 and 1716. Although work stopped on the Earl's death in 1738 and Castle Howard was never completed to Vanbrugh's design, it is still important as the first great baroque design in England, and one of the most impressive houses ever conceived.

Vanbrugh and Hawksmoor worked together again on the monumental Blenheim Palace in Oxfordshire, built in 1706–22 by a grateful nation for the Duke of Marlborough, who in effect had stopped Louis XIV from conquering Europe. They had almost as much trouble finishing Blenheim as they did at Castle Howard; but the result was an extraordinary, if not necessarily attractive, building. As the architectural historian David Watkin explains in his book *English Architecture*: 'Vanbrugh and Hawksmoor were thinking grandly in terms of masses, planes and volume in a way that Inigo Jones had never done, and Wren only rarely'.

Besides becoming the very incarnation of baroque, Vanbrugh also had English influences that anticipated the 'picturesque' movement of years to come. He liked, he said, to give his houses 'something of the Castle Air', and his later projects – such as Seaton Delaval in Northumberland, built in 1720-28 and the last house he designed – have an eccentric, slightly abstract and distinctly castle-like outline. He also tried to retain the old Woodstock Manor as a romantic ruin in the grounds at Blenheim, and is thought to have been behind the creation of the 'Arcadian' parkland at Castle Howard – both very much in the spirit of the picturesque movement that would flourish in the following century.

The last of the baroque architects worthy of mention is James Gibbs, whose best-known creations are the London churches of St Mary-le-Strand, built in 1714–17, and St Martin-in-the-Fields, built in 1720–6, as well as the Radcliffe Camera in Oxford. Gibbs was a Scottish Catholic who in 1703, aged 21, went to Rome to train for the priesthood; but he abandoned his studies after a year to become a pupil of Carlo Fontana, Italy's leading baroque architect of the age; which meant that by the time he came back to Britain, in 1709, he was one of the most up-to-date architects in the country. He was to suffer,

Chatsworth
1687–96 (remodelled)

William Talman

Hampton Court,
William & Mary wings
1689–94

Sir Christopher Wren

Castle Howard
1700–38

Sir John Vanbrugh

Blenheim
1706–22

Sir John Vanbrugh

Ragley Hall
1750–58
(remodelled)

James Gibbs

however, from the political rivalries which divided the ruling classes in the early 1700s. Even though Vanbrugh and most of his clients had been Whigs, the baroque style was increasingly considered a reactionary, Tory style, and the Whigs were championing the cause of the next big thing, Palladianism. As a Tory and a Catholic, Gibbs found himself barred from public office – in 1716, after the Jacobite rising of the previous year, he was removed from his position as one of two surveyors to the Commissioners for building Fifty New Churches in London.

Thereafter his commissions were mostly country houses for Tory landowners, often conservative in external appearance, but distinguished by their flamboyant, status-marking baroque interiors with extravagant use of plasterwork, often by the Italian craftsmen Arturi and Bagutti. An example is Ragley Hall in Warwickshire, which Gibbs fitted out for Lord Hertford in 1750–58.

The Palladian revolution, 1721–1772

The new young architects of the age rejected the old-fashioned baroque style, strongly associated with Tories, Catholics and other reactionary forces, and returned instead to the principles of Palladio that Inigo Jones had found so intriguing. And in doing so, they displayed a puritanical zeal. They believed that there was a right way of building, and only by following it could a truly harmonious result be assured; and also that the right way was a law derived from nature, in contrast with the artificiality and falseness of baroque. It is this same belief in the natural that also led to the rise of the landscape movement, which, by the second half of the century, would see Lancelot 'Capability' Brown building hills and digging lakes in just about every park in the country.

A pioneer of the new Palladians was the Scottish architect Colen Campbell, a member of the little clique that gathered around the 'Architect Earl', Richard Boyle, 3rd Earl of Burlington. In 1715, Campbell published a survey of English architecture since the time of Inigo Jones entitled *Vitruvius Britannicus*, which set out the guiding principles of Palladianism; in the same year, the first English translation of Palladio's *Four Books* was published (and both, incidentally, were dedicated to the new Hanoverian king, George I). Among

Campbell's earliest creations was Stourhead in Wiltshire, built in 1721–5 for the London banker Henry Hoare; it has been altered since, but the pure Palladian principle is still evident in the proportions of the rooms Campbell created.

Lord Burlington made a fascinating experiment in pure Palladianism in his own Chiswick House, London, a charming little jewel-casket of a house, built in 1726–9. In 1719 – the year in which he replaced James Gibbs with Colen Campbell as the architect of his central London home, Burlington House – the earl had travelled to Italy to study the buildings of Palladio and his heir, Vincenzo Scamozzi, whom Inigo Jones had met in Venice in 1614. Palladio's Villa Rotonda and Scamozzi's Rocca Pisani, near Vicenza, both of which had central domes, were the chief influences for Chiswick.

Burlington came back from Italy with a large collection of Palladio's drawings and also, perhaps more importantly for the future of British country house architecture, with the second-rate painter William Kent, who worked with the Earl at Chiswick and developed, under his patronage, into one of the most creative and influential architects of the age. Kent's first great creation was the spectacular Holkham Hall in Norfolk, built in 1734–62 and designed with input from both Lord Burlington and Holkham's owner, Lord Leicester, who wanted an appropriately 'antique' setting for the paintings and classical sculpture he had gathered on the Grand Tour.

The big problem that faced Kent at Holkham – and the Palladians generally – was one that Palladio had struggled with: although he was determined to recreate classical houses, there was no information on what their interiors had looked like. The obvious thing was finish the interiors in the latest style; so Inigo Jones's new wing at Wilton had extravagant baroque interiors. At Holkham, William Kent followed a different path, taking ideas from interiors of an appropriate age and style even if they weren't domestic. As a result, his extraordinary entrance hall has vast marble columns, an enormous coffered ceiling and a richly carved frieze, variously derived from temples, basilicas and churches – and, wonderful though it is, scarcely feels like a house at all.

As his career progressed, it became clear that Kent could successfully turn his hand to just about anything. He created splendid baroque interiors for Sir Robert Walpole's house at Houghton in Norfolk in 1725–35; he designed influential furniture, as well as ladies' dresses and even a baby's pram; he was a pioneer of the new natural style of garden design, working on such famous gardens as Rousham near Oxford and Stowe in Buckinghamshire; and he also produced some of the first buildings in the 'gothic' style that would become so popular later in the century.

Other neo-Palladians followed, notable among them being James Paine, whose house at Nostell Priory, Yorkshire, built in 1735–65 for Sir Rowland Winn, is a rather heavy, ponderous thing, and John Carr of York, whose consistently tidy and pleasing creations, most of them in Yorkshire, include Harewood House, near Leeds. Significantly, though, at both Nostell Priory and Harewood the interiors would be completed by the leading figure of the generation that left Palladio behind and looked to an increasingly diverse range of classical sources – Robert Adam.

Neo-classicism and Adam, 1758–1797

The next generation of architects wanted to see Rome for themselves, not filtered through Palladio's eyes. They were helped by the increasing interest in archaeology in the 1750s – when, for example, Robert Wood published his drawings of late Roman buildings in Syria – and by the founding in 1733–4 of the Society of Dilettantes, a wealthy and influential group dedicated to promoting 'Greek taste and Roman spirit' and prepared to put their money where their mouths were by acting as patrons to architectural projects.

One of the first results was an increase in interest in the buildings of ancient Greece; this led to a strong theoretical movement that favoured Greek over Roman models, typified by James 'Athenian' Stuart, who, with his associate Nicholas Revett, made the first survey of the ancient buildings of Athens in 1751–5. This movement would not, however, achieve widespread acceptance until the following century.

Instead, the new classical revival was led in an altogether less constricted and theoretical fashion by the greatest architect of the age, Robert Adam. The son of the leading Scottish architect William Adam,

Stourhead
1721–5

Colen Campbell

Chiswick House
1726–29

Lord Burlington,
William Kent

Holkham Hall
1734–62

William Kent

Nostell Priory
1735–65

James Paine

Harewood
1759–72
(remodelled 1840s)

John Carr of York

Robert was no doubt familiar from an early age with the ideas behind by his father's advanced, Palladian-influenced layouts for houses such as the House of Dun, near Montrose, built in 1730–43 for the judge David Erskine. Robert trained, along with his two brothers, in his father's practice in Edinburgh, before setting off on a Grand Tour in 1754 at the age of 28. He spent three years abroad, mostly in Italy, examining and drawing ancient buildings; and on his return, in January 1758, he established himself in London and quickly started to earn the commissions through which, in the course of the next five years, he would develop the uniquely delicate and sophisticated style that made him the most fashionable designer of the next three decades.

One of his first commissions was Hatchlands Park in Surrey, already built in a plainish style by the Palladian architect Leadbetter for Admiral Edward Boscawen. It's fascinating to see Adam's first exploration of the ideas he had brought back from Italy, with much of the flair and understanding that he would later show already evident, but not the delicacy of touch he would soon achieve.

All too often Adam was asked to create new interiors for older houses, as at the Duke of Northumberland's Syon House, London (remodelled in 1762–69) and the banker Robert Child's Osterley Park, also in London (1763–80), both of which are among his finest creations. His struggle to make old rooms at least *seem* to have the sort of harmonious proportions he thought proper is particularly evident at Osterley, where his greatest neo-classical flourish is the open portico that breaks through one side of the Tudor house.

AT KEDLESTON HALL in Derbyshire, a brand new building he completed for Sir Nathaniel Curzon in 1760–65, Adam had more of a free hand, although the house had already been started by James Paine. Kedleston is one of the purest and most complete of neo-classical houses, and in its layout and function is typical of the way in which great houses now worked (and had, indeed, throughout the baroque and Palladian periods). The first thing to note is that the main house is a public space, not a private one; the family lived in a separate wing, and the main house spent most of the time locked and shuttered, with the furniture and fittings covered. The main rooms are those on the first floor, called, in the Italian tradition, the *piano nobile* and distinguished, to anyone looking at the outside, by larger windows.

Steps lead up under an impressive portico to the main entrance, also on the first floor, and into the entrance hall – which, along with the other main reception room, the saloon, runs through the centre of the house from front to back. Echoing its role as the great hall in Jacobean and earlier houses, the entrance hall was still the place to make a bold statement about the wealth, prestige and taste of the owner – at Kedleston, the hall is a lofty and slightly mysterious space where light filters down through high windows and casts shadows behind tall marble columns. It was used for parties, balls and gatherings of all kind, while the saloon, beyond, though equally impressive, was a slightly more intimate space. The saloon at Kedleston is one of Adam's most stunning creations: inspired by the Pantheon in Rome, it is completely circular, with doors that follow the curve of the walls and a vast domed, coffered ceiling.

To the left of the entrance is the music room, with the drawing room and library beyond; to the right of the entrance is the dining room, behind which, somewhat unexpectedly, is a bedroom and the accompanying dressing room, 'wardrobe' and ante-room, making up a state apartment. Such state apartments had been a crucial part of any great house in the 1600s, when royal patronage was always to be sought; and though they were now self-consciously old-fashioned, force of tradition meant they had to be kept, and they were seen primarily as 'rooms of parade', where elegant furniture and fine paintings could be shown off to guests.

Also abundantly evident at Kedleston is another of the qualities that make Adam's work so satisfying: his immense attention to detail. He would design every aspect of a room, right down to the door handles; in the library at Kedleston, he even designed the curtain pelmets. He designed furniture, which he had made by Thomas Chippendale, and carpets to echo his ceilings, to be made by Thomas Whitty at Axminster. His drawings of the walls of a room would show where paintings would hang and what size they would be, and he would build frames of wood or plaster into the wall; he insisted that dining rooms were never hung with fabric, since it would retain odours.

One final aspect of Adam's work that must be mentioned is that he could not have been so prolific without a large team of skilled assistants at the office he shared with his brother James, at least one of whom, Joseph Bonomi, went on to become a noted architect in his own right; and nor could he have achieved such consistent quality without a highly skilled team of artists and craftsmen, including the painters Antonio Zucchi, Angelica Kaufmann (who married Zucchi) and Biagio Rebeca; and, perhaps above all, the plasterer Joseph Rose the Younger of York, who turned the designs of Adam's famous ceilings into reality.

Jospeh Rose earned such a reputation that he was asked to act as a consultant on the house built at Sledmere in North Yorkshire by its owner, Sir Christopher Sykes, in the 1780s, helping to create its wonderful, long-gallery-like first-floor library; and he was also greatly in demand from the many imitators of Adam who inevitably followed. The most successful of these was probably James Wyatt, with whom Rose worked at Castle Coole in Northern Ireland, built for the Earl of Belmore in 1790–97; it is one of the few houses to echo Adam's saloon at Kedleston by having, in its oval saloon, doors that curve with the walls.

The picturesque return of Gothic, 1776–1893

James Wyatt went on to become one of the most prolific architects of the late 1700s. Like Adam, who created a number of 'castle style' houses in Scotland in the 1770s and onwards (the most famous being Culzean Castle in Ayrshire, started in 1776 for the Earl of Cassilis and incomplete when both men died in 1792), Wyatt also made considerable experiments in the gothic style – the main difference being that Wyatt's buildings showed a picturesque asymmetry that Adam, it seems, could not bring himself to try.

Wyatt's gothic creations – among them the legendary, long-vanished Fonthill Abbey in Wiltshire, built in 1796–1812 for the eccentric writer William Beckford, and Belvoir Castle in Leicestershire, with its wonderful cathedral-like halls, which Wyatt remodelled for the Duke of Rutland in 1801–16 – had earned him a considerable reputation by the early 1800s; one which he would probably still enjoy were it not

Kedleston Hall
1760–65

Robert Adam

Osterley Park
1763–80

Robert Adam

Culzean Castle
1776–92

Robert Adam

Castle Coole
1790–97

James Wyatt

Belvoir Castle
1801–16

James Wyatt

for his disastrous restoration work at a number of the finest English cathedrals, which instead left him labelled as 'Wyatt the Destroyer'. But his work paved the way for the great architectural movement of Victorian times – the gothic revival.

The building that perhaps summed up the age was the new Palace of Westminster, designed by Sir Charles Barry with the help of AWN Pugin in 1835. Those competing to design it were told that only gothic or Elizabethan styles would be considered appropriate for a great national institution – perfectly illustrating the influence that the past exerted on the architectural thinking of the day. Pugin's gorgeous polychromatic medieval interiors for the House of Lords earned him a commission in 1847 to do a similar job at Eastnor Castle in Herefordshire, built in an almost too realistically brutal style by Robert Smirke for Earl Somers in 1810–24.

The most dramatic of all the pretend castles, however, was the neo-Norman extravaganza built by Thomas Hopper at Penrhyn in North Wales in 1820–45 for George Hay Dawkins-Pennant. On a truly massive scale, castle-like outside but with a cathedral-like grand hall, and decorated with beautifully authentic carved stonework in a medieval monastic style, particularly at the top of the grand staircase, Penrhyn is essentially a huge folly. But it has to be said that, apart from its size, it was also a very practical house, with such modern luxuries as hot and cold running water in every room.

What Penrhyn has in common with so many of the other great houses of the Victorian age is a love of the quality of medieval craftsmanship, which, thanks in part to industrial techniques and in part to the wealth that their industry had earned, the Victorians were able to reproduce. Similar influences – love of the medieval and of things made by the hands of craftsmen – inspired the Arts and Crafts movement, led by William Morris, which flourished in the 1860s and 1870s, and eventually produced the great architect of the early 20th century, Sir Edwin Lutyens.

Precisely the same love of craftsmanship, of buildings built with no conscious sense of 'design', was what drove the Cheshire architect Edward Ould, who built one of the finest of all Arts and Crafts houses, Wightwick Manor near Wolverhampton, in 1887–93 for the paint manufacturer Theodore Mander. In the earlier part of the house, Ould was a little conservative; but when it came to building an extension, having got to know his client well, he was able to let himself go. Drawing on the black-and-white timber-framed Tudor and Elizabethan houses of the North West, particularly Little Moreton Hall in Cheshire and Speke Hall near Liverpool, Ould created a structure that was entirely timber-framed and embellished it with touches copied directly from the older buildings. Decorated by Morris's company and hung with Pre-Raphaelite art, Wightwick is superbly evocative of the Arts and Crafts period.

A GREAT INFLUENCE on William Morris was the artist and philosopher John Ruskin, whose books *The Seven Lamps of Architecture* (1849) and *The Stones of Venice* (1851–3) had a tremendous impact on the gothic revival. For Ruskin, as for Pugin, producing the right kind of architecture was almost a moral crusade. Besides putting a romantic emphasis on the spirit of a building and on the hand of the craftsman, which is what inspired Morris, Ruskin also held that the pattern and colour in Italian and French gothic was immensely superior to anything produced in Britain. It was to continental models that the architects to come chiefly looked.

Among the greatest of those architects were Sir George Gilbert Scott, perhaps best known for the Albert Memorial (1863–72) and the Midland Hotel at St Pancras (1868–74); and, more interestingly as far as houses in Britain are concerned, the wayward, opium-crazed genius William Burges. Burges was employed by the richest man and most prolific architectural patron of the age, John Patrick Crichton-Stuart, the 3rd Marquess of Bute, to remodel Cardiff Castle in 1868–81 and create a new castle-like house at Castell Coch, not far from Cardiff, in 1875–81. A less complete example of Burges's work, lacking the crazily colourful fairytale interiors of the other two, is Knightshayes Court in Devon, which he built in 1869–72 for the industrialist Sir John Heathcoat Amory; but Sir John got cold feet when it came to letting him loose on the interiors.

The culmination of the movement towards French and Italian gothic – in terms of houses, at least – is another building for the Marquess of Bute: his home at Mount Stuart on the Isle of Bute, built in 1878–86 by Sir Robert Rowand Anderson, a former pupil

of George Gilbert Scott and the leading Scottish architect of his day. It is one of the largest and most dramatic houses ever built, its central hall a cathedral-like space surrounded by marble columns. It was also one of the most technologically advanced houses of the time, the first in Scotland lit by electricity and the first anywhere to have an indoor swimming pool.

Technology was also a feature of Cragside in Northumberland, built (or rather extended) for the industrialist William Armstrong in 1869–93 and the first house in Britain to have electric lights. It was the work of one of the greatest architects of houses of the period, Richard Norman Shaw, a Scot who had trained with the master of the Scots baronial style, William Burn, before setting up his own practice in London.

Norman Shaw made his name creating pretty, red brick, tile-hung houses in the 'Old English' style in Kent and Sussex – above all with a house called Leyswood at Groomsbridge in West Sussex, which he built in 1868–9 for the shipping magnate J.W. Temple. Cragside, set on a rocky slope in wild Northumberland hill country, was a very different proposition; but the towering, dramatic result is one of the most pleasing houses in Britain, with a strong Arts and Crafts flavour to its interiors.

ONE LAST THING to note is that gothic was not the only style of architecture to enjoy a revival in the 19th century. Far from it. The early 1800s finally saw the Greek revival that James 'Athenian' Stuart had hoped for back in the 1750s. The style was most popular in public buildings in the north of England and Scotland, but had its impact on houses, too: most notably the astonishingly pared-down Belsay Hall in Northumberland, built in 1807–17 by its owner, Sir Charles Monck, following a visit to the Temple of Theseus in Athens; and the handsomely original suburban villa of Holmwood House in Glasgow, built for paper-mill owner James Couper in 1857–8 by Alexander 'Greek' Thomson.

Nor had Italian classicism had its day. The picturesque, asymmetrical Italianate villas designed in the 1830s by Sir Charles Barry, the architect of the Palace of Westminster, soon spawned a host of imitators – not least the London builder Thomas Cubitt, who was employed by Queen Victoria and Prince Albert in 1844–51 to create an Italianate villa on a grand scale as their private home, Osborne House on the Isle of Wight.

Castle Howard, Yorkshire, by Sir John Vanbrugh: built in 1700–38 for the Earl of Carlisle, a former First Lord of the Treasury

Introduction, part two: the owners

Who lived in a place like that?

For most of the past 1,000 years, no one except the extremely wealthy could contemplate building a great house; but that wasn't always quite the case. In the earliest days, land and labour were more important; and that remained true much more recently in the outlying areas of Britain. In 1380–1400, when John Domulton built a timber-framed manor at Lower Brockhampton in Herefordshire, he was able to do so because he owned the land. The labour to build it was supplied by the workers on his estate; the timber from which it was made was selected from trees growing on the estate.

That, however, is a rare exception. Generally a house meant money, and money would usually come from one of three sources: the builder might inherit it; or marry it; or work for it.

The most obvious source of a regular income was land, but trade and commerce have a surprisingly large part to play from the earliest days. The builder of Stokesay Castle in the 1280s, Lawrence of Ludlow,

was, as we have already seen, the wealthiest wool merchant in England. Up in the north-east of Scotland some 300 years later, the builder of Craigievar Castle, completed in 1626, was an Edinburgh-born merchant named William Forbes, who traded so successfully with the Baltic that he earned the nickname 'Danzig Willie'.

Owning your own bank was also a good start. Henry Hoare, who built the Palladian villa at Stourhead in Wiltshire in 1721–25, had inherited Hoare's Bank from his father, Sir Richard; but Sir Richard had come from humble origins as the son of a London horse-dealer and, apprenticed to a goldsmith at the age of 17, had eventually taken over his master's business, a part of which involved lending money at vast rates of interest to Charles II's government. Similarly, Robert Child was able to employ Robert Adam to remodel the family home at Osterley Park in London from 1763 to 1780 thanks largely to the £30,000 a year he made as titular head of Child's Bank, although he didn't dirty his hands by getting involved in running it. His good fortune he could attribute to his distant ancestor Sir Francis Child, who again had developed a goldsmith's business into a banking one, doing particularly well out of financing William III's War of the Grand Alliance in the 1690s.

One of the saddest of financiers' stories is that of Frederick Sharp, who built a handsome little house at Hill of Tarvit in Fife in 1906. His father earned a fortune from processing jute into sackcloth, used to make sandbags by both sides in the American Civil War; but Frederick made his own fortune first from venture capital and then in the railways, as a director of the London, Midland and Scottish. Tragically, his only son, Hugh, was killed in 1937 in one of Britain's worst ever railway disasters, at Castlecary near Falkirk. Hugh had only been travelling by train because his fiancee, whom he was on his way to visit, had insisted that the weather was too bad to drive.

Industry was also, from surprisingly early times, a good way to make a pile. The Moretons, who built Little Moreton Hall in Cheshire in the 1480s and improved it in the 1560s, may have earned most of their income through farming, but they also owned an iron mill and a coal pit. Down in Cornwall, the tin industry was the primary source of the wealth of the Godolghans, who built Godolphin in stages from the 1470s to the 1630s. And though Sir Ralph Bankes, who built Kingston Lacy in Dorset in 1663, had inherited the wealth that allowed him to do so from his father, Sir John Bankes had earned the money he passed on to his son through a successful legal career in London – with a little help from the graphite mines his Cumbrian family had passed on to him.

Industry was also, of course, the route to a lovely big house in the country for many self-made men of the 1700s and 1800s. William George Armstrong, who turned Cragside in Northumberland into one of the most remarkable houses of the Victorian era in 1869–83, started off making hydraulic cranes for the docks at Newcastle and Liverpool, and ended up making artillery for anyone in the world who could pay for it. He also had a hand, incidentally, in the mechanism that raised and lowered Tower Bridge in London.

Armstrong died without children, but another great industrialist, John Heathcoat, who invented a machine for making lace in 1808 and built a thriving textile business around it, was unfortunate only in that he had no son. However his daughter, Anne, married one of his employees; and her son, Sir John Heathcoat-Amory, was eventually able to fulfil the dream all self-made men

Duncombe Park, Yorkshire: built in about 1713 by Thomas Duncombe after he inherited the estates of his uncle, Sir Charles Duncombe, a banker who was said to be England's richest commoner

Mount Stuart, Isle of Bute: left incomplete on the death of the 3rd Marquess in 1900, it was abandoned and put up for sale in 1920. Since the 1980s, the Bute family has embarked on the task of finishing it

had for their sons by turning his back on business and living the life of a country gent. Sir John bought a country estate in Devon and built a splendid new house, Knightshayes Court, in 1869–72; but that was probably mainly to keep his wife happy. All he cared about was huntin' with one of his three packs of hounds on Exmoor, shootin' at his estate in Perthshire and fishin' at his lodge in Norway.

ANOTHER TOP-NOTCH way of acquiring land and, with it, a good income was to do the King a favour. The lovely old stone manor of Cotehele in Cornwall was begun in 1485 by Sir Richard Edgcumbe, after he was handsomely rewarded by Henry Tudor for the loyalty he showed at the Battle of Bosworth. Up in Scotland, Sir Henry Preston had the good fortune to capture the English knight Ralph de Percy at the battle of Otterburn in 1388; and in 1391, when his king, Robert III, offered to swap the hostage for the lands and the Castle of Fyvie, he would have been foolish to refuse.

But an even easier way to make money from the King was by being appointed to a position of trust, holding the nation's purse-strings. In 1603, Thomas Howard, Earl of Suffolk, set about building the largest and grandest house in the kingdom at Audley End in Essex; it is said to have cost the immense sum of £200,000 to complete (compare that with Hatfield, built by his successor as Lord Treasurer, Robert Cecil, for just £12,000). Exactly where Suffolk got the money from is not certain, but in 1614 he was made Lord Treasurer of England by James I; and in 1618 he was relieved of his office, found guilty of 'extorcion and bribery' and thrown in the Tower along with his Countess.

BY FAR THE EASIEST way of making money, however, was to marry it. The instances of an impoverished gentleman's new house being started shortly after his marriage to a wealthy heiress are too numerous to list; but in fact the greatest exponent of the art of marrying well was probably a woman – Elizabeth, Countess of Shrewsbury, better known as Bess of Hardwick.

The daughter of minor gentry who inherited £26 on her father's death in 1528, Bess married a cousin, whose family were slightly wealthier, in about 1543, when she was 16. He was already ill when they married and died a few months later, leaving her an annual income that by 1588 was worth £66 a year. Her second husband, in 1547, was Sir William Cavendish, an elderly and very rich courtier. To please her, he sold the lands he had acquired all over England as one of the commissioners for the Dissolution of the Monasteries, and bought estates in Derbyshire and Nottinghamshire instead. When he died in 1557, after she had given him eight children, he left her a substantial part of his property.

Two years later she married again, this time a rich landowner from the West Country, Sir William St Loe. When he died five years later, he also left most of his property to Bess, much to the disgust of his family. By now, at the age of 37, she was probably the most eligible widow in the kingdom, and there was much gossip about who she might marry next. The winner, in 1567, was George Talbot, Earl of Shrewsbury, the head of one of the oldest, grandest and richest families in England, who not only made vast sums from farming but also owned coal mines, glassworks, ironworks, lead mines and ships. Their marriage was almost like a business merger – signed in triplicate, with one of her sons marrying one of his daughters, and one of her daughters marrying one of his sons.

Bess overreached herself in 1574 when she married her daughter Elizabeth to Charles Stuart, the brother-in-law of Mary, Queen of Scots; which meant that the daughter of the marriage, Arabella Stuart, was in line to the English throne. The queen was furious; so was Bess's husband; and with the marriage collapsing, she retired to her family's old estate at Hardwick. Still, she certainly had the money to build a new house in a lavish style.

IN THE TWENTIETH CENTURY, the problem of money was a different one: not where to get funds to buy or build anew, but how to scrape together the pennies to hang on to the old place and keep it from falling down. The troubled times began with the First World War, which took young men who had been estate workers and household staff off to France and left them there, buried under foreign soil. Rents from the estate could no longer support most big houses, and the newly introduced death duties were enough to finish them off; in the 1920s, many were offered for sale and demolition (including, unbelievably, the astonishing Mount Stuart, on the Isle of Bute), while others had their roofs removed so that rates were no longer payable and were left to rot or burn down. Hundreds vanished.

For many owners, the first glimmer of hope came in 1937 with the National Trust's Country Houses Scheme, by which a house could be given to the Trust while the owners and one generation of descendants continued to live there. Equally, delicate negotiations with the government enabled the transfer of an unwanted property to the Trust to be offset against the enormous sums often requested in inheritance tax.

Luckily, too, there was already a tradition of visits to private historic houses: Cotehele in Cornwall had attracted regular ferry trips up the Tamar in the 1820s. Thanks to the efforts of owners in attracting visitors – Woburn Abbey became the originator of 'the stately home business', as the Duke of Bedford himself put it, when it opened to the public in 1955 – and to the preservational instincts of the National Trust, there are still plenty around to enjoy; and some, even, are not just standing still, but are still changing and growing ever more interesting.

Wilton House, Wiltshire: the south wing (left of picture) was added by Inigo Jones's assistant, Isaac de Caux, in 1636–53 for Philip, 4th Earl of Pembroke, a close friend of King Charles I. The Earl's family had been in royal favour since the 1530s, when William Herbert, the 1st Earl, married Anne Parr, the sister of Henry VIII's wife Catherine. Henry gave the 1st Earl the lands of the dissolved abbey of Wilton in 1544

Britain's historic houses

Kedleston Hall, Derbyshire

How to use this book
Practical information: ownership, prices, directions, opening times

Ownership

Many of the finest historic houses are in the care of the National Trust, in England, Wales and Northern Ireland, or its sister organisation in Scotland, the National Trust for Scotland. Members of these organisations are admitted free of charge to their properties (and also to the properties of the sister organisation), so joining can be well worthwhile.

Some older houses, especially ruins, are in the care of the national heritage organisations English Heritage, Cadw (Wales), Scottish National Heritage and the Environment and Heritage Service in Northern Ireland. Again, members of these organisations gain free admission to their properties and, after the first year, free admission to properties operated by sister organisations (half-price admission in the first year).

The Historic Houses Association (HHA) is an umbrella organisation to which surprisingly many privately owned houses belong. Friends of the HHA gain free admission to the properties of HHA members, and becoming a friend is not as expensive as joining the National Trust. I would recommend it.

Privately owned houses are very often run as charitable trusts, so the profits earned from admission fees and sales in gift shops and tearooms are ploughed back in to the upkeep of the property. This is often the case with houses that aren't maintained by charitable trusts, too, of course.

Just a few properties are operated by local councils. These tend to be subsidized and so are good value, but often have an educational role or act as a museum, and inevitably lack the 'lived-in' feel of a private home.

Prices

It is impossible to give exact prices, because this book will remain in print for a number of years. What I have done instead is use a simple system of pound signs to indicate not only how expensive admission to a property is, but also whether or not it represents good value for money, as follows:

£   Very cheap, probably a pound or less.

££   Fairly cheap (a few pounds) or very good value for money.

£££   Represents decent value, but may be quite expensive.

££££ Sufficiently expensive to be a disincentive; perhaps not good value for money.

The majority of houses in this book inevitably fall into the £££ category. Historic houses are very expensive to maintain and can, as a result, be quite expensive to visit by comparison with other heritage sites.

Directions

The directions accompanying each of the main entries should be enough to get you there if you have a road atlas. I have tried to indicate if a property is not clearly signposted, and give additional directions.

Opening times

Again, it is impossible to give exact opening times and hours.

Generally, most houses are open from April to October.

A few important points:

Bank holidays – many houses that are not normally open on a Monday will be open on a bank holiday Monday, and some also on the preceding weekend. By the same token, some that usually are open may be closed. It's worth telephoning to ask.

Opening season – many properties open for the first time at Easter, so the season can start earlier than stated if Easter falls early in the year. The season may start or end a few days earlier or later than the rough indication I've been able to give.

Hours – the majority of houses are open only in the afternoon, although some, particularly those in the care of the national heritage organisations, have very long hours.

Guided tours – houses that only offer tours generally have them at specified times. With the smaller houses, there may be only two or three tours in an afternoon. It is worth telephoning to find out.

Please note

I have done everything I can to ensure that all the details given are correct at time of going to press, but I'm afraid that we cannot accept responsibility for any loss or inconvenience caused by errors.

South West
Cornwall, Devon

Bristol *Channel*

Lundy

Ilfracombe   Lynmouth

Arlington Court

Barnstaple

Hartland Abbey

Great
Torrington

Knightshayes Court

Tiverton

Bude

Killerton

Shute Barton

Tintagel

Okehampton

Exeter

Castle Drogo

Powderham Castle

Sidmouth

Prideaux Place

Wadebridge

Launceston

Tavistock

Exmouth

Padstow

Pencarrow

Cotehele

Bodmin

Buckland Abbey

Torquay

Newquay

Lanhydrock

Plymouth

Torbay

Trerice

Antony

Totnes

Coleton Fishacre

Redruth

St Austell

Saltram

St Ives

Mount Edgcumbe

Dartmouth

Truro

Penzance   *Godolphin*

Salcombe   Start Point

St Michael's Mount   Falmouth

Land's End

Lizard Point

ENGLISH CHANNEL

0 miles   20

0 kilometres   30

Antony, Cornwall

National Trust • £££ • Open Apr to Oct, Tu-Th (also Jun to Aug, Su)

It is always pleasing when a stately home also feels like a family home. This is not often the case with National Trust houses, but it certainly applies to Antony, still occupied by descendants of the Carew family, who have lived in this place since the 1440s.

Nowhere is this more apparent than in the bedrooms upstairs, roped off so that visitors must peer into them from the central corridor that runs the length of the house: the bedside tables are stacked with books, clothes hang here and there, and it feels as if the family has tidied up quickly before clearing off for the day.

The downstairs rooms, although inevitably somewhat more showy and formal, are also a delightful mix of the historic and the personal. The Carews were a Pembrokeshire family who came to Cornwall after Sir Nicholas Carew married the heiress to Antony, Joan Courtenay, and thereafter intermarried with all the prominent Cornish families. In the hall hangs a portrait painted in 1586 of Richard Carew, a scholar and antiquarian who wrote a survey of Elizabethan Cornwall; in the library is a painting from about 1630 of Sir Alexander Carew, which was slashed from its frame by his disappointed Royalist family when he supported Parliament, but was stitched back in after he tried to change sides and was executed.

The house was built in 1718–25 by Sir Alexander's grandson, Sir William Carew, a confirmed Jacobite who was imprisoned in 1715–16 on suspicion of plotting for the return of the exiled Stuarts. It's in a deliberately archaic style, but robust and well-balanced, and made of a local stone that has a delightful silver sheen in sunshine.

The interiors are never spectacular, but are richly redolent of the family history, with lots of dark wood panelling and many portraits, and consistently cosy and warm in feel – none more so than the library, where the temptation to sit down and pick up a book is almost too much to resist.

Carew Pole Woodland Gardens (open Mar to Oct, Tu-Th, S & Su), extensive and interesting gardens, tearoom, shop.

Signposted on A374 Torpoint to Looe road, 2 miles west of Torpoint.

Arlington Court, Devon

National Trust • £££ • Open Apr to Oct, M, W-F, S & Su

A most unusual house, built in 1820 in an almost excessively plain Greek Revival style by an architect from Barnstaple, Thomas Lee, for Colonel John Chichester; with a long, low, rustic-looking service wing added in the 1860s by Sir Bruce Chichester. Inside, however, the chief influence

Antony: said to be the most splendid house in Cornwall, built in 1718–25 by the Carew family and still occupied by their descendants, with a lovely lived-in feel

Arlington Court: a plain Greek Revival house of 1820 with a service wing added in the 1860s

on the way the house looks today was Sir Bruce's daughter, Rosalie, an enthusiastic traveller and compulsive collector – especially of pewter and model ships – who lived here alone after her mother remarried in 1883, and with a paid companion, Miss Chrissy Peters, from 1912 to her death in 1949.

The rooms on the ground floor, grouped around the immense central stair hall, are decorated in a lavish French-influenced style, much of it not altered since 1839. Particularly fine is the suite of morning room, ante-room and white drawing room, divided by clever mirrored folding screens. All are littered with items from Miss Chichester's collections; in the last of these three rooms her parrot, Polly, was allowed to fly free. Don't miss, either, the looking-glass of the 1690s in the boudoir.

The only mild disappointment is the upstairs, which, except for Miss Chichester's bedroom, is not shown in anything like its original state.

Collection of more than 50 carriages in the stables, cave with roosting bats, church, parkland with lakeside walks, walled gardens (open as house, also Jun to Aug, Tu), tearoom, shop.

Signposted on minor road off A39 Barnstaple to Lynmouth road, 8 miles north-east of Barnstaple.

Buckland Abbey, Devon

National Trust and local council • £££ • Open Apr to Oct, M-W, S & Su, Nov to late Dec and mid-Feb to Mar, S & Su

The former home of the great Elizabethan courtier, naval captain and pirate Sir Francis Drake, converted from a former Cistercian abbey following the dissolution. Sir Richard Grenville bought the abbey from Henry VIII in 1541 to provide an estate for his son and heir, Sir Roger, who drowned while captaining the king's ill-fated new flagship, the *Mary Rose*, in 1545. Not until the 1570s did Roger's younger brother, another Richard, get around to making the abbey into a home. Unusually for a post-dissolution monastic conversion, the house was based on the actual church, rather than on the accommodation ranges grouped around the cloister.

Tucked away in a little valley overlooking the River Tavy, Buckland has a delightfully rustic feel, with chickens wandering among the old stone farm buildings. A superb ancient monastic barn is one of the treats on offer in the gardens and grounds. The house itself is, for the most part, disappointingly un-house-like, since the largest rooms are devoted to museum-style displays covering Drake's life and times, but there are a few real treats on offer, most notably the great hall.

Created by Richard Grenville on the ground floor of what was the main body of the church, the hall has wooden panelling with a frieze carved with extraordinary, almost savage figures, including the bizarre fertility figures known as sheila na gigs. Carvings of this sort feature a great deal in Elizabethan houses in Devon and Cornwall, still untouched, in those days, by urban sophistication. Also striking are the plaster friezes, particularly one that shows a knight resting under a tree, his weapons laid aside, perhaps suggesting that, at the age of only 34, Grenville had had enough of the warlike life.

That apart, look out for some nice details surviving from the original abbey church – especially the pillars from the crossing hidden behind hinged panels in the hall.

Estate walks, barn, Elizabethan garden, restaurant, craft shops, shop.

Signposted on minor road off A386 Plymouth to Tavistock road, 11 miles north of Plymouth.

Buckland Abbey: the home of Sir Francis Drake, converted from a Cistercian abbey church in the 1570s

Castle Drogo: a marvellous neo-Norman fantasy, created by the great Sir Edwin Lutyens in 1911–27

Castle Drogo,
Devon

National Trust • £££ • Open Apr to Oct, M, W-F, S & Su

A fascinating mock-castle built in 1911–27 by Sir Edwin Lutyens for Julius Drewe, who made a pile as joint founder of a successful shop, the Home and Colonial Stores in London, in the 1880s. It's not as big as one imagines (or as was originally planned), but is extraordinary for its uncompromising appearance and the scale and craftsmanship of the bare stone interiors.

The servants' quarters and the kitchens are highlights, and there is lots of interest, too, in such technical trickery of the period as the electric candlesticks on the dining room table.

Extensive gardens with croquet lawn, tearoom, shop.

Signposted on A382 Newton Abbot to Okehampton road, 5 miles south of A30.

Coleton Fishacre,
Devon

National Trust • £££ • Open Apr to Oct, W-F, S & Su

Very different from the general run of National Trust houses, this is a small, comfortable and relatively modern house, built in 1923–6 by Oswald Milne, a former assistant to Lutyens, as a seaside holiday home for Rupert D'Oyly Carte, son of the theatrical impresario who put on Gilbert and Sullivan's operettas and founded a business empire that included the Savoy and Claridge's.

The house is only sparsely furnished, making it feel almost as if someone has just moved out, but the few pieces left behind when Rupert's daughter, Bridget, sold the house in 1949 are clean, simple designs that match the art deco style of the fixtures – most pleasing of which are the Lalique light fittings in the dining room, the tiles in the bathroom and, in the library, the wind dial set into a bird's eye view of the house painted by George Spencer Hoffman. Best of all, though, is the stroll down through the gardens to the beach below.

Extensive gardens, access to coastal footpaths, tearoom, shop.

Signposted on minor road off B3205 Brixham to Kingswear road, 3 miles east of Kingswear.

Coleton Fishacre: the seaside retreat of the D'Oyly Carte family, built in 1923–6, with art deco interiors

Cotehele, Cornwall

National Trust • £££ • Open Apr to Oct, M-Th, S & Su

More than with most old houses, a trip to Cotehele is like a journey into the past. It's not that the old stone house is unaltered since it was first built in the late 1400s and early 1500s, because it has been, many times; but electricity has never reached it, and the dark and ancient feel of the wood-panelled and tapestry-covered interiors is wonderfully unspoiled. Even the approach to it, through a maze of little lanes that wind along the steep-sided valley of the River Tamar, has a mysterious and indefinable air of travelling back in time.

The house was begun in 1485 by Sir Richard Edgcumbe, who had been handsomely rewarded by Henry Tudor for the loyalty he showed at the Battle of Bosworth, and continued after his death four years later by his son, Sir Piers, who in 1493 married a wealthy local heiress, Joan Durnford.

These were still turbulent times in the West Country, so the defensive layout of gatehouse and courtyard in front of the main house was no mere frivolity. The Edgcumbes' house was based, in traditional style, around a great hall in which daily life took place and a solar block with the lord's private apartments.

Piers's son, Richard, built a new house at Mount Edgcumbe, overlooking Plymouth Sound, but Cotehele was not abandoned; a new castellated tower was added in about 1620 and further changes were made in the mid-1600s when Colonel Piers Edgcumbe, a staunch Royalist, lived here. But from the late 1600s the family moved to the new house and Cotehele was left pretty much untouched. Today, not much Tudor furnishing remains; the house has a distinct flavour of the 17th century.

As early as the late 1700s, Cotehele's antiquarian delights were appreciated by George, 1st Earl of Edgcumbe, a friend of Horace Walpole; and by the 1820s regular ferry trips up the Tamar from Plymouth brought parties of visitors to look round the house.

The plainest and lightest rooms are the great hall – unaltered in its basic form, but without its original raised dais and decorated in mock-archaic mode with a motley collection of weapons and armour – and the chapel, where the clock, installed in the 1480s, is the earliest in England unmodified and in its original position. The rest of the house is dominated by oak panelling, a wealth of tapestries (most of them English or Flemish, from the 1660s to 1680s, and cheerfully cut up and squeezed in wherever they would fit) and oak furniture with heavy, almost grotesque carving – seldom beautiful, but often fascinating.

Walks to Cotehele Quay and National Maritime Museum with preserved boats, working watermill; gardens (open daily, all year), restaurant, craft gallery, shop.

Signposted on minor roads off A390 Tavistock to Liskeard road, 8 miles south-west of Tavistock.

Cotehele: bluntly defensive manor house built in the late 1400s and early 1500s, altered in the 1600s, with a wonderfully dark and ancient feel to its interiors

Godolphin: the many-columned loggias of the 1630s give a Renaissance touch to a manor of the 1400s

Godolphin, Cornwall

Privately owned (HHA) • £££ • Open late Apr to Sep, Th-F, Su (also late Apr, Jul and Aug, Tu)

One of the most modest houses open to the public in Britain, but also one of the most welcoming, where the visitor is likely to be greeted by members of the family who own the house and have taken on the daunting task of restoring it. There's a delightful feeling of rustic, haphazard antiquity to Godolphin, which in places is more like a ruined castle than a house, but that doesn't obscure the fact that this was, in its time, the most graceful and sophisticated courtier's residence west of Wilton in Wiltshire.

Essentially it consists of parts of a house built in the late 1470s by John Godolghan, whose family had made a fortune in the tin industry, with later remodelling throughout the 1500s, culminating in a curtailed attempt, in the 1630s, to create a small but grandly classical residence. Its most striking and engaging feature is the north range, built on top of and around a courtyard wall and entrance gate of the late 1500s, with simple, powerful Tuscan columns creating both inward and outward facing loggias; on the first floor was placed a large reception room and two suites of apartments.

Many satisfying details include beautiful plasterwork of 1610 in the withdrawing room, depicting flowers, and the fine overmantel in the king's chamber, moved there when the great hall was demolished in about 1800.

Continuing restoration of Elizabethan gardens (open as house), cafe, shop.

Signposted on minor road near Godolphin Cross, off B3302 Hayle to Helston road.

Hartland Abbey, Devon

Privately owned (HHA) • £££ • Open Apr to Oct, W, Th, Su (also Jul and Aug, Tu)

Sitting in the flat bottom of a steep-sided valley that runs down to the sea – the long walk to see the pebbly shore and dramatic cliffs is a must – this is a pleasing house that is a mixture of work from a number of different periods.

Its origins are medieval and monastic: the abbey was given by Henry VIII to his Sergeant of the Wine Cellar, William Abbott, who built a house from one and a half ranges of the cloisters. But it owes its character today to three stages of rebuilding: first by Paul Orchard, who inherited by marriage in 1704; next in the 1750s to 1770s, by his son, another Paul, who built in the fashionable Strawberry Hill Gothic style; and finally from 1862 by Sir George Stucley, who employed George Gilbert Scott to give the place a thoroughly medieval revamp.

Just slightly ramshackle and old-fashioned in the way it presents itself to the public, Hartland is less a showpiece and more a family home.

Many of its best pictures are family portraits, among them paintings by Romney of both the Paul Orchards; outstanding among its contents are various pieces of furniture picked up over the years, including a clever multi-leaved table in the dining room and a rare and delicately carved suite in oak by Hepplewhite.

By far its most striking features, however, are the interiors created by Sir George Gilbert Scott. Scott is at his most extravagant in the linking corridor that runs the length of the house, its vaulted ceiling decorated with brightly coloured stencilling inspired by the Alhambra Palace in Granada; Sir George at his most grandiose in the drawing room, influenced by Pugin's work at the House of Lords, with linenfold panelling and murals in a charming sub-Pre-Raphaelite style showing scenes from the lives of Sir George's ancestors.

Extensive gardens, tearoom, shop.

Signposted off B3248 in Hartland, 15 miles west of Bideford.

Hartland Abbey (below): remodelled in gothic style in the 1750s to 1770s, and in the 1860s

Killerton: a plain little house of 1778–9, with many later alterations and lavish Edwardian interiors

Killerton, Devon

National Trust • £££ • Open Apr to Oct, M, W-F, S & Su

Killerton is not large and has nothing outstanding about its design either inside or out, but it is a friendly little place and, as the guidebook points out, comfortable enough to make the visitor feel it would be a good house to live in. The welcoming atmosphere is reinforced by an invitation to all comers to play the piano in the music room, next door to the entrance hall.

The house was built in 1778–9 as the centrepiece of a substantial agricultural estate belonging to Sir Thomas Dyke Acland: elsewhere on the estate, the Trust shows a 1950s post office, a working watermill, a medieval 'cob' house and a fine set of farm buildings (now housing an equestrian centre, carriage museum and pets' corner). The house was meant to be a temporary measure while a larger one was built higher on the hill, but in the end that never came about.

Instead, Killerton was remodelled and extended many times, with the biggest expansion coming in the early 1800s to accommodate the expanding family of Sir Thomas Acland, a prominent politician.

Major changes were also made in the early 1900s, when the 'essentially feudal' Sir Charles and his wife Gertrude reorganized the ground floor to suit the lavish scale of Edwardian entertaining, and following a fire in 1924.

Much of Sir Thomas's extension is not open to the public, since it now houses the Trust's regional offices. Of the original small house, the upstairs rooms are devoted to changing exhibitions of dresses from a vast collection of costumes, mostly of the 1700s and 1800s, donated to the Trust by the collector.

What remains, then, is a small sequence of rooms in three stages: the wonderfully welcoming entrance hall of the 1920s; the imposing Edwardian music room, staircase hall and drawing room; and two rooms on the west side of the house that retain their original form from the 1770s, if not their functions and decoration.

These last two are by far the most pleasing and the nicer is the library, an airy room where a secret door is hidden behind several shelves of imitation books with amusingly appropriate made-up titles.

Laundry, park and extensive gardens with long walks, ice house, follies, views (open all year, daily), restaurant, tearoom, shop.

Signposted on minor road off B3181 Exeter to Cullompton road, 7 miles north of Exeter.

Knightshayes Court, Devon

National Trust • £££ • Open mid-Mar to Oct, M-Th, S & Su

It could have been one of the most splendid and extravagant examples of the Victorian fascination with medieval gothic, but its builder could not, in the end, either afford such extravagance or persuade himself to live amongst it. All the same, it is a handsome house with plenty of fascinating detail inside and out.

The builder was Sir John Heathcoat Amory, grandson of the textile manufacturer John Heathcoat, who secured the family fortunes with his brilliant invention in 1808 of a machine for making lace – until then done by hand. In 1816, after his factory in Loughborough, Leicestershire, was destroyed by Luddites, Heathcoat moved the entire operation to Tavistock, many of his workers walking the 200-odd miles to join him. Not only did his business flourish, but he became known as a kind and caring employer, insisting on the education of the children who worked for him.

Sir John, the son of John's daughter, Anne, took no personal interest in the business, pursuing a parliamentary career before retiring to the life of a country squire: shooting on his estate in Perthshire, fishing at his lodge in Norway and hunting on Exmoor. In 1868 he bought the estate at Knightshayes and demolished an existing house. It may have been his wife, Henrietta, who chose to employ the most obsessive of gothic revival architects, William Burges, best known for his rebuilding of Cardiff Castle, begun in 1865. Burges's wildest ideas were fuelled as much by his addiction to opium as by his passion for medieval architecture; his golden rule was that there were no rules except 'whatever looks best is best'. There's a superb photograph of him in the guide book, dressed in the motley of a medieval jester.

All began well enough, the only major change to Burges's plans for the exterior being the removal of a huge tower. The shell of the house, built in dark red Hensley stone with dressings in yellow Ham stone, was begun in 1869 and finished by 1872. But Burges's designs for a fairytale interior were thought too much, and instead the firm of JD Crace was employed to complete the decoration. Even then, Sir John later had some of Crace's painted friezes removed.

Despite being a limited version of the original vision, Knightshayes is at its most glorious where it is most unrestrained: particularly in the medieval-style great hall, used by the family only for taking tea, with beautiful carved stone corbels supporting the roof. Almost as marvellous is Crace's dining room, now restored to its full splendour by the Trust. And one bedroom was, just for fun, decorated in 2002 in the style proposed by Burges, and features the bed he designed in 1879 for his own house in London.

Extensive gardens and grounds (also open early Mar, S & Su), restaurant, shop.

Signposted on A396 Tiverton to Minehead road, 2 miles north of Tiverton.

Knightshayes Court: superb gothic extravaganza of the 1860s and 1870s designed by William Burges, but without the full fairytale interiors Burges planned

Lanhydrock: Jacobean house of the 1620s and 1630s, remodelled in the 1880s as a Victorian ideal home

Lanhydrock, Cornwall

National Trust • £££ • Open Apr to Oct, Tu-F, S & Su

A fascinatingly complete example of a house of a particular period: not the Jacobean manor it first seems, from its low, plain, stone-built ranges and beautifully frivolous Renaissance gatehouse, but a High Victorian country residence in which the layout of the rooms reflects the strict social order of the times. It is also one of the most-visited National Trust properties and is, of course, especially busy in summer.

The lovely parkland in which it stands was originally a possession of the Priory of St Petroc at Bodmin, complete with a sacred well and a small stone church of the late 1400s. After the Dissolution it passed through various hands until, in 1620, it was bought by Sir Richard Robartes, whose family had become wealthy through supplying wood as fuel for the tin industry and by using the profits to establish a moneylending business.

Sir Richard began building the house, which was completed by his son, John, a key figure in Cornish affairs during the Civil War. The house consisted of four ranges around a long, rectangular courtyard, three of which survive. In 1857 it was remodelled by Thomas, 1st Baron Robartes, and his wife, Juliana, under the auspices of the most fashionable architect of the time, George Gilbert Scott. Scott left much of the work in the hands of his assistant Richard Coad, a local man; and after the house burned down in 1881, the family asked Coad, who by now had his own practice, to redevelop the house again, retaining its Jacobean character but giving it all the modern conveniences required by a well-off Victorian family.

Inside, the main survival from the original house is the long gallery, with superb plasterwork in its barrel-vaulted ceiling dating from about 1642. Coad gave the other public rooms an appropriately Jacobean feel, but of more interest are the extensive and wonderfully well-preserved service wings, the separate quarters for male and female servants, and the nursery wing, where the children could be neither seen nor heard.

Equally redolent of Victorian life is the male preserve of billiard room and smoking room, but best of all is the maze of larders and sculleries next to the kitchen, with beautifully contrived technology to keep everything running smoothly – such as the elaborate arrangement of running water in troughs that cools the dairy, or the steam jets in the scullery, used to scour greasy pots.

Parkland, gardens, church (open all year, daily), restaurant, shop.

Signposted off B3268 Bodmin to Lostwithiel road, 3 miles south-east of Bodmin.

Mount Edgcumbe, Cornwall

Local council • £££ • Open Apr to Sep, M-Th, Su

The house built in 1547–50 by Sir Richard Edgcumbe, formerly of Cotehele (see above), was a castle-like affair in red stone, with round towers at each corner and an innovative layout involving a great hall at the centre instead of a courtyard. Several of its original ogee-headed windows survive, but the majority was remodelled from 1644, after being set alight by Parliamentarian attackers in the Civil War, and in the early 1700s, when octagonal towers replaced the round ones. Gothic modifications followed in the 1800s, then the whole thing was destroyed by incendiary bombs in 1941.

Rebuilt in 1958–64, the house now has a freshly decorated feel, but the grand 1800s interiors have been convincingly recreated, and it is this aspect that gives Mount Edgcumbe its particular appeal.

Extensive parkland with walks, deer, follies and forts (open all year, daily, free), gardens (open as house), restaurant, shop.

Signposted on B3247 Torpoint to Cremyll road, 8 miles from Torpoint.

Mount Edgcumbe: built in 1547–50, remodelled in the early 1700s, destroyed in 1941, rebuilt in the 1950s

Pencarrow, Cornwall

Privately owned (HHA) • £££ • Open Apr to Oct, M-Th & Su, guided tours only

The approach, along a drive lined with the rhododendrons for which the gardens at Pencarrow are justly famous (there are more than 700 varieties), is spectacular; the house, a tidy but unimaginative ochre-stuccoed Palladian creation of the 1750s to 1770s, is much less so.

Inside it's a little musty and dusty in feel, but the fact that admission is by tour only – often a problem – means that visitors really do make the most of what's here.

Started by Sir John Molesworth (whose grandfather, a Vice-Admiral of northern Cornwall, was knighted by Charles II) and finished by his son, another Sir John, the house is still lived in by the family and has a sprinkling of pleasingly offbeat touches, such as the fine array of hats that adorn the busts in the inner hall.

None of the rooms is especially remarkable for its architecture or decoration and, perhaps as a result, the tour tends to pay much attention to detail, with a great deal of pointing-out of china and furniture. There are a few interesting stories, too, mind you: in the nicest room in the house, the music room, where visitors are invited to play the piano, much of the operetta *Iolanthe* was composed. Mostly, though, it's paintings and objects that attract the attention: not least two views of London in 1755 by Samuel Scott and a wonderful Chinese *famille rose* bowl in the ante-room.

Extensive and beautiful gardens (open Mar to Oct, daily), tearoom, shop.

Signposted on minor road from A389 Wadebridge to Bodmin road, 4 miles north-west of Bodmin.

Pencarrow: an unexciting Palladian-influenced house of the 1750s to 1770s, set in superb gardens

Powderham Castle, Devon

Privately owned (HHA) • £££ • Open Apr to Oct, M-F & Su, guided tours only

One of the oddest houses you're likely to visit, but certainly not without interest. From the outside, it still looks very much like the fortified manor of 1390–1490 that it fundamentally is – and is very tidy and well-looked-after, too. Inside, however, it is a hotchpotch of later additions and alterations, and in one or two places feels as though it could do with a bit of money spent.

Powderham was originally built by Sir Philip Courtenay, whose descendants, the Earls of Devon, still live here today. The castle was altered and added to many times over the years, and in its present form is largely the creation of William, 10th Earl of Devon, who inherited in 1835 and employed an Exeter architect, Charles Fowler, to tidy the place up. Grandest of the rooms they created together is the convincingly medieval great hall, with a superb gothicky fireplace and linenfold panelling added by William's son.

Even more striking, however, is an earlier addition, the immense, theatrical music room, built by the fashionable architect James Wyatt in 1794–6. The Adam-like carpet in contrasting pastel colours was designed especially for the room by Thomas Whitty, the founder of the Axminster factory.

Variety continues to be the theme throughout. There are cunning devices (secret doors in bookcases, windows concealed by sliding panels); there are things of beauty, and things of grotesque fascination (the hideous plasterwork of the 1750s and the garish blue paint in the stair hall). And you may meet the castle's oldest resident, a tortoise aged 160 by the name of Timothy.

Grounds with walks, Victorian rose garden (open as house, also Mar, Su), estate yard with working forge and wheelwright's workshop, tearoom, shop.

Signposted on A379 Exeter to Dawlish road, 6 miles south-west of Exeter.

Powderham Castle: a fortified manor of 1390–1490 with many later changes, including a Victorian revamp

Prideaux Place, Cornwall

Privately owned (HHA) • £££ • Open Easter and May to Oct, M-Th & Su, guided tours only

A rather wonderful combination of an E-plan Elizabethan house – complete with extraordinary carved wood panelling in the great hall, and a superb plasterwork ceiling in the great chamber above – with additions of the late 1700s and early 1800s in charmingly frivolous Strawberry Hill gothic style. The only thing that might spoil it for you is a dull tour guide. It does happen.

Built by Sir Nicholas Pridcaux in 1592, the older parts of the house retain fascinating details: the carved figures of women, with moveable arms, in the dining room, are unique and puzzling.

Gardens, tearoom.

Signposted on minor road just to the north of Padstow.

Prideaux Place: a fascinating blend of an Elizabethan manor of 1592 with gothic additions of the 1800s

St Michael's Mount, Cornwall

National Trust • £££ • Open Apr to Oct, M-F (access by causeway at low tide, ferry at high tide, weather permitting)

This magical setting, on a tidal island just off the beach of Penzance Bay, deserves a castle: but in fact it has a former Benedictine priory, a daughter house of the even more spectacular Mont St Michel in Normandy, which, thanks to its natural defences, slipped into use as a fortress after the dissolution. Since 1660, after being held by Royalist forces in the Civil War, it has been the home of the St Aubyn family – and inevitably has been much altered over the years as comfort became a priority.

Most pleasing of its surprisingly few rooms are the hall in the former refectory, with a superb plasterwork frieze of the mid-1600s depicting hunting scenes, and the blue drawing room, redecorated in a delicate rococo gothic style in about 1740–50. That apart, it's really the location that matters.

Church, gardens, restaurant, shop.

Signposted on shore road, off A390 Helston to Penzance road, 3 miles east of Penzance.

St Michael's Mount: originally a Benedictine priory, later a fortress that slowly developed into a house

Saltram, Devon

National Trust • £££ • Open Apr to Oct, M-Th, S & Su

A handsome house, Tudor in origin but given a comprehensive Palladian revamp after 1743, when it was inherited by John Parker, a country squire. Parker's marriage to Lady Catherine Poulett, the daughter of Queen Anne's Secretary of State, gave him enough money to build in fairly extravagant style – although not enough to demolish the old house and start again, as he had hoped. It was then remodelled internally in neoclassical style by Robert Adam in the 1770s, and again, in Regency fashion, in about 1820.

The result is a house that has remarkable moments, but doesn't quite satisfy as a whole. A number of wonderful features survive from the first remodelling in the 1740s, particularly the superb rococo plasterwork in the entrance hall; but, perhaps inevitably, it is the sheer class of Robert Adam's work that steals the show. The finest room is his saloon, which he designed, as usual, down to the tiniest detail, with a ceiling painted by Antonio Zucchi, a carpet that reflects the ceiling's patterns, armchairs and sofas by Chippendale, and Adam's own pier-glasses and side-tables. Only the chimneypiece is older.

Elsewhere in the house, the greatest treats are the handpainted wallpaper of the early 1700s in the Chinese dressing room and the collections of china and paintings, with fine portraits by Reynolds and Angelica Kauffmann.

Gardens (open all year, M-Th, S & Su), gallery, tearoom, shop.

Signposted off A38 at junction with A374, 4 miles east of Plymouth city centre.

Saltram: a Tudor house remodelled in Palladian style in the 1740s, with later interiors by Robert Adam

Shute Barton, Devon

National Trust • ££ • Open Apr to Oct, W & S, guided tours only

Although Shute Barton is, as one of the tour guides cheerfully described it, little more than a kitchen with a few extra things attached, the feeling of antiquity is immense and the well-informed guides make a visit into a fascinating exercise in puzzle-solving. And it really is a splendid kitchen, too, with what is said to be the largest chimney flue in the country.

It's the remnant of a large, unfortified manor house, built in stages between 1380 and the late 1500s, first by Sir William Bonville, a landowner and local bigwig of Norman descent, then by his son and grandson, and then, after the Wars of the Roses, by the Grey family, who inherited by marriage.

It became a tenanted farmhouse after a new house was built in the 1780s, and has been modernized and is still lived in today. The tour visits only a few rooms, but the kitchen is easily the star of the show.

Signposted on minor road off A35 Honiton to Axminster road in Shute village, 3 miles south-west of Axminster.

Shute Barton: the remnant of a huge manor built between 1380 and the late 1500s, with a fine kitchen

Trerice, Cornwall

National Trust • £££ • Open Apr to Oct, M, W-F, Su (also mid-Jul to early Sep, Tu)

A terribly pretty little Elizabethan manor house in an equally pretty garden setting, unfortunately much altered inside, but still with some of the original features that make houses of this era a delight. It was rebuilt from an earlier dwelling in the few years before 1573 by Sir John Arundell IV, a soldier and gentleman who served as Sheriff of Cornwall in 1574. His military career in the Low Countries may have been where he picked up the idea for the unusual Dutch gables. His son, another Sir John, famously held Pendennis Castle for the Royalists in the Civil War.

By far the most impressive room is the great hall, the traditional centrepiece of an Elizabethan house, separated from the entrance by a screens passage. Its strapwork plaster ceiling is intact, but was restored in the 1840s; the room is lit by a superb large window, with 576 panes of glass, many of them original. The minstrels' gallery is most unusual, screened from the hall by a series of low arches.

Almost as striking as the hall is the great chamber, the main reception room, on the first floor of the block beside the hall. It has wonderful plasterwork, both in the barrel-vaulted ceiling and in the overmantel above the fireplace, perhaps by the same craftsman who worked at Buckland Abbey (above). Other rooms are largely later additions or restoration.

Gardens, lawnmower museum (open as house), tearoom, shop.

Signposted on minor road off A3058 Newquay to St Austell road, 3 miles south-east of Newquay.

Trerice: rare survival of an Elizabethan manor in Cornwall, built about 1573 and restored in the 1950s

See also...

A La Ronde
Exmouth, Devon
National Trust, £££, open Apr to Oct, M-Th & Su
Very unusual little 16-sided house built in 'gothick' style in 1798, with shell-encrusted gallery.

Berry Pomeroy Castle
Near Totnes, Devon
English Heritage, ££, open Apr to Oct, daily
Interesting ruin picturesquely set in a steep valley, with walls and gatehouse of the 1400s and the shell of an Elizabethan house built in about 1560–1600 by the Seymour family.

Bickleigh Castle
Tiverton, Devon
Privately owned (HHA), £££, open Easter to Sep, Wed & Sun
A small Norman castle of about 1100 that has been lived in and much updated over the years.

Bradley Manor
Newton Abbot, Devon
National Trust, £££, open Apr to Sep, Tu-Th
Small medieval manor, still lived in and with limited access.

Berry Pomeroy Castle, below: walls and towers of the 1400s with an Elizabethan house behind

Cadhay
Ottery St Mary, Devon
Privately owned (HHA), £££, open late spring, M & Su, Jul-Aug, Tu-Th
Attractive stone-built Tudor manor incorporating fragments of a medieval priory, restored in 1910.

Caerhayes Castle
St Austell, Cornwall
Privately owned (HHA), £££, open late Mar to early May, daily
Mock-castle of early 1800s built by John Nash, in woodland gardens noted for camellias and rhododendrons.

Chambercombe Manor
Ilfracombe, Devon
Privately owned, ££, open Easter to Sep, M-F & Su, tours only
Small, atttractive manor house with great hall of the 1100s.

Compton Castle
Marldon, Paignton, Devon
National Trust, £££, open Apr to Oct, M, W-Th, tours only
Rather splendid fortified manor house of 1300s to 1500s, restored and still occupied.

Flete
Privately owned, £££, open May to Sep, W-Th
Smart Elizabethan manor with Victorian gothic update; converted into flats, so with limited access.

Fursdon
Cadbury, north of Exeter, Devon
Privately owned (HHA), ££, open one week in each of Apr, May, Jun, Aug, tours only
Very old home, possibly of 1200s, enlarged in the 1730s and given a new facade in 1815.

Haldon Belvedere
Near Dunchideock, Devon
Devon Historic Buildings Trust, £, open Mar to Oct, Su & bank hols
Triangular folly tower of 1700s. Not really a house, but rather good fun.

Hemerdon House
Plympton, Devon
Privately owned (HHA), £££, open on a few specified dates in May to Sep
Comfortable Georgian and Victorian home with naval connections.

Kirkham House
Paignton, Devon
English Heritage and local trusts, ££, open Jul to Aug, Su and on a few specific dates in Apr, May and Sep
A fascinating town house of the 1400s, but with limited opening.

Lawrence House
Launceston, Cornwall
National Trust and local council, free, open Apr to Oct, M-F
Georgian house now in use as a local museum and civic centre.

Marker's Cottage, Killerton
Broadclyst, near Exeter, Devon
National Trust, ££, open Apr to Oct, M-Tu & Su
A rather fine medieval cob house (built from mud) with medieval painted screen in cross-passage.

Oldway Mansion
Torbay, Devon
Local council, free, open all year, M-S (also Easter to Oct, Su)
Built in the 1870s by a sewing machine entrepreneur.

Overbecks Museum
Salcombe, Devon
National Trust, £££, open Apr to Sep, M-F & Su (also Aug, S, Oct, M-Th & Su)
Edwardian house containing unusual collections of scientist Otto Overbeck.

Sand

Sidmouth, Devon

Privately owned (HHA), £££, open on a few specified dates in Apr and Sep

Elizabethan manor rebuilt from an earlier house in the 1590s and extended in Tudor style in 1900s.

Tapeley Park

Instow, Bideford, Devon

Privately owned, £££, open Easter to Oct, M-F & Su

Much-altered Queen Anne house with gardens and park.

Tintagel Old Post Office

Tintagel, Cornwall

National Trust, ££, open Apr to Oct, daily

More interesting than it sounds, a delightful little stone-built manor house of the 1300s. One room contains the Victorian post office.

Tiverton Castle

Tiverton, Devon

Privately owned (HHA), £££, open Easter to Sep, Th & Su (also Jul and Aug, M-W)

Sizeable Norman castle of 1106 with many later alterations.

Torre Abbey

Kings Drive, Torquay

Local council, ££, open Apr to Oct, daily

Former abbey remodelled as a country house, now an art gallery.

Trewithen

Off A390 between Truro and St Austell, Cornwall

Privately owned (HHA), £££, open Apr to Aug, M-Tu

Palladian house of mid-1700s by Thomas Edwards of Greenwich, lived in by the family for 250 years.

Ugbrooke Park

Ideford, north of Newton Abbot, Devon

Privately owned (HHA), £££, open mid-Jul to early Sep, Tu-Th, limited number of tours only

Four-square house of the late 1700s by Robert Adam, with a neo-Norman facade added in the late 1800s. Terraced gardens, Capability Brown landscaped park.

Compton Castle: an attractive fortified manor with ruined medieval kitchens and a restored great hall

And...

Boconnoc

Lostwithiel, Cornwall

Privately owned, ££, open only to groups by appt

Very tidy country house bought in 1717 with the famous Pitt Diamond and home to three prime ministers. Tours visit limited parts of the house and the grounds (including church and Georgian bath house).

Bowhill

Near Exeter, Devon

English Heritage, ££, limited access

A mansion of about 1500 with restored great hall. Only open very occasionally for tours.

Exeter Customs House

The Quay, Exeter

Local council, free, limited opening for tours

Customs house built in 1680–2.

Dartington Hall,

Totnes, Devon

Privately owned, ££, open only to groups by appt

Manor of 1388 with noted gardens, now a hotel.

Hemyock Castle

Cullompton, Devon

Privately owned, ££, open only on bank holiday Mondays

Attractive little former fortified manor house, later a farm.

Puslinch

Yealmpton, Devon

Privately owned, ££, open only to groups by appt

Queen Anne/Georgian house of 1720.

Trelowarren House and chapel

Near Helston, Cornwall

Privately owned, ££, limited opening, details change annually

Tudor and 1600s house; chapel and main rooms open.

Wessex

Somerset, Dorset, Wiltshire, Hampshire, Isle of Wight

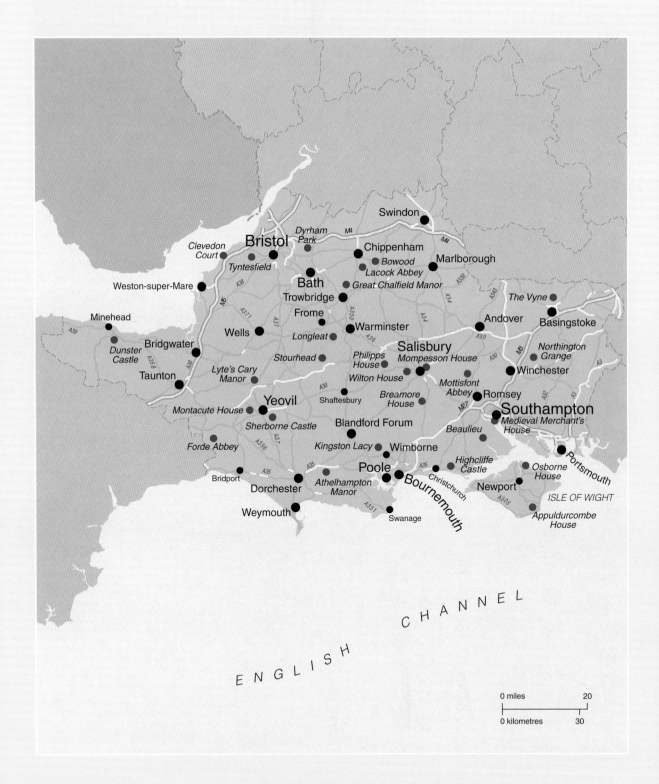

Swindon

Clevedon
Court
Bristol
Dyrham
Park
M4

Chippenham
Bowood
Marlborough

Tyntesfield
Lacock Abbey
Great Chalfield Manor
A34

Weston-super-Mare
Bath
The Vyne
Basingstoke

Trowbridge
A350
Andover

Frome
A36
A34

Minehead
A39
Wells
Warminster
Salisbury
Northington
Grange

Longleat
Mompesson House
Winchester

Bridgwater
Stourhead
Philipps
House
Romsey

Dunster
Castle
Lyte's Cary
Manor
Wilton House
Mottisfont
Abbey
Southampton

Taunton
A30
Breamore
House
M27
Medieval Merchant's
House

Yeovil
Shaftesbury
Beaulieu

Montacute House
Sherborne Castle
Blandford Forum
Highcliffe
Castle
Portsmouth

Forde Abbey
A37
A356
Kingston Lacy
Wimborne
Osborne
House

Bridport
A35
A35
Poole
Christchurch
Newport
ISLE OF WIGHT

Dorchester
Athelhampton
Manor
Bournemouth
A305

Weymouth
A351
Swanage
Appuldurcombe
House

E N G L I S H   C H A N N E L

0 miles   20
0 kilometres   30

Appuldurcombe House, Isle of Wight

English Heritage • ££ • Open mid-Feb to mid-Dec, daily

An engaging and romantic ruin, tucked away behind woods at the bottom of a small bowl of a valley, it provides both a simple lesson in architecture and an enjoyable wander in a peaceful spot.

Appuldurcombe was built by Sir Robert Worsley in 1701–13 and extended between 1723 and 1782, with the addition of a grand arched porte cochere – a covered carriage entrance – in the early 1800s. It has been abandoned since 1909. The back of the house is pretty ruinous; but the main entrance front to the east, which features a great deal of beautiful carved ornamentation, is still in fine condition, with glazing restored to the windows to help keep them from deteriorating.

Whereas later Palladian houses had an emphasis on the first floor, the piano nobile, with smaller windows above, this is in the baroque style, with equal weight given to the two main floors. Also typically baroque are the picture-frame-like mouldings around the windows, with bold triple wedge-shaped keystones above.

Grounds by Capability Brown, tearoom, shop, falconry centre (additional fee).

Signposted from B3327 near Wroxall.

Athelhampton: a small but beautiful manor, built around the great hall of 1485 and restored after 1891

Athelhampton, Dorset

Privately owned (HHA) • £££ • Open Mar to Oct, M-F & Su, Nov to Feb, Su

It's always pleasing to discover an ancient house that has changed little over the years; but the next best thing is a medieval house that has been sensitively restored in late Victorian times, when the quality of the original craftsmanship was both valued and equalled.

So it is with Athelhampton, which was going to ruin when bought in 1891 by Alfred Cart de la Fontaine. He not only renovated the house but also enhanced its interiors with fittings and furniture in the gothic revival style, some of it designed by AWN Pugin. He also laid out the beautiful gardens, which are now Grade I listed.

Central to the house is the great hall with its original timber roof, built in 1485. Like much of the rest of the house, it has beautiful panelling around the walls; the tall bay window is filled with heraldic glass of the Martyn family, builders of the hall, whose crest was a chained ape and whose motto, oddly, was 'He who looks at Martyn's ape, Martyn's ape shall look at him'.

Next door, up on the first floor, is the library, a perfect example of the way the Victorian adaptations chime in with the house's medieval feel. For this is a billiard room, a very Victorian idea, and though the snooker table and its 'killer pool' scoreboard dominate the room, its new oak panelling and chairs by Pugin give it an appropriate feel.

Cross-era highlights include the carved beams of the 1600s in the green parlour and the ceiling in the great parlour, copied in 1905 from one at the Reindeer Inn in Banbury.

Formal gardens, woodland gardens and riverside gardens, restaurant, shop.

Signposted from A35 Dorchester to Poole road, 6 miles east of Dorchester.

Appuldurcombe House: a view of the more ruinous rear, showing the porte cochere of the early 1800s

Beaulieu, Hampshire

*Privately owned (HHA) • ££££ •
Open all year, daily*

You might expect that the famous motor museum here would be the main attraction, with the house something of an afterthought, and you'd be quite right. Even though it is an interesting building – adapted from the abbey gatehouse and developed greatly in the 1870s, when the opportunities this sort of place provided for gothic revivalism were most appreciated – and even though it is still a lived-in family home, it is far smaller than you would expect and has the feel of a cross between a museum and a hotel. Perhaps it's simply down to the sheer number of visitors who now cross its threshold. Lord Montagu and his family have a private suite in the Victorian wing.

It is not, however, entirely without charm. The rebuilding of the 1870s made as much use as possible of old monastic features, and the baronial style of the dining room and lower drawing room, with their original vaulted ceilings, is very satisfying. There are some good portraits, too.

Motor museum, abbey ruins, large gardens (all open as house), restaurants, shops.

Clearly signposted on B3054 at Beaulieu, 8 miles south-west of Southampton.

Palace House, Beaulieu: built from the medieval abbey gatehouse, and given a gothic revival in the 1870s

Bowood, Wiltshire

*Privately owned (HHA) • £££ •
Open Apr to Oct, daily*

A peculiar house, largely because it isn't strictly speaking a house at all. It's actually the wing of a house built between 1720 and 1760, and demolished in 1955. The new wing was designed by Robert Adam, no less, in the 1760s, principally to house an orangery and conceal the service courtyard, and was originally attached to the main house by a vast drawing room, which has also gone.

The wing was made grander yet in the 1800s when the 3rd Marquess of Lansdowne – whose Prime Minister father had employed Adam – commissioned CR Cockerell to design the chapel and alter the library, and Sir Charles Barry to add a few external flourishes. So it's an oddity, but such a grand and pleasing one that it hardly matters.

Perhaps inevitably, it does seem more like a museum than a house. The orangery is like a long picture gallery with glazed arcades, leading into a smaller sculpture gallery with several pretty Victorian statues. From the orangery open the chapel, the library (in which Cockerell swept away most of Adam's work in favour of a blunter neoclassicism) and, believe it or not, a laboratory, in which Dr Joseph Priestley identified oxygen gas in 1774.

Upstairs is a series of exhibition rooms displaying assorted objects and, strangely, entire reconstructed rooms behind glass, with a superb collection of watercolours by Turner, Varley and others, and a wonderful series of sketches made mostly in Africa by the adventurous Richard Parkes Bonington.

Gardens, grounds and parkland walks, restaurant, shop.

Signposted on A4 Chippenham to Calne road, 2 miles west of Calne.

Bowood: the wing of a now-demolished house, designed by Robert Adam to contain a library and orangery

Breamore House, Hampshire

Privately owned (HHA) • ££ • Open May to Sep, Tu-Th, S & Su • Tours only

A classic Elizabethan manor house – one of the most satisfying kinds of English architecture – built of red brick, with large windows and tall, prominent chimneystacks, and laid out in the 'E' plan always said to have been intended to flatter Queen Elizabeth by reflecting the initial of her name (though surely the design has more to do with symmetry and the benefits of the projecting bays bringing light into the house).

Externally, the house looks much as it did when built in 1583 by Sir William Dodington, although one prominent feature – the eccentric water-tower behind the house – is a notable later addition. Incidentally, the murder of his mother at Breamore by Sir William's grandson, Henry, in 1629 is said by some to be the reason behind the house's most persistent ghost story.

Inside a fair bit has changed over the years, but then this is a family home, still lived in by the Hulse family, who bought it in 1748, and is no less appealing for its blend of early features and later modifications. The tour is not extensive, visiting the principal rooms on the ground floor and two bedrooms before concluding in the kitchens, but is very pleasant in tone and focuses quite interestingly on the paintings and furnishings gathered by the Hulses in the course of the past 250-odd years.

The most impressive of the rooms for its original character is the great hall, exactly four times as long as it is wide. The fact that the original door (a later entrance at the back of the house is now used) is placed right in the middle of the central bay and leads straight into the middle of the great hall shows how advanced this house was in comparison to others of the period, where the medieval concept of the hall, with offset entrance and screens passage, was still adhered to (compare, for example, the equally handsome red brick manor at Burton Agnes in Yorkshire).

Among the most striking of the works of art on show are a pair of Brussels tapestries of about 1630 in the great hall, designed by the artist David Teniers and showing a fishing scene and a harvest, and a bizarre but fascinating series of portraits seized from a Spanish galleon depicting the results of various kinds of inter-racial liaisons.

Tearoom, shop, maze and Breamore Countryside Museum with collections of tractors and traction engines (admission included with house).

Signposted on the A338 Ringwood to Salisbury road just north of Fordingbridge.

Breamore House: a classic Elizabethan manor house – the red brick construction, tall chimneys and large windows all spoke of wealth and status

Clevedon Court: a stone-built manor house of the 1320s, with later additions but its original rooms intact

Clevedon Court, Somerset

National Trust • £££ • Open Apr to Oct, W, Th & Su

A rare and rather splendid stone-built manor house of the 1320s, much of which survives beneath various later additions. It was built by Sir John de Clevedon, lord of the manor and a direct descendant of the man who took over the lands here at the Norman Conquest. One of its most unusual features is a private chapel, 'hanging' on the first floor, which may have been put in because the church, two miles away, was inaccessible in winter across flooded marshes.

The manor incorporates two earlier buildings, a thick-walled defensive tower of the mid-1200s and a hall of about 1300 (now the museum, containing a collection of Elton Ware pots and Nailsea glass). The new manor was set alongside both, forming a tiny triangular courtyard with the well in it.

The great hall survives, with a screens passage at one end running between front and back porches – the halls of the time nearly always had a direct through-route to a rear courtyard. The chimney-like vents that once let smoke escape from the open hearth (proper fireplaces were added in the time of Henry VIII) can still be seen outside.

The other rooms of the 1320s have been buried or altered in later rebuilding, all except the chapel, with its eccentrically beautiful tracery window.

The few rooms open to visitors are only sparsely furnished, but a number of paintings recall the days of Sir Charles Abraham Elton, poet, friend of Thackeray and member of a literary circle that included the Wordsworths, Southey and Coleridge. His good works included bringing gas lighting to the area: 'not merely useful, but ornamental'.

Signposted on B3128 just to the west of Clevedon town centre.

Dunster Castle, Somerset

National Trust • £££ • Open Apr to Oct, M-W, S & Su

Looking gothically picturesque from a distance, but a little plain close up, this is a pretend-castle created in 1868–72 by the leading gothic architect of the day, Anthony Salvin, for the Luttrell family, who had lived here since the late 1300s. Salvin's castle incorporated parts of a medieval castle, of which the original gatehouse survives, but is based mostly on a house of the 1600s built within the old walls. Salvin, an expert in the 'Tudorbethan' style as well as in pseudo-medieval castles, retained features from the Jacobean house, including fine plasterwork and a handsome oak and elm staircase.

The interiors are very mixed, with some good Chippendale furniture among the highlights. Best of all, though, are the painted leather hangings in the gallery, which date from the mid-1600s and depict the story of Anthony and Cleopatra, and the servants' wing created by Salvin; although the latter is, sadly, not always open.

Parkland with walks, interesting gardens, tearoom, shop.

Signposted on A39 Minehead to Bridgwater road, 3 miles south-east of Minehead.

Dunster Castle: on the site of a Norman fortress, built by Anthony Salvin for the Luttrells in 1868–72

Dyrham Park, Somerset

National Trust • £££ • Open Apr to Oct, M-Tu, F, S & Su

There's something frustrating and something endearing about Dyrham, and both boil down to exactly the same thing: it is simply not in the best possible taste. It was built between 1692 and 1704 as a stage-by-stage adaptation of an existing Tudor house, carried out in a Dutch-influenced baroque style that even in its day was already behind the times.

Its owner was William Blathwayt, a top-ranking civil servant known as 'the Elephant' for the plodding nature of his jokes, but a lover of books and music. His early career as private secretary to the British ambassador in Holland proved his competence and left him fluent in Dutch: this skill was to prove invaluable after the fall of James II

Dyrham Park: rebuilt from a smaller Tudor house in 1692–1704, in an old-fashioned baroque style

in 1688, when the new Dutch king, William II, found that Blathwayt was too valuable a servant to dismiss, even though he had loyally supported the old king. In 1692, Blathwayt was made Secretary of State on a salary of £2,200 and at last had the money to rebuild Dyrham, which he had inherited by marriage in 1686. Sadly, his wife, whom he seems to have married for her money but then fallen in love with, had died the year before.

His descendants had neither the money nor the inclination to improve the house, so it remains structurally much as he left it, but the interiors were changed here and there in the 1840s, and given a little fashionable updating by the tenant from 1936 to 1948, Anne, Lady Islington. The exterior is handsome enough; the interiors tend towards dark wood panelling and heavy classical ornamentation.

The two great difficulties for a visitor to Dyrham is that the route around the house is confusing, and enough changes have been made to leave a haphazard impression, dominated by Blathwayt's rich tapestries and furniture, but never quite as he left it. The rooms that stand out are the halls and stairs, where the lack of furnishing is a relief and the original glory of woodwork and plaster still sings.

A real highlight is the superb perspective painting of a Dutch (naturally) interior painted in 1662 by Samuel Van Hoogstraten.

A treat at the end of the visit, too, is the servants' quarters, modernized in 1844–5. The fountain to cool the dairy is a lovely touch.

Gardens (open as house), parkland with walks (open daily, all year), tearoom, shop.

Signposted on A46 Bath to Stroud road, 8 miles north of Bath.

Forde Abbey, Dorset

Privately owned • £££ • Open Apr to Oct, Tu-F & Su

A fascinating blend of styles and periods, but more than anything else an Italian palazzo created in the mid-1600s in the trendiest of Renaissance styles, inside the shell of a former abbey.

The abbey was grand enough in itself, having been rebuilt between 1521 and 1539 by Abbot Chard, clearly a man of great pretensions and little restraint. The great hall is much as he left it, a vast room flooded with light from huge windows – although in fact it was shortened and the windows on one side were blocked in subsequent rebuilding. Equally pleasing is the one cloister surviving from the abbot's time, now used as a sort of conservatory.

After the abbey's dissolution in 1539, it decayed gradually for more than a century until in 1649 it was bought by Edmund Prideaux, Cromwell's Attorney General. He converted the abbot's lodgings into a family home, created an immense saloon from the lay brothers' quarters, with an impressive staircase leading up to it, and put in state apartments above the cloister.

It was once thought that Prideaux had the help of Inigo Jones, and indeed the architecture is very

Forde Abbey: grand monastic lodgings, converted into a palatial Renaissance house in about 1650

much in Jones's grand classical style. The saloon is by far the most splendid of Prideaux's rooms, on an extraordinary scale for its time, with a superb plaster ceiling and excellent tapestries (the latter, based on a set of cartoons by Raphael and woven in Mortlake in the 1620s, are possibly the abbey's greatest treasures).

Famous and extensive gardens (open all year, daily), restaurant, shops.

Signposted off B3162 Chard to Bridport road, 4 miles south-east of Chard.

Highcliffe Castle, Dorset

Local council • ££ • Open Mar to Dec daily

A fascinating phoenix rising from the ashes of fires in 1967 and 1968, for long a neglected ruin but now slowly being restored. It is a most unusual gothic house of 1830–35 incorporating quantities of genuine medieval gothic stonework shipped over from France, some of it from the Norman abbey at Jumieges.

The first house at High Cliff was built in 1773 by Robert Adam for the retired former Prime Minister Lord Bute, who bought land here long before the Victorian resort of Bournemouth was established, after discovering the area on a botanical expedition. Unfortunately his son demolished the house in 1794, then sold the estate. The land was bought back by the diplomat Lord Stuart de Rothesay, who built the new house.

The roofs are back on, but the house is little more than a shell. None the less, the architectural details are fascinating. To add interest, there are art exhibitions and history displays.

Grounds with seaside walks (open all year), tearoom, shop.

On A337 Christchurch to Lymington road, 3 miles east of Christchurch.

Highcliffe Castle: a fascinating Victorian gothic house incorporating genuine, imported gothic stonework

Great Chalfield Manor, Wiltshire

National Trust • £££ • Open Apr to Oct, Tu-Th, guided tours only

A lovely spot to visit, the ancient manor having settled quietly into the landscape over the course of more than 500 years, surrounded by a still-thriving miniature estate consisting of farm buildings, cottages and parish church.

The moat and the low remnants of a defensive wall – which, like parts of the church, dates from the 1300s or even earlier – show that this was once a fortified manor, but the delicate oriel windows on the north front of the house suggest a more gracious and less warlike age. This side, from which visitors approach the house, still looks much as it did when it was built by Thomas Tropnell between about 1467 and 1480.

Tropnell, the son of a family of not very wealthy local landowners, became steward to the far more powerful Hungerfords, who set him up for a seat in Parliament. He was able to successfully pursue a series of lawsuits that eventually brought him the manor at Great Chalfield, thanks to a family connection with its previous owners, the Percies, that dated back to the early 1200s. Through good management of his properties and a sound knowledge of the law, Tropnell eventually built up an estate consisting of more than seven manors.

Thomas is thought to have started building at Great Chalfield in about 1467, and was certainly living here by 1480. The house he created was based around a great hall, with private apartments at either end. Behind it was a walled courtyard with two ranges of buildings, of which only the foundation walls now survive. To the front of the house, on the right, a long, low service range was added at some unspecified time after Thomas's house was finished, connecting with an ancient gatehouse.

As is often the case, the gradual decline and decay of the manor had reached an almost terminal stage by the early 1800s when Thomas Larkin Walker, a pupil of Pugin, made a number of accurate drawings of the architecture. In 1838, the east (left-hand) side of the house was pulled down, but luckily leaving intact the facade with the oriel window. Larkin's drawings proved the saving of the place when, in 1905–12, it was rebuilt by the architect Sir Harold Brakspear for Robert Fuller, whose family still lives in the house.

Everything to the left of the hall – essentially just the solar on the first floor, now used as a living room – is a beautifully accurate reconstruction, while everything to the right – the parlour (now dining room) on the ground floor and the bedchamber above, both still with the same use – is original, but updated. Of most interest is the hall itself, with beautiful roof timbers and traces of stone benches around the walls; its rarest and most intriguing feature is a set of three 'looking-masks' set over openings in the walls, through the eyes of which someone standing behind could peer into the hall.

Church, gardens, stables and outbuildings.

On minor road from Bradford Leigh to Great Chalfield, off B3109 Corsham road 4 miles north-east of Bradford-on-Avon.

Great Chalfield Manor: the north front still looks much as it did when built in 1480, although much of the house behind the facade was rebuilt in 1905–12

Kingston Lacy: even prettier than when it was first built, having been restored in the 1830s

Kingston Lacy, Dorset

National Trust • £££ • Open late Mar to Nov, W-F, S & Su

Not only is it one of the most attractive of Britain's grand country houses, Kingston Lacy also has a superb art collection and tells rather vividly the stories of a number of its occupants.

Built in 1663 for Sir Ralph Bankes, who had rebuilt the fortunes of his staunchly Royalist family (owners of Corfe Castle) after the Civil War, it was long thought to have been the work of Inigo Jones, the first great English architect. In fact it is by Sir Roger Pratt, a follower of Jones who was equally influential at the end of the century. It has a pleasing exterior, friendly as well as imposing, with a touch of the doll's house.

Kingston Lacy owes its present looks, inside as well as out, to the taste and style of William Bankes, who inherited in 1834. A close friend of Byron and a man whose wealth allowed him to indulge his passions for art, travel and archaeology (the obelisks in the grounds are real), William restored the house after an earlier rebuilding and redesigned the interiors as a splendid setting for his collections.

Unfortunately for him, in 1841 William was accused of consorting with a guardsman in Green Park and had to flee the country. In exile in Italy, he commissioned statues and furnishings of the highest quality and sent them home with strict instructions to his sister as to how they should be placed. The result is a house that drips with quality, with astonishing craftsmanship in such details as the carved boxwood doors in the dining room.

Sadly William could never return to show off his house to guests, but he is said to have made secret visits. He also bought some truly great paintings, including a Titian and an unfinished masterpiece by the Renaissance artist Sebastiano del Piombo which attracts experts from all over the world.

The last owner of Kingston Lacy, another Ralph Bankes, used just three rooms – an office off the entrance hall and a bedroom and bathroom upstairs – as a bizarre sort of two-up, two-down. His Victorian carved bed, with a wizard sitting at its foot, is a highlight.

Don't miss, either, the superb avenue of beech trees – originally there were 365 pairs, one for each day of the year, planted by William just after he inherited as a birthday present for his mother – that runs past the iron age hill fort of Badbury Rings.

Victorian laundry, gardens, estate walks (open Feb to Dec), children's play areas, restaurant, shop, herd of Red Devon cattle.

On B3082 Wimborne to Blandford road, 2 miles west of Wimborne Minster.

Lacock Abbey, Wiltshire

National Trust • £££ • Open Apr to Oct, M, W-F, S & Su

Of all the many houses built from (or on top of) the remains of a dissolved abbey, Lacock stands out because so much of the original monastic fabric survives. It was a nunnery for Augustinian canonesses until its suppression in 1539, when William Sharington bought it and converted the accommodation ranges around the cloister into a house, demolishing the church.

Sharington employed top-quality craftsmen to complete the conversion in the most up-to-date Renaissance style. The house was remodelled in the 1750s, when it was one of the very earliest to get the gothic revival treatment, and in the 1800s by the house's famous occupant, the photographic pioneer William Henry Fox Talbot, and his son.

The fabric of the building is, consequently, of more interest than its contents, the interiors mostly being a characterless fusion of styles from the mid-1700s onwards.

Fox Talbot Photography Museum, cloisters, garden (all open Apr to Oct, daily), shop.

Signposted in Lacock village, off A350 Chippenham to Melksham road.

Lacock Abbey: the cloister buildings were made into a house in the 1540s but many original details survive

Longleat, Wiltshire

Privately owned (HHA) • £££ • Open Apr to Dec, daily, Jan to Mar, S & Su

One of the greatest Elizabethan houses, its interiors vastly remodelled over the years, but retaining much of its original character on the outside, where the broad expanses of stone and glass – the huge windows look almost like those of a factory – must have been a striking statement of wealth and privilege when it was first built. Now, of course, it is as well known for its safari park and many other tourist attractions, but the house is, none the less, both a family home and a pleasant place to visit.

Longleat was built in 1568–80 by Sir John Thynne, by then quietly retired after a turbulent career that had seen him rise from clerk of the kitchen at the Tudor court to become one of the wealthiest and most powerful men in the kingdom. Its facades are thought to have been designed by Robert Smythson and Allen Maynard, and give it an unusually gracious, serene look.

The home of the Thynne family ever since, it is now owned by the mildly eccentric 7th Marquess of Bath, whose text for the guidebook is nicely warm and informative. Inside, the only real survival of the Elizabethan era is the great hall; dominant from here on in are the influences of Sir Jeffrey Wyattville, who remodelled the house in the early 1800s, and the designer JD Crace, who created superb gilded and painted ceilings in the style of an Italian palace for the 4th Marquess in the 1870s and 1880s.

There are many little treats and treasures, notable amongst them being a superb Titian stolen in 1995 and now back in its rightful place.

Safari park (separate admission), many other attractions, restaurants and shops.

Signposted off A362 Frome to Warminster road, 3 miles west of Warminster.

Longleat: one of the greatest and most beautiful Elizabethan houses, built in 1568–80 for Sir John Thynne

Lytes Cary Manor, Somerset

National Trust • £££ • Open mid-Apr to Oct, M, W, F, Su

A charming little Tudor manor house – or at least what remains of it – built in the early 1500s around a great hall of the mid-1400s. It survives largely unaltered because it was more or less abandoned by the late 1700s, and it only survives at all – the north range was pulled down before 1810 and the west range disappeared not long after – to its purchase in 1907 and subsequent sensitive restoration by Sir Walter Jenner (the son of Queen Victoria's doctor) and his wife Flora.

The house gets its name from the nearby River Cary and the family who lived here, the Lytes, whose most famous son was the Elizabethan scholar and botanist Henry Lyte. An original copy of his *Niewe Herbal* of 1578, illustrated with 870 woodcuts of the plants described in it, is on show in the great hall.

The hall is the finest room in the house as well as the oldest, its beautiful roof with three tiers of curving windbraces and carved heraldic angels giving it an almost church-like feel. Also impressive is

Lytes Cary Manor: to the left is the chapel of 1348; the door leads into the great hall of the mid-1400s

the great chamber, the original plaster ceiling of which survives.

The manor has been kept as the Jenners – whose children both died young – left it, furnished with an interesting collection of items of appropriate date and style. For such a small place – only six rooms – there is plenty to see.

Gardens (open as house), riverside walk.

Signposted from A372 at junction with A303 and A37, 3 miles south-west of Somerton.

Mompesson House, Wiltshire

National Trust • £££ • Open Apr to Sep, M-W, S & Su

In a lovely setting beside a green not far from Salisbury's famous cathedral, this is a quiet gem of a town house, built in 1701 by Charles Mompesson and decorated with extravagant and beautifully executed plasterwork some 40 years later by his brother-in-law, Charles Longueville.

If it fails to satisfy the visitor entirely, that's largely because the florid decoration – a little archaic in its own time – is not to everyone's taste, and the original layout and use of each room is not known, so that it doesn't quite give a complete or convincing impression of a grand 18th-century household.

Very amusing, though, are the descriptions of the decorative experiments of the house's last owner, Denis Martineau. Turquoise and strident pink? The little library he created has been left as it was, as a backhanded compliment – clumsy, ill-proportioned, gaudily coloured and actually rather cosy.

Garden (open as house), tearoom.

In Choristers' Green, Cathedral Close, Salisbury, pedestrian access only.

Mompesson House: on the outside, at least, a pleasing and well-proportioned town house of 1701

Montacute House, Somerset

National Trust • £££ • Open Apr to Oct, M, W-F, S & Su

This exuberantly attractive Elizabethan manor house, built of warm, yellow limestone from the quarries at nearby Ham Hill, has justly been described as the most beautiful of its age in England – yet it's easy to forget that in its own time, when people were not as used to tall buildings as we are now, it must also have seemed incredibly impressive and grand.

Laid out symmetrically on the classic 'H' plan, the house was originally just one room wide, but in the 1780s it was widened by the addition of a new west front using stonework from another house at Clifton Maybank near Yeovil.

The east front, on the other hand, is almost exactly as it was when Montacute was built. This was the main entrance front, separated from the road by a walled courtyard with pavilions at the corners and a gatehouse; all but the gatehouse has survived intact. The facade of the house has acres of glass, another statement of wealth and status, and is enlivened with statues in niches, small pointy obelisks, chimneys shaped like columns and curving Flemish gables topped with amusing little animal figures.

Inside, Montacute retains enough of its Elizabethan layout to give a good impression of how a house of its age would have functioned, from the great hall in which the servants would still have eaten and passed their leisure time, to the great chamber upstairs (now the library) in which the lord and his guests would have dined and the withdrawing room next door (now divided in two as the crimson bedroom suite) to which they would have retired after the meal.

In addition, a great deal of the original decoration survives, with highly entertaining plasterwork friezes in the great hall (depicting an errant husband being paraded around the village astride a pole) and in the parlour (showing animals both native and exotic, including a rather sweet camel) plus remarkable woodwork and fireplaces throughout.

Inevitably the most stunning room is the long gallery at the top of the house, the longest of its type surviving, with beautiful oriel windows at either end. It is used to display portraits of appropriate age from the collections of the National Portrait Gallery.

Montacute was finished in 1601, built by a prolific and influential Somerset stonemason named William Arnold for Edward Phelips, a lawyer and judge who was knighted by King James I and served as Speaker of the House of Commons. He was notoriously intolerant of Roman Catholics, once condemning a man to death 'simply for entertaining a Jesuit', and opened for the prosecution at the trial of Guy Fawkes in 1605.

Garden (also open winter, W-F, S & Su), restaurant, shop.

Signposted from A3088 and A303 4 miles west of Yeovil.

Montacute House: the west front was added in the 1780s using stonework from another house. Elsewhere, the house is much as it was when finished in 1601

Mottisfont Abbey, Hampshire

National Trust • £££ • Open Mar to Oct, M-W, S & Su (also mid to late Jun, daily, Jul and Aug, Th)

Best known for its gardens, and especially its collection of old-fashioned rose varieties, Mottisfont stands in pleasant lawns on the banks of the River Test. It's an odd little house, built from the church and small parts of the cloister of a priory of Austin canons after its dissolution in 1536 by William, 1st Lord Sandys of The Vyne, a former Lord Chamberlain to Henry VIII who took the land here in exchange for the villages of Paddington and Chelsea near London. Perhaps his descendants might wish he had hung on to them.

It was completely rebuilt in the 1740s and little remains of either the priory or the Tudor house. Indeed, the feel of the Georgian house does not survive in the interiors, which were redecorated in a vaguely kitsch neo-classical style after its purchase in 1934 by Gilbert Russell – a descendant of the Duke of Bedford and also, he later discovered, of the founder of the priory – and his wife Maud.

The house is now used principally as a gallery space for

Mottisfont Abbey: a house of the 1740s based on a medieval priory, now principally a modest art gallery

the eclectic art collection put together by Maud, who was a patron of many major artists in the first half of the 20th century. She also commissioned Rex Whistler to paint the eccentric gothic decorations on the walls of the drawing room of the house, which remain its most interesting feature.

Walled gardens (open as house, also Mar, S & Su), tearoom, shop.

Signposted off A3057 Romsey to Andover road, 4 miles north of Romsey.

Northington Grange, Hampshire

English Heritage • Free • Open all year, daily

Architecturally one of the most interesting houses in Britain, as reflected in the fact that half a million pounds has recently been spent on its restoration, and well worth seeing, even though visitors can only admire the exterior. Created in 1804–09 by the architect William Wilkins for Henry Drummond, it was the epitome of the Greek revival style and has been called 'the most complete Greek-temple house of all time'.

Wilkins' house is essentially just a refacing of a mansion built in about 1670 by William Samuell, and said to have been one of the first houses to use a Palladian-style layout; it belonged to the Barings banking family. The Prince of Wales, later George IV, lived there for a while and in Victorian times Carlyle, Thackeray, Kingsley and Wilberforce were regular guests.

The house is set in a landscaped park with lakes; the attractive orangery of 1825 has also been restored.

Signposted on minor road off B3046 New Alresford to Basingstoke road, 4 miles north of New Alresford.

The Grange, Northington: the finest Greek-style house in Britain, built in 1804–09 by William Wilkins

Osborne House, Isle of Wight

English Heritage • £££ • Open Apr to Oct, daily

Whatever your feelings about Queen Victoria, it's impossible to not be amused by the Italianate villa the Queen and Prince Albert built between 1844 (four years after their marriage) and 1851 as their private home, away from the everyday stresses of their three official residences: Windsor Castle, Buckingham Palace and the Royal Pavilion at Brighton.

Osborne was designed by the London building contractor Thomas Cubitt in the Italianate style popularized by Charles Barry in the 1830s. It might not seem it today, but the Queen and the Prince Consort considered this style absolutely right for its seaside setting with views over the Solent, which apparently reminded the Prince of the Bay of Naples.

Inside, the house is exactly the mixture of opulence with a splash of kitsch that you might expect, but there are surprises, too. For one thing, all the stories of Victorian table-leg-covering prudery don't prepare you for the extensive collections of very un-covered-up classical statues, clearly not chosen for their coyness; nor for the vast fresco at the top of the stairs, *Neptune Resigning the Empire of the Seas to Britannia*, painted by William Dyce in 1847, with its voluptuously naked figures.

Equally unexpected is that some of the rooms are really rather lovely – particularly the principal drawing room, with its rich yellow damask curtains, cosy as well as very ornately decorated – while others show a fascination with classical decoration – such as the grand corridor, a combination of entrance hall and sculpture gallery, where the walls and ceilings are painted with classical motifs in rich reds, blues and greens.

Yet more surprises come in Victoria's private apartments, where her own paintings are on display (sentimental subjects, but her technique is quite decent) and where the room in which she died in January 1901 was treated as a kind of private shrine, complete with memorial stone, by the family. An iron gate installed by Edward VII blocked access to the suite of rooms to all but royal visitors.

Also strangely fascinating are the portraits (including one of the Queen's Indian secretary, who taught her Urdu) and collections in the Durbar wing, built in 1890–1. They betray an unexpected respect for and interest in the Empire's far-flung subjects.

Formal terraced gardens and extensive grounds (open as house), Swiss Cottage (the royal children's playhouse), children's museum, children's play fort and barracks, Victoria's bathing machine, tearooms, shop.

On A3021 1 mile north of East Cowes.

Osborne House: built by Queen Victoria and Prince Albert in 1844–51 as their private home, and given to the nation in 1902 by King Edward VII

Philipps House and Dinton Park, Wiltshire

National Trust • ££ • Open Apr to Oct, M, S

A little gem that might take only ten minutes to visit – unless, that is, you get chatting to the friendly, well-informed guides – but is still very much worth the trip. Completed in 1820 and designed by Sir Jeffrey Wyattville for William Wyndham, an educated country gentleman, it is a handsome villa in the neo-Grecian style fashionable at the time – plainer and simpler than the Palladian villas of the previous century.

The interior is an essay in elegance, the six rooms of the ground floor – all that visitors see – each connecting with the high, square staircase hall at the centre. The stair itself is a thing of beauty: its treads of Portland stone, cantilevered out of the wall, are amazingly thin.

The same kind of attention to detail is evident in all the fabric of the house, including the lovely mahogany doors and delicate plaster cornices. The rooms are sparsely furnished, making such details all the easier to appreciate.

Signposted on B3089 Wilton to Mere road, 9 miles west of Salisbury.

Philipps House: a modestly sized, impeccably elegant neo-Grecian villa built in 1820 by Jeffrey Wyattville

Sherborne Castle, Dorset

Privately owned (HHA) • £££ • Open Apr to Oct, Tu-Th, S & Su

One of the most eccentric-looking houses in Britain, built as a tall, hexagonal-turreted, tower-like structure by Sir Walter Raleigh in 1594 and extended in the 1620s by the addition of four wings with more turrets at their ends, creating the complex outline that survives to this day. Its rendered exterior looks a little glum in dull weather, but again is as it was originally.

Many details survive from Raleigh's time, such as the plaster ceiling in his great chamber (now the green drawing room) on the first floor of the tower. The room is dominated by Victorian decoration and furnishings, but in themselves these are now quite rare survivals, and certainly not lacking in quality. A similar blend of periods and styles, dotted with occasional objects or fittings of outstanding interest – such as the tobacco pipe Raleigh was given by native Americans – prevails throughout the house.

The wings were added by the diplomat Sir John Digby, who bought the house from King James in 1617, the land having been forfeited to the Crown after Raleigh's execution for treason. In one of these wings is the house's least-altered room, the oak room, its original panelling and interior porch still intact. The cracked hearthstone is said to have been damaged by the weight of the printing press on which William of Orange produced his proclamation leaflets in 1688.

Garden and grounds (open as house), tearoom, shop.

Signposted off A352 Sherborne to Dorchester road on south-west side of Sherborne.

Sherborne Castle: the central block was built by Sir Walter Raleigh in 1594, the wings added in the 1620s

Stourhead, Wiltshire

National Trust • £££ • Open Apr to Oct, M-Tu, F, S & Su

A far more prominent attraction than the house is the famous and theatrical gardens, described as 'an outstanding example of the English landscape style', with classical temples set around a lake to offer a series of changing vistas. Yet the house, though modest in its appeal, also has a great deal of interest.

The interior was mostly destroyed by a disastrous fire in 1902, after which it was restored in a debased version of the original, and today many of the rooms are Edwardian in flavour and comfortable rather than spectacular. What makes it interesting, however, is the underlying structure: Stourhead was one of the first country villas in a pure Palladian style, built in 1721–5 for the London banker Henry Hoare by Colen Campbell. Campbell's book *Vitruvius Britannicus*, the first volume published in 1715, helped kick off the Palladian craze.

In designing Stourhead, Campbell used the idea that rooms with simple mathematical proportions would be harmonious and pleasing. Thus the entrance hall is a 30-foot cube, while the rooms on each side – the music room and cabinet room – are both 30 feet by 20 feet.

Campbell was supported by the architect earl Lord Burlington (see Chiswick House, London), who banked with Hoare. In addition, Hoare's brother-in-law was William Benson, successor to Sir Christopher Wren as Surveyor-General, who appointed Campbell as his deputy. Hardly surprising, then, that Campbell should end up as the architect of Hoare's house.

The entrance front was enlarged considerably in 1792 when Sir Richard Colt Hoare, one of the first archaeologists to study Wiltshire's prehistoric monuments, added two wings in a restrained and sympathetic style to contain his library and picture gallery. These rooms escaped the fire and are among the finest examples of

Regency interiors in England. Sir Richard also commissioned a great deal of furniture from Thomas Chippendale, much of which is still in the house, and paintings from the young JMW Turner, nearly all of which, sadly, have been sold – although Sir Richard's fascinating collection of paintings by the Swiss artist Louis Ducros is still in place.

The gardens were created by Henry Hoare's son, also Henry, known as 'Henry the Magnificent'. He married twice, but after the death of his second wife, Susanna, in 1743 his gardens became his main preoccupation. He commissioned sculptures from Michael Rysbrack and the follies were designed for him by Henry Flitcroft, yet another protege of Lord Burlington.

Gardens (open all year, daily), restaurant, shop. Also estate walks including visits to two iron age hill forts, and 160ft-high folly built in 1772, King Alfred's Tower (open Mar to Oct daily).

Signposted from A303 on B3092 Frome to Gillingham road, 2 miles north of Mere.

Stourhead: a fascinating early Palladian villa, built in 1721–5 by Colen Campbell. The portico was added in 1838, but was part of Campbell's original plan

Tyntesfield, Somerset

National Trust • £££ • Open Apr to Oct,
initially by pre-booked guided tour only

This extraordinary Victorian gothic revival house and its estate, complete with home farm and sawmill, was acquired by the Trust in 2002 after a high-profile fund-raising campaign and, thanks to a last-minute deal with the taxman, with its entire contents intact – though not exactly just as it had been left by the last owner, since everything had been packed up ready for sale at auction.

In a new departure, the Trust has decided to open Tyntesfield to the public during its initial restoration. This means that access to both the house and the gardens will be limited in the first years to guided tours booked in advance, moving to 'free-flow' visits, probably with timed tickets to control numbers. Another new idea is that contractors working on the restoration have been asked to take on trainees, in order to pass on skills and knowledge that are in danger of being lost.

Tyntesfield, completed in 1865, was designed by the Bristol-born

Tyntesfield: one of the finest Victorian country houses, mostly unaltered and with its original contents

architect John Norton, a pupil of Benjamin Ferrey, who in turn had been taught by the master of the gothic revival, AWN Pugin. Norton was employed by William Gibbs, the son of a merchant family with a long history of trading with Spain and South America. In 1842 the family firm acquired a monopoly on exporting guano – dried-out bird droppings, rich in nitrogen and a powerful fertiliser – from Peru, which brought in so much money that William could have built a new Tyntesfield every year.

William was already 75 when the house was finished and died 10 years later, followed in 1887 by his wife, Matilda. Their son, Antony, spent three years and £50,000 on remodelling the house (it had cost £70,000 to build), making major changes to the dining room, billiard room, halls and staircase, before moving in in the summer of 1890.

His son George inherited in 1907 and with his first wife, Via, made more changes, particularly to the decoration of the drawing room and the bedrooms. When George died in

1931, his eldest son, Richard, was just three and the house was presided over by Richard's mother, George's second wife, Ursula, Lady Wraxall, until her death in 1979. Richard left the house alone but worked hard to maintain the estate and gardens. When he died in 2001, having lived alone at Tyntesfield with most of the house shuttered and closed, his younger brother had no wish to take over, and so the entire estate was put up for sale.

Currently visits are limited to just a handful of rooms, including the superb oak-roofed library, like a medieval hall, and the beautiful private chapel. Even so, it's a lovely place to visit, but eventually far more should be opened up, starting with the well-preserved service rooms and moving on to the bedrooms – and there are yet more ambitious plans afoot, such as the rebuilding of the huge conservatory in the garden.

Gardens (by separate tour), shop.

Access initially by minibus from Nailsea, as directed when booking.

Southampton Medieval Merchant's House, Hampshire

English Heritage • ££ • Open Apr to Oct, daily

A fascinating example of the sort of surprisingly cramped and modestly furnished town house in which even a quite a wealthy medieval merchant would have lived – and not just in a major port like Southampton, but in smaller ports and inland towns up and down the country.

It was built in about 1290 by John Fortin, a wine merchant whose trade was mostly with Bordeaux; and although it had undergone many later alterations, these have been removed and the house has been restored to look much as it would have in the mid-1300s.

The layout of the rooms and how they were used is fascinating; the furnishing is sparse and mostly plain, although there are some brightly painted pieces; and wall hangings make the private rooms cosy.

Signposted for pedestrians in French Street, on south side of Southampton city centre.

The Vyne: a Tudor house with some splendid original features, remodelled many times over the years

The Vyne, Hampshire

National Trust • £££ • Open Apr to Oct, M-W, S & Su

In a gently beautiful setting beside a lake in which big fish swim and herons fish, this is an ancient house that has developed piece by piece over the years, creating a patchwork of styles and impressions. It is at its most pleasing where the work of one particular period dominates, such as in the remarkable Tudor gothic chapel, where the elaborate carved wood stalls and stained glass of the early 1500s are of the finest quality, or in the comically theatrical staircase hall, designed in 1769–71 by the then owner, John Chute, and crammed with columns in an unintentional classical pastiche.

Fundamentally it is still the Tudor house built by William, 1st Lord Sandys, Lord Chamberlain to Henry VIII, but the greatest influence that shows today is that of John Chute, an antiquarian and amateur architect, and a close friend of Horace Walpole, who helped design Walpole's influential neo-gothic villa at Strawberry Hill, near Twickenham. He restored or updated many of the Tudor rooms at The Vyne, leaving behind the mish-mash of styles evident today.

Overall, none of the rooms is as pleasing as the two mentioned, except the long gallery, a very rare survival of the early 1500s, its beautiful oak panelling carved with heraldic emblems. But the place is littered with objects of interest, not least the miniature camera obscura that Martha Chute used to make drawings of the interiors in the 1860s.

Grounds with woodland and lakeside walks (open as house, also Feb and Mar, S & Su), restaurant, shop.

Signposted on minor road off A340 Basingstoke to Tadley road, 4 miles north of Basingstoke.

The Medieval Merchant's House, Southampton: built in about 1290 by John Fortin, a wine merchant

Wilton House, Wiltshire

Privately owned (HHA) • £££ •
Open mid-Apr to Oct, daily

In common with many of the greatest houses, Wilton is not all of a piece, built at one time and in one style, but developed its current form gradually over the years, being rebuilt from time to time as fashions changed. Nonetheless, it is most renowned for one particular phase of its construction, the south wing, built between 1636 and 1653, which is one of the earliest examples of Palladian architecture in Britain and possibly the only surviving example of domestic architecture by the first great English architect, Inigo Jones.

A Benedictine abbey on the site was dissolved in 1536 and the estate given to William Herbert, 1st Earl of Pembroke, who in 1543 set about building himself a grand Tudor house. The Pembrokes have lived here ever since. Remnants of the original house include the east tower (the archway through it, blocked to form the gothic hall in about 1815, was the main entrance to the inner courtyard) and the Holbein porch, a splendidly ornate example of the Renaissance influence on English buildings of the time, which was dismantled and moved to the private gardens in the early 1800s (it can be glimpsed from the path to the Palladian bridge of 1737).

The last major phase of change started not long after 1800, when James Wyatt was employed to improve the privacy of and access to the main rooms by building a corridor around the courtyard. Perhaps mindful of the house's monastic origins, he designed it as a gothic cloister. Unfortunately his commitment to his work was poor and in 1815 he was sacked, and other men employed to finish the cloister and the 'Tudor' library.

Still the most impressive feature of the house, however, are the state rooms in Inigo Jones's south wing. Jones himself was busy at Greenwich in the 1630s, so work started here under his assistant, Isaac de Caus. The original plans had to be scaled down at the start of the Civil War, and then a fire in 1647 meant that rebuilding had to take place, directed by Jones's nephew, John Webb. By the time work finished, all three of the men who had conceived the project – King Charles I, who persuaded the 4th Earl to build the new wing, the 4th Earl himself, and Inigo Jones – were dead.

Two of Jones and Webb's state rooms are particularly famous, and alone make a visit to Wilton worthwhile: the double cube room, which is 30 feet wide, 30 feet high and 60 feet long, and the single cube room, 30 feet in each direction (these precise and harmonious proportions were used time and again in later Palladian houses). The former was a formal dining room, while the latter served as its ante-room. Both are splendidly decorated in an ornate baroque version of the classical style, with superb painted ceilings and a great deal of gilding, and now house a notable collection of portraits by Van Dyck and Sir Peter Lely.

Museum in indoor riding school of 1755, reconstructed Tudor kitchens and Victorian laundry, extensive gardens, tearoom, shop.

Signposted from A3 at Wilton, 3 miles west of Salisbury.

Wilton House: noted above all for the state rooms in the south wing, to the left, designed by the great Inigo Jones and his nephew John Webb in 1636–53

See also...

Avebury Manor
Avebury, Wiltshire
National Trust, £££, open Apr to Oct, Tu-W, Su
Stone manor of the 1500s, with parts of monastic origin and Queen Anne alterations, restored in early 1900s. Also famous gardens composed of 'rooms' with box hedges (*open as house, also F & S*).

Barrington Court
Near Ilminster, Somerset
National Trust, £££, open Mar to Oct, Th-F, S & Su (also Apr to Sep, M-Tu)
Tudor manor house restored in the 1920s and now used as an antiques showroom. The real attraction is the garden, by Gertrude Jekyll.

Broadlands
Near Romsey, Hampshire
Privately owned, £££, open early Jun to Aug, daily
Elegant Palladian house of the mid-1700s, the former home of Lord Mountbatten and once the country residence of Lord Palmerston.

Clouds Hill
Near Wareham, Dorset
National Trust, ££, open Apr to Oct, Th-F, S & Su
Lovely little brick cottage with sparsely furnished interiors, lived in by TE Lawrence.

Fiddleford Manor: remnant of a medieval manor house, with superb beamed roof and carved stonework

Coleridge Cottage
Nether Stowey, Somerset
National Trust, ££, open Apr to Sep, Th-F, S & Su
The home of the Romantic poet from 1797 to 1800, where he wrote *The Rime of the Ancient Mariner*.

Fiddleford Manor
Sturminster Newton, Dorset
English Heritage, free, open Apr to Oct, daily (during working hours)
Remaining part of a medieval manor house with superb beamed roof and interesting details. Well worth a visit.

Hardy's Cottage
Near Dorchester, Dorset
National Trust, ££, open Apr to Oct, M, Th-F, S & Su
Attractive cob-built thatched cottage in which Thomas Hardy was born in 1840, and in which he wrote several of his novels. Set in cottage garden with pleasing period feel.

Highclere Castle
Highclere, Hampshire
(near Newbury, Berkshire)
Privately owned (HHA), £££, open Jul to Aug, Tu-F, S & Su
Splendid, square-towered, soaring gothic mansion built in the 1830s by Sir Charles Barry for the 3rd Earl of Caernarvon, with interiors in styles from gothic to rococo to Moorish; also archeological exhibits relating to the 5th Earl of Caernarvon, who discovered Tutankhamun's tomb.

Hinton Ampner
Near Alresford, Hampshire
National Trust, £££, open Apr to Sep, Tu-W (also Aug, S & Su)
Small neo-Georgian manor of the 1930s, remodelled from an earlier house, now lived in by a tenant, with furniture collection of Ralph Dutton, Lord Sherborne. The real attraction, however, is Dutton's famous garden (*open Apr to Sep, M-W, S & Su*).

Horton Court: the great hall (left of picture) survives from a Norman rectory, the oldest in England

Horton Court
Near Chipping Sodbury, Gloucestershire
National Trust, £££, open Apr to Oct, W & Su
Not large, but very interesting great hall of the Norman period, the remnant of what is thought to be the oldest rectory in England. Also early Renaissance loggia with stucco roundels depicting classical figures.

Jane Austen's house
Chawton, near Alton, Hampshire
Privately owned, ££, open Mar to Nov, daily, Dec to Feb, S & Su
Modest Georgian red brick house where Austen wrote or revised six of her novels.

King John's Hunting Lodge
Axbridge, Somerset
National Trust and local council, free, open Apr to Sep, daily
Interesting early Tudor merchant's house, recently restored and now used as a local museum.

Little Clarendon
Dinton, Salisbury, Wiltshire
National Trust, £££, open Apr to Oct, M & S
Cosy little Tudor manor altered in the 1600s and restored in the early 1900s.

Lulworth Castle
Lulworth, Dorset
English Heritage, ££, open all year, M-F & Su
Wonderful 'play-castle' hunting lodge of early 1600s, recently restored.

Max Gate
Dorchester
National Trust, £££, open Apr to Sep, M, W, Su
The house Thomas Hardy designed and lived in from 1885.

Old Basing House
Basingstoke, Hampshire
Local council, £, open Apr to Sep, W-F, S & Su
Ruins of a Tudor palace with interesting Civil War history.

The Priest's House, Muchelney
Muchelney, Somerset
National Trust, ££, opening arrangements vary
Medieval hall house built in 1308.

The Treasurer's House, Martock
Martock, Somerset
National Trust, ££, open Apr to Sep, M-Tu, Su
Small medieval house with great hall of 1293, earlier solar with wall painting.

Westwood Manor
Bradford on Avon, Wilts
National Trust, £££, open Apr to Sep, Tu-W, Su
Stone manor house of 1400s with various later alterations.

Wolfeton House
Dorchester, Dorset
Privately owned (HHA), £££, open mid-Jul to mid-Sep, M, W-Th
Medieval and Elizabethan manor house in water meadows, with various other ancient buildings.

And...

Cranborne Manor gardens
Cranborne, Dorset
Privately owned, ££, open Mar to Sep, W
Charming, romantic little Jacobean manor built as a hunting lodge in 1608–11 by Lord Salisbury. The house is not open, but the exterior can be seen from the historic gardens, laid out in the early 1600s.

The Manor House, Purse Caundle
Purse Caundle, Dorset
Privately owned (HHA), open Apr to Oct, Th, by appt only
Charming small stone manor of 1429 expanded in 1500s with hall and great chamber.

Prior Park Landscape Garden
Bath, Somerset
National Trust, ££, open Feb to Nov, M, W-F, S & Su, Dec to Jan, F, S & Su
The Palladian mansion is now a school, but the beautiful gardens created by Ralph Allen with the help of Alexander Pope have been restored.

Lulworth Castle: a romantic hunting lodge of the early 1600s, gutted by fire in 1929 and recently restored

Gravesend

Margate

Rochester

Ramsgate

Weybridge

Canterbury

Woking

Deal

Sevenoaks

Knole

Maidstone

Walmer Castle

Hatchlands Park

Polesden Lacey

Ashford

Clandon Park

Reigate

Chartwell

Loseley Park

Guildford

Ightham Mote

Dover

Hever Castle

Tonbridge

Leeds Castle

Chiddingstone Castle

Penshurst Place

Folkestone

Crawley

Royal Tunbridge Wells

Eurotunnel

Horsham

Standen

Tenterden

Midhurst

Haywards Heath

Bateman's

Rye

Petworth House

Uckfield

Petworth

Battle

Uppark

Lewes

Hastings

Chichester

Bexhill

Worthing

Brighton

Eastbourne

Bognor Regis

Littlehampton

Newhaven

ENGLISH CHANNEL

0 miles	20
0 kilometres	30

Bateman's, East Sussex

National Trust • £££ • Open Apr to Sep, M-W, S & Su

A delightful little Jacobean stone manor, built about 1634 (the date over the door) and lived in from 1902 by the writer Rudyard Kipling, who described it as 'all untouched and unfaked', as it pretty much remains to this day.

It's such a modest house that it might not, perhaps, be open to the public if it weren't for its famous occupant, but it certainly has its own merits, too, and the combination of the two makes it a very enjoyable place to visit. Little is known of its early history, beyond a tradition that it was built by a Sussex ironmaster and was certainly lived in by an iron dealer in the late 1600s.

Largely unmodernized, it retains many original features, such as the wood panelling and simple fireplace in the entrance hall. Just as pleasing are the comfortable furnishings and the Kipling memorabilia, such as the illustrations for the first edition of the *Jungle Book*.

Gardens (open as house, also Mar, S & Su), working watermill, tearoom, shop.

Signposted on minor road off A265 Heathfield to Hurst Green road, 1 mile south-west of Burwash.

Chartwell: the home of Sir Winston Churchill, adapted in the 1920s from a red brick Victorian mansion

Chartwell, Kent

National Trust • £££ • Open late Mar to early Nov, W-F, S & Su (also Jul and Aug, Tu)

The home of wartime Prime Minister Winston Churchill from 1922, standing in a wonderful position at the head of a small, enclosed valley with distant views over the Kentish Weald and surrounded by gardens Churchill himself designed, lakes and a swimming pond he engineered and many a brick wall he personally built, as well as his studio, with a permanent exhibition of his paintings.

It is in effect a new house of the 1920s, although converted from an odd-looking, red brick Victorian mansion, which in turn was based on a much older manor (it even had a room in which Henry VIII was said to have slept). Churchill's architect, Philip Tilden, was keen to retain certain features of the Victorian house of which he approved, such as the carved brick mullioned windows. In the house's most appealing and most evocative room, Churchill's study, he opened up the ceiling to reveal the ancient beams of the original house.

The owner was eager to make the most of the views, so Tilden's main contribution was to add a new wing to the east (on the right in the photograph above), which contains some of the most successful rooms: the dining room in the basement, the drawing room on the ground floor and, at the top, the bedroom of Churchill's wife, Clementine.

After Churchill's death, Clementine gave the house to the Trust on condition that it be shown as it was in the 1920s and 1930s. Light and pleasantly decorated, with a great deal of contemporary furniture, it features many excellent paintings and many evocative objects gathered by Sir Winston over the years.

Country walks, extensive gardens (open as house), Churchill's studio, tearoom, shop.

Signposted on minor road off B2026 Westerham to Edenbridge road, 2 miles south of Westerham.

Bateman's: a Jacobean manor of 1634, largely unaltered when bought by Rudyard Kipling in 1902

Chiddingstone Castle, Kent

Privately owned (HHA) • £££ • Open Jun to Sep, W-F & Su

An eccentric and somewhat odd place to visit. It's a very handsome building, based on a house of about 1675 but remodelled in about 1805 for Henry Streatfield, whose family had lived on the site since the 1550s, by the architect William Atkinson, a pupil of James Wyatt, in the fashionable 'castle style'.

By the 1950s, after serving as both a military headquarters and a school, Chiddingstone was abandoned and partially derelict, but it was bought by the art collector Denys Bower, who wanted it as a place to display his collections and hoped to restore it and open it to the public. Only after his death in 1977 did his dream finally come true.

In places the architecture is very pleasing, but really the house is now more an art gallery, with Bower's collections taking centre stage. Highlights include a superb nude study of Nell Gwynne painted by Sir Peter Lely for Charles II, and a truly wonderful array of Japanese lacquer.

Gardens, tearoom, shop.

On minor road off B2027 Edenbridge to Tonbridge road, just west of Chiddingstone.

Chiddingstone Castle: an older house remodelled in medieval gothic style in 1805, now an art gallery

Clandon Park, Surrey

National Trust • £££ • Open Apr to Oct, Tu-Th & Su

A fine house on a splendid scale, built in the early 1720s by the Venetian architect Giacomo Leoni for Lord Onslow, whose marriage to a wealthy Jamaican heiress in 1708 had given him the money to indulge his fantasies. It's worth coming just for the extraordinary double-height entrance hall, known as the marble hall, with its wonderful plaster ceiling by Giuseppe Artari and marble reliefs carved by John Michael Rysbrack; but sadly this room is one of the few to accurately reproduce Leoni's vision: even the splendid saloon is spoiled by later redecoration and an unfortunate restoration in the 1960s.

Clandon has notable collections of china, from all the major English makers, and porcelain, with a great number of Meissen figures.

Gardens with grotto and Maori house (open as house), church, museum of Surrey Regiment, tearoom, shop.

Signposted on A247 at West Clandon, 3 miles east of Guildford.

Clandon Park: an immense classical house designed by the Venetian architect Giacomo Leoni in the 1720s for Lord Onslow, with a superb entrance hall

Hatchlands Park, Surrey

National Trust • £££ • Open Apr to Oct, Tu-Th & Su (also Aug, F)

A fascinating house for three reasons, two of them rather specialized. First, its decoration was an early commission for the young Robert Adam, freshly returned from Italy in 1757. His designs here are based rather slavishly on their classical originals and lack the lightness of touch he later achieved, but will interest anyone who admires his work.

Second, it is now home to an extraordinary collection of keyboard instruments, many of which were owned by famous composers or musicians. And third – and this is the non-specialized reason – the house is leased to a tenant who has furnished it in his own individual style. This makes it seem an exceptionally welcoming and cosy house, and among its rewards is a fine collection of paintings including the famous Reynolds portrait of Mrs Siddons.

Park (open late Mar to early Nov, daily), gardens (open as house), tearoom, shop.

Signposted on A246 Guildford to Leatherhead road, just east of East Clandon.

Hatchlands: an unremarkable house of the 1750s, enlivened by some of Robert Adam's earliest interiors

Hever Castle, Kent

Privately owned (HHA) • £££ • Open Mar to Nov, daily

A gorgeous little fortified, moated manor house, built in about 1270 and converted into a more up-to-date and convenient dwelling in about 1500; most famous as the home of Anne Boleyn, second wife of Henry VIII and mother of Queen Elizabeth I, who was beheaded in 1536, at the age of just 35.

Inevitably, it is a popular attraction and frequently busy, but the little house is charming in its fabric – restored following its purchase by the American millionaire William Waldorf Astor in 1903 – and packed with objects of interest relating to the Tudors, including two prayer books inscribed by Anne.

The castle came into the Bullen (as it was originally spelt) family by the efforts of Geoffrey Bullen, a man of humble Norfolk origins who worked his way up to become Lord Mayor of London in 1459, was knighted, amassed a great fortune and bought both Hever and Blickling Hall in Norfolk. His grandson, Thomas, made a good marriage to Elizabeth Howard, the daughter of the Duke of Norfolk, in 1498 and it was he, Anne's father, who built the Tudor house.

Inside, the wood panelling and strapwork ceilings are largely modern reproductions, but beautifully done; much of the furnishing is Edwardian, too, but with a scatter of superb 16th- and 17th-century items. One of its finest possessions is a French tapestry of about 1522 showing the marriage of Henry VII's sister, Mary, to the French king Louis XII.

Extensive gardens including Italian garden, rose garden and maze, restaurants, shops.

Signposted on minor road between B2027 and B2026, 4 miles south-east of Edenbridge.

Hever Castle: a moated manor house of about 1270 updated in about 1500 by Anne Boleyn's father

Ightham Mote, Kent

National Trust • £££ • Open late Mar to early Nov, M, W-F & Su

Aptly described in the guidebook as 'one of the loveliest and most interesting of the medieval and Tudor manor houses to survive in England', Ightham is a fascinating and, above all, beautiful mixture of buildings from many periods, which despite its piecemeal origins seems almost as if it had all been built at one time. In common with Knole (below), it is one of the finest ancient places within easy reach of London.

Its setting is one of the most picturesque imaginable, nestling at the bottom of a steep-sided valley through which runs a stream that was dammed to form lakes and the moat that surrounds the house. The oldest parts, built about 1340, are the great hall, a chapel with a crypt beneath and two solars or private apartments. It is not known

who built them, but by about 1360 it was owned by Sir Thomas Cawne, a soldier from Staffordshire who married a local woman.

After Sir Thomas's time, the house expanded slowly until it consisted of four ranges around an open courtyard, filling the area inside the moat. Surprisingly, it's actually a rather large house, with 72 rooms, some of them on a very generous scale; not all of them are open to the public.

Even after the house reached its present size, it continued to be altered and improved right into the late 1800s, the final years of its ownership by the Selby family, whose ancestor Sir William Selby had bought it in 1591. The architect Norman Shaw was employed to make a number of sensitive improvements, among them the conversion of a buttery beside the great hall into an entrance hall, so that, for the first time in its life, the house's principal entrance was no longer directly into the hall.

A great deal of the interest lies in the fabric of the building, which has been the subject of a massive restoration project over the last 10 years and more, and in the way it has changed under different owners. So, in the great hall, as well as Norman Shaw's little touches, one can see stained glass installed by the courtier Richard Clement, who bought Ightham in 1521, its heraldic panels celebrating the marriage of Henry VIII with his first wife, Catherine of Aragon.

Perhaps the most noticeable of its owners, however, is the American paper magnate Henry Robinson, who bought it in 1953 and left it to the Trust in 1985. The furniture and pictures in the house were mostly gathered by him.

Estate with woodland walks (open all year, daily), gardens (open as house), tearoom, shop.

Signposted on minor road off A227 Borough Green to Tonbridge road, 3 miles south of Ightham.

Ightham Mote: a wonderful moated manor house with a hall built in about 1340 and other ranges that developed piecemeal over the following three centuries

Knole,
Kent

National Trust • £££ • Open late Mar to Oct, W-F, S & Su

Truly one of the most astonishing buildings in Britain – vast, sprawling and at times castle-like, it was the palace of an archbishop and later of Henry VIII. Its oldest parts date from the late 1400s but it was enlarged and improved in the early 1600s by Thomas Sackville, 1st Earl of Dorset, a favourite of Elizabeth I. It has a beautiful setting, too, in one of the loveliest deer parks in England.

The estate was bought in 1456 by Thomas Bourchier, Archbishop of Canterbury. It is not known whether a house already stood on the site, but certainly the earliest buildings visible today are those built by Bourchier in about 1460. It's not always easy for a visitor to make sense of Knole, so large and sprawling is it; but essentially once you've walked through the outer gatehouse and across the green court, you reach the archbishop's original house. It consisted of the second gatehouse – known as Bourchier's Tower, with a fine oriel window lighting the oratory – and

the smaller courtyard behind it, where two timber-framed ranges connected the gatehouse to the archbishop's great hall.

Knole passed to successive Archbishops of Canterbury, until in 1538 Thomas Cranmer was obliged to give it 'voluntarily' to Henry VIII. Henry spent little time here – he had 60 royal residences – but he built the outer gatehouse and the low accommodation ranges around the green court, none of which is open to the public.

After Henry's death in 1547, the house was granted to various occupants by Edward VI, Mary I and then Elizabeth, until finally, in 1605, Thomas Sackville acquired the freehold. Sackville was a man whose fortunes had swung wildly but was now, as Lord Treasurer, at the peak of his career – and ideally placed to get his hands on a royal estate.

Thomas added graceful classical touches to the medieval exterior and revamped the interior. He put a new ceiling and an ornate wooden screen in the great hall and created the great staircase, with its wonderful painted Renaissance decoration, which leads to a maze of dark wood-panelled apartments beyond. These apartments contain much

superb early English furniture acquired by the 6th Earl, who as Lord Chamberlain of the Household to William III from 1689 to 1697 was allowed to take away anything thought to be worn out or outdated. Thus he collected many pieces owned by James I and Charles I, as well as James II's glorious state bed, still with its original hangings – its odd smell is due to the fact that its mattress is stuffed with old wigs. Nearby is a billiard table of the 1600s.

Thomas saved his greatest extravagance for the main reception room, the great chamber (now the ballroom), where the plasterwork decoration created by the King's craftsmen is simply extraordinary, though somewhat grotesque to modern tastes. Off the cartoon gallery next door, which has a superb and delicate ceiling, is the *piece de resistance* – the King's chamber. Now lit by subdued electric lights to keep the fabrics from fading, it is a glowing treasure-vault of the richest furniture the late 1600s could offer, including another state bed of James II.

Parkland with walks, tearoom, shop.

Signposted on A225 Sevenoaks to Tonbridge road on south-east side of Sevenoaks.

Knole: a medieval palace of about 1460, extended by Henry VIII and turned into a palatial Elizabethan home after 1605 by Thomas Sackville, Earl of Dorset

Leeds Castle: a royal possession of Edward I from 1278, restored as a medieval fantasy in the 1920s

Leeds Castle, Kent

Privately owned • ££££ • Open all year, daily

A medieval royal castle that slipped into use as a home but was transformed after 1926, when it was bought by Lady Olive Baillie, a wealthy socialite of American birth. With the aid of two French interior decorators she turned it into a fantasy reflecting the English Arts and Crafts movement's fascination with the medieval, but with a touch of Hollywood to it, too. On her death in 1974, she left the castle to a trust with the aim of keeping it open to the public.

Leeds became a royal castle when it was acquired by Edward I in 1278, and Henry VIII spent a lot of money on it, building a banqueting hall with a superb ebony floor. In the early 1700s it was used as a prison, but in the next two centuries it was improved for use as a house, until Lady Olive's transformation stripped away the recent past and exposed its medieval origins, as well as adding 1920s mod cons. An odd blend, but a pleasant place to visit.

Extensive gardens, maze, aviary, museum of dog collars, restaurant, tearoom, shop.

Signposted off A20 Maidstone to Ashford road, 2 miles east of Maidstone.

Loseley Park, Surrey

Privately owned (HHA) • £££ • Open Jun to Aug, W-F, S & Su, guided tours only

A rather nice Elizabethan manor house, built in 1562–8 to the classic E-plan (and surprisingly narrow as a result, the great hall having windows at both front and back) using stone 'quarried' from the ruin of nearby Waverley Abbey.

The manor of Loseley was bought by Sir Christopher More, Sheriff of Surrey and Sussex, during the reign of Henry VII and the house was built by his son, Sir William, a trusted adviser of Queen Elizabeth, who stayed here on four occasions.

Their ancestors, the More-Molyneux family, live here still, and their presence helps make this a friendly place to visit, with recent family photos scattered among the ancestral portraits. The guided tours are among the most well-informed and mercifully short-winded you are likely to encounter.

Although there have certainly been changes over the years, the house as a whole has a wonderfully ancient feel and retains many original features. Some of the decoration and furnishing is even older than the house: the great hall is adorned with painted panelling from Henry VIII's Nonsuch Palace, demolished in the 1680s. In the same room hang portraits of King James I and his Queen, thought to have been presented to Loseley's owners after a visit by the king, and a fine portrait of the boy king Edward VI.

The superb plasterwork ceiling of the drawing room was gilded for James I's visit; the handsome frieze below it depicts cockatrices, moorhens and mulberry trees, all family emblems. The extraordinary ornate chimneypiece in the same room, from a design by Holbein, is carved from chalk.

Walled gardens and rose garden (open May to Sep, W-F, S & Su), restaurant, tearoom, shop.

Signposted on minor road off B3000, 2 miles south-west of Guildford.

Loseley Park: an Elizabethan manor house built in 1562–8 using stone from the ruin of Waverley Abbey

Penshurst Place: a fortified manor with a superb great hall built in 1341 and Elizabethan modifications

Penshurst Place, Kent

Privately owned • £££ • Open Apr to Oct, daily, also Mar, S & Su

The great hall at the fortified manor house of Penshurst is one of the most impressive and celebrated medieval structures in England. It was built in 1341 by John de Poultney, four times Lord Mayor of London, and is little altered, still having its original beamed roof – chestnut, not oak – and even the central hearth.

The house was given by Edward VI to Sir William Sidney in 1552 and has been the home of the Sidney family ever since. It has seen many changes over the years, including a substantial revamp in late Elizabethan times, with the building of a long gallery in 1601.

The fabric of the building feels beautifully ancient, with superb stonework and surviving details, such as the original panelling in the gallery, but most of the furnishing is comfortably modern.

Extensive and historic gardens, adventure playground, toy museum (all open as house), tearoom, shop.

Signposted on B2176 at Penshurst, 6 miles north-west of Tunbridge Wells.

Petworth House, West Sussex

National Trust • £££ • Open Apr to Oct, M-W, S & Su

A long, narrow, house with a plain baroque exterior, home of a branch of the Percy family, built largely by the 6th Duke of Somerset in 1688–1702, based on an earlier house. It's not an architectural gem inside, either, although it has its moments, notably the grand stair with wall-paintings by Laguerre.

Far more importantly, however, Petworth offers three treats: the lovely deer park by Capability Brown; a separate service wing with fascinating kitchens; and a remarkable art collection, as well as links with a number of noted artists, in particular JMW Turner.

Most striking of the rooms are the carved room, with sublime decoration by Grinling Gibbons and four paintings commissioned from Turner, and the Victorian picture gallery, a tribute to the efforts of George, 3rd Earl of Egremont, as a patron of the arts.

Pleasure ground (open as house), deer park with extensive walks (open daily all year), restaurant, shop.

Signposted on A283 (and from A272) 1 mile north of Petworth village.

Petworth House: the west front, looking much as it did when built in 1688–1702, with Capability Brown's deer park running right up to its French windows

Polesden Lacey: a luxurious Edwardian villa in a splendid hilltop setting with superb southerly views

Polesden Lacey, Surrey

National Trust • £££ • Open late Mar to early Nov, W-F, S & Su

A house with a most individual style and character, not representative of a particular type of architecture, but richly redolent of early-20th-century high society and bursting at the seams with *objets d'art* of the highest quality.

Underneath, it is a Regency house, rebuilt from an earlier building in 1735–48 and inhabited in the early 1800s by the playwright Richard Brinsley Sheridan, who called it 'The nicest place, within a prudent distance of town, in England,' and relished the simple pleasures of a small, working country estate. But its present character is entirely Edwardian, since Polesden was remodelled in 1906–9 by the architects of the newly built Ritz Hotel, Mewes and Davis, for Maggie Greville, a society hostess whose husband had died young.

Cecil Beaton called Mrs Greville 'a galumphing, greedy, snobbish old toad who watered at the chops at the sight of royalty,' but her friends appreciated her 'skilfully malicious' wit and the warmth of her hospitality. Certainly she did aim to attract royal visitors and, just as certainly, she succeeded: King Edward VII, who stayed here in 1909, was a close friend, Queen Mary came often and the future King George VI and Queen Elizabeth spent part of their honeymoon here in 1923.

The house was excellently suited to its role as a royal resort, having all modern conveniences as well as a luxuriously historical flavour. In the entrance hall, for example, the carved wooden reredos from Wren's church of St Matthew's, Friday Street, demolished in 1883, makes a grand statement, while opposite on the staircase landing is a collection of rare and valuable maiolica earthenware – and yet, for all this artistic clutter, it is still a room of warm and comfort.

It was considered essential, for privacy and convenience, to have corridors in late Victorian and Edwardian country houses, rather than interconnecting rooms. Here the corridor that runs around three sides of the central courtyard was given Jacobean-style oak panelling and a curved, barrel-vault ceiling copied from the long gallery at Chastleton House, Oxfordshire (see below), and was used as a picture gallery. It is hung with an appealing collection of paintings including 14th-century altarpieces, Renaissance portraits and 17th-century Dutch landscapes.

In the saloon, dripping with gilt, red velvet and mirrors, and splendid in its camp excess, are some of the finest pieces from Mrs Greville's extensive collections – an eclectic mix of Faberge trinkets, Chinese ceramics, porcelain figures from Meissen, Derby and Chelsea, and much more besides.

Gardens with walled rose garden, parkland with walks (open daily, all year), tearoom, shop.

Clearly signposted from A246 Leatherhead to Guildford road, 2 miles south of Great Bookham.

Standen,
West Sussex

National Trust • £££ • Open late Mar to early Nov, W-F, S & Su

One of the finest houses to come out of the Arts and Crafts movement, built in 1892–4 for a successful London solicitor, James Beale, whose role as a Parliamentary agent was crucial in gaining approval for the Midland Railway's London terminus at St Pancras Station.

Standen was one of the last houses designed by William Morris's close associate Philip Webb, a pupil of the leading gothic revivalist George Edmund Street. The first house Webb ever designed was Morris's Red House at Bexleyheath, London. What makes Standen special is not the building itself, although it is both welcoming and attractive, and the details of Webb's approach are fascinating – he insisted on retaining the old farm buildings on the site, worked around several mature trees, and specified materials in great detail by reference to other local buildings. All the same, the appeal lies largely in the furnishing and decoration, much of which is original to the house.

It's worth coming here just for one beautiful chair, designed for Morris & Co by the artist Dante Gabriel Rossetti, on show in the Larkspur Bedroom. But there are wonderful things scattered throughout the house, many designed and supplied by Morris & Co, who were employed to complete the decoration and were brought back to redecorate in 1906, while the Beales were on a round-the-world holiday.

Many of the famous Morris wallpapers are in evidence in the bedrooms upstairs, but panelling and textiles predominate in most of the downstairs rooms. James's wife, Margaret Beale, was a great needlewoman and embroidered many of the textiles herself to Morris's designs, while her daughter, Maggie, trained in fine art, produced her own designs.

Among the many splendid paintings and decorative objects gathered later by the house's curator are a wonderful tapestry by Morris and Burne-Jones, and ceramics by William de Morgan.

Woodland walks, gardens (open as house, also Nov to late Dec, F, S & Su), restaurant, shop.

Signposted on minor road off B2110, 2 miles south of East Grinstead.

Standen: one of the great Arts and Crafts houses, built in 1892–4 and decorated by Morris & Co

Uppark,
West Sussex

National Trust • £££ • Open Apr to Oct, M-Th & Su

The house that rose, phoenix-like, from the ashes, destroyed by fire in 1989 and since given the most astonishingly complete restoration. A good deal of the interest lies in following the story of what is original (very little, in fact) and what reconstructed, and in admiring the great skill with which the reconstruction was effected.

It was a house worth saving, too, not just for its little-changed exterior, built in about 1690, but also for its twice-remodelled interiors. The builder was the colourful Ford, 3rd Lord Grey of Warke, the son of a Northumbrian gentleman who had married into the family that owned Uppark.

Ford was a notoriously duplicitous character whose exploits including marrying Mary, daughter of the Earl of Berkeley, then eloping with her sister Henrietta. He was almost executed for his part in Monmouth's rebellion against James II in 1685, but he managed to survive by giving evidence against his friends and paying out vast sums of money, and eventually he became a trusted and prominent member of

Uppark: built in about 1690, altered in the 1740s and early 1800s, burned down in 1989

the government of William and Mary. He was made Earl of Tankerville in 1695.

Uppark was bought in 1747 by Sir Matthew Featherstonhaugh, who had inherited £400,000 the previous year. An art collector and man of learning, he made many changes at Uppark, perhaps aided by the architect James Paine, who built his London house. His son, Sir Harry, was famous for his affair with Emma Hamilton and for marrying, in 1825, aged more than 70, his 20-year-old dairymaid. He made further changes in the early 1800s with the help of Humphrey Repton.

Inevitably, then, the interiors are a mix of styles and periods, but there is some superlative work. Probably the finest of the work attributed to Paine is the ceiling of the saloon, painted white and gilded, its delicate classical design anticipating Robert Adam.

Just as interesting are the service rooms in the basement, with tunnels leading to the stable block and dairy on one side and the service block and kitchen on the other.

Woodland walks, gardens (open as house), dairy, restaurant, shop.

Signposted on B2146 Petersfield to Havant road, 2 miles south of South Harting.

Walmer Castle, Kent

English Heritage • £££ • Open Apr to Oct, daily, Mar and Nov to Dec, W-F, S & Su, Jan to Feb, S & Su

Built by Henry VIII as part of a series of small, round artillery castles intended to protect the south coast from French invasion, Walmer became the official residence of the Lords Warden of the Cinque Ports in 1708 and was converted into a surprisingly pleasant and comfortable home. Its most famous occupants include William Pitt the Younger, Lord Warden from 1792 to 1806, who laid out the gardens and grounds, and the Duke of Wellington, Lord Warden from 1829, who died here in September 1852.

The work of converting the castle into a residence was started by the first Lord Warden to use it as such, the Duke of Dorset, who extended the central keep out over the bastions. Several subsequent holders of the title made further alterations, but the last to make major changes to the structure of the building was Earl Granville, Lord Warden 1865–91, who employed the architect George

Devey, known for his sensitive work on country houses, to build extra rooms over the gatehouse bastion. This he did using stone from nearby Sandown Castle, which was being demolished at the time.

The castle has not been used as a permanent residence since the 1930s and, rather than trying to recreate a particular phase of its past, English Heritage has decided to keep it in the state in which it had naturally arrived at that time. Until 1891, when the bookshop founder WH Smith became Lord Warden, there was a tradition that new wardens should purchase the existing furniture from the family of the previous occupant, but there was no obligation to do so. Smith set up a trust to preserve the contents, ensuring that furniture and mementoes belonging to Pitt and Wellington have survived.

Wellington's room is by far the most evocative in the castle, its simple furniture including his campaign bed, with its original horsehair mattress, and the armchair in which he died in 1852.

Gardens (open as house), tearoom, shop.

Signposted on minor road near seafront at Walmer village, off A258 Deal to Dover road, 2 miles south of Deal.

Walmer Castle: an artillery fort of 1539, converted after 1708 for the Lords Warden of the Cinque Ports

See also…

Alfriston Clergy House

Alfriston, Brighton, East Sussex
National Trust, ££, open mid-Mar to early Nov, M, W-Th, S & Su
A small, thatched Wealden hall house of the 1300s; in 1896 it became the first historic building acquired by the National Trust.

Anne of Cleves House

Lewes, East Sussex
Sussex Past, ££, open all year, Tu-F, S (also Mar to Oct, M)
Timber-framed Wealden hall house of the 1500s, given to Anne as part of her divorce settlement from Henry VIII in 1541.

Arundel Castle

Arundel, West Sussex
Privately owned, ££££, open Apr to Oct, daily
Home of the Dukes of Norfolk. The 'shell keep' survives of the castle of the 1100s; the rest was remodelled in baronial gothic style in the late 1800s and early 1900s.

Belmont

Faversham, Kent
Privately owned (HHA), £££, open Apr to Oct, S & Su
Handsome neoclassical house of late 1700s by Samuel Wyatt, in delightful grounds. Unusual clock collection.

Charleston

Near Lewes, East Sussex
Privately owned, £££, open Apr to Oct, W-F, S & Su
Attractive farmhouse lived in from 1916 by Virginia and Leonard Woolf and various friends, decorated with the help of Bloomsbury Group artists. Good garden.

Firle Place

Lewes, East Sussex
Privately owned (HHA), £££, open May to Sep, W-Th, S
Unassuming but elegant house in pale Caen stone, remodelled from a Tudor manor in the late 1700s. Decent art collection, strong on Sevres porcelain.

Glynde Place

Lewes, East Sussex
Privately owned (HHA), £££, open Jun to Sep, W & Su (also Jul-Aug, Th)
Attractive and impressive Elizabethan manor house built in 1559 of local flint and Caen stone, with fine views over the South Downs.

Goodwood House

Chichester, West Sussex
Privately owned (HHA), £££, open Apr to Sep, M & Su (also Aug, Tu-Th)
Elegant house developed from a Jacobean hunting lodge in the late 1700s by James Wyatt. Fine art collection and French furniture.

Great Dixter

Northiam, East Sussex
Privately owned (HHA), £££, open Apr to Oct, Tu-F, S & Su
One of the largest timber-framed halls in England, built about 1450, with additions by Lutyens; also a hall house of about 1500 dismantled and moved from a nearby village, plus one of England's finest gardens.

Lamb House

Rye, East Sussex
National Trust, £££, open Apr to Oct, W, S
Nice early 1700s brick house, the home of the novelist Henry James from 1896 to 1916.

Lullingstone Castle

Edenbridge, Kent
Privately owned (HHA), £££, open May-Aug, S & Su
Elegant Queen Anne remodelling of a Tudor manor, with the original Tudor gatehouse surviving.

Michelham Priory

Near Hailsham, East Sussex
Sussex Past (HHA), ££, Open Mar to Oct, Tu-F, S & Su
Part of an Augustinian priory made into a house in the 1590s, later a farm. Medieval gatehouse, watermill, yard with workshops and reconstructions of prehistoric houses.

Monks House

Rodmell, near Lewes, East Sussex
National Trust, ££, open Apr to Oct, W, S
Small weather-boarded house, the home of Virginia and Leonard Woolf until 1969.

Oakhurst Cottage

Hambledon, Godalming, Surrey
National Trust, ££, open Apr to Oct, W-Th, S & Su
Small timber-framed cottage of 1500s, restored as a labourer's dwelling, with Victorian garden.

Old Soar Manor

Plaxtol, Kent
National Trust, free, open Apr to Sep, M-Th, S & Su
Solar block of a knight's dwelling of the 1200s. Tiny, but very interesting.

Michelham Priory: parts of the refectory and abbot's lodgings were turned into a house in the 1500s

Owletts
Cobham, Gravesend, Kent
National Trust, ££, open Apr to Sep,
W-Th, tours only
Modest red brick Charles II house,
famous as the home of the architect
Sir Herbert Baker, a contemporary of
Lutyens. Shown by tenant.

Parham Park
Pulborough, West Sussex
Privately owned (HHA), £££, open
Apr to Oct, W-Th & Su
Classic E-plan Elizabethan stone
mansion of 1557 with fine hall and
long gallery. Excellent gardens.

The Priest's House
West Hoathly, West Sussex
Sussex Past, ££, open Mar to Oct
daily
Timber-framed hall house of the
early 1400s with stone roof; restored
formal gardens and herb garden.

The Royal Pavilion
Brighton, East Sussex
Local council, £££, open all year,
daily
Wonderfully exotic Oriental creation
by John Nash for King George IV,
with magnificently voluptuous
restored interiors.

Quebec House
Westerham, Kent
National Trust, £££, open Apr to Oct,
Tu & Su
Red brick house of 1600s in which
General Wolfe was born.

Saint Mary's House
Bramber, West Sussex
Privately owned (HHA), £££, open
Easter to Sep, Th & Su
Attractive timber-framed medieval
house, originally a monastic inn
founded by the Bishop of Winchester
for pilgrims travelling to Canterbury.
Animal topiary in the garden.

Sissinghurst Castle
Near Cranbrook, Kent
National Trust, £££, open late Mar to
Oct, M-Tu, F, S & Su
Surviving 'prospect tower' of
Elizabethan house, but the main
attraction is the famous garden laid
out by Vita Sackville-West.

Old Soar Manor: the surviving solar block (private apartments) of a knight's residence of the 1200s

Smallhythe Place
Tenterden, Kent,
National Trust, £££, open Apr to Oct,
M-W, S & Su
Half-timbered house of the early
1500s, lived in by the Victorian
actress Ellen Terry, with the
Barn Theatre next door.

Stansted Park
Near Rowlands Castle, Hampshire
Privately owned (HHA), £££, open
Apr to Oct, M-W & Su
Elegant Charles II house with
magnificent grounds and lots of
extras to appeal to visitors, including
falconry displays.

Stoneacre
Otham, Maidstone, Kent,
National Trust, ££, open Apr to mid-
Oct, W, S
Half-timbered yeoman's house of late
1400s with great hall, tenanted.

Squerryes Court
Westerham, Kent
Privately owned (HHA), £££, open
Apr to Sep, W, S & Su
Tidy William & Mary house with
good collection of Italian and Dutch
paintings and partially restored 1700s
Anglo-Dutch gardens.

Titsey Place
Oxted, Surrey
Privately owned, ££, open mid-May
to Sep, W & Su, tours only
Pleasant Elizabethan and later manor
featuring paintings from the National
Portrait Gallery.

Wakehurst Place
Ardingly, near Haywards Heath,
West Sussex
National Trust, £££, open all year,
daily
The vast gardens, the rural branch of
the Royal Botanic Gardens, Kew, are
the real attraction; the Elizabethan
manor contains explanatory displays.

And...

Boughton Monchelsea Place
Near Maidstone, Kent
Privately owned, open all year for
groups by arrangement only
Pretty stone manor of 1500s with
many later alterations.

Dickens Centre, Eastgate House
Rochester, Kent
Local council, ££, open all year, daily
Greatly altered house of 1500s with
museum of Charles Dickens's life,
also his Swiss chalet.

London

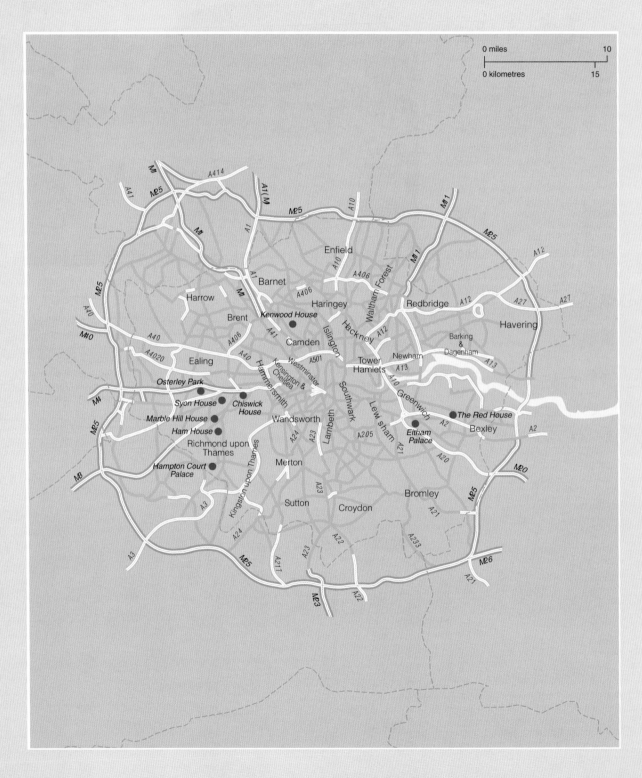

Kenwood House

Osterley Park

Syon House
Chiswick House

Marble Hill House
Ham House
Richmond upon Thames
Hampton Court Palace

The Red House
Eltham Palace

Harrow

Barnet

Enfield

Brent

Camden

Haringey

Waltham Forest

Redbridge

Havering

Ealing

Westminster

Islington

Hackney

Tower Hamlets

Newham

Barking & Dagenham

Kensington & Chelsea

Hammersmith

Southwark

Greenwich

Bexley

Wandsworth

Lambeth

Lewisham

Kingston upon Thames

Merton

Sutton

Croydon

Bromley

Chiswick House: this small, square villa, finished in 1729, was an early bid for true Palladian glory

Chiswick House, Chiswick

English Heritage • ££ • Open Apr to Oct, W-F, S & Su

A very entertaining little villa, one of the earliest and most influential experiments in Palladian design, created in 1726–9 by 'the Architect Earl', Richard, 3rd Earl of Burlington, in cooperation with his protege William Kent. The latter went on to become one of England's foremost architects and landscape designers, producing such astonishing Palladian masterpieces as Holkham Hall and Houghton Hall, both in Norfolk.

When it was built, the villa stood alongside the earl's existing Jacobean house, connected to it by a two-storey link; but in 1788 the old house was demolished and new wings were added to the villa to make it into a proper mansion. These additions have now been taken down and the villa returned to its original state.

Designed around a central octagonal saloon under the distinctive dome, the interiors are compact but beautifully proportioned. The decoration is brightly coloured and highly ornate in a baroque style, but always elegant. Most of the original contents have gone, a lot of them to Chatsworth in Derbyshire, and the interiors are still mostly bare of furniture, but some pieces have been returned and copies of more made. There are some striking paintings, too, particularly the vast canvases in the saloon, which have hung here since at least 1740.

Extensive gardens and grounds with follies (open all year, free), tearoom.

Signposted from A4 just west of junction with A316 in Chiswick, west London.

Eltham Palace, Eltham

English Heritage • £££ • Open Feb to late Dec, W-F, Su

A bizarre but fascinating combination of a medieval royal palace, complete with its original great hall, and an unrestrained art deco house of the 1930s. The palace started life as a moated manor house, bought in 1305 by the future King Edward II and remodelled by Edward IV, who built the great hall in the 1470s.

Eltham went into decline in the late 1500s after Greenwich Palace was built; it was used as a farm for 200 years after the Civil War and was almost derelict – although the hall's superb 'false hammerbeam' roof was still intact – when bought by Stephen and Virginia Courtauld in 1933. They commissioned the architects Seeley and Paget to restore the hall and build a flashy new art deco home.

As the only large example of a home of the type, it has undoubted allure. The clean lines, bold shapes and minimalist approach to colour, as well as the undoubted quality of craftsmanship, will strike a chord with many a 21st-century visitor.

Gardens, shop.

Signposted from the A20 (Lewisham to M20/M25) in Eltham, south-east London.

Eltham Palace: a fascinating combination of a royal hall of the 1470s and an art deco house of the 1930s

Ham House, Richmond

National Trust • £££ • Open Apr to Oct, M-W, S & Su

One of the most fascinating 17th-century houses in England, retaining a dark and ancient feel in a good many of its interiors. It's not that the house, built in 1610 for Sir Thomas Vavasour, a successful Elizabethan naval captain, has not been altered at all since, because it has: first in 1637–9 by William Murray, a close friend of Charles I, and again in 1672–4 by John Maitland, 2nd Earl of Lauderdale, and his wife Elizabeth, who built new rooms in the gaps between the bays of the south front.

Lauderdale was an unpleasant and uncultured character, coarse and ruthless and incapable of telling a joke without getting it wrong, yet he was a favourite of

King Charles II and a member of his 'Cabal' ministry (Clifford, Ashley, Buckingham, Arlington and Lauderdale).

Many of the rooms from Lauderdale's version of Ham survive intact, complete with their original furniture. The house was described in his time as 'esteemed as one of the beautyful and compleat seats in the kingdome' and 'furnished like a Great Prince's', and although the original glory of the decoration and furnishings is now dulled and darkened with age, the house is all the more atmospheric as a result.

This sense is at its height in the three suites of state apartments: the Duke's and Duchess's on the ground floor, and the Queen's on the first floor, prepared for a visit by Queen Catherine of Braganza in 1673. Particularly notable is the attention paid to the wooden floors, with their elaborate parquetry.

Equally ancient in feel, however, is the picture gallery that runs through the middle of the house from back to front – unchanged since 1639 and hung with portraits by Van Dyck and Lely, among others – and the tiny green closet next door, designed especially for the display of miniature paintings. It is a very rare survival.

Several other rooms demand attention, including the cramped, musty library, fitted out in the 1670s and little changed since and the great staircase, built in 1638–9 and hung with some of the house's most interesting paintings, among them a copy of Correggio's *The School of Love* that may have been given to William Murray by Charles I.

Extensive gardens (open all year, M-W, S & Su), still-house (where plant essences were distilled), tearoom, shop.

Signposted from the A307 Richmond to Kingston road, south-west London.

Ham House: built in 1610 and remodelled in 1672–4 by the 2nd Earl of Lauderdale, a favourite of Charles II, its interiors have a dark and ancient splendour

Hampton Court Palace: built by Cardinal Wolsey between 1514 and 1528, remodelled by Henry VIII, rebuilt by Wren for William and Mary in 1689–94

Hampton Court Palace, Richmond

Historic Royal Palaces • £££ • Open all year, Tu-F, S & Su

One of the most remarkable historic buildings in Britain, a combination of a Tudor palace begun by Cardinal Wolsey in 1514 and completed by Henry VIII in the 1530s, and a classical palace of 1689–94 built by Sir Christopher Wren for King William and Queen Mary.

Like the colleges at Oxford and Cambridge universities, Wolsey's palace consisted of low ranges of living accommodation built around courtyards, with halls in which the residents would gather. The part of the early palace that survives best is the base court, the vast outer courtyard built to house his guests. The gatehouse originally had about eight guest suites, while the ranges around the cobbled courtyard had a total of 40 guest lodgings, each consisting of an outer room and an inner room with a garderobe toilet. Equally well preserved are the Tudor kitchens, where a fire still often burns in the immense hearth.

Wolsey inevitably fell out of favour with his king when he was unable to secure Henry's divorce from Catherine of Aragon, and in 1528 he was obliged to give Henry his house – easily the largest in the kingdom – as part of a desperate bid to avoid the fatal consequences of the disagreement. Within six months, Henry had the builders in. He spent £62,000 in the next 10 years, remodelling the royal accommodation, building a huge new great hall and immense kitchens. He also created the Great House of Easement, a communal toilet that could sit 28 people. Most of Henry's lodgings were later rebuilt, but his hall and much of the kitchen court survives.

The palace was a popular royal resort and underwent many more changes before, in 1689, William III decided to make it his principal residence. The plan he agreed with Sir Christopher Wren would have swept away all the earlier work except the great hall, but money was short and, after Mary's death in 1694, William lost heart; so in the end only the main royal apartments on the south and east sides were rebuilt. The gracious exteriors and superb painted walls and ceilings by Sir James Thornhill inside the new wings make this part of the palace a baroque treat.

Perhaps the finest aspect of the sparsely furnished state apartments is that they retain their original decoration and most of the art collected by the palace's royal owners is still in place. Particularly notable are Henry's tapestries and the fine collection of paintings amassed by Charles I, with Dutch and Italian masters featuring strongly.

Extensive historic gardens, famous maze, restaurant, tearooms and shops.

Signposted on A308 between Kingston upon Thames and M3 junction 1.

Kenwood House, Hampstead

English Heritage • Free • Open all year, daily

On the outside is one of the most beautiful facades in England, famous for its role as a backdrop in the film *Notting Hill*, created by Robert Adam in 1764–79, when he remodelled the original brick house for Lord Mansfield, one of the nation's leading legal men. On the inside, it is really more an art gallery than a house: Kenwood and its collection of paintings was given to the nation by the brewing magnate the Earl of Iveagh in 1927, on the condition that it be opened to the public free of charge.

The only room of real interest for its architecture is Adam's library in the right-hand wing, its classical decoration a typical blend of extravagance and restraint. That apart, the main attraction is the pictures, including a wonderful view of the medieval London Bridge.

Above all, though, the house makes a superb destination for a walk on Hampstead Heath, starting from either Hampstead tube or the bus stops at Parliament Hill Fields.

Grounds with sculptures, woodland walks, restaurant, shop.

Signposted on B519 Hampstead to Highgate road, 1 mile east of Hampstead.

Kenwood House: one of the finest neoclassical facades in England, created in 1764–79 by Robert Adam

Marble Hill House, Twickenham

English Heritage • ££ • Open Apr to Oct, W-F, S & Su

Like Chiswick House (above), this is a jewel casket of a house, an essay in small-scale perfection. It was built in 1724–9 by the innovative Palladian architect Colen Campbell under the direction – as at Chiswick – of 'the Architect Earl', Lord Burlington, for Henrietta Howard, the mistress of the Prince of Wales, later King George II. Its setting beside the Thames was not only an attractive one in an area popular with the aristocracy, but also convenient for town at a time when river boats were the taxis of their day.

Henrietta, the daughter of Sir Henry Hobart of Blickling Hall in Norfolk, married Charles Howard, a younger son of the Earl of Suffolk, in 1706 at the age of 18. When he turned out to be a violent, drunken gambler, she fled, with her young son, Henry, to Hanover, where she eventually became a Lady of the Bedchamber to Caroline, Princess of Wales, Throughout her time as George's mistress, the two women seem to have remained on good terms; indeed, it is not even certain that George and Henrietta's relationship was a sexual one.

The house is only sparsely furnished, but has a good many interesting paintings, and is in any case notable mainly for its extravagant carved and gilded decoration in a showy baroque style, much of the imagery of which may have been conceived by Henrietta's friend, the poet Alexander Pope.

Park, cafe, shop.

Signposted on Richmond Road, Twickenham.

Marble Hill House: built in 1724–9 by Colen Campbell and Lord Burlington for Henrietta Howard

Osterley Park, Isleworth

National Trust • ££ • Open Apr to Oct, W-F, S & Su (also Mar, S & Su)

Nothing could be more obvious than that Osterley is a Tudor house (four wings of red brick around a central courtyard, with a pointy-topped tower at each corner) with 18th-century alterations – the vast neo-classical 'transparent' portico banged through one side to open the courtyard up. What makes it really special, though, is that the modifications are by Robert Adam, whose wealthy clients gave him a the opportunity to express his ideas to the full in the interiors.

Not only is the house full of extraordinary examples of Adam's attention to detail, but also many of the original drawings and plans – for anything from ceilings to furniture – survive in the Sir John Soane Museum in London. Adam

was commissioned in 1761, three years after his return from the Grand Tour and at the height of his early popularity, by Francis Child, the owner of Child's Bank. When Francis died suddenly in 1763, his brother Robert and Robert's new wife, Sarah, determined to complete the changes to the house.

One thing that makes Adam's work at Osterley particularly intriguing is the way in which he has worked around the limitations imposed by the original structure of the Tudor house. In the marble-floored entrance hall, semi-circular alcoves at either end are intended to reduce the length and so increase the apparent height of a room that is really too low.

The development between the earlier rooms and the later is equally fascinating. The first rooms finished were the eating room and its twin at the other side of the house, the drawing room, both of which were completed piecemeal. Then came

the library, finished in 1776 and a perfect whole – ceiling restored to its original plain white colouring, pictures painted for the room by Antonio Zucchi and furniture made for it by John Linell.

The later rooms include a state apartment suite – tapestry room, state bedroom and Etruscan-style dressing room – that the guidebook describes as 'the only surviving example of the high-water mark of Adam's decoration complete with the furniture he designed for it'.

And on top of the glory of all these perfect and perfectly preserved Adam interiors, Osterley Park is an oasis of countryside at the heart of town and a fine escape.

Parkland with walks, pleasure grounds (both open all year), gallery of modern art in basement (open as house, free), 16th-century stables (open summer Sunday afternoons), tearoom, shop.

Signposted from A4 between Hounslow and Hammersmith, west London.

Osterley Park: set in parkland next to fields where cows graze and without a high-rise in sight, the house features some of Robert Adam's finest interiors

Syon House: the plain exterior, with carriage portico added in the 1800s, belies the splendour of the interior, remodelled by Robert Adam in the 1760s

Syon House, Brentford

Privately owned (HHA) • £££ • Open Apr to Oct, W, Th, Su

Like nearby Osterley Park, Syon is not only a showcase for some of Robert Adam's most glorious interiors, but also a green oasis in the city – cows graze the fields and the meadows behind the house are flooded by the tidal Thames.

The most striking of Adam's rooms are the vast entrance hall and the equally classical ante-room next door, but his decorative skill is also seen in the long gallery, which retains its Tudor shape.

Unlike Osterley, the house is still lived in, being the London home of the Duke of Northumberland, and so has a warmth its neighbour lacks. The Adam rooms are kept for show; the dining and drawing rooms used by the family have Victorian decor and are not as splendid, but are still full of interest. The visit is topped off with the bedrooms, including a suite remodelled for Princess (later Queen) Victoria and her mother in 1832.

Gardens with splendid 1820s conservatory (open daily all year), ice house, garden centre, tearoom, shop.

Signposted from A312 between Brentford and Twickenham, south-west London.

The Red House, Bexleyheath

National Trust • £££ • Open Apr to Nov daily, booking required, tours only

One of the National Trust's most recent acquisitions, opened to the public for the first time in 2003, the Red House was the first home of William Morris and his wife Jane, built on land he bought in 1858, the year before they married.

It was also the first house designed by Morris's architect friend Philip Webb, who went on to bigger and better things (Standen in West Sussex, also owned by the Trust,

was his last house). Sadly all the contents of the Red House have been dispersed over the years and most of the vivid decorative work by Morris and his friends – almost every wall was painted – has gone. All that remains are a few glazing panels by Morris and Burne-Jones, three mural panels also by Burne-Jones, and the traces, in a cupboard, of an uncompleted mural by Rossetti's wife, Lizzie Siddal.

Only if more can be uncovered during restoration will a visit become truly worthwhile.

Signposted from A226 on west side of Bexleyheath; access on foot only.

The Red House: William Morris's first home, but not much of his decorative genius is in evidence

See also...

Apsley House
Hyde Park Corner, W1
V&A Museum, £££, open all year, daily
Robert Adam house of 1771–8, bought by the Duke of Wellington in 1817 and extended, known as 'No 1 London'. Restored 1992–5. Sumptuous interiors, vast and splendid collection of art.

The Banqueting House
Whitehall, SW1
Royal Palaces, £££, open all year, M-F, S (but can be closed for Government functions)
Inigo Jones's wonderful creation of 1619–22, built as an extension to the Tudor Palace of Whitehall, which was destroyed by fire in 1698.

Buckingham Palace
Green Park, SW1
Royal Palaces, ££££, limited opening (state rooms and grounds, Aug and Sep, daily; Queen's Gallery, all year, daily; Royal Mews, Mar to Oct, daily)
Famous royal palace, converted from an earlier house in 1825–30 by John Nash for King George IV. Only a few public rooms can be visited.

Danson House
Bexley, Kent
English Heritage, prices and opening times to be confirmed
Simple Palladian City merchant's house built 1762–7, currently being restored and conserved.

Fenton House
Windmill Hill, Hampstead
National Trust, £££, open Mar, S & Su, Apr to Oct, W-F, S & Su
Pleasing merchant's house of late 1600s with renowned collection of keyboard instruments (played on occasional demonstration days).

Fulham Palace
Bishops Avenue, Fulham
Local council, ££, open Mar to Oct, W-F, S & Su, Nov to Feb, Th-F, S & Su
Tudor palace of Bishops of London, with Georgian additions, Victorian chapel, and museum.

Kensington Palace
Kensington Gardens, W8
Royal Palaces, £££, open all year, daily
State apartments of royal residence built in 1689, where Queen Victoria was born. Lavish interiors, interesting painted staircase of George I era, costume collection featuring dresses worn by Elizabeth II and Diana, Princess of Wales.

Kew Palace
Kew Gardens
Royal Palaces, prices and opening times to be confirmed
An attractive red brick house with Dutch gables set in Kew Gardens; built as The Dutch House in 1631 for a City merchant. A royal residence from 1728, lived in by George III. Currently being restored. Also Queen Charlotte's Cottage, a *cottage orné* of 1770 (not normally open).

The Queen's House
Greenwich Park, Greenwich
Royal Observatory and National Maritime Museum, free, open daily, all year
One of only four buildings known for certain to have been designed by Inigo Jones and, of those, the only house; built in 1616–35 and altered by John Webb in the 1660s.

Ranger's House
Chesterfield Walk, Blackheath
English Heritage, £££, open all year, W-F, S & Su
Red brick villa on the edge of Greenwich Park, recently became the home of Sir Julius Wernher's art collection (mostly from Bath House, some from Luton Hoo).

Southside House
Wimbledon Common
Privately owned (HHA), ££, open Jan to Jun, W, S & Su, tours only
Built 1665, but much adapted; with artistic associations.

Sutton House
Homerton High St, Hackney
National Trust, ££, open early Feb to late Dec, F, S & Su
Tudor house built by a courtier in 1535, with many original features.

And...

Blewcoat School
Caxton St, Westminster, SW1
National Trust, free, open all year, M-F
Built in 1709 by a local brewer to give poor children an education, now the National Trust's main London gift shop and information centre.

Boston Manor House
Brentford
Local council, free, open Apr to Oct, S & Su
Jacobean house of 1623 set in parkland (*free, open all year, daily*).

Bruce Castle
Lordship Lane, Tottenham
Local council, free, open all year, W-F, S & Su
Manor house of 1500s, now home to a museum and local history archive.

Burgh House
New End Square, Hampstead
Local council, free, open all year, W-F & Su
House of 1703 with panelled rooms, terraced gardens, home to the Hampstead Museum.

Eastbury Manor House
Eastbury Square, Barking
National Trust and local council, ££, open Mar to Dec, first S of month
Rare example of a medium-sized Elizabethan manor house, used mostly for a range of local arts and heritage activities.

18 Folgate St
Spitalfields, E1
Spitalfields Historic Buildings Trust, ££, open twice a month, two days, M (lunchtime) & Su (afternoon)
'Time capsule' Georgian town house restored in authentic style, with sounds and even smells, to tell the story of a Huguenot silk-weaving family from 1725 to 1919.

Forty Hall
Forty Hill, Enfield
Local council, free, open all year, S & Su
Jacobean manor with fine plaster ceilings, nature trails, local museum.

Gunnersbury Park Museum

Gunnersbury Park, W3
*Local council, free, open all year,
daily (Victorian kitchens, S & Su)*
Grand family house of 1802 restored
by Sydney Smirke for the Rothschilds.

Lindsey House

Cheyne Walk, SW10
*National Trust, free, open four days
in year only, by appt only*
Fine house of 1600s, only entrance
hall, staircase and gardens open.

Pitshanger Manor

Walpole Park, Ealing
*Local council, free, open all year,
Tu- F, S*
Regency villa owned and rebuilt by
Sir John Soane in his own inimitable
way, restored, with contemporary art
gallery in a modern extension.

Rainham Hall

Rainham
*National Trust, ££, open Apr to Oct,
W only*
Elegant Georgian house of 1729,
occupied by a tenant.

Spencer House

St James's Place, SW1
*Privately owned, £££, open Feb to
Jul and Sep to Dec, Su, tours only*
Built 1756–66, said to be London's
most magnificent private palace.

Strawberry Hill

Waldergrave Rd, Twickenham
*Privately owned, £££, open May to
Sep, Su only*
Famous and highly influential gothic
revival home of Horace Walpole.

Houses with famous owners

Carlyle's House

Cheyne Row, Chelsea, SW3
*National Trust, ££, open Apr to Oct,
W–F, S & Su*
Queen Anne house with Victorian
decoration intact, the home of
Thomas Carlyle for 47 years until his
death in 1881.

The Charles Dickens Museum

48 Doughty St, WC1
*Privately owned, £££, open all year
daily*
Victorian terrace house where the
writer and his family lived 1837–9,
still in original state.

Down House

Near Biggin Hill, Kent
*English Heritage, £££, open early
Feb to late Dec, W-F, S & Su*
The home of Charles Darwin, still
much as it was when he lived here.

Freud Museum

Maresfield Gardens, Hampstead
*Privately owned, £££, open all year,
W-F, S & Su*
Home to Sigmund Freud after he left
Austria to escape the Nazis, with his
study intact (and his famous couch).

Handel House Museum

Brook St, W1
*Privately owned, £££, open all year,
Tu-F, S & Su*
The house in which George Frederick
Handel lived for 36 years to his death
in 1759, and composed his *Messiah*.
Only composer's museum in London.

Hogarth's House

Great West Road, Chiswick
*Privately owned by trust, free, open
all year, Tu-F, S & Su*
House of late 1600s lived in by the
painter, engraver and satirist from
1749 to his death in 1764.

Johnson's House

Gough Square, EC4
*Privately owned, £££, open all year,
M-F, Sat*
House of the 1700s in which Dr
Samuel Johnson, the writer and
lexicographer, lived.

Keats House

Keats Grove, Hampstead
*Corporation of London, ££, open all
year, Tu-F, S & Su*
Regency home of the poet.

Leighton House Museum

Holland Park Road, W14
*Local council, free, open all year,
M, W-F, S & Su*
Built 1864–79, home of the painter
Frederic, Lord Leighton, with
opulent Victorian interiors.

Lindley Sambourne House

Stafford Terrace, W8
*Local council, £££, open May to Oct,
S & Su, guided tours only*
The home of the *Punch* cartoonist
Edward Lindley Sambourne, with its
original interiors undisturbed.

Sir John Soane's Museum

Lincoln's Inn Fields, WC2
*Privately owned, free, open all year,
Tu-F, S & Su*
Wonderfully eccentric house built in
1812 by the famous architect,
containing his fascinatingly eclectic
collections of paintings, sculpture
and antiquities.

2 Willow Road

Hampstead, NW3
*National Trust, £££, open Apr to Oct,
Th-F, S (also Mar and Nov, S)*
Modernist house in a terrace of three
designed in 1939 by the architect
Erno Goldfinger; his own home, with
fine collection of 20th-century art.

*2 Willow Road, left: built in 1939 by the
architect Erno Goldfinger as his own home*

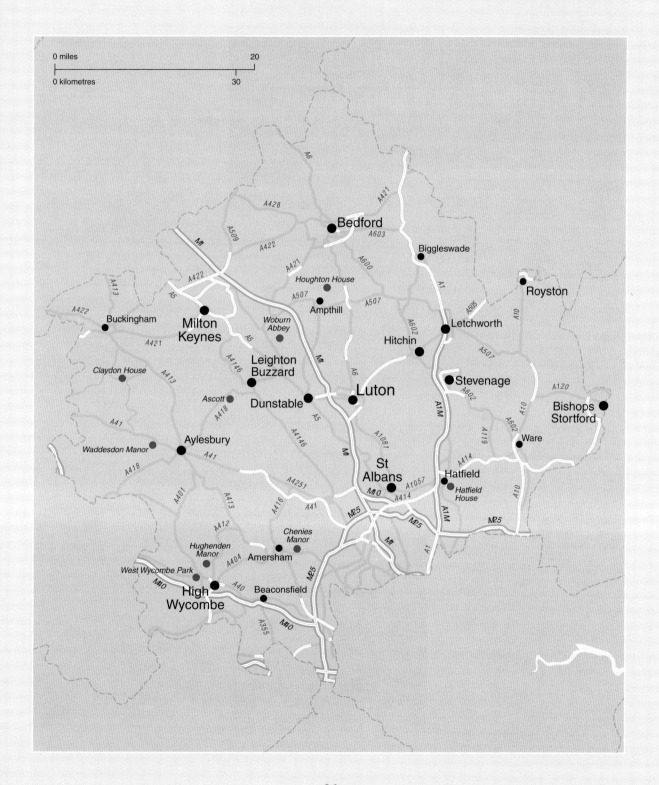

0 miles 20
0 kilometres 30

A6
A421
A428
A509
A422
Bedford
A603
Biggleswade
A421
M1
A422
A421
A600
A1
Houghton House
A507
A507
Royston
A505
A413
A5
Ampthill
A602
Letchworth
A10
A422
Buckingham
Milton Keynes
Woburn Abbey
A5
Hitchin
A507
A421
Leighton Buzzard
A4146
M1
Stevenage
A120
Claydon House
A413
A6
A602
Bishops Stortford
Ascott
A418
Dunstable
Luton
Aylesbury
A41
A5
A1M
A119
A602
Ware
Waddesdon Manor
A41
A4146
A1081
A10
A418
A4251
St Albans
A414
Hatfield
A401
A416
A41
M25
M10
A1057
Hatfield House
A10
A413
A412
Chenies Manor
A414
A1M
M25
Hughenden Manor
A404
Amersham
M1
A1
M40
West Wycombe Park
M40
A40
Beaconsfield
M25
High Wycombe
A355
M40

91

Ascott: a comfortable house built after 1873 for Leopold de Rothschild, with a superb art collection

Ascott, Buckinghamshire

National Trust • £££ • Open Apr and Aug to mid-Sep, Tu-F, S & Su

Although there is a Jacobean farmhouse at its heart, this is really a Victorian house in a half-timbered 'Tudorbethan' style, built after 1873 by the architect George Devey for Leopold de Rothschild, son of the wealthy banking family. It is still lived in by his grandson, Sir Evelyn de Rothschild, and one of the beauties of this comfortable and welcoming house is that time does not stand still here; improvements to the decoration (and even to the layout – Devey's entrance was reinstated as recently as 1988) are constantly being made, the most striking being the painted *trompe l'oeil* tiling in the dining room, the work of Italian designer Renzo Mongiardino, which was added in the last few years.

The fabric of the building, then, is not historic; but the extraordinary art collection certainly is. A good deal of it was inherited by Leopold from his father, Baron Lionel de Rothschild; it's good to be able to admire the paintings, sculpture and ceramics in a setting that feels like a cosy home, rather than a gallery. A fun game to play is to ask the room guides what their favourite object is; they all seem to have thought long and hard about which they'd take

home, given the chance. There's plenty of choice, particularly among the smaller statues, but the modern-looking Chinese ceramics of the Han and Tang periods, between 1,000 and 2,200 years old, are hard to beat.

Also unmissable are the gardens, a blend of the formal and natural, laid out in the 1880s after Leopold's marriage, which is celebrated in the Venus and Cupid fountains and an inscription on the sundial.

Extensive gardens (open as house).

Signposted on A418 Leighton Buzzard to Aylesbury road, just east of Wing.

Chenies Manor, Buckinghamshire

Privately owned (HHA) • £££ • Open Apr to Oct, W & Th

The pretty gardens at Chenies, famous for their tulips in spring and featuring an interesting mathematical yew maze planted in 1991, are of more appeal than the house itself. Although it does have substantial medieval work in it, it was largely restored in recent years as a family home and the rooms retain little of their original form and none of their contents.

Most of the interiors are a comfortable mix of 17th-, 18th- and 19th-century furnishings against a largely 19th-century backdrop of quiet panelling and loud wallpaper. More interesting is the structure of the house, with an odd double outer wall creating tiny closets off the upstairs rooms, among them a privy, an oratory and a priest's hole. Best of all, though, is the exterior, with superb chimneys of carved brick.

Chenies was built in the mid-1400s and extended in 1523–6, and was the principal seat of the Russell family until they moved to Woburn after the Restoration.

Gardens (open as house), shop, tearoom, art exhibitions in Pavilion gallery.

Off A404 Amersham to Rickmansworth road, in Chenies village.

Chenies Manor: surviving hall (mid-1400s) and lodgings wing (1520s), much altered over the years

Claydon House: built in the 1760s as one wing of a planned mansion, attached to a vast central rotunda

Claydon House, Buckinghamshire

National Trust • ££ • Open Apr to Oct, M-W, S & Su

The extraordinary thing about Claydon is that the present house, with its unrestrainedly sumptuous decoration in a mix of rococo and neo-classical styles, is merely one surviving wing of an immense mansion started in 1754 by Ralph, 2nd Earl Verney, and still incomplete on his death in 1791.

The Verneys had lived on the estate here since 1620, when it was owned by Sir Edmund Verney, one of the greatest and most respected courtiers of his day, who was the royal standard-bearer in the Civil War and was killed at the battle of Edgehill in 1642.

Ralph seems to have been quiet and conscientious in his youth, studying hard at Cambridge and then managing the family estates, but after he inherited in 1752, the vast family fortune – augmented by good marriages to wealthy heiresses made by his elder brother, who died young, and by Ralph himself – seems to have gone to his head. He set out on a political career that put him into direct rivalry with his near neighbour Earl Temple, and decided to build a house to equal Temple's at Stowe.

In fact the surviving part of Claydon, which contains the state rooms, probably started out as a house in its own right; but even before the structure was finished in 1768, Ralph had plans to add an enormous rotunda as an entrance hall and a matching wing on the other side to contain a ballroom.

By this time Ralph had fallen out with his architect, Luke Lightfoot, really a stonemason and woodcarver, whose 'extravagant and freakish decors', as the guidebook puts it, were filling the house. Ralph called in Sir Thomas Robinson, a respectable Palladian architect, who disliked Lightfoot, calling him 'an ignorant knave, with no small spice of madness in his composition', but worked alongside him for a year before it finally emerged that Lightfoot was fraudulent as well as haphazard in his methods and the latter was dismissed.

Robinson employed Joseph Rose, Robert Adam's favourite plasterer, to do the ceilings, and really it's the combination of Lightfoot's crazed rococo genius and Rose's elegant classicism that makes the sparsely furnished interiors special. One of the finest rooms is the staircase, with stuccoed walls and ceiling by Rose and the stairs by Lightfoot, with an ironwork balustrade so delicate that it rustles when someone walks up.

Ralph's fortunes dipped after a series of bad investments, and his ballroom was still unfinished at the time of his death. It was pulled down within months by his successor, his niece Mary, whose portrait shows a stern and practical-looking lady.

Grounds (open as house), secondhand bookshop. Also church, cafe (not NT).

Signposted from A413 Buckingham to Aylesbury road and from A41, 4 miles south-west of Winslow.

Hatfield House: the south front of this splendid Jacobean house shows a Renaissance influence

Hatfield House, Hertfordshire

Privately owned • £££ • Open Apr to Sep, daily (by guided tour on weekdays)

Possibly the finest of the grand houses of the Jacobean age, and in remarkably original condition. Hatfield was built in 1607–11 by Robert Cecil, 1st Earl of Salisbury and chief minister to King James I. After the new king arrived from Scotland, he took a shine to Cecil's house at Theobald's and decided that Cecil would no doubt be delighted to swap it for the old royal palace at Hatfield.

Cecil pulled down three-quarters of the ancient palace – where a young Elizabeth had been more or less imprisoned during the reign of her sister Mary and where, while reading under an oak tree in the park, she heard the news of her succession – to make way for a new house as grand as Theobald's. The architect was Robert Lyminge, designer of Blickling Hall in Norfolk, but with input from, among others, a young Inigo Jones.

The result is an 'E'-plan house of severe and impressive plainness on the entrance front and slightly more frivolity at the back, its red brick and acres of glazing speaking of wealth and status. Inside, it retains a great deal of its original layout and decoration, starting in the lofty marble hall, a typically Jacobean development of the medieval great hall, separated from the entrance hall by an enormous carved wooden screen, with a minstrels' gallery at the opposite end of the room. All the woodwork is original.

This sets the tone for the rest of the interiors, all classically Jacobean in form and equally impressive in scale. The grand staircase is one of the finest of its period and, unusually for such an ancient stair, is still used; its wealth of decoration includes a relief portrait of a gentleman with a rake, basket and vase of flowers, said to be John Tradescant, one of the earliest professional gardeners, who worked for Robert Cecil at Hatfield and for Charles I.

The great chamber has a Victorian feel to its decoration but retains its Jacobean proportions and much original detail, including a fireplace with a life-size statue of James I. The long gallery is original in every respect, except that the delicately handsome ceiling was gilded in the early 1800s. It does look fine, though, so no disrespect to the 2nd Marquess of Salisbury, who did a great deal to restore the house's Jacobean appearance.

Scattered throughout the house are remarkable and world-famous early paintings, including the 'Rainbow' and 'Ermine' portraits of Queen Elizabeth. Of equal interest is a series of four tapestries made in 1611 in Warwickshire, depicting everyday scenes of rural life in absorbing detail.

Extensive gardens (open as house), shop, restaurant, model soldier collection, banqueting house of Tudor palace.

Signposted from A1, on A1000, on east side of Hatfield.

Houghton House, Bedfordshire

English Heritage • Free • Open all year, daily

An interesting ruin, notable even in its degraded state for the way that a traditional Jacobean house built in about 1615 – of red brick, with wings and gables – was given trendy Renaissance flourishes as it was being completed. On two sides there are open loggias two storeys high, their arches still graceful even though the stonework has been badly corroded by airborne pollution from the nearby brickworks in the last century. It is possible that Inigo Jones was the architect responsible for adding these elegant touches.

The house stood on land granted by King James I to Mary, Dowager Countess Pembroke, the sister of Sir Philip Sidney, and is said to have inspired the House Beautiful in Bunyan's *The Pilgrim's Progress*. It was dismantled in 1794, when panelling was ripped out and wall paintings were destroyed.

It is a pleasant spot to visit, set on a hillside with extensive views (but no avoiding those brickworks).

On B530 Ampthill to Bedford road, 1 mile north of Ampthill. Short walk to property.

Houghton House: ruin of a Jacobean manor of about 1615, with classical details attributed to Inigo Jones

Hughenden Manor, Buckinghamshire

National Trust • £££ • Open Apr to Oct, W-F, S & Su (also Mar, S & Su)

The country retreat of Victorian prime minister Benjamin Disraeli is notable mainly for its associations with the flamboyant politician, but also for the easy-going Gothic style in which he had it remodelled after buying the house in 1848, with comfort and practicality clearly priorities. This is evident at once in the arcade protecting the front door, tiled and fitted with plate-glass windows, and in the pretty plaster fan-vaults of the entrance hall.

The rooms have been restored as closely as possible, including the Disraelis' bedroom, so that it is easy to get a real sense of the place as a functioning family home. Least altered of the rooms is Disraeli's upstairs study, looking almost exactly as it did in a photograph taken in 1881. Here Queen Victoria spent a few moments alone when she visited after her favourite politician's death that same year.

The house, built in about 1740, is not large or grand, and does not really have much to offer anyone not interested in its most famous owner. But it is hard not to become interested once you visit, since he was such a fascinating character and so closely involved in fashionable society as well as in politics; read, for example, the story behind the portraits of Count D'Orsay and the Countess of Bessington that hang in the drawing room.

Gardens (open as house), parkland and woodland walks (open all year, daily), shop, restaurant.

Signposted on A4128 High Wycombe to Great Missenden road, 2 miles north of High Wycombe.

Hughenden Manor: bought by Disraeli in 1848, the year before he became leader of the Conservatives

Waddesdon Manor, Buckinghamshire

National Trust • £££ • Open Apr to Oct, W-F, S & Su

The only French chateau in England, built in 1877–83 on a greenfield site – a hilltop on an estate purchased from the Duke of Marlborough – by Baron Ferdinand de Rothschild (the title was conferred on the five Rothschild brothers in 1822 by the Austrian emperor), son of the international banking family who consolidated their fortune by shipping gold secretly from all over Europe to fund Wellington's army in Spain in the run-up to the victory at Waterloo in 1815.

Intending to create a house to, as Lord Rothschild puts it in the guidebook, 'delight and surprise the small circle of Baron Ferdinand's friends', he employed the French architect Gabriel-Hippolyte Destailleur, who had recently renovated the 16th-century Chateau de Mouchy near Beauvais. The job was an immense one and involved laying 11 miles of pipe to bring water from Aylesbury, building a gasworks (and a railway to supply it) at Westcott, levelling the hilltop for the north avenue, which leads up to the front door, and digging down 30 feet through clay to find solid ground for the foundations.

The original plans were for a house almost twice the length, but this was too much for Ferdinand. He later regretted having ignored his architect's advice that 'one always builds too small' and in 1889–91 added an extension for the morning room, equipped with five desks and writing-tables, in which, as he put it, visiting friends 'could all meet, and read and write without disturbing each other'.

Inside, Waddesdon is a jewel box of sumptuous decoration and a treasure-house of fine furniture and works of art. The emphasis is distinctly French, with Sevres porcelain scattered liberally around the place, a set of 18th-century panelling put to good use in the breakfast room and stacks of ormolu furniture (decorated with gilded metalwork), much of which was once owned by French kings. The French decor finds a nice counterpoint in fine English portraits, with a particularly good collection of paintings of female sitters by Reynolds, Gainsborough and Romney in the Baron's study.

Somehow the Baron's rooms contrive to be comfortable as well as richly ornamented, but none the less it is pleasing to find a more robust atmosphere in the bachelors' wing (open only on weekdays), where male guests could skulk in the billiards room or puff away in the smoking room – like a grandee's version of a traditional pub.

Gardens, parterre, aviary, wooded grounds (open Mar to Dec, W-F, S & Su), shop, restaurants, wine cellars and wine shop.

Signposted on A41 Aylesbury to Bicester road, 6 miles north-west of Aylesbury.

Waddesdon Manor: built in 1877–83 in the style of a French chateau for Baron Ferdinand de Rothschild, it is an extraordinary statement of wealth and taste

Woburn Abbey: built on the site of a Cistercian abbey in the 1600s, it was redeveloped in the 1740s and 1780s in a slightly old-fashioned classical style

West Wycombe Park, Buckinghamshire

National Trust • £££ • Open Jun to Aug, M-Th & Su, tours only

An eccentric version of the smart 18th-century Palladian mansion, its interiors having more panache than taste – but thoroughly entertaining none the less. It is still lived in (which dictates its limited opening season) by the Dashwood family, descendants of the infamous Sir Francis Dashwood, founder of the Bacchanalian dining society known as the Hellfire Club, whose own entertaining eccentricities are laid bare during the tour.

Set in a lovely rococo landscaped garden, the house looks sensible enough from the north, bar its rich yellow colour, but the extraordinary Greek-revival portico at the west end, created by Nicholas Revett in 1771, and the Italianate double colonnade of the south front are strikingly individual statements.

Equally remarkable is the main feature of the classically influenced interiors: most of the ceilings and many of the walls are painted, with a great deal of *trompe l'oeil* work. Most of it was done in the 1750s to 1770s by the Italian artist Giuseppe Borgnis and his son Giovanni.

Grounds (open Apr to Aug, M-Th & Su).

Off the A40 Oxford road on western side West Wycombe village.

Woburn Abbey, Bedfordshire

Privately owned (HHA) • £££ • Open Apr to Sep, daily (also Jan to Mar and Oct, S & Su)

One of the top echelon of Britain's 'public' great houses, best known for its safari park and deer reserve. The home of the Russells, Earls (and later Dukes) of Bedford, it grew up in the 1600s on the site of a Cistercian abbey, but owes its present form to rebuilding after 1747 by Henry Flitcroft and then from 1786 by Henry Holland.

The state rooms on the first floor – starting with the bedroom used by Queen Victoria on her visit in 1841 and continuing through the saloon, with its extraordinary coffered ceiling, to the library and long gallery – are decorated in a Victorian-buffed version of highly gilded 18th-century extravagance that is rich but seldom very exciting. Of more interest are the paintings, with quantities of Van Dycks and – for many, the highlight of the house – an entire room of Canalettos.

Elsewhere Woburn suffers from a museum-like quality, with collections of porcelain, silver and gold hidden behind glass in the basement. A rare treat, though, is the shell-lined grotto of the early 1600s in the loggia.

Grounds, deer park, maze, sculpture gallery, antiques centre, pottery, shops, restaurant.

On A4012 Bedford to Leighton Buzzard road south of Woburn village.

West Wycombe Park: the south front, built in about 1756, with its theatrical Italianate double colonnade

See also…

Gorhambury House
St Albans, Hertfordshire
Privately owned (HHA), £££, open May to Sep, Th
Palladian house of 1700s, with ruin of Tudor manor house in the park (Old Gorhambury, *English Heritage, free, access at reasonable times by two-mile walk on permissive footpath*).

Knebworth House
Knebworth, Hertfordshire
Privately owned (HHA), £££, open Easter, spring half-term, Jul and Aug, daily
Pleasing Tudor mansion of 1492, gothicized in the late 1800s, with formal gardens, deer park and adventure playground.

Nether Winchendon House
Aylesbury, Buckinghamshire
Privately owned (HHA), £££, open odd days in May and Aug, tours only
Medieval and Tudor manor house with fine original plasterwork, with 'Gothick' alterations of late 1700s.

Shaw's Corner
Ayot St Lawrence, Hertfordshire
National Trust, £££, open Apr to Oct, W-F, S & Su
Edwardian Arts and Crafts house lived in by George Bernard Shaw from 1906 to his death in 1950.

Stowe House
Stowe, Buckinghamshire
Privately owned, open Easter and summer school holidays, W-F, S & Su, guided tours only
Vast and elegant Palladian mansion of late 1700s, now a school. The real attraction is the landscape garden of the early 1700s with buildings by Vanbrugh, Gibbs, Kent and Leoni (*National Trust, £££, open Mar to late Dec, W-F, S & Su*).

Wrest Park Gardens
Near Shefford, Bedfordshire
English Heritage, £££, open Apr to Oct, S & Su
Fascinating formal gardens of early 1700s with numerous garden buildings, also chateau-style house of 1830s (not normally open).

And…

Chicheley Hall
Newport Pagnell, Buckinghamshire
Privately owned (HHA), £££, open all year, groups by appt only
English Baroque house of 1719–23 with interesting interiors.

Cliveden
Taplow, Buckinghamshire
National Trust, £££, open mid-Mar to Dec, daily (estate and garden), Apr to Oct, Th & Su (house)
Great estate with famous gardens and grounds overlooking the Thames. The house was built in 1851 by Sir Charles Barry for the Duke of Sutherland; it is now a hotel and opening is limited to a few rooms.

Princes Risborough Manor
Princes Risborough, Buckinghamshire
National Trust, ££, open Apr to Oct, W, by appt only
Red brick house of the early 1600s with original features; only hall, Jacobean staircase, drawing room and garden open.

Old Gorhambury House: the ruins of a large Elizabethan manor with considerable Renaissance decoration, in the park of a fine Palladian mansion

Heart of England
Berkshire, Oxfordshire, Gloucestershire

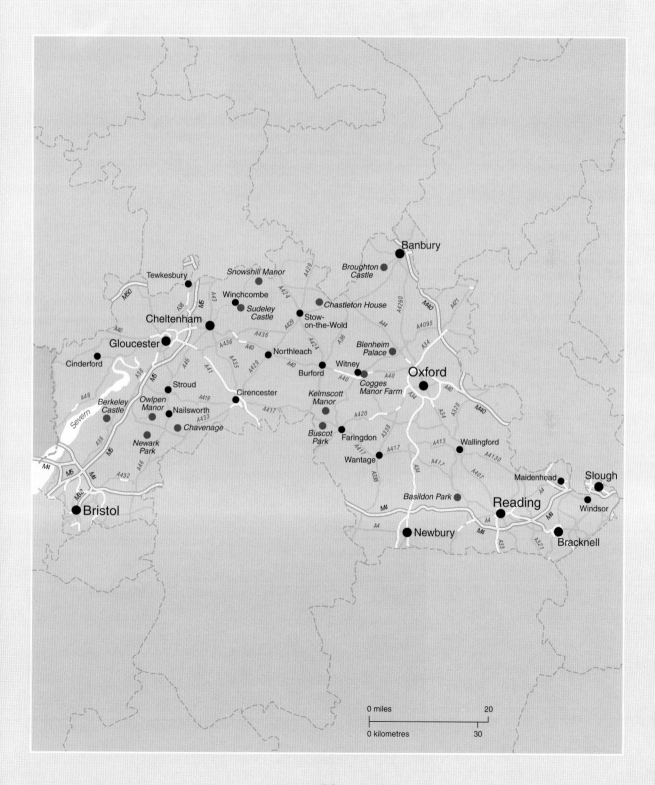

Tewkesbury

Snowshill Manor

Broughton
Castle

Banbury

Winchcombe

Chastleton House

Sudeley
Castle

Cheltenham

Stow-
on-the-Wold

Gloucester

Blenheim
Palace

Cinderford

Northleach

Witney

Oxford

Stroud

Burford

Cogges
Manor Farm

Berkeley
Castle

Owlpen
Manor

Cirencester

Kelmscott
Manor

Nailsworth

Chavenage

Buscot
Park

Faringdon

Wallingford

Newark
Park

Wantage

Maidenhead

Slough

Reading

Windsor

Basildon Park

Bristol

Newbury

Bracknell

Severn

M50 A38 M5 A43 A424 A429 A4260 M40 A421 A4095 A44 A34 A40 A436 A436 A40 A424 A46 A41 A435 A429 A40 A40 A40 A329 M40 A48 A419 A417 A420 A338 A34 A413 A4130 A38 A433 A417 A417 A417 A4 M5 A432 A338 A34 A407 M4 M5 M4 M4 A4 M4 A33 A321 M32

0 miles 20

0 kilometres 30

Basildon Park: one of the finest Palladian facades in England, built in 1776–83 by John Carr of York

Basildon Park, Berkshire

National Trust • £££ • Open Apr to Oct, W-F, S & Su

Graced with one of the most restrained and stately Palladian facades in Britain, Basildon was built in 1776–83 by John Carr of York for Sir Francis Sykes, who made his fortune working for the East India company in Bengal and decided to settle in a part of the country that had been nicknamed 'the English Hindoostan' because so many of his fellow venturers had retired there.

The remarkable thing about Basildon, however, is that it still exists at all; because it was sold in 1929, having been empty for almost 20 years, to a property developer who stripped out many of the fittings – chimneypieces, doors, doorcases and even small sections of the plasterwork (to be used as patterns for other houses) – before advertising it for sale in America at one million dollars, inclusive of dismantling, shipping and re-erection. There were no takers, and it was left abandoned and decaying until in 1952 it was bought by Lord and Lady Iliffe.

The new owners set out to learn about Carr's other houses, such as Harewood in Yorkshire, and bought original fittings from one in Lincolnshire that was about to be demolished, discovering that Carr's designs and the work of his craftsmen were so precise that doors fitted straight into sockets and the pins that held chimneypieces slotted into existing holes.

The result is a fascinating reconstruction, full of little puzzles, never quite the same as the original but also, since it is essentially a modern home, with a lived-in and comfortable feel. None of the rooms is a masterpiece, but there is plenty of interest – including one upstairs room filled with an oddly appealing collection of shells.

Gardens, parkland with walks (both open as house), estate walks, restaurant, shop.

On A329 between Pangbourne and Streatley, 7 miles north-west of Reading.

Berkeley Castle, Gloucestershire

Privately owned (HHA) • £££ • Open Apr to Sep, W-F, S & Su, also Oct, Su

A charming and intriguing example of a medieval castle that survives in very much its ancient form and has stayed in use as a residence over the years. Berkeley is a compact and powerful little castle, its oldest parts dating back to 1117 and its prominence in history having almost as long a run: in 1327 King Edward II was murdered here after being held captive for some time in a 'drop 'em in and forget 'em' type of dungeon, into which visitors can peer. You can also see the bowling green on which Queen Elizabeth played when she stayed here.

What's surprising is that such an old-fashioned structure can also make a comfortable house, but the castle has been modified gently over the years and is still the home of the Berkeley family. As a result it combines the defensive fascinations of a Marcher fortress – trip steps and murder holes – with far more modern touches of class, such as the famed collections of silver and some excellent Dutch paintings, including a series of sea paintings by Van de Velde.

Butterfly house, Elizabethan terraced gardens, tearoom, shops.

Signposted on B4066 off A38 Bristol to Gloucester road, 6 miles west of Dursley.

Berkeley Castle: little changed but much mellowed since it was completed in 1153 on the orders of Henry II

Blenheim Palace: an immense and weighty baroque monument, built using Crown money to reward the Duke of Marlborough's victories over the French

Blenheim Palace, Oxfordshire

Privately owned (HHA) • ££££ •
Open mid-Mar to Oct daily

This immense, hugely aspirational residence is always said to have been built by a grateful nation for John Churchill, 1st Duke of Marlborough, after his victory at Blenheim in 1704 had prevented the French army of Louis XIV from invading Austria; and to be the masterpiece of the playwright-turned-architect Sir John Vanbrugh. But it isn't quite that simple.

The royal estate of Woodstock was given to the Duke as a reward for his services by Queen Anne, who had come to the throne in 1702 and who promised £240,000 for the building of a house. At the time, Marlborough's wife, Sarah, was the Queen's closest friend; but by 1710 the two women had fallen out and by 1712 work on the new house ceased altogether, with £220,000 already spent and £45,000 owing to the various craftsmen and designers working on it (among

them Vanbrugh's assistant, Nicholas Hawksmoor; the same chief stonemasons who had worked on St Paul's Cathedral in London; and Grinling Gibbons). The duke decided to complete the house with his own money, but refused to offer the Crown rates that had been paid previously. In 1716 work restarted without the big names; within months Vanbrugh had walked out and left in charge was the cabinet-maker James Moore. Only after the duke's death in 1722 did Hawksmoor return to build the triumphal arch.

None the less, Blenheim stands as Vanbrugh and Hawksmoor's great baroque statement, massively weighty and sober but with bizarre flourishes atop the corner towers and, in keeping with its origins, more the feel of a public monument than a house. Inside, too, it is more like a museum than a place to live, especially since the most famous son of the Churchill line, Winston, Britain's wartime prime minister, is commemorated in a series of gallery-like rooms that includes the room in which he was born. There are some fine paintings of his, too.

The drawing-rooms and state rooms are an essay in baroque grandeur, with original gilded ceilings by Hawksmoor and opulent marble doorcases by Gibbons. The most splendid of the rooms are the entrance hall, a vast space lit by the high windows of Vanbrugh's clerestory, with carved stonework by Gibbons and a painted ceiling by Sir James Thornhill, and the saloon, its walls and ceiling painted by Louis Laguerre. The more intimate rooms have fine family portraits by Kneller, Romney and Reynolds, while the three state rooms feature a series of tapestries commissioned by Marlborough, depicting his victorious battles in great detail – in the end, they are probably the greatest treasure of Blenheim.

Parkland landscaped by Capability Brown with walks, lake, bridge by Vanbrugh, cafe (open all year, daily). Italian garden and water terraces (open as house), restaurant, shop. Also Pleasure Grounds (open as house, separate admission) with maze, adventure playground, butterfly house.

Signposted from A44 Oxford to Chipping Norton road in Woodstock village.

Broughton Castle, Oxfordshire

Privately owned (HHA) • £££ •
Open mid-May to mid-Sep, W & Su
(also Th in Jul and Aug)

Not as defensible as the name implies, despite the picturesque gatehouse flanked by battlemented walls and the moat surrounding the well-kept gardens, Broughton is essentially a Tudor manor house, developed in the 1550s from a more heavily fortified manor built in the early 1300s. It was, however, besieged by Royalist troops in 1642 following the nearby Battle of Edgehill; its then owner, William, 8th Lord Saye and Sele, had been active in Parliamentarian plotting long before the outbreak of war, and a small room in the house is said to be where he and his fellow conspirators gathered between 1629 and 1640 to plan their opposition to Charles I.

Today it's a tidy and well-cared-for little house with rooms that evoke a number of different periods without ever having been frozen in time. For instance, the great hall is an Elizabethan creation that incorporates the medieval hall of about 1300, with a handsome Jacobean-style ceiling that was actually put in in the 1760s. In the

Broughton Castle: really a Tudor manor, but the gatehouse of the late 1300s survives (left of picture)

king's chamber, meanwhile, a sophisticated French-influenced chimneypiece of 1553 happily co-exists with 18th-century handpainted Chinese wallpaper.

There's also a rare private chapel of the early 1300s and, in the great parlour, a smashing Elizabethan ceiling of 1599.

Gardens, gatehouse, park (open as house), medieval church, tearoom.

On B4035 Banbury to Shipston-on-Stour road, 3 miles south of Banbury.

Buscot Park, Oxfordshire

National Trust • £££ • Open Apr to Sep, W-F

More an art gallery than a house, Buscot – a small, tidy Palladian mansion of 1779–83 – is now home to the eclectic collections of Gavin Henderson, 2nd Lord Faringdon, an original champagne socialist who was prominent in the Labour Party, together with that acquired by his wealthy financier father. It's a right old mix, sprinkling serious, heavyweight works by Rembrandt, Murillo, Rubens and Jordaens in among a froth of frivolous and unusual modern pictures.

By far the most striking room in the house is the saloon, which not only retains its plasterwork ceiling of the 1780s but is dominated by Edward Burne-Jones's *The Legend of the Briar Rose*, a series of paintings running around three walls, in architectural frames designed by the artist. This and the Italianate formal gardens laid out 1904–13 by the leading garden designer Harold Peto are, by some distance, the highlights of a visit.

Grounds with avenue walks, Italianate water garden and walled garden (open as house, also M-Tu), tearoom, shop.

Signposted on A417 Lechlade to Faringdon road, 3 miles east of Lechlade.

Buscot Park: built in 1779–83, redecorated greatly in the 1930s and now home to an unusual art collection

Chastleton House: built in 1607–12, and one of our most attractive and interesting Jacobean houses

Chastleton House, Gloucestershire

National Trust • £££ • Open Apr to Oct, W-F & S, admission by timed ticket, advance booking recommended

One of the best Jacobean houses in England, preserved in a slightly run-down but beautifully unaltered state that makes it a thoroughly satisfying place to visit. When it was first opened to visitors in the 1940s, the then owner, Mrs Irene Whitmore-Jones, would explain its lack of gloss and polish by saying that the family had lost its money 'in the war', by which she meant the Civil War, 300 years before.

It was built between 1607 and 1612 by Walter Jones, a lawyer descended from a south Welsh family who had settled near Witney in Oxfordshire in the mid-1400s and made their money in the wool trade, then England's principal and most profitable export. Walter was a prominent figure in political life in Worcester, but may have settled here because of his friendship with Ralph Sheldon, the owner of the tapestry workshops at Barcheston in Worcestershire. Sheldon was owed money by Chastleton's previous owner, Robert Catesby, the leader of the Gunpowder Plot of 1605, so he was probably in a position to do William a favour.

One of the greatest treasures of Chastleton is a set of Flemish tapestries of the 1590s, their design sharing many details with Sheldon tapestries. They hang in a room that bears the Sheldon name and has the Sheldon arms over the fireplace – William's aim being not just to honour his close friend, but also to show off the friendship to impress guests.

There are numerous original features in the tall, handsomely designed house, including superb chimneypieces and ceilings, two rather wonderful wooden staircases and a set of vividly patterned 'flamestitch' hangings in one of the bedroom closets. There are also lots of fascinating objects, among them the bible said to have been used by Charles I's chaplain at the king's execution in 1649.

But the unique thing about the house is the way it has been kept as it was when given to the Trust, with an air of daily use and impoverished practicality. A bundle of plant labels lies on a table, handy for the garden; to reach the long gallery at the top of the house – a glorious room with a fabulous barrel-vaulted ceiling – visitors pass through an attic room with bare joists and water tanks.

Even the dark, damp vaulted basement is interesting, complete with a decaying ladder 66ft long, supplied in the 1850s and used to climb to the roof and clear gutters.

Elizabethan and Jacobean-style gardens.

Signposted on minor road from A436 Chipping Norton to Stow-on-the-Wold road, 6 miles north-east of Stow-on-the-Wold.

Chavenage: this pretty Elizabethan Cotswold stone manor looks much as it did when completed in 1576

Chavenage, Gloucestershire

Privately owned (HHA) • ££ • Open May to Sep, Th & Su, guided tour only

An attractive little Elizabethan manor built from Cotswold stone and looking much as it did when completed by a gentleman named Edward Stephens in 1576. The real beauty of Chavenage today, however, is that visitors are welcomed in and shown around by members of the family that owns it. Their detailed and intimate knowledge of the house and its contents, as well as their gregarious and friendly disposition, makes it feel as if you've dropped in to see a good friend who is eager to introduce you to the delights of a home in which he takes great pride.

Apart from a plain Edwardian wing at the back containing a ballroom, the rooms shown are still largely Elizabethan in character and furnishing. The most striking are the great hall, with its elaborate carved oak screen and vast floor-to-roof windows, and a tapestry-lined bedroom known as Cromwell's room, where Chavenage's favourite ghost story is recounted.

The tapestries are one of the great treasures of Chavenage, and the house is full of Civil War relics, too; but more importantly it is scattered with objects that have an interesting or amusing story attached, such as the hinged picture frame in the oak room (used to conceal a risque picture behind a respectable one) and the designs by Sir Jeffrey Wyattville for the interiors of Windsor Castle, discovered accidentally in 1970.

Signposted on minor road off B4014, 2 miles north-west of Tetbury.

Cogges Manor Farm, Oxfordshire

Local council • ££ • Open Apr to Nov, Tu-F, S & Su

The real raison d'etre of the manor farm museum is to entertain school groups, but there is plenty here to keep adults interested, too, even before you take the house itself into account: there are traditional breeds of farm animals (you have to have a hard heart not to be amused by Gloucester Old Spot piglets) and 18th-century barns containing displays of agricultural implements and machinery, as well as a cottagey walled kitchen garden.

Parts of the manor house date back as far as the 1300s, but much of it was updated in the 1670s and there is a nice bit of 17th-century *trompe l'oeil* painted panelling in one of the upstairs rooms. However the manor is shown largely as a farmhouse of the 1800s. It's at its best in the kitchens and associated service rooms, where the Victorian range is often fired up for cooking and the implements that litter the shelves can be identified with the help of a beautifully simple pictorial system like a children's book.

Agricultural exhibits and demonstrations, animals, kitchen garden, shop, tearoom.

Signposted on south-east side of Witney.

Cogges Manor: a medieval moated manor given a grander air in the 1670s and shown as a Victorian farm

Kelmscott Manor, Gloucestershire

Privately owned by trust (HHA) • £££ • Open Apr to Sep, W (and some S)

A lovely Tudor farmhouse in Cotswold stone, the home of William Morris, his wife Jane and their daughters Jenny and May from 1871, when the Morrises left the Red House in Bexleyheath, on the south-eastern fringes of London, and retired to the country. It was not simply a family home, however; Morris leased Kelmscott jointly with Dante Gabriel Rossetti, whose affair with Janey he discreetly allowed to flourish, disappearing on a trip to Iceland as soon as the family, and Rossetti, moved in.

Although the well-kept, white-painted interiors are just a tiny bit sterile, feeling at times a little more like an art gallery than a home, Kelmscott is still flooded with the superb Arts and Crafts furnishings and decoration gathered by Morris, much of it his own work or that of his friends, including Rossetti and Edward Burne-Jones. The most intimate rooms are, perhaps not surprisingly, Janey and William's bedrooms upstairs: Janey's looking much as it did in a Victorian photograph, with her beautiful jewel casket painted by Rossetti and his wife, Lizzie Siddal; and William's

Kelmscott: a beautiful Cotswold stone farmhouse packed with the treasures of William Morris and friends

with a four-poster bed of the early 1600s, its hangings embroidered with one of his own poems.

Other highlights include the beautiful drawings by Rossetti of Jane Morris and the sketches by Burne-Jones for his 'Signs of the Zodiac' panels (now in the V&A).

Gardens, outbuildings (including three-seater outside lavatory), tearoom, shop.

In Kelmscott village, off the A417 east of Lechlade.

Newark Park, Gloucestershire

National Trust • £££ • Open Jun to Oct, W-Th, S & Su (also mid-to-late Feb, S & Su, for snowdrops; Apr and May, W-Th)

An eccentric little house in a superb setting, perched at the edge of a 40-foot cliff above a wooded valley with a view that has scarcely changed in hundreds of years. It owes its peculiar tall, narrow shape to the fact that it was built as a hunting lodge in about 1550, then extended as a H-plan house in the 1670s and finally improved by the architect James Wyatt in the 1790s.

This varied history gives the house its most interesting features: Wyatt's gracious entrance hall, with its elegant classical decoration; the late-1600s barrel-vaulted ceiling of the gallery at the top of the house; a scattering of Tudor details in the upstairs rooms; the early-16th-century kitchens in the basement. More than this, though, the house is lived in and loved and decorated with an eclectic and friendly mix of modern art and period furniture – and throughout, the most is made of those glorious views.

Signposted on minor road from A4135 Dursley to Tetbury road at junction with B4058, 2 miles east of Wotton-under-Edge.

Newark Park: an unusual, friendly little house, developed from a Tudor hunting lodge, with superb views

Owlpen Manor, Gloucestershire

Privately owned (HHA) • ££ • Open Apr to Sep, Tu-F, S & Su

'A singularly romantic and sequestered spot,' said a visitor in 1807, and little has changed since. Owlpen Manor achieved a kind of fame in late Victorian and early 20th-century England, admired by the likes of Gertrude Jekyll and Vita Sackville-West not just for its pretty little garden, described by Sir Geoffrey Jellicoe as possibly the earliest domestic garden in England to survive in something approaching completeness, but also as the archetype of the sort of romantic medieval manor that was much admired in the years after the Arts and Crafts movement.

Tucked away in a steep-sided valley with hanging woods behind, Owlpen is also an unusual example of a small Cotswold estate. Its fortunes declined in the 1830s with the collapse of the local cloth industry, leaving the house in steady decline until it was bought in 1925 by Norman Jewson, an architect and craftsman who was a prominent member of the Cotswold

Arts and Crafts movement, and sensitively restored.

It's this recent history of love and appreciation, continued by the Mander family who own and live in the house today (and expressed to the full in the excellent guidebook), that makes the tiny manor such a friendly place to visit. It is not large, but its few rooms give a rich impression of its haphazard development, added to and rebuilt between about 1450 and 1720, and are full of engaging details. Pieces of furniture by the Cotswold Arts and Crafts designers not only feel absolutely at home in their Tudor setting, but also add an extra layer of interest; they include a high-backed settle made for Ernest Gimson by Sidney Barnsley.

Barely any of the contents of the house are original to it, with the notable exception of one real rarity: a set of painted cloth wall-hangings, once common as a cheap alternative to tapestries, which date from the late 1500s or early 1600s and hang in a bedroom upstairs.

Terraced gardens, Cyder House restaurant in former medieval barn, Victorian church, holiday cottages in mill and court house.

Signposted from B4066 just north of Uley.

Snowshill Manor, Gloucestershire

National Trust • £££ • Open Apr to Oct, W-F, S & Su (also M in Jul & Aug)

It hardly matters that Snowshill is a Cotswold manor house of about 1500, extended in about 1600 and given a regular classical facade in about 1720, since the house is little more than a backdrop for the bizarre and eclectic collections amassed in the early 20th century by the eccentric artist and craftsman Charles Paget Wade.

Wade trained as an architect, qualifying in 1907, and started his working life with the practice of Parker and Unwin, leading exponents of the Arts and Crafts movement and responsible for Hampstead Garden Suburb in north London. On the death of his father in 1911, he inherited a private income from the family estates in St Kitts in the West Indies, and left his job, concentrating mainly on book illustration.

After serving during the First World War in a workshop company of the Royal Engineers, he bought Snowshill and restored it from top to bottom before starting to fill it

Owlpen Manor: a pleasingly haphazard little house that grew up organically from about 1450 to 1720

Snowshill Manor: the main house is on the right with the Priest's House, lived in by the collector Charles Paget Wade, to its left

with the collections that, having started as a hobby in childhood, were increasingly becoming his obsession. At first he concentrated on simple household objects, mostly English, but with time he grew fascinated with European furniture and Far Eastern crafts.

The result is a house crammed from entrance hall to attics with a colourful and bewildering array of items: dozens of tiny watch cocks in a frame on the wall, a room full of Japanese armour with fearsome face-masks, an attic stuffed with ancient bicycles and models of haywagons from around England.

Wade filled up the house and lived in the cottage next door, a former monastic lodging called the Priest's House. Downstairs are his kitchen-cum-sitting-room and his workshop, upstairs his bedroom and bathroom; it's a charming and characterful little home.

Lovely walled gardens and outbuildings, restaurant, shop.

Signposted on minor road 2 miles south of Broadway.

Sudeley Castle, Gloucestershire

Privately owned (HHA) • £££ • Open Apr to Oct daily

In the mid-1400s, a palatial castle-residence was built at Sudeley by Ralph Boteler, a military commander in France and Normandy under Henry V and one-time Captain of Calais Castle who in 1443 became High Treasurer of England under Henry VI. His luck changed when he was on the losing side in the Wars of the Roses, and the new king, Edward IV, took away his property and gave it to the future King Richard III. It remained in royal ownership, visited in 1535 by Henry VIII and Anne Boleyn, until in 1547 it was given to Sir Thomas Seymour, later Lord High Admiral, lover of Katherine Parr before her marriage to Henry VIII and her husband after the king's death. Their story is one of the great fascinations of Sudeley today.

This whirlwind romp through history – complete with a visit by Queen Elizabeth in 1592 – comes to an end in 1649, following the Civil War, when parliament ordered the castle to be slighted. Thereafter it lay in ruins, neglected apart from the discovery in 1782 of the grave of Katherine Parr and in it a coffin containing a body wrapped in linen and apparently uncorrupted.

In 1837, the romantic ruin was bought by the Dent brothers, wealthy glovemakers of Worcester, who set about making a house from the Elizabethan ranges of the outer courtyard. They decided to leave much of the earlier buildings alone as picturesque ruins, including the tall, many-windowed banqueting house added by Richard III. It is this sensitive choice that gives Sudeley and its gardens their special character today.

Inside, the rooms that are open to the public are not used by the family, and the house feels rather more like a museum than a home. It's most impressive, however, that so much appropriate historic material has been gathered here over the years, from intricate Elizabethan tapestries that would have William Morris drooling to Katherine Parr's own prayer-book.

Superb gardens (also open Mar, daily), Tudor chapel (St Mary's church) restored in 1863, ruined barn, shop, coffee shop.

Signposted in centre of Winchcombe.

Sudeley Castle: a Victorian house built from the picturesque ruins of a castle with a fascinating history

See also...

Ashdown House
Lambourn, Berkshire
National Trust, ££, open Apr to Oct, W, S, guided tours only
Impressive Dutch-style house of the 1600s associated with Elizabeth of Bohemia, Charles I's sister; but only the hall, stairs and roof are shown. Also woodland walks (*free, open all year, M-Th, S & Su*) and car park for scenic walks on downs.

Ardington House
Wantage, Oxfordshire
Privately owned (HHA), £££, open certain days in May and Aug, guided tours only
Terribly elegant little baroque house of the early 1700s, the home of the Baring banking family.

Dorney Court
Windsor, Berkshire
Privately owned (HHA), £££, open Aug, M-F & Su
Beautiful little Tudor manor house with fine great hall, comfortably furnished and welcoming.

Fawley Court
Henley-on-Thames, Oxfordshire
Privately owned, £££, open May to Oct, W-Th & Su
Handsome classical house of 1684 designed by Sir Christopher Wren, with Grinling Gibbons woodwork and James Wyatt remodelling. Museum of Polish kings and army.

Greys Court
Rotherfield Greys, Henley, Oxfordshire
National Trust, £££, open Apr to Sep, W-F
A picturesque house of the 1500s, based on a fortified manor of the 1300s, with various later alterations. Only part of ground floor open.

Kingston Bagpuize House
Abingdon, Oxfordshire
Privately owned (HHA), £££, open Feb to Oct, certain days only, guided tours only
Elegant red brick house of the 1660s remodelled in the early 1700s, with decoration and furnishings of various periods since. Grounds, gardens.

Lodge Park and Sherborne Estate
Aldsworth, near Cheltenham, Gloucestershire
National Trust, £££, open Apr to Oct, M, F & Su
Picturesque Cotswold estate with remarkable and unusual 'grandstand' of 1634 – an elegant lodge for watching hunting, with accompanying deer course and park.

Mapledurham House
Mapledurham, Oxfordshire
Privately owned, £££, open Easter to Sep, S & Su
Charming red brick Elizabethan manor with original plaster ceilings, plus Strawberry Hill gothic chapel of 1797 and restored, working watermill of the 1400s.

Milton Manor House
Near Abingdon, Oxfordshire
Privately owned, open mid to end Jul and mid to end Aug, also bank hol w/ends from Easter to Aug
Tall, slightly eccentric red brick house said to have been designed by Inigo Jones in the mid-1600s, with loveable 'Gothick' library.

Rodmarton Manor
Cirencester, Gloucestershire
Privately owned (HHA), £££, open May to Aug, W, S
Attractive Victorian Arts and Crafts Cotswold stone manor house.

Rousham House
Steeple Ashton, Bicester, Oxfordshire
Privately owned, ££, open Apr to Sep, W & Su
Stone house of 1635, but the real attraction is the gardens, early landscape design of early 1700s by William Kent with romantic follies.

Stonor
Henley-on-Thames, Oxfordshire
Privately owned (HHA), £££, open Apr to Sep, Su (also Jul and Aug, W)
Parts of this pleasing house, including the Catholic chapel, date back to the 1100s, with 1300s additions – but the whole was handsomely remodelled in red brick with gothic touches in the 1700s. Deer park, gardens.

Taplow Court
Near Maidenhead, Berkshire
Privately owned (HHA), free, open end May to mid-Sep, Su
Wonderfully mad-looking tall, Elizabethan-style house remodelled in the mid-1800s by William Burn, set above Thames with splendid views.

Woodchester Mansion
Stroud, Gloucestershire
Privately owned, £££, open Easter to Sept, Su (also Jul and Aug, S, and first S of Apr, May, Jun, Sep)
House started in 1856 but abandoned incomplete in 1870, giving insights into traditional building techniques.

And...

Buscot Old Parsonage
Buscot, Faringdon, Oxfordshire
National Trust, open only occasionally by written appt
Early 1700s Cotswold stone house.

Ditchley Park
Enstone, Oxfordshire
Privately owned, groups by appt only
Baroque house of mid-1700s by James Gibbs.

26A East St Helens Street
Abingdon, Oxfordshire
Oxford Preservation Trust, open by appt only
Well-preserved merchant's hall house of the 1400s with later alterations.

Frampton Court and Manor
Frampton on Severn, Gloucestershire
Privately owned, groups by appt only
Vanbrugh house of 1732 and medieval/Elizabethan timber-framed manor on a site occupied by the Cliffords since Norman times.

Kingston Lisle Park
Wantage, Oxfordshire
Privately owned, groups by appt only
Smart Palladian house of late 1700s.

Welford Park
Newbury, Berkshire
Privately owned, £££, open May, Jun & Aug, groups by appt only
Queen Anne house, attractive grounds with riverside walks, cream teas.

East Anglia
Cambridgeshire, Norfolk, Suffolk, Essex

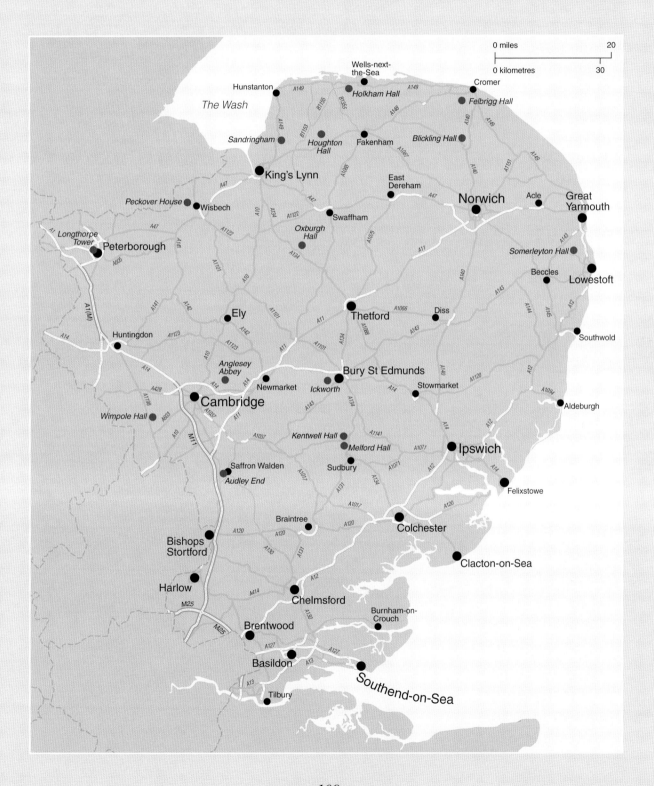

0 miles 20
0 kilometres 30

Wells-next-the-Sea

Hunstanton

The Wash

A149

Holkham Hall

Cromer

A149

Felbrigg Hall

A140

A149

B1155

B1355

A148

Sandringham

B1153

Houghton Hall

Fakenham

Blickling Hall

A140

A1151

A149

A149

King's Lynn

A1065

A1067

East Dereham

Norwich

Acle

Great Yarmouth

A47

A47

Peckover House

Wisbech

A10

A134

A1122

Swaffham

A47

A1075

A143

A11

A140

Somerleyton Hall

A1

Longthorpe Tower

A47

A1122

Oxburgh Hall

A134

A11

Beccles

Lowestoft

Peterborough

A1(M)

A47

A10

A1101

A140

A143

A1144

A146

A12

A605

A141

A142

A1101

A134

Thetford

A1066

Diss

A143

A605

Ely

A142

A11

A1101

A11

A1088

A143

Southwold

Huntingdon

A14

A1123

A1123

A140

A1120

A12

A1094

A14

A10

Anglesey Abbey

A14

Bury St Edmunds

A134

Stowmarket

A14

Aldeburgh

A428

A14

Newmarket

Ickworth

A143

A134

A14

A12

A1198

Cambridge

A1307

A11

Kentwell Hall

A1141

A1071

Ipswich

A14

Wimpole Hall

A603

A10

Melford Hall

A1071

A12

M11

A1057

Sudbury

A134

Felixstowe

Saffron Walden

A1017

A131

A1017

A120

Braintree

A120

Colchester

Audley End

A120

M25

A120

Bishops Stortford

A130

A131

A12

Clacton-on-Sea

Harlow

A414

Chelmsford

Burnham-on-Crouch

M25

M25

A130

Brentwood

A127

Basildon

A13

Southend-on-Sea

A13

Tilbury

Anglesey Abbey: a Jacobean house based on a 13th-century priory, heavily remodelled in the 1920s

Anglesey Abbey, Cambridgeshire

National Trust • £££ • Open Apr to Oct, W-F, S & Su

An unusual and eccentric house, consisting of parts of an Augustinian priory dating from about 1240 and a heavily remodelled Jacobean house, plus a bizarre art gallery extension built in 1958. Essentially it reflects the equally eccentric character of its former owner, Huttleston Broughton, 1st Lord Fairhaven, a wealthy Anglo-American whose family had made their money in oil.

Huttleston and his brother Henry bought the house in 1926, primarily for the good pheasant-shooting nearby and the proximity of Newmarket races. The initial redevelopment of the house took place over the following two years, but in 1932, when Henry married, Huttleston bought out his brother's half share and took up residence

permanently, gradually remodelling the place as a showcase for his considerable art collection and creating gardens that are now world famous.

Today it's the gardens that really make a visit to Anglesey special, but the house is also rewarding. Lord Fairhaven, who died in 2000, gave it to the Trust with the enjoinder that gardens, house and furnishings should all be kept exactly as they were on his death, 'representative of an age and way of life that is quickly passing'. Anglesey is still used by his family, however – and as a result both of this and of its relatively recent modifications (it is, after all, basically a house of the 1920s onward), has a very comfortable and home-like feel.

This welcoming personality comes across in many small details (such as the notice on the post-box reminding visitors not to ask when

the post goes, since no one else knows either) and is especially noticeable in the guest bedrooms – bedrooms are often disappointingly artificial in 'preserved' houses.

After the cosified Jacobean feel of the main living rooms, the huge plain space of the two-storeyed art gallery of 1958 comes almost as a shock. On display here are some of Lord Fairhaven's most impressive paintings, including two Claude landscapes; but in truth the eccentric collections elsewhere in the house are far more entertaining, notable amongst them being the paintings of British birds by Charles Collins in the panelled lobby and the prude-defying nudes by Victorian painter William Etty in the library corridor.

Superb gardens (open as house), restored working watermill, restaurant, shop.

Signposted from A14, on B1102 six miles north-east of Cambridge.

Audley End, Essex

*English Heritage • £££ • Open Apr to Oct,
M-W, S & Su (S & Su only in Oct)*

Built between 1603 and 1614 by
Thomas Howard, 1st Earl of Suffolk
and Lord Treasurer to King James I,
Audley End had a fair claim to be
the largest and grandest house in
England. Indeed, the king visited in
1615 and remarked that it was too
great a house for a king, but might
suit a Lord Treasurer.

Perhaps the king's suspicions
were aroused, but in 1619 Thomas
was convicted of corruption and
thrown into the Tower of London.
His release nine days later involved
a fine of £7,000 and his debts – the
house had cost a vast £200,000 to
build – were to prove fatal to the
fortunes of his family.

Now just a third of the original
immense house remains, and much
of its Jacobean character has been
lost. In the 1750s a large part was
demolished; in the 1760s a great
deal of remodelling was carried out
by Robert Adam; in the 1780s, a
possible visit by the king led to the
creation of a sumptuous suite of
state rooms; in the 1820s this suite
was swept away to make room for
modern entertaining rooms in a
lavish mock-Jacobean style, and
Adam's rooms on the ground floor
were subdivided as bedrooms.

Audley End: once the grandest house of Jacobean England, but now just a third of its original size

The result is an unsatisfactory
mish-mash of styles, with tempting
traces of the original (the glorious
Jacobean ceiling in the saloon) and
occasional bursts of fascination
(the gothick chapel of the late
1700s; the restored Adam rooms,
beautifully decorated but too cramped
in their proportions to have ever
been a true expression of the
maestro's talents).

*Landscaped grounds with follies, parterre
garden and organic kitchen garden, shop.*

*Signposted from the B1383 and B1052
1 mile west of Saffron Walden.*

Blickling Hall, Norfolk

*National Trust • £££ • Open Apr to Oct,
W-F, S & Su*

The Jacobean splendour of
Blickling is best appreciated from
the outside. It was built between
1619 and 1625 by Robert Lyminge,
the architect of the splendid Hatfield
Palace in Hertfordshire, for Sir
Henry Hobart, who like many other
great men of his age had made his
fortune as a lawyer in London.
Unlike the interiors, the exterior was
changed very little when the house
was remodelled in the 1760s
(although the fanciful clock-tower is
a replacement of the 1820s).

Inside, the best and most
rewarding elements are the few
Jacobean remnants, including the
wonderful ceilings of the south
drawing room (originally the great
chamber) and the long gallery.
Rather less enjoyable is the
seemingly piecemeal updating,
including a striking but faded state
bedroom of the 1780s by the
estimable architect Samuel Wyatt,
all of which leaves Blickling as an
odd patchwork of impressions.

*Extensive gardens and parkland (open all
year, but garden limited in winter), shop,
second-hand bookshop, restaurant.*

*Signposted on minor road north-west of
Aylsham, off the A140 Norwich to Cromer.*

Blickling Hall: the attractive exterior looks much as it did when the house was completed in 1625

Felbrigg Hall, Norfolk

National Trust • £££ • Apr to Oct, M-W, S & Su

An interesting mixture of Jacobean and Restoration styles built on top of an earlier Tudor house that had been the home of the Windhams since about 1450.

Satisfyingly, the south front still looks very much as it did when it was built – between 1621 and 1624, almost certainly with the input of the architect Robert Lyminge, who had been working at nearby Blickling Hall since 1619 (the two houses have many details in common). Inside, the original layout of the Jacobean house is still obvious, with its entrance into a screens passage with the great hall to the left and the butteries, pantry and kitchen to the right.

The great hall remains, but the service rooms were swept away in the mid-1680s, when work began on a new west wing designed by the architect William Samwell, who was largely responsible for the fascinating Ham House in London. Built of red brick in an superbly clean classical style, the new wing contrasts pleasingly with the older part of the house.

It was built for William Windham and his wife Katherine, whose life at Felbrigg seems to have been very quiet and contented. William eschewed politics and society, instead taking 'delight in my nursery and garden', and left behind detailed records which constitute one of the most valuable insights into estate management in the late 1600s. Katherine, for her part, widowed in 1689, wrote in the early 1700s a book of cookery and housekeeping which is an equally fascinating glimpse into the domestic life of a wealthy family. Husband and wife are both shown in portraits by Sir Peter Lely and his studio in the dining room.

Inside the remodelled house, no expense was spared on decoration, and superb ceilings in a florid, ornate rococo style survive in the drawing room (originally the great parlour, the main living and dining room) and the cabinet (the 1680s drawing room). These ceilings are by a master craftsman of the era, Edward Goudge. Much of the rest of the interior, however, was redesigned in the 1750s for William's grandson, also William, by James Paine.

The results are respectful of the character of the old house but a little heavy, including a restoration of the great hall in an amusingly clumsy neo-Tudor style. Best of the rooms are the cabinet, crammed with the collection of Grand Tour paintings assembled by William II, still hung to the original plan, and the book room next to the upstairs library, in which there is a changing display of fascinating volumes from the library shelves.

Gardens and walled garden (open as house, but also Th & F in high summer), estate walks (open all year), shop, bookshop, restaurant and tearoom.

Signposted from A148 Holt to Cromer road 2 miles south-west of Cromer.

Felbrigg Hall: the south front retains its Jacobean character, but behind is a new wing of the 1680s, and the interior was redesigned in the 1750s

Holkham Hall: built not of stone, but of yellow brick, it is one of the finest examples of mid-18th-century Palladian architecture, designed to impress

Holkham Hall, Norfolk

Privately owned (HHA) • £££ • Open late May to Sep (also limited opening in Apr & early May), M, Th-F, S & Su

An outstanding example of Palladian architecture at its most extravagant and awe-inspiring, designed by William Kent and built between 1734 and 1762 for Thomas Coke, first Earl of Leicester, as a temple of the arts in which his unrivalled collections of paintings and sculpture could be displayed. Thomas died three years before the house was completed, but he left detailed instructions as to how it should be decorated, down to the exact positions in which marble busts should stand and paintings hang.

The result is a house of two scales – grandeur in the size of the rooms and the perfection of their finishing, with a museum-like intensity of interest in the works of art on display. There's not much here that speaks of domestic life,

since the rooms open to the public are principally the state rooms, but the house is all the more remarkable for the fact that it is still privately owned and lived in.

The state rooms are in the central block, with four wings attached – service wing, family wing (for day-to-day living), chapel wing (with accommodation for the children) and strangers' wing, containing the guest bedrooms. A couple of the rooms in the strangers' wing are open to the public when not in use, which adds a satisfyingly intimate note to a visit. Otherwise, though, jaw-dropping splendour is more the order of the day.

The two most uncompromisingly classical rooms are the vast marble hall – the formal entrance to the house, its imposing ceiling from a design by Inigo Jones – and the nearby statue gallery, lined with ancient Greek and Roman marble figures that form one of the finest collections of classical sculpture in private hands. Very beautiful too.

There follows an opulent series of state rooms all of which are largely unchanged since the 1780s, and yet are not faded and decayed. In the saloon – the grandest of the reception rooms, and still used for entertaining – the crimson velvet is original; while in the green state bedroom, where Queen Victoria stayed, the bed designed by William Kent has its hangings of Genoa velvet.

Everywhere you look, there are great paintings – here a set of Italian Renaissance works, there a Rubens, everywhere portraits by such noted artists as Van Dyck and Gainsborough. One room is crammed with landscapes by Claude and Poussin, rehung in 1996 to the original layout of 1773.

Bygones museum of agricultural and domestic exhibits, church, deer park, pottery, shop, tearoom.

Signposted on A149 Hunstanton to Sheringham road 2 miles west of Wells-next-the-Sea.

Houghton Hall: built in 1722–35 for Sir Robert Walpole, with splendidly ornate interiors by William Kent

Houghton Hall, Norfolk

Privately owned (HHA) • £££
• Open mid-Apr to Sep, W, Th & Su

'Still dominated by the ebullient personality, energy and taste of Sir Robert Walpole,' says the present owner, David, 7th Marquess of Cholmondeley, in his introduction to the guidebook. Houghton was built in 1722–9 for Britain's first true Prime Minister, designed by James Gibbs with the later input of Colen Campbell; and the interiors were created between 1725 and 1735 by William Kent, the architect of nearby Holkham Hall. No one seems quite sure how Walpole was able to afford it (although he was Lord Treasurer at the time) and he destroyed all records that might betray its cost, although he is said to have confided in a neighbour that £200,000 was pretty near the mark.

Both Campbell and Kent were arch exponents of full-on Palladianism, yet this house has a baroque flamboyance both on the outside, where Gibbs's domes at each corner give it its characteristic drama, and within. And it does indeed remain largely as it was in Walpole's day, thanks to the efforts of the family in first preserving it unaltered and with its contents intact, and then restoring it from the 1920s onwards.

The interiors lack the classical dignity of Holkham, but they have a richness and exuberance all of their own. The rooms open to visitors are the state rooms on the ground floor, plus just one of the private rooms, the common parlour, which has a plain ceiling and lacks the gilding that is such a feature of the rest of the main rooms.

The most extraordinary statement of the interiors is made by the double-height stone hall with gallery, based on a design by Inigo Jones and with lavish sculpted decoration by Rysbrack, but there is almost equal splendour throughout the house. In the style of its period, Houghton has state bedrooms even though these were already an outdated idea, still with the furniture designed by Kent as well as his painted ceilings.

Deer park with herd of white deer, church, gardens, stable block with carriages, museum of model soldiers, shop, tearoom.

Signposted from A148 King's Lynn to Fakenham road 8 miles west of Fakenham.

Ickworth, Suffolk

National Trust • £££ • Open Apr to Oct, M-Tu, F, S & Su

It was perfectly usual for a grand country house of the 18th century to have a central block containing state rooms and designed as a backdrop for an art collection; but it was perfectly unusual for the central block to be an enormous rotunda. Thus Ickworth, described by its builder's wife as a 'stupendous monument of folly', reflects the eccentric character of its creator, Frederick, 4th Earl of Bristol and Bishop of Derry, a man who, despite the nature of his calling, once tipped a tureen of spaghetti over a procession of the Blessed Sacrament because he had 'a particular aversion to the tinkling of bells'.

The Earl-Bishop passed most of his time in Italy, spending the income from his church estates on an art collection that took over 30 years to acquire. Work started on a house in which he could display his collection in 1795, but in 1798 the whole lot was captured by Napoleonic troops invading Rome. The Earl died in 1803 without recovering his art and with only the shell of Ickworth complete.

Ickworth (right): built to house the art collection of the 4th Earl of Bristol, but at his death his art had been stolen and the house was unfinished

His son, the 1st Marquess of Bristol, employed the architect John Field to redesign the east wing, planned as galleries, as a family wing; it is now a hotel. Field decorated the state rooms on the ground floor of the rotunda in what the guidebook justly describes as 'an austere Regency style'. Smaller than one might expect, they never quite deal with the problem of the curving walls, and have a cramped and dowdy feel.

By far the most pleasing of the rooms is the Pompeian room in the middle of the curving west wing (which contains the orangery). It was decorated in 1879 by JD Crace with designs based on the painted walls of the Villa Negroni in Rome, and is a small slice of perfection in a fascinating but ill-conceived house.

Italianate gardens (open Jan to Oct daily, Nov to Dec M-F), parkland with walks, deer enclosure, Georgian summerhouse, lakes, canal, church (open all year, daily), restaurant, shop.

Signposted on A143 Bury to Haverhill road, 3 miles south-west of Bury St Edmunds.

Kentwell Hall, Suffolk

Privately owned (HHA) • £££ • Open mid-Apr to Sep, W, Th & Su (also M-F and Su mid-Jul to Aug, Su in Oct and Nov)

Another beautiful and welcoming example (like Burton Agnes in Yorkshire and Breamore in Hampshire) of an Elizabethan house where most of the original fabric is untouched, but time has not stood still, and the house is still lived in and thriving.

A classic Elizabethan E-plan manor, its construction probably started before his death in 1562 by William Clopton, Kentwell still has its moat and retains most of the original service rooms, including a remarkable kitchen, in the west wing,

Kentwell Hall (left): a beautiful Elizabethan manor house built in about 1560, with its original moat, kitchens and service rooms

but the east wing was remodelled by Thomas Hopper after a fire in 1826. The most striking of Hopper's rooms is the main dining room, created in a weighty Tudor Gothic style in imitation of a great hall.

The present owners have lived here since 1971 and have spent their time restoring the older parts and making the rest into a cosy home with considerable artistic flair, with the result that new work, such as the remodelled bedrooms upstairs and the painted ceiling of 1997 in the drawing room, sits comfortably with the old and is just as pleasing.

Restored formal gardens with maze, Elizabethan moat house (originally a brewhouse and service building), camera obscura, home farm with rare breeds, tearoom.

Off A1092 1 mile north of Long Melford.

Longthorpe Tower: not much to look at, but inside are the finest medieval wall-paintings in England

Longthorpe Tower, Cambridgeshire

English Heritage • ££ • Open Apr to Oct, S & Su

Only this small tower remains of a 14th-century fortified manor house, but it contains one of the greatest treasures of English domestic interior design – an elaborate series of wall-paintings of the early 1300s, without equal in England and with very few rivals in Europe.

The paintings were discovered in the 1940s under layers of limewash by the tenant, who sensibly stopped decorating and called the authorities. Thus they were able to reveal the whole set, covering all four walls and the vaulted ceiling of the first-floor great chamber. The colours are faded to pale red and ochre; the subjects are largely religious, but with a scattering of birds (a particular love of the English in the 14th century, apparently) and beasts, and one wall is given over to a heraldic theme.

The paintings are thought to have been done for Robert Thorpe, Steward of Peterborough Abbey from 1310 to 1329.

Signposted from A47 in Longthorpe, 2 miles west of Peterborough.

Melford Hall, Suffolk

National Trust • £££ • Open Jul to Sep, Tu-F & S (also S in Apr, Jun and Oct)

Practically across the road from Kentwell Hall (see previous page), this is another attractive and, externally at least, largely unaltered Elizabethan red brick manor house, built some time before 1578 by Sir William Cordell, who held high office under both Queen Mary and Elizabeth I. Inside, however, it's a different story, since the interior was remodelled in the 1730s and 1740s and again in 1813–20 by Thomas Hopper (best known for Penrhyn Castle in north Wales) for Sir William Parker.

Sir William was the son of a distinguished naval family: his uncle gave the signal at the Battle of Copenhagen that prompted Nelson to put a telescope to his blind eye, and his cousin captained the first steamship, HMS *Firebrand*. The library is something of a shrine to Sir William's grandfather, Vice-Admiral Sir Hyde Parker, who was visited on his ship by King George III after his victory against the Dutch at Dogger Bank in 1781, but turned down the King's offer of a knighthood, suggesting boldly that an investment in younger officers and better ships would be a far more useful idea.

The portrait of Sir Hyde Parker by Romney and the paintings of some of his naval engagements by Dominique Serres, marine painter to George III, are among the highlights of the house, which is mostly decorated in a restrained and unremarkable Georgian style. The only room at all redolent of the Elizabethan period is the great hall, which retains its original size and shape but not its original decoration.

What Melford Hall does have to offer, however, is a strong connection with Beatrix Potter, who was a cousin of Ethel, Lady Hyde Parker, the grandmother of the present owner, and often came to stay. One upstairs room has been set aside for the display of her sketches, many of them of the hall and grounds, together with the model of Jemima Puddleduck she used to draw from. She always stayed in the charming, comfortable west bedroom, overlooking the garden, with a turret that she saw as the ideal place to keep any small animals she had with her.

Gardens (open as house) with small Tudor banqueting house, park walk.

Off A134 1 mile north of Long Melford.

Melford Hall: the turrets and spires of its attractive exterior are little changed since the 1570s

Oxburgh Hall: built in about 1482, with its moat and splendid gatehouse intact, but remodelled within

Oxburgh Hall, Norfolk

National Trust • ££ • Open Apr to Oct, M-W, S & Su

Yet another of the region's superb red brick manor houses, but older, built in about 1482. Like Melford Hall (opposite), it was considerably altered inside in the early 1800s, but with the difference that the 're-edifying' work – carried out by the antiquarian architect JC Buckler for Sir Henry Paston-Bedingfield, a descendant of the man who built the house – was perfectly matched to the original building.

Oxburgh still has its moat, which adds greatly to the beauty of the exterior (and is full of fish, too). It also has its imposing gatehouse, described as 'one of England's most enchanting pieces of architectural pageantry' and still looking almost exactly as it did when it was built more than 500 years ago.

The rooms inside the gatehouse retain more of a medieval feel than the rest of the house and in the remodelling of 1830 were treated with respect, just romanticized slightly by the addition of oak linenfold panelling and tapestries on the walls. The first-floor room has been known as the King's room ever since Henry VII stayed here in 1487. Above it, up a superb brick-built spiral stair (its cunningly wrought brickwork ceiling painted, oddly enough, to look like brick), is the Queen's room, where there hangs an extraordinary tapestry map of Oxfordshire and Berkshire woven in about 1647. On up the stairs is the roof, with fine views.

Elsewhere, the house does not have such a genuinely medieval feel, and the first few rooms visitors see are actually something of a disappointment. The original great hall was demolished in the 1780s and a neo-classical saloon built instead, and this in turn was given a gothic twist in the 1830s; it's not an especially happy mix.

Before long, however, things start warming up. The Tudor-style ceiling in the west drawing room, painted by JD Crace in the 1850s, is a delight, while the heavier gothic style of the library and the dark, floridly carved wooden panelling of the small dining room are all redolent of early Victorian mock-medieval taste.

Oxburgh's greatest treasure is a set of embroidered hangings worked in 1569–84 by Mary, Queen of Scots and Bess of Hardwick, whose husband was Mary's warder for most of her 18-year captivity in England. There is much exuberant detail, especially in the many different animals portrayed, and a close study is well rewarded.

Gardens with French parterre of 1845, woodland walks, Catholic chapel of 1836, restaurant, secondhand bookshop, shop.

Signposted on minor road off A134 Thetford to King's Lynn road near Stoke Ferry, 7 miles south-west of Swaffham.

Peckover House: a Georgian gentleman's residence of 1722, noted for its rococo plaster and woodwork

Peckover House, Cambridgeshire

National Trust • £££ • Open Apr to Oct, W, S & Su (also Th, May to Aug)

Town houses inevitably lack the scale and extravagance of their country cousins, but there is interest in the period detail that survives in this elegant Georgian residence of 1722, named after the banker who owned it from 1794. Particularly striking are the rococo woodwork and plaster decorations, but equally intriguing are such unusual fixtures as the 'snob screens' obscuring the lower parts of the windows.

Almost more of an attraction than the house are the two-acre Victorian gardens with orangery, summer houses and fernery.

Gardens (open Apr to Oct, M-Th, S & Su), tearoom, shop.

North Brink, Wisbech. Pedestrian access only from Chapel Road car park.

Sandringham, Norfolk

Privately owned • £££ • Open mid-Apr to mid-Jul and Aug to Oct, daily

The Queen's rural retreat was built in 1870 for Edward Albert, Prince of Wales, later King Edward VII, and his wife, Princess Alexandra of Denmark, to replace the cramped home on the estate they had lived in since 1863.

Rather pleasingly, it's exactly what you would expect of a Victorian-built royal country house – beautifully kept, grand in a not entirely tasteful but very comfortable way and filled to the brim with horse- and dog-related knick-knacks, family photographs, art that shows an interest in wildlife and guns to kill it with.

Visitors have access only to the ground-floor public rooms, all splendidly decorated by the best Italian craftsmen and packed with expensive ornaments and china.

Gardens (open as house; walled gardens by tour only), parkland walks, museum in former stables, steam launch, garages with royal cars, tearoom, shop.

Signposted from A148 King's Lynn to Fakenham road, on B1440 6 miles north-east of King's Lynn.

Sandringham: the Queen's private country house, built in 1870 for the future King Edward VII and his wife Alexandra, is richly but comfortably furnished

Somerleyton Hall: a Victorian Italianate mansion, built in the 1840s around an earlier Jacobean house

Somerleyton Hall, Suffolk

Privately owned (HHA) • £££ •
Open mid-Apr to Oct, Th & Su
(also Jul and Aug, Tu-W)

Underneath somewhere are traces of a Jacobean house, but rebuilt in 1844–51 by Sir Morton Peto – a self-made man who started out as a bricklayer and ended up as the world's largest construction contractor – as a weighty Victorian Italianate mansion. The design was by John Thomas, a protege of Sir Charles Barry who was primarily an ornamental mason, his best-known work being the stone lions that guard the Britannia Bridge across the Menai Straits.

The interiors were changed again in the 1920s, when Sir Morton's grandest statement, a two-storey hall, was turned into the present library with bedrooms above. Visitors only see a handful of rooms, most satisfying of which are the oak room, which has a Jacobean feel it owes largely to panelling from the original house, and the small entrance hall with its bonkers Victorianism enhanced by a pair of stuffed, rearing polar bears.

Extensive gardens with Paxton glasshouses, maze (open as house), shop, restaurant.

Signposted from A143 Great Yarmouth to Beccles road, on B1074, 4 miles north-west of Lowestoft.

Wimpole Hall, Cambridgeshire

National Trust • £££ • Open late Mar to Oct, Tu-Th, S & Su (also F in Aug, Su in Nov)

The best things about Wimpole Hall are on a vast scale, starting as you stand outside the entrance with with the stunning south avenue, two parallel lines of trees 90 yards apart running for two miles off into the distance. The original elms had to be replanted with limes in the 1970s, but even in its reduced state it's astonishing. The history of the house is on an equally epic scale, with a huge cast of characters.

It was originally built in the mid-1600s by Thomas Chicheley, a prominent royalist who flourished under Charles II, but has been altered many times since. The most notable of the changes were carried out in 1713–32 by James Gibbs, whose chief surviving contributions are the remarkable library and the chapel, decorated entirely with *trompe l'oeil* murals by Sir James Thornhill; and in the early 1790s by Sir John Soane, whose yellow drawing room is one of the most extraordinary rooms in any country house. To make room for it, Soane knocked through rooms on the first floor and in the attics, creating a church-like space of arches and apses topped by a dome. The puzzle of how the gas chandelier in the dome was lit has a clever answer.

Home Farm of 1742 with rare breeds (separate admission, open as house but also daily in Feb and Apr, S & Su in winter), gardens (open as farm), parkland (open all year), restaurant, shop.

Signposted from A603, 8 miles south-west of Cambridge.

Wimpole Hall: an untidy mix of styles and periods, with some stunning rooms of the early and late 1700s

See also...

Bridge Cottage
Flatford, Suffolk
National Trust, £££, open Jan and Feb, S & Su, Mar to Apr and Nov to Dec, W-F, S & Su, May to Oct, daily
Thatched cottage of the 1500s with exhibitions on the life of the artist John Constable.

Christchurch Mansion
Ipswich, Suffolk
Local council, free, open all year, Tu-F, S
Tudor house set in parkland near the centre of Ipswich.

Cromwell's House
Ely, Cambridgeshire
Local council, £££, open all year, daily
Small house of the 1600s, the home of Lord Protector Oliver Cromwell.

Dragon Hall
Norwich, Norfolk
Norfolk & Norwich Heritage Trust, ££, open all year, M-F (also Apr to Oct, S)
Merchant's home of the 1400s with living hall, screens passage, timber-framed great hall with crown post roof and carved, painted dragon.

Elizabethan House Museum
Great Yarmouth, Norfolk
National Trust and Norfolk Museums Service, ££, open Apr to Oct, daily
House of 1500s with rooms in the styles of later periods (Tudor bedroom, Victorian kitchen) to reflect the lives of people who have lived here.

Elton House
Peterborough, Cambridgeshire
Privately owned, £££, open Jun, W, Jul and Aug, W-Th & Su
Splendid-looking late 1700s and 1800s gothic development of a house of the 1600s, with excellent library containing Henry VIII's prayer book, gardens with new gothic orangery.

Euston Hall
Thetford, Norfolk
Privately owned (HHA), £££, open Jun to Sep, Th only
House of 1700s with good collection of paintings, pleasure grounds by John Evelyn and William Kent, riverside walk and watermill.

Gainsborough's House
Sudbury, Suffolk
Privately owned, £££, open all year, Tu-F, S & Su
Georgian red brick town house, birthplace of the portrait painter Thomas Gainsborough (1727–88) with the world's largest collection of his paintings.

Hylands House
Chelmsford, Essex
Local council, £££, open all year, M & Su
Very smart neoclassical villa of the late 1700s, largely restored (but still an interesting work in progress), with Georgian and Victorian interiors.

Ingatestone Hall
Ingatestone, Essex
Privately owned (HHA), £££, open mid-Apr to Sep, S & Su (also late Jul to Aug, W-F)
Handsome stone-built mansion of 1500s set in formal gardens, built by Sir William Petre, Secretary of State to four Tudor monarchs. Still lived in by his descendants.

Layer Marney Tower: a vast Tudor mansion was planned, but only the impressive gatehouse was built

Layer Marney Tower
Near Colchester, Essex
Privately owned (HHA), £££, open Apr to Sep, M-F & Su
Remarkable, vast Tudor brick-built gatehouse with fine Renaissance terracotta ornamentation, thought to have been intended as the first stage of a house to rival Hampton Court, but left incomplete when Henry, Lord Marney, died, followed two years later by his son (1525).

Manor House Museum
Bury St Edmunds, Suffolk
Local council, ££, open all year, W-F, S & Su
An elegant Georgian town house built in 1736–7 by the Earl of Bristol for his wife, Elizabeth.

Old Merchant's House
Great Yarmouth, Suffolk
English Heritage, ££, open Apr to Oct, daily, guided tours only
One of two neighbouring examples of the distinctive Great Yarmouth 'row house' of the 1200s, unique to the town. Nearby are remains of a Franciscan friary of the 1100s with traces of wall paintings (see Row 111 House, Great Yarmouth, below).

Paycocke's
Coggeshall, Essex
National Trust, £££, open April to mid-Oct, Tu, Th & Su
Beautiful merchant's house of about 1500 with rich panelling and woodcarving, also cottage garden. Joint ticket with nearby medieval grange barn.

Row 111 House
Great Yarmouth, Suffolk
English Heritage, ££, open Apr to Oct, daily, guided tours only
One of two neighbouring examples of the distinctive Great Yarmouth 'row house', damaged by bombing in 1942–3 (see Old Merchant's House, Great Yarmouth, above).

South Elmham Hall
St Cross, Harleston, Norfolk
Privately owned, £££, open May to Sep, Th, guided tours only

A small medieval manor house in a moated enclosure, much altered in 1500s, so well looked after that it looks like a nice Victorian imitation; with walks through grounds to South Elmham Minster, a ruined Norman chapel with Saxon origins.

Valence House Museum
Dagenham, Essex
Local council, free, open all year, M-F, S

Manor house of 1400s surviving in the middle of the modern town, still partially surrounded by moat.

Wingfield Old College
Near Stradbroke, Suffolk
Privately owned (HHA), £££, open Easter to Sep, W, S & Su
Attractive house remodelled in 1700s in a characterful local style, with medieval great hall. Also gardens, contemporary arts centre.

And...

Angel Corner
Bury St Edmunds, Suffolk
National Trust, open by appt only
Queen Anne house still in use and containing parlour used by the town's mayor, hence the limited opening.

Belchamp Hall
Belchamp Water, Sudbury, Suffolk
Privately owned, open May to Sep, Tu, Th & bank holidays, only to groups by appt
Charming red brick Queen Anne house with interesting grounds.

Copped Hall
Epping, Essex
Privately owned by trust, open only to groups by appt, plus occasional open days
Shell of a Palladian manor with many outbuildings, gardens and park, all being restored.

Gosfield Hall
Near Halstead, Essex
Privately owned, £££, open May to Sep, Wed & Th
Tudor house of 1545 arranged around a courtyard, converted into apartments so access is limited.

Hengrave Hall
Bury St Edmunds, Suffolk
Privately owned, open only for tours by appt
Lovely Tudor stone and brick house, built 1525–38.

Hill Hall
Epping, Essex
English Heritage, ££, open Apr to Sep, W, tours only
Elizabethan mansion with fine Renaissance architecture and rare wall paintings, parts only open.

Island Hall
Godmanchester, Cambridgeshire
Privately owned, open May to Jul and Sep, only to groups by appt
Nice Georgian mansion.

Kimbolton Castle
Near Huntingdon, Cambridgeshire
Privately owned, open only one day in Mar and one in Nov
Late Stuart house developed from 1300s fortified manor, with work by Vanbrugh and Hawksmoor and Robert Adam gatehouse.

The Manor, Hemingford Grey
Huntingdon, Cambridgeshire
Privately owned, open May, daily, guided tours only
Oldest continuously occupied house in Britain, built about 1130.

Thorington Hall
Stoke by Nayland, Suffolk
National Trust, open only by appt
Oak-framed house of c 1600 with later additions.

Wolterton Park
Near Eppingham, Norfolk
Privately owned (HHA), £££, open May to Oct, F only
Red brick and stone house of 1700s with park and lake.

East Midlands

Northamptonshire, Leicestershire, Rutland,
Lincolnshire, Nottinghamshire, Derbyshire

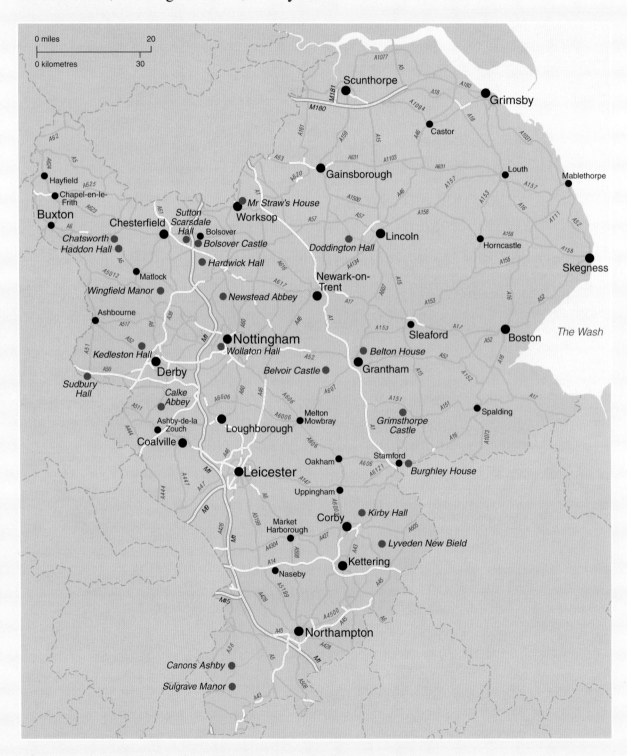

0 miles 20
0 kilometres 30

Hayfield
Chapel-en-le-Frith
Buxton
Chesterfield
Sutton Scarsdale Hall
Bolsover
Bolsover Castle
Chatsworth
Haddon Hall
Hardwick Hall
Matlock
Wingfield Manor
Ashbourne
Kedleston Hall
Derby
Sudbury Hall
Calke Abbey
Ashby-de-la-Zouch
Coalville
Scunthorpe
Grimsby
Castor
Gainsborough
Louth
Mablethorpe
Worksop
Mr Straw's House
Lincoln
Doddington Hall
Horncastle
Skegness
Newark-on-Trent
Newstead Abbey
Sleaford
Boston
The Wash
Nottingham
Wollaton Hall
Belton House
Grantham
Belvoir Castle
Loughborough
Melton Mowbray
Grimsthorpe Castle
Spalding
Oakham
Stamford
Burghley House
Leicester
Uppingham
Corby
Kirby Hall
Market Harborough
Lyveden New Bield
Naseby
Kettering
Northampton
Canons Ashby
Sulgrave Manor

Belton House, Lincolnshire

National Trust • £££ • Open Apr to Oct, W-F, S & Su

Described (in the National Trust handbook) as 'the crowning achievement of Restoration country house architecture', Belton is a robust house built in 1685–8 by 'Young' Sir John Barlow, the great nephew of 'Old' Sir John, who made sufficient money as a landowner and sheep-farmer to have sacks of cash lying around his houses.

Belton was altered in the 1770s under the direction of the architect James Wyatt, and again in 1809–20 by his nephew Sir Jeffrey Wyattville, noted for his work at Windsor Castle. The result is a heavy blend of ornate rococo plaster and dark wood panelling with rich Georgian decoration which never really achieves particular grace or drama. On the whole, the gardens and grounds are much more fun.

Parkland (open all year), wildlife centre (open weekends and school summer holidays), miniature railway, gardens with maze and adventure playground (open as house, also Nov to late Dec, S & Su), church, restaurant, shop.

Signposted on A607 Grantham to Lincoln road, 3 miles north of Grantham.

Belton House: a smart Restoration country house of 1685–8, but somewhat lacking in beauty within

Belvoir Castle, Leicestershire

Privately owned (HHA) • £££ • Open late Apr to Sep, daily

The seat of the Dukes of Rutland since their move from Haddon Hall in Derbyshire (see below) in 1703, Belvoir is a fascinating blend of architectural styles from different periods, but above all is a joyful example of early-19th-century mock-medieval, its gothic stonework as cathedral-like on the inside as it is castle-like on the outside.

The castle was inspired by Elizabeth Howard of Castle Howard, who in 1799 married the 5th Duke and in 1801 engaged James Wyatt to rebuild Belvoir as a turreted medieval fantasy. The work was overseen by the duke's friend and chaplain, the Rev Sir James Thoroton, who had increasing input after a fire in 1816.

The result of their efforts is a house of astonishing scale and splendour, decorated with lashings of red and gold in the trendy 'Louis Quatorze' style which the architectural critic Pevsner described as 'a neo-baroque, neo-rococo mixture'. It may be a little over the top, but it works beautifully in this instance – particularly so in the Elizabeth Saloon, named in tribute to the duchess, where a statue of her in white marble drifts in a sea of gold ornamentation. Equally impressive is Wyatt's Regent's room, adapted from the old long gallery with the addition of a semi-circular bay in a tower.

Belvoir is also a friendly place to visit, still lived in and used. It has its eccentricities – the unavoidable visit to the regimental museum of the Queen's Royal Lancers is not everyone's cup of tea – but has plenty to please, including superb paintings by Holbein, Rubens and Reynolds, as well as Gobelin and Mortlake tapestries.

Gardens and sculpture garden (open as house), restaurant, shop.

Signposted off A607 Grantham to Melton Mowbray road and A52 Nottingham to Grantham road, 7 miles west of Grantham.

Belvoir Castle: on the site of a Norman fortification stands a gothic revival fantasy of the early 1800s

Bolsover Castle, Derbyshire

English Heritage • £££ • Open Apr to Oct daily, Nov to Mar M, Th-F, S & Su

Truly one of the most remarkable houses in Britain. It looks like a castle – and indeed is built on the site of a medieval castle, perched above a steep slope on the edge of a ridge, with superb views over what was once a pastoral idyll but has since been transformed by mining and a motorway into a kind of industrial countryside – but it is really two very different things: the ruin of a grand and unusual house of the early 1600s, plus a sumptuous and fascinating 'pleasure house' in the Norman-style 'keep'.

There is, of course, as with so many houses in the area, a link with Bess of Hardwick (see Hardwick Hall, below): the work of building it was started by Bess's son, Charles Cavendish, with the help of Robert Smythson, the greatest architect of the age, although it was completed after the deaths of both men (in 1617 and 1614 respectively) by their sons, William and John.

William Cavendish went on to become a major figure in the kingdom, but achieved unwanted fame in the Civil War as the commander of the Royalist forces crushed at the Battle of Marston Moor in 1644. None the less, it was his aspirations that led to the creation of Bolsover as we see it today.

It consists, essentially, of two ranges: one contains a riding school built in the 1630s (William took his horsemanship very seriously), while the other, known as the terrace range, consists of an excessively ostentatious set of state rooms, also built in the 1630s, intended to attract royal interest and preferment. Both are now ruinous, although the riding school has been re-roofed. Their most notable feature is the exterior of the terrace range, topped with Dutch gables and ornamented with strange bulbous pillars that show John Smithson (he preferred a more modern spelling of his name) picking up ideas from the newly trendy 'mannerist' architecture.

The star of the piece, however, is the keep, known as the Little Castle, which is now unfurnished but is otherwise intact. Covered with odd classical flourishes picked up by John Smithson on his travels, it is an essay in chivalry and courtly love, decorated throughout with the most extraordinary wall paintings commissioned by William as well as splendidly showy chimneypieces designed by John and many other little treats – not least the gothic vaults of the hall and the ceiling of the great chamber, painted in an unusual shade of pale blue and decorated with gilded stars.

Designed purely for show, the Little Castle got a royal audience in July 1634, when King Charles and Queen Henrietta Maria were entertained at vast expense and a masque written just for the occasion by the playwright Ben Jonson, a friend of William's, was performed.

Reconstructed period gardens with Venus fountain, restaurant, shop.

Signposted off A632 Chesterfield to Ollerton road, in the centre of Bolsover.

Bolsover Castle: the keep-like Little Castle, to the left of the picture, is the most remarkable example in Britain of an early 17th-century 'pleasure house'

Burghley House: one of the most splendid of Elizabethan houses, designed and built by the Queen's most trusted advisor, Sir William Cecil, in 1555–87

Burghley House, Lincolnshire

Privately owned (HHA) • £££ • Open Apr to Oct, daily

Spectacular inside and out, Burghley is still fundamentally the splendid Renaissance extravaganza created in 1555–87 by Sir William Cecil, Queen Elizabeth I's private secretary and Lord Treasurer, and her senior and most trusted advisor. Some alterations were carried out for his descendant, the 9th Earl of Exeter, in 1756–79 by Lancelot 'Capability' Brown, whose skills as an architect are less well known than his ubiquitous achievements as a landscaper. Brown made the south front more regular and designed the interiors of several of the principal rooms on that side of the house.

The third man involved in making Burghley what it is today was John, the 5th Earl, who married the heiress Anne Cavendish of Chatsworth, daughter of the 3rd Earl of Devonshire. Together they spent most of their considerable wealth on grand tours of the cultural centres of Europe during which they collected over 300 paintings and many other *objets d'art*, most of which are still on show in the house, and they also secured the services of the Italian painter Antonio Verrio and his equally esteemed French contemporary Louis Laguerre to decorate the walls and ceilings of the state rooms in a truly astonishing style.

By far the most astounding of the paintings are in a drawing room known as the heaven room, said to be Verrio's masterpiece and including a self-portrait among the dozens of figures of gods, voluptuously naked goddesses and mythological creatures, and on the hell staircase, where Verrio shows the mouth of hell as the gaping jaws of a huge cat. By the time he got round to this latter work, Verrio was heavily in debt and was obliged to dismiss his assistants, so he worked mainly alone, taking 11 months to finish. When the 5th Earl died in 1700, he left debts that hamstrung the estate for decades.

The treats of the painted rooms come at the climax of a visit to the house, which starts quietly with the largely unaltered Elizabethan kitchens, where hangs a bizarre painting of a butchered ox by the animal artist Frans Snyders. Equally restrained in its appeal is the next room visited, the chapel, with a pleasing ceiling in Jacobean style designed by Lancelot Brown; but here is your best chance to take a look through a window at the architecture of the courtyard, with the extraordinary clock tower topped by a tall, obelisk-like spire and embellished with a host of Renaissance flourishes – all designed by Cecil, who was his own architect.

Throughout the rest of the house, the thing that stands out is the quality and variety of the paintings, with works by many Italian and Dutch masters and fine portraits.

Deer park, landscaped parkland and sculpture gardens (open all year, daily, admission free), private gardens (open Apr, daily), restaurant, shop.

Signposted from A1 on B1443 Stamford to Peterborough road, 1 mile east of Stamford.

Calke Abbey: built in the early 1700s, not quite elegant on the outside, beautifully decaying within

Calke Abbey, Derbyshire

National Trust • £££ • Open Apr to Oct, M-W, S & Su

A wonderful experiment in preserving a house in exactly the state in which it was handed over to the National Trust – with, as the guide book puts it, its 'potent but fragile atmosphere of quiet decay'. Far from being an easy option, this has meant painstaking conservation almost as difficult and expensive as complete restoration, involving such delicate tasks as varnishing peeling plaster into place.

It works because of the unusual history of Calke. Essentially the house had been going into gradual decline over more than 150 years, with its owners, the Harpur Crewe family, gradually shutting up more and more rooms and using fewer and fewer. But the family were also avid collectors over several generations and hardly ever threw anything away, so that many of the closed rooms are piled high with an odd mix of junk and treasure.

It was an eccentric enough house anyway, built in baroque style in the early 1700s on the foundations of an Elizabethan house that itself replaced the original abbey. It followed the lines of old walls, so the classical balance and symmetry to which it aspired never came off. It was remodelled in 1789–1810 with the addition of the Greek-style portico, then overhauled internally in the 1840s by Sir George Crewe. And then it wasn't touched save for the connection of a phone in 1928 and electricity in 1962.

Sir George was a principled and hard-working man, but his father had been a little offbeat, painfully shy and fond of wild animals, and his son, Sir John Harpur Crewe, turned out to be another typical English eccentric, attached to the quiet life and an avid collector of stuffed birds and geological specimens. The mix of Sir George's grand Victorian decor and Sir John's collections gave the house's interiors their musty, museum-like atmosphere, only increased by the gathering dust of the last century.

One treasure stands out among the piles of things found in the attics when the Trust took over: a superb state bed of about 1715, probably a wedding present given in 1734 by Princess Anne, the daughter of King George II, to the wife of Sir Henry Harpur. It had never been unpacked from its boxes and its Chinese silk hangings glow like new.

Other treats include the kitchens, scattered with equipment as if simply abandoned in mid-use at some indefinite time in the last 100 years, and the long, dark, gloomy servants' tunnel by which visitors leave after seeing the house.

Parkland with extensive walks (open all year, daily), garden, church (open as house), restaurant, shop.

Signposted from B5006, off A514 Derby to Swadlincote road, 10 miles south of Derby.

Chatsworth, Derbyshire

Privately owned • £££ • Open Apr to late Dec, daily

Consistently coming top in polls of the nation's favourite stately homes and tourist attractions, Chatsworth deserves its popularity.

Part of the attraction is the beautiful grounds, with a marvellous water cascade and 'willow' fountain created by the 1st Duke of Devonshire in the 1690s, to which have been added landscaping by Capability Brown and the works of Joseph Paxton, the designer of the Crystal Palace, whose cunningly wrought inventions include the glasshouses on which he based his design for the halls in which the Great Exhibition of 1851 took place and the 'emperor' fountain, the tallest in the world fed by gravity.

Equally appealing, though, is the sense that Chatsworth is a living (and lived-in) place, constantly changing even now. As the guide book points out, only four rooms are in their original form: the chapel and state dining room of the 1690s, and the great dining room and sculpture gallery from the 1830s.

Underneath is the house built in 1552 by Bess of Hardwick (see Hardwick Hall, below) and her second husband, Sir William Cavendish. From that union are descended three lines of dukes, including the Cavendish family, Dukes of Devonshire, who still live here today. Sir William was made responsible for the house arrest of Mary, Queen of Scots and put her up at various of his places: the rooms here in which she stayed are open occasionally to the public for a small extra fee, but of course have changed a great deal and are notable mainly for the Chinese hand-painted wallpaper put up in 1830, an amusing collection of toys and a display about the renowned Georgiana, Duchess of Devonshire.

The two major remodellings of the house were carried out in the 1690s by the 1st Duke, given his title for the part he played in bringing William of Orange to the English throne, and in the 1830s for the 6th Duke, Georgiana's son, by Sir Jeffry Wyattville, who added the long north wing with its odd 'belvedere' tower.

By far the most striking feature of the treasure-packed house are the painted walls and ceilings of the 1st Duke's great hall and state rooms, by two of the finest masters of this kind of work, Antonio Verrio and Louis Laguerre. The state rooms are scattered with superb furniture by William Kent and fine paintings by the likes of Sir Peter Lely.

The efforts of the 1st and 6th Dukes come together in the library, an attractive room built as a long gallery and converted to its present use by Wyattville. In the new dining room, added by Wyattville, hangs Gainsborough's famous painting of Georgiana in a huge black hat.

Parkland (open all year), gardens and grounds (open as house), farmyard and adventure playground (open as house, separate admission fee), restaurant, shop.

Signposted on B6012, off A619 Bakewell to Chesterfield road or A6 Bakewell to Matlock road, 3 miles east of Bakewell.

Chatsworth: built in 1552 by Bess of Hardwick, but owing its present appearance largely to remodelling in the 1690s, with the long north wing added in the 1830s

Canons Ashby, Northamptonshire

National Trust • £££ • Open Apr to Oct, W-M, S & Su

A modest but interesting example of a manor house belonging to Elizabethan minor gentry. The home of the Dryden family since 1551, it has a richly authentic feel in many of the rooms and has been little altered over the years, apart from a mild revamp by Edward Dryden in 1708–17, when the red brick exterior was refaced in stone, a grand new doorway was added and large sash windows were fitted to the rooms on the south front.

The Drydens are aptly described in the guide book as 'modest squires, bookish, conservative-minded and often short of money'. It was John Dryden who established the family's presence here in the 1550s, having inherited a farmhouse on the site, which he spent 30 years transforming into a manor of three wings, with an impressive great hall and a mildly showy staircase tower.

John's son, Erasmus, added an extra range in the 1590s to enclose the courtyard, while his grandson, Sir John, put up the deliciously over-the-top domed plasterwork ceiling in the great chamber (now known as the drawing room), above his father's equally excessive stone fireplace.

These two features are among the house's finest – particularly the chimneypiece, on which survive considerable traces of the original brightly coloured paintwork. But there are also many other pleasing details elsewhere, including a rare and fascinating set of Elizabethan 'grisaille' murals (painted in shades of grey) in a room named after the poet Edmund Spenser, a first cousin by marriage of Sir Erasmus, who often stayed in the house.

Best of all, however, is the Elizabethan painted decoration on the walnut panelling of the winter parlour, a room added in about 1580. The decoration, discovered under layers of cream paint by restorers in the 1980s, depicts the crests and devices of the Dryden family, together with those of other families they married into and noteworthy local nobles.

Gardens (open as house, also Nov to late Dec, S & Su), church, tearoom, shop.

Signposted on minor road off A361 Banbury to Daventry or B4525 Banbury to Towcester roads, 8 miles north-east of Banbury.

Canons Ashby: an Elizabethan manor of the 1550s to 1590s, with stone facings and windows of about 1710

Doddington Hall, Lincolnshire

Privately owned (HHA) • £££ • Open May to Sep, W & Su

Completed in 1600, this is a superb example of a smaller manor by Sir Robert Smythson, the greatest architect of the Elizabethan age. Its lines are typically plain, almost brutal, but its scale and practicality, as well as 400 years of gentle ageing, give it an approachability that some of his larger houses lack. It has not been altered at all externally since it was built, and it still has its original matching gatehouse and walled courtyard at the front.

Internally, however, it has been changed enough to lose most of its Elizabethan feel. For the most part the decoration is undistinguished, although the house, which is still lived in, does have a warm and welcoming atmosphere. Of most appeal are the rooms that retain, in their scale, at least, a sense of their original grandeur; particularly the long gallery, which occupies most of the top floor, and the great hall, in the central range of the ground floor. This room is pleasantly

Doddington Hall: built by Sir Robert Smythson in 1600 and unchanged externally since

arranged, with many beautiful modern craft objects.

Gardens with Elizabethan-style formal areas and wild areas, maze, tearoom, shop.

Signposted on B1190 Lincoln to Torksey road, 5 miles west of Lincoln.

Grimsthorpe Castle, Lincolnshire

Privately owned (HHA) • £££ • Open Apr to Sep, Th & Su (also Aug, M-W)

A rather fascinating revamp of a Tudor house carried out by Sir John Vanbrugh between 1722 and his death in 1726, which has been described as his last masterpiece. There was a castle of sorts on the site from as early as the late 1100s, parts of which remain in the structure of a corner tower known as King John's tower; but the majority of the house was built hurriedly by Charles Brandon, Duke of Suffolk, in time for a visit by Henry VIII in 1541.

Suffolk was an important figure at court and married the king's sister, Mary, the widow of King Louis XII of France, in 1515. He was also legal ward to Katherine Willoughby, heiress of Grimsthorpe, whose father died in 1526, when she was seven; and in 1533, when Mary died, Suffolk married Katherine and got his hands on the Grimsthorpe estate.

Vanbrugh was called in to remodel the house in 1715 by Robert Bertie, newly created 1st Duke of Ancaster and Kesteven by George I, but did not start work until the 2nd Duke, Peregrine Bertie, inherited in 1723. Vanbrugh added a typically extravagant but beautiful baroque facade on the entrance front – like so many of his designs, it has a rhythmical quality, but is also very geometric – flanked by tower-like pavilions and walls. His designs for the other faces of the house, sketches of which survive, were never executed, so these still have their Tudor randomness.

Inside, Vanbrugh's spectacular entrance hall with, like the facade, two layers of arcades (sets of arches) all round, easily steals the scene. The only room to rival it is the state dining room, with extravagant rococo decoration of the 1730s including a marble chimneypiece that was probably carved by the sculptor Sir Henry Cheere.

The rest of the house pales by comparison, with a messy blend of decoration in the styles of various later periods; but it is, none the less, a comfortable house, with a lived-in feel, and there are many items of interest to see.

Deer park, adventure playground, gardens (open as house), restaurant, shop.

Signposted on A151 Bourne to Grantham road, 4 miles north-west of Bourne.

Grimsthorpe Castle: a Tudor house built in 1540–41 with a marvellous baroque facade – even more impressive up close – added by Sir John Vanbrugh in 1722–26

Haddon Hall, Derbyshire

Privately owned (HHA) • £££ • Open Apr to Sep, daily, Oct, Th-F, S & Su

A most unusual and enjoyable place to visit, very different from the usual run of stately homes that are privately owned and lived in. Haddon is a castle-like fortified manor dating largely from the 1300s and 1400s, but with a few surviving Norman parts and some notable Elizabethan alterations, restored in the early 20th century after almost 200 years during which it was left empty but kept structurally intact. Today it is only sparsely furnished, but the main interest is in the fabric of the building itself – although it also has a notable collection of tapestries.

Haddon was the home of the Vernon family from the 1100s, but only some traces that go this far back remain, including Norman arches and pillars in the chapel. In about 1370 Richard de Vernon started work on a new great hall that formed the centrepiece of his revamped house: its beautiful wooden-beamed roof was renewed in the 1920s. The kitchens next door, equally ancient, are among the most fascinating of the period in Britain, full of interesting fixtures and features, with a bakehouse and butchery alongside.

The parlour next to the hall was modified in about 1500, split into a lower and an upper floor to form a dining room below and great chamber above. At about the same time, the chapel was remodelled and the north-west tower, through which visitors enter the courtyard, was added; the apparently haphazard set of arches and corbels, known as 'squinches', by which the new tower was linked to an earlier range, is very pleasing.

The glorious long gallery, with very fine panelling of the early 1600s, was added in the late 1500s by Sir George, last of the Vernons, who had no male heir. Haddon passed, through his daughter's marriage, to the Manners family, created Earls of Rutland in 1641. In 1703, when the Dukedom of Rutland was conferred upon the family, the 1st Duke moved his household to Belvoir Castle and Haddon was abandoned until in 1920 work began to restore it under the auspices of the 9th Duke.

Surprisingly, even when the house was empty, its collection of tapestries was left in storage here. A fire in 1925 destroyed the room in which most were stored, burning about 60. Of the comparatively few that survived, the most important are the five Mortlake tapestries of the early 1600s, thought to have been owned by Charles I, which are scattered around the house. More enjoyable, though, are the Flemish works hung in the state bedroom: look out for the horse depicted treading on a pike-bearer's foot.

Gardens (open as house), restaurant, shop.

Signposted on A6 Bakewell to Matlock road, 2 miles south of Bakewell.

Haddon Hall: a fascinating castle-like fortified manor, Norman in origin but based around a great hall of about 1370, with notable Elizabethan additions

Hardwick Hall: a splendid house of 1590–9, built by Elizabeth of Shrewsbury and adorned with her initials

Hardwick Hall, Derbyshire

National Trust • £££ • Open Apr to Oct, W-Th, S & Su (also Jul and Aug, M)

One of the most extraordinary houses in Britain, its plain shape – like a number of cardboard boxes stacked against each other – and its enormous windows giving it something of the look of a 1920s modernist factory. It is one of the Elizabethan 'prodigy houses', built in 1590–9 by the greatest architect of the age, Sir Robert Smythson, for the formidable Elizabeth, Countess of Shrewsbury, better known as Bess of Hardwick.

Born at Hardwick in 1527, the daughter of minor gentry, Bess made two very advantageous marriages. Her second husband, Sir William Cavendish, had made a pile serving Henry VIII and picked up land all over England, which he sold to buy new estates in the Midlands. He and Bess built a splendid new house at Chatsworth, which he bought in 1549. Her fourth marriage, in 1567, was to George Talbot, Earl of Shrewsbury, a favourite of Queen Elizabeth. By now Bess was one of the wealthiest and most powerful women in the land, but she soured relations with both the Queen and her husband in 1574, when she married one of her daughters to a relative of Mary Queen of Scots, so ensuring that her grand-daughter, Arabella, was in line to the throne.

The Queen was furious; Bess's husband hardly less so. Bess moved to Hardwick and started to rebuild her family's old house, before the earl's death in 1590 gave her the money to start a new house of innovative style and splendour.

The most remarkable of its dark and ancient interiors, which have survived largely unaltered, are the state rooms on the top floor – and particularly the high great chamber, with a beautiful frieze of painted plaster depicting a forest filled with animals and the court of the goddess Diana, the huntress. Really there are simply too many treasures to even begin to list, but chief among them are the tapestries and a fine collection of historic needlework.

Parkland with walks (open all year, daily), fine walled gardens (open Apr to Oct, M, W-F, S & Su), restaurant, shop.

Signposted on minor road from A6175 west of J29 of M1, 7 miles west of Mansfield.

Hardwick Old Hall, Derbyshire

English Heritage • ££ • Open Apr to Oct, M, W-Th, S & Su

Bess's revamping of the old house, completed in 1591 and used, after the new hall was built, to house servants and less important guests. Ruinous, but a few fine details.

Directions as for 'new' Hardwick Hall.

Old Hardwick Hall: the ruin of the older house Bess had rebuilt stands right next to the new hall

Kedleston Hall, Derbyshire

National Trust • £££ • Open Apr to Oct, M-W, S & Su

It's something of a surprise to go in search of the ultimate in grand Palladian houses and find it on the outskirts of Derby – but Kedleston is indeed close to perfection. Designed by Robert Adam, with interiors by Adam and a landscaped park with lake, bridge and fishing pavilion all by Adam, it has justly been called 'one of the masterpieces of mid-18th-century English architecture'.

Anyone who enjoys visiting a house that feels like a home may, however, be disappointed: the haughty splendour of this remarkable house is all about display and ostentation, and has little to do with comfort. Indeed, the main house was always more a public space than a private one. It was perfectly usual for gentlemen

who found themselves near a large country house to call in and ask to be shown round, and in this sense Kedleston has been open to visitors since it was completed in 1765. The comment by Dr Johnson that 'It would do excellently for a town hall' will strike a chord with some.

In fact, the main day-to-day living spaces were in the family wing to the north-east, with the kitchens and service rooms in a matching block to the north-west, both joined to the main house by elegant, curving covered corridors (in the family corridor, the oak floorboards are curved to match, but the servants had to make do with straight floorboards). There were to have been two matching wings at the back of the house, one a music pavilion, the other containing a conservatory, but the money ran out.

The immense rooms at the centre of the house are decorated with the relentless elegance of Adam at his

best, and the attention to detail is extraordinary, right down to door furniture and curtain pelmets: admire the immense curved doors of the saloon, which are too heavy for hinges and instead pivot on metal cones.

The house was built for Sir Nathaniel Curzon, offshoot of a wealthy landowning family, who was not ashamed to demolish the village that once stood here, leaving only the church. Luckily his descendants were too impoverished to ever change Kedleston much; the only notable family offshoot was Lord Curzon, Viceroy of India from 1899 to 1905, whose life and times are remembered in a fascinating museum in the basement.

Gardens, parkland walks (open all year), fishing pavilion, tearoom, shop.

Signposted from A38 (travelling east) 3 miles north-west of Derby city centre – watch for turning to Quarndon.

Kedleston Hall: the Palladian elegance of the exterior is reflected in the equally elegant interior of Robert Adam's masterpiece, completed in 1765

Kirby Hall: extensive ruin of an Elizabethan house given a stunning classical update in 1638–40, with splendid stonework. It was left to decay in the 1800s

Kirby Hall, Northamptonshire

English Heritage • ££ • Open all year, Apr to Oct, daily, Nov to Mar, S & Su

One of the most extensive and spectacular of England's ruins, this is the remains of a house begun in 1570 by Sir Humphrey Stafford and completed later in the same century by Sir Christopher Hatton, one of Queen Elizabeth's favourite courtiers. Like so many houses of the time, it was built in extravagant style in the hope that the Queen would favour its owner with a visit.

In fact, what makes it impressive is not its size, but the ornamentation of the exteriors, and particularly the stonework of the inner faces of the four ranges grouped around the inner courtyard. Best of all is the classical loggia, with pilasters and a statue of Apollo, added by the mason Nicholas Stone for Sir Christopher Hatton III in 1638–40.

Some rooms have been re-roofed, the most striking being the great hall and the four bedchambers on the ground and first floors, with their enormous bay windows.

Part-restored gardens of late 1600s, shop.

Signposted on minor road off A43 Corby to Stamford road, 4 miles west of Corby.

Lyveden New Bield, Northamptonshire

National Trust • ££ • Open all year, Apr to Oct, W-F, S & Su, Nov to Mar, S & Su (also daily in Aug)

Another very fine ruin, and within easy reach of Kirby Hall (left): the two make a fine day out in winter, when many houses are closed.

Actually Lyveden has not been ruined, but was never finished; work stopped in 1605 on the death of its builder, Sir Thomas Tresham, a staunch Catholic throughout the Protestant years of Elizabeth I's reign. The still-crisp stonework of its exterior is carved with many religious scriptures and a frieze telling the story of the Passion.

Next to the house, the structural elements of the Elizabethan garden survive: terraces, moats and spiral 'snail' mounts. Fascinating.

Gardens (open as house).

Signposted on minor road off A6116 Corby to Thrapston road, and off A427 Corby to Oundle road, 4 miles south-west of Oundle.

Lyveden New Bield: built 1595–1605 for the Catholic Sir Thomas Tresham, left unfinished on his death

Mr Straw's House, Nottinghamshire

National Trust • £££ • Open Apr to Oct, Tu-F & S, advance booking essential

The youngest house to make it into the National Trust's care on the basis of architectural interest, not because it had a famous occupant (though Paul McCartney's childhood home in Liverpool, a terraced house of the 1950s, is said to be a fine example of its period). It is a typical Edwardian suburban semi-detached house, built in about 1906, and bought in 1920 by a local grocer, William Straw, who had it totally redecorated before moving in with his family three years later.

What makes it unusual is that his sons, William and Walter, lived here as bachelors from the time of their mother's death in 1939 until William died in 1990, aged 92, making no alterations at all, never even acquiring a radio, telephone, television or central heating, and hardly ever throwing anything away, so that the house and its contents survive as a microcosm of the interwar years.

Clearly it's not at all grand, but the question is, is it interesting? Well, it depends who you are. Those old enough to remember the

Mr Straw's House: the right-hand of a pair of semis built in about 1906 and very little changed since 1923

ancient foodstuffs in the store cupboard or whose gran 'had one of those' seem to find it fascinating, as do youngsters for whom it is already ancient history. Others might find it a musty relic of a cramped, restrictive era.

Garden with greenhouse, outside lavatory.

Signposted on B6045 Worksop to Blyth road, on north side of Worksop.

Newstead Abbey, Nottinghamshire

Local council • £££ • Open Apr to Sep, daily

The house in which the rakish poet Lord Byron lived and kept his famous pet bear is bound to exert a certain fascination, but it is also of interest as a house in its own right. After its dissolution, the Augustinian priory of Newstead was granted by the king in 1540 to Sir John Byron of Colwick, who demolished the church and made the ranges around the cloister into a house.

It was empty and almost in ruins when Byron inherited in 1798, but had retained its medieval character. When Byron was forced to sell it, in 1818, to Thomas Wildman, a friend whose family had grown rich through plantations in Jamaica, the buyer was able to give it a pleasing gothic restoration with the help of the architect Norman Shaw.

It is largely unfurnished today, but full of engaging architectural details, both ancient and modern.

Parkland with walks, extensive gardens (open all year, daily), shop.

Signposted on B683 Ravenshead to Hucknall road, off A60 Mansfield to Nottingham road, 5 miles south of Mansfield.

Newstead Abbey: the home of the poet Lord Byron, whose ancestor Sir John Byron was given the abbey in 1540 and converted the cloister ranges into his house

Sudbury Hall: built from 1661 to the 1690s by Sir George Vernon, in a fascinatingly archaic style

Sudbury Hall, Derbyshire

National Trust • £££ • Open Apr to Oct, W-F, S & Su

A handsome and unusual house of the Restoration period – that is, built during the reign of Charles II – but looking back, in its design, to the Jacobean era. It was owned by George Vernon, whose ancestors had once lived at Haddon Hall (see above) and had, over several generations, accumulated a great deal of money and land largely through advantageous marriages to wealthy heiresses.

George inherited the estate at Sudbury in 1660 at the age of 24 or 25 (the exact year of his birth is not known) and decided to build a new house on a fresh site. Work started almost straight away but took more than 30 years to complete, and new ideas seem to have been picked up as the work progressed; which perhaps explains why a building with a fundamentally Jacobean plan and layout is topped off by a hipped roof and cupola in a far more up-to-date style, influenced by Sir Christopher Wren, Inigo Jones and Sir Roger Pratt (compare the cupola with that of Pratt's house at Kingston Lacy, Dorset), and why the interiors are decorated in the latest baroque fashion as pioneered by Wren in his London churches.

Whatever the reasons, Vernon's house has many features that are very old-fashioned for its time yet work rather beautifully, including a distinctly anachronistic long gallery that is one of the most pleasing rooms in the house. Its ceiling, completed in about 1676 by the renowned plasterers Bradbury and Pettifer, is said to be the finest of its type in England. The weight of its bold, high-relief ornamentation is lightened by its sheer liveliness; it incorporates busts ostensibly of Roman emperors, but thought to be caricatures of notable men of the time, including Charles II and James II; and grasshoppers dance around its central rosette.

Indeed, it is the quality of the finishing throughout that makes Sudbury a treat. Vernon started by using local craftsmen, but ended up employing some of the finest artists of the age. There are unbelievably delicate and detailed woodcarvings by Grinling Gibbons – although the subject matter, dead game and fish (as well as fruit and flowers) will probably not appeal to all – over the chimneypiece in the drawing room; there are equally fine but very different carved wood panels by Edward Pierce in the saloon; and the whole was topped off in the 1690s, when the house was finally being completed, by murals and ceilings painted by Louis Laguerre.

The furnishing is sparse, but there is an interesting variety of paintings, including portraits of the late 1600s by the English artist John Michael Wright, in the long gallery.

Museum of Childhood (open as house, also late Mar, W-F, S & Su, and early Dec, S & Su), grounds (open as house, also late Mar, W-F, S & Su), tearoom, shop.

Signposted from A50 Stoke-on-Trent to Derby road, 6 miles east of Uttoxeter.

Sulgrave Manor: the remaining parts of a modest house built by George Washington's ancestors in 1539

Sulgrave Manor, Northamptonshire

Privately owned • £££ • Open Apr to Oct, Tue-Th, S & Su, tours only

The remaining parts, after its later conversion to a farmhouse, of a small Elizabethan manor house built in 1539 of local stone, and a later wing added in about 1700. The house is notable mainly for the fact that it was the seat of the ancestors of one of the founding fathers of the United States of America, George Washington: among its proudest possessions is a portrait of George by the American artist Gilbert Stuart. It is no coincidence that the Washington family arms – which are seen throughout the house, notably in copies of stained glass windows dating from the late 1500s – consist of a pattern of stars and stripes.

It is not a particularly thrilling house in its own right, but there are pleasing details both outside and inside the main surviving part of the original house, which contains the great hall. As with the rest of the house, the hall has been furnished in a style appropriate to the period, which in this case means an oak refectory table and a scattering of chairs.

Best of the other rooms is the kitchen, where the fascinating array of ancient fixtures and equipment was brought in wholesale from a manor house in Hampshire.

Sadly, the manor is not well suited to presentation by guided tour, which does it no favours at all.

Gardens, restaurant, shop.

On minor road to Sulgrave, off B4525 Banbury to Towcester road, 5 miles east of Banbury.

Sutton Scarsdale Hall, Derbyshire

English Heritage • Free • Open all year, daily

A mostly unremarkable ruin, except for the attractive and dramatic neoclassical facade on the east side, which now looks out over open fields. The house was built in about 1720 by Nicholas Leke, 4th Lord Scarsdale, on the site of an earlier house. His architect was Francis Smith of Warwick.

The Leake family had lived on the Sutton estate from the 1400s – the family's most famous daughter being Elizabeth Leake, who was married to John of Hardwick in about 1508 and subsequently had one son and four daughters, one of whom was the famous Bess of Hardwick.

Nicholas died without an heir and the house passed through numerous hands, including those of Richard Arkwright, son of the inventor of the spinning jenny, until finally, in the 1920s, it was sold for scrap to a building firm who shipped off its fine Adam-style fireplaces and staircases to America and ripped out stone and timber for re-use locally. It was saved in 1946, just three days before it was due to be demolished.

On minor road between A632 Chesterfield to Bolsover road and A617 Chesterfield to Mansfield road, 5 miles east of Chesterfield

Sutton Scarsdale: ruin of a house of about 1720, with a superb east front by Francis Smith of Warwick

Wingfield Manor, Derbyshire

English Heritage • ££ • Open Apr to Oct, W-F, S & Su, Nov to Mar, S & Su

Britain's largest and most interesting ruin of a pre-Elizabethan house. Wingfield was planned around two courtyards, the first for servants' quarters, the second for the lord's residence with great hall, great chamber and private apartments.

It was built in about 1439 by Ralph, Lord Cromwell, who served as Lord Treasurer to Henry VI from 1433. He was clearly no shrinking violet – his motto was 'Have I not the right?' – and he expressed his wealth and status in building not just this house, but also, at about the same time, the dramatic red brick keep at Tattershall Castle, Lincolnshire.

In the 1570s, Wingfield was owned by George Talbot, Earl of Shrewsbury (see Hardwick Hall, above), who was responsible for keeping Mary, Queen of Scots under lock and key at his various houses; it was during one of her three stays here that she is supposed to have hatched a plot to overthrow Elizabeth.

Shop.

Signposted on B5035, off A615 Matlock to Alfreton road or A6 Matlock to Belper road, 11 miles south of Chesterfield.

Wollaton Hall: one of Britain's most extraordinary houses, built in 1580–8 by Sir Robert Smythson

Wollaton Hall, Nottinghamshire

Local council • Free (M-F), £ (S & Su) • Open all year, daily

One of the most remarkable houses in Britain, and all the more so for the fact that it is Elizabethan, built in 1580–8 by the greatest architect of the age, Sir Robert Smythson, for Sir Francis Willoughby, the highly educated and immensely wealthy son of one of the country's leading families. Willoughby's ancestors had made a fortune in the late 1400s from industry, especially coal mining, as well as from their loyalty to Henry VII.

Smythson had just finished working at Longleat in Wiltshire, and would later build Hardwick Hall in Derbyshire: the first is much more horizontal and elegant than Wollaton, the latter far plainer. Wollaton's unusually lavish ornamentation, a haphazard blend of Dutch, gothic and Renaissance influences, was probably required by the client, who knew a little about architecture; and its most peculiar feature, the huge high hall on top, was almost certainly a last-minute addition at Willoughby's insistence.

The hall is now used as a local natural history museum, and the interiors do not in any way reflect their original Elizabethan splendour, with the exception of the carved stone screen in the great hall, for which Smythson's design survives. There is a project under way to restore it authentically, which would be a superb achievement.

Deer park (£ parking charge, open all year, daily), steam engine house, art gallery, cafe, shop.

In Wollaton, 3 miles west of Nottingham city centre.

Wingfield Manor: ruin of a vast manor house of about 1439, built by Ralph Cromwell, Lord Treasurer

See also...

Althorp
Near Northampton
Privately owned, ££££, open Jul to Sep, daily (booking advised)
Impressive mansion of Tudor origin, remodelled first in classical and then in Palladian style, in the late 1600s and early 1700s. The home of the Spencers, with burial place of the late Diana, Princess of Wales.

Ayscoughfee Hall
Spalding, Lincolnshire
Local council, free, open all year, Mar to Oct, daily, Nov to Feb, M-F
Late medieval wool merchant's house, home to local museum.

Boughton House
Kettering, Northamptonshire
Privately owned (HHA), £££, open Aug, daily
Impressive house around seven courtyards developed from Tudor monastic building, culminating in a French-style addition of 1695. Visits place an interesting emphasis on the house's relationship with its working estate.

Bradgate Park
Newtown Linford, Leicestershire
Privately owned, £ (parking fee), open all year, daily
Ruin of a brick-built medieval house, the childhood home of Lady Jane Grey, set in a medieval deer park, now a country park, with walks in woodland (walk of just over a mile to the house ruins).

Clumber Park
Worksop, Nottinghamshire
National Trust, ££ (parking charge), open daily, all year
A grand estate minus its house, which was pulled down in 1938. Also kitchen garden with splendid glasshouses (£, *open Apr to Oct, W-F, S & Su*) and gothic revival chapel.

Cottesbrooke Hall
Cottesbrooke, Northamptonshire
Privately owned (HHA), £££, open May and Jun, W-Th, Jul to Sep, Th
Queen Anne house with little alteration. Renowned picture collection strong on sporting and equestrian subjects; gardens with collections of magnolia, acer and cherry trees.

Deene Park
Corby, Northamptonshire
Privately owned (HHA), £££, open Jun to Aug, Su (also Easter to Aug, Su & M of bank holidays)
Interesting house developed from a medieval manor arranged around a courtyard, with Tudor additions and Georgian remodelling, restored gradually since the 1950s.

Donington-le-Heath Manor
Donington-le-Heath, Leicestershire
Local council, free, open Mar to Nov, daily, Dec to Feb, S & Su
Small manor house of the 1280s, altered in the early 1600s, restored with appropriate furnishings.

Eyam Hall
Eyam, Derbyshire
Privately owned (HHA), £££, open Jun to Aug, W-Th & Su
Small, intimate manor house in famous plague village, the home of the Wright family since 1761.

Gainsborough Old Hall
Gainsborough, Lincolnshire
English Heritage and local council, ££, open all year, Easter to Oct, daily, Nov to Easter, M-F, S
Fascinating large, brick-built medieval house of about 1460, consisting of two wings flanking great hall. Interesting kitchens and good views from tower.

Holdenby House
Holdenby, Northamptonshire
Privately owned (HHA), £££, open only certain days in Apr, May, Aug
Fine Elizabethan stone house, the largest in England when it was built, with notable gardens (restored by Rosemary Verey and Rupert Golby) and falconry centre.

Holme Pierrepont Hall
Near Nottingham
Privately owned (HHA), £££, open Jun, Th, Jul, W-Th, Aug, Tu-Th
Castle-styled red brick late medieval manor house.

Rufford Abbey: a house of the 1600s, with a ruined wing built from the refectory of a Cistercian abbey

Kelmarsh Hall

Kelmarsh, Northamptonshire
Privately owned (HHA), £££, open mid-Apr to Sep, Su (also Aug, Th)
Red brick Palladian house built 1732, designed by James Gibbs, with parkland and notable gardens.

Lamport Hall

Northampton
Privately owned (HHA), £££, open Easter to Sep, Su
Originally of 1560s, but dominated by facade of late 1600s/early 1700s by John Webb and Smith of Warwick, with additions of 1800s. Garden said to have been home to England's first garden gnomes in mid-1800s.

Lyddington Bede House

Lyddington, Rutland
English Heritage, ££, open Apr to Oct, daily
The wing of a medieval palace of the Bishops of Lincoln, converted into almshouses in 1600. Attics with fascinating roof structure.

The Prebendal Manor House

Nassington, Northamptonshire
Privately owned, £££, open Easter to Sep, W & Su
Manor dating from the early 1200s with many medieval features, also tithe barn and medieval fishponds.

Rufford Abbey

Ollerton, Nottinghamshire
English Heritage and local council, £ (parking charge), open all year, daily
Ruined wing of a house of the early 1600s built from the refectory of a Cistercian abbey.

Southwick Hall

Near Oundle, Northamptonshire
Privately owned (HHA), £££, open Apr to Aug, Su and M of bank holidays only
Medieval house of 1300 with Tudor and 1700s additions, exhibitions of Victorian and Edwardian life, agricultural items, local archeology.

Stanford Hall

Lutterworth, Leicestershire
Privately owned (HHA), £££, open mid-Apr to Sep, F & Su, (also bank holiday weekends, F, S & Su, M)

Tattershall Castle: built in the 1440s, and one of the earliest brick-built structures in Britain

House of 1690s by the Smiths of Warwick, also motorcycle museum.

Stoke Park Pavilions

Stoke Bruerne, Northamptonshire
Privately owned, ££, open Aug, daily
Two pavilions from a house of about 1630 thought to have been designed by Inigo Jones.

Tattershall Castle

Tattershall, Lincolnshire
National Trust, £££, open Apr to Oct, M-W, S & Su, also Mar and Nov to early Dec, S & Su
One of the earliest brick buildings in Britain, built by Ralph Cromwell, Lord Treasurer in the 1440s; state apartments, some original decoration.

Upton Park

Near Newark, Nottinghamshire
Privately owned (HHA), £££, open Apr to Oct, Tu-F, S & Sun
Fine country house, originally of the 1500s but with extensive 1800s alterations; the home of the British Horological Institute, with museum of clocks and watches.

Woolsthorpe Manor

Near Grantham, Lincolnshire
National Trust, ££, open Apr to Sep, W-F, S & Su (also Mar and Oct, S & Su)
Attractive stone manor house of the 1600s where Isaac Newton was born and produced his early work, with apple orchard, editions of his books and reconstructions of his inventions.

And...

Aynhoe Park
Aynhoe, Northamptonshire
Privately owned, £££, open Apr to Sep, W-Th
Elizabethan house rebuilt after the Civil War, with elegant later work by Thomas Archer and Sir John Soane. Converted to flats, access limited.

Carlton Hall
Carlton-on-Trent, Nottinghamshire
Privately owned, £££, open by appt only
Handsome house of mid-1700s with stables by John Carr of York.

Carnfield Hall
Near Alfreton, Derbyshire
Privately owned (HHA), £££, open by appt only
Stone-built Elizabethan manor with classical update of early 1600s.

Catton Hall
Walton-on-Trent, Derbyshire
Privately owned, ££, open Apr to Oct, M, tours only
Tidy red brick mansion of 1745.

Grantham House
Grantham, Lincs
National Trust, ££, open Apr to Sep, W only, by appt only
House in mixed styles, oldest parts of which date from 1380.

Lyddington Bede House: the wing of a medieval palace of the Bishops of Lincoln

Gunby Hall
Near Spilsby, Lincolnshire
National Trust, ££, open Apr to Sep, W only
Only ground floor and basement shown of red brick house of 1700.

Harlaxton Manor
Near Grantham, Lincolnshire
Privately owned, £££, open Jul, first and last Su and for groups by appt
Remarkable neo-Elizabethan house of 1800s by Anthony Salvin.

Marston Hall
Near Grantham, Lincolnshire
Privately owned, ££, open Mar to Jun, Aug, Oct, certain days only

Ancient house with Norman, Tudor and Georgian elements.

The Old Manor, Norbury
Near Ashbourne, Derbyshire
National Trust, ££, open by appt only
Stone-built hall of 1200s and 1400s, of specialist interest only.

The Priest's House
Easton on the Hill, Northamptonshire
National Trust, free, open all year, keys from keyholder as advertised on noticeboard at property
Pre-Reformation priest's lodge said to be of specialist interest only.

Renishaw Hall
Sheffield, Derbyshire
Privately owned (HHA), £££, open Apr to Sep, for groups by appt only (gardens ££, open Apr to Sep, Th-F, S & Su)
Characterful stone manor of 1625 with Georgian additions, also gardens and art galleries.

Thrumpton Hall
Thrumpton, Notts
Privately owned (HHA), £££, open all year for groups by appt only
Lovely little Jacobean manor with Renaissance touches.

Tissington Hall
Ashbourne, Derbyshire
Privately owned (HHA), £££, open late Jul to Aug, Tu–Fr (also certain days in Apr and Jun), tours only
Stone-built manor of the 1500s.

Woolsthorpe Manor: small manor of 1600s in which Isaac Newton was born, complete with apple orchard

West Midlands

Hereford and Worcester, Warwickshire,
West Midlands, Shropshire, Staffordshire

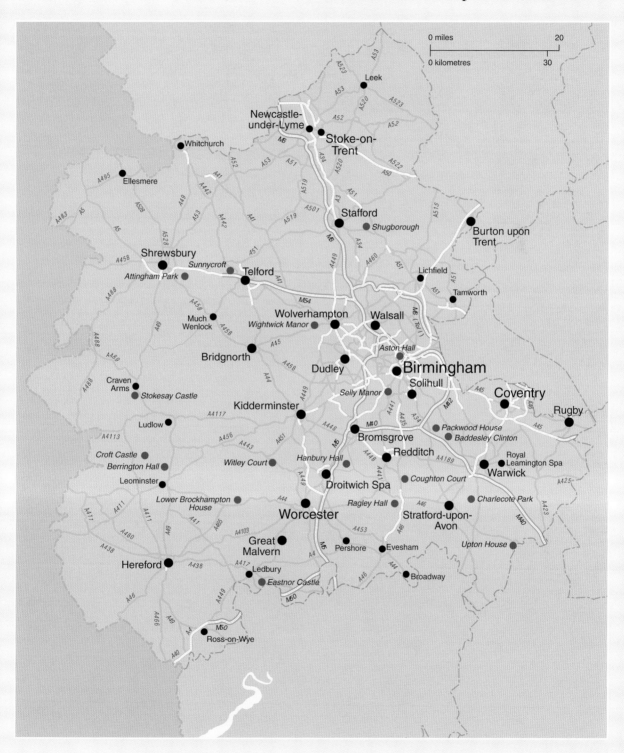

Aston Hall, Birmingham

Local council • Free • Open Apr to Oct, Tu-F, S & Su

If this remarkable Jacobean manor, one of the finest of its kind in the country, were set in rolling acres of parkland in open countryside, it would surely be far better known than it is. Instead, its urban location just a goal-kick's flight from the Aston Villa football ground, in a park with a definite air of neglect, does it no favours at all. Even a little attention paid to the park would make no end of difference.

It is, however, a fascinating building with its Jacobean structure and many original features intact, and all the better for the fact that there is no charge at all for entry. The house was built in 1618–35 for Sir Thomas Holte, heir to a family that had owned estates at Aston, Duddeston and Nechells (now a part of inner-city Birmingham) since the 1300s. As one of Warwickshire's leading landowners, he was also something of a social climber,

knighted by King James in 1603 and buying a baronetcy in 1618. The hall was a self-conscious expression of his wealth and status, described by a neighbour as 'a noble fabrick, which for beauty and state much exceedeth any in these parts'. An engraving after a drawing of about 1640 shows it looking much as it does now, but surrounded by fields.

The house was altered slightly in the late 1600s and again in the 1700s, but even this early in its life its owners seem to have taken great care to preserve as much as possible of its Jacobean character. The estate was sold in 1817, when a complex succession split it among several heirs who needed money more than they needed land. From 1819 to 1848 the house was rented by the younger James Watt, son of the eminent engineer, but then it remained empty until it was bought in 1864 by Birmingham Corporation. Thus it survived the Victorian era without any further alteration.

Little of the original furniture has found its way back to the house, but a programme of restoration in the 1980s has seen it furnished as far as

possible in accordance with the 17th- and 18th-century inventories. This attention to detail gives it an archaic feel that suits it well and makes it feel more convincingly of the period than just about any other in Britain.

One of the finest features is the great stair, an unusually bold design for its era in that it is cantilevered, with beautifully carved woodwork. Even more impressive is the plaster ceiling and frieze of the great dining room (everything in the house seems to be called 'great'), with grotesque masks lurking in the strapwork of the ceiling and large, robustly modelled Renaissance-style figures of warriors standing out of the frieze.

The long gallery is also pretty remarkable, again with an intricate strapwork ceiling, but as pleasing as any individual feature is that visitors can roam over most of the house, right up to the attics, with fresh discoveries lurking in every corner. It's a joy to explore.

Signposted off A38(M) and A38 in Aston, just north of Birmingham city centre.

Aston Hall: superbly unaltered and well-restored Jacobean manor built in 1618–35 by Sir Thomas Holte, let down only by its unappealing urban location

Attingham Park: built in 1782–5 to a beautiful design by George Steuart, but never finished as planned

Attingham Park, Shropshire

National Trust • £££ • Open Apr to Oct, M-Tu, F, S & Su

Time has not been especially kind to this elegant Palladian mansion, and nor have its previous owners. It was built in 1782–5 for Noel Hill, 1st Lord Berwick, by George Steuart, a former assistant and rival of Robert Adam, to a most unusual symmetrical plan, with a series of rooms to the right of the entrance intended for Lady Berwick, and those to the left for his lordship.

Visitors start with the 'feminine' side of the house, where Steuart's original decorative scheme is best preserved in all its delicate Adamesque beauty, culminating in the wonderful circular boudoir. This, however, is one of the few rooms to have been completed before the death of the 1st Lord Berwick in 1789. His son finished things off in a more robust French-influenced classical style, with lots of gilding everywhere, and it all went downhill from there.

In 1805, the 2nd Lord Berwick, whose chief pleasure lay in buying and commissioning art, brought in John Nash to insert a massive picture gallery into the house. It's a fascinating room, approached by an enchanting winding stair, but made a nonsense of the layout of the house, destroying the proportions of Steuart's entrance hall.

Other, later occupants, including an adult education college, did the house no favours either, and the 'masculine' side still feels neglected. The gradual process of restoration is still under way, however. In the meantime, Attingham is a patchwork that lacks enough of quality to be really satisfying.

Landscaped deer park with riverside walks (open all year, daily), tearoom, shop.

Signposted off B4380 Shrewsbury to Ironbridge road, 4 miles east of Shrewsbury.

Berrington Hall, Herefordshire

National Trust • £££ • Open Apr to Oct, M-W, S & Su

Set in parkland landscaped by Capability Brown and designed by his son-in-law, Henry Holland, Berrington is a squat, square house of dark red sandstone, the severity of its appearance lifted only slightly by the arched windows on the top floor. Inside, however, it is a different story altogether: a light and cheery adventure into the French-influenced neo-classical style that was trendy at the time.

It was built for Thomas Harley, a London banker who bought the estate to retire to in his mid-40s. His daughter Anne married the son of Admiral Rodney, whose victories are commemorated in a series of paintings in the dining room.

Finest of the house's comfortably sumptuous interiors is the glorious staircase hall, delightfully open and airy downstairs and almost playful in its use of columns upstairs.

Service court with stables, laundry and dairy, gardens (open as house), parkland walk to lake (open Jul to Oct, M-W, S & Su), restaurant, shop.

Signposted on A49 Leominster to Ludlow road, 3 miles north of Leominster.

Berrington Hall: designed by Capability Brown's son-in-law, Henry Holland, in about 1778

Baddesley Clinton: a lovely moated manor built in the 1400s, rebuilt about 1600, and altered since

Baddesley Clinton, Warwickshire

National Trust • £££ • Open Mar to Oct, W-F, S & Su

A most attractive and welcoming little moated manor house, established in the mid-1400s, rebuilt in the late 1500s and remodelled from time to time since, growing gradually and organically into the pleasing shape seen today. It consists of three ranges around a courtyard, with the rectangular moat running close to the walls; the courtyard is now open on the fourth side, but this is thought to have been where the medieval great hall stood.

If it is the sort of place the visitor can immediately imagine living in, this is probably down to the cosiness of the Artsy Craftsy touches added in the late 1800s by its four occupants of the time, known as 'the quartet': the owner, Marmion Edward Ferrers; his wife, Rebecca; her aunt, Lady Georgiana Chatterton and her husband, Edward Heneage Dering. In 1885, after the deaths of their respective partners,

Rebecca and Edward married. After his death in 1892, Rebecca continued to live at Baddesley until 1923.

The comfortable furnishings and the understated decoration are chiefly down to the four friends, who also embellished the house with heraldry and stained glass. In this they were continuing the tradition of Henry Ferrers 'the Antiquarian', the Elizabethan man of learning who owned Baddesley from 1564 to 1633.

In the early 1600s Henry rebuilt the house in a more up-to-date style, adding the great parlour above the gatehouse, but before this, from about 1586, he let it, and it became a refuge for Jesuit priests. A number of hidey-holes can still be seen, the largest being in a room used as the kitchen since the early 1700s; basically part of the medieval sewer system, it could only be reached from a garderobe toilet on the first floor. A dramatic account by a priest who hid here in October 1591 is reproduced in the guidebook.

Throughout the house are scattered details from Henry's time, although not always in their original position – such as the immense stone chimneypiece now in the great hall, which began life in the great parlour. His bedroom still has the elaborate wooden chimneypiece that he oversaw the creation of in 1629, as described in detail in his diary.

Really, though, the appealing thing about Baddesley is the way such ancient features are jumbled up with later additions, so that an early 20th-century icebox in the kitchen seems just as appropriate as the court cupboard of 1683 in the drawing room, and the use of cut-about Charles II oak chests to hide the central heating radiators installed in 1923 seems not vandalistic, but entirely in keeping.

Gardens and grounds with stewponds, lakeside walk, nature walk (open Mar to mid-Dec, W-F, S & Su), restaurant, secondhand bookshop, shop.

Signposted off A4141 Solihull to Warwick road, 8 miles north-west of Warwick.

Charlecote Park, Warwickshire

National Trust • £££ • Open Mar to Oct, M-Tu, F, S & Su

A pretty red-brick Elizabethan manor house, built after 1551 by Sir Thomas Lucy, a local worthy caricatured by Shakespeare as Justice Shallow in Henry IV Pt II. Although it retains its original appearance on the outside, made all the more picturesque by the charming gatehouse of about 1600, inside the house was greatly modified in the 1830s by George Hammond Lucy following his marriage to Mary, a mining heiress.

It stands, then, as a fine example of an early-19th-century romantic interior in the Elizabethan revival style – more solid and not as subtle as the original, but satisfying none the less. Equally notable is a collection of objects bought in 1823 from William Beckford's hugely eccentric house at Fonthill Abbey, most striking being a 16th-century inlaid marble table formerly in the Borghese Palace in Rome.

Parkland with riverside walks, gardens (open as house, also Nov and Dec, S & Su), brewhouse, coach house with carriage collection, restaurant, shop.

Signposted on B4088, off B4086 Stratford-upon-Avon to Wellesbourne road, 5 miles east of Stratford.

Coughton Court: a manor of the early 1500s with a dramatic gatehouse, with interiors of many periods

Coughton Court, Warwickshire

National Trust and privately owned (HHA) • £££ • Open Apr to Sep, W-F, S & Su (also Jul and Aug, Tu), mid to end Mar and Oct, S & Su

Still lived in by the Throckmortons, whose home it has been since 1409, when John Throckmorton, later Under-Secretary of England, married the heiress to the estate, Coughton is essentially a Tudor fortified manor built in the early 1500s by Sir George Throckmorton, but it has been modified here, there and more or less everywhere in the years since. It is now a pleasing synthesis of bits and pieces of various styles and ages, all of it blending happily.

Its ancient origins are more apparent from the rear, where two brick-built wings with timber-framed upper storeys flank the noble stone gatehouse. From the front, it has the gothic flavour of the late 1700s, and indeed the beautiful, delicate fan vault inside the gatehouse is of this date.

This is just the first of many treats inside the house, continuing with the climb to the gatehouse roof, from where the views across the low-lying park are excellent. The most authentically ancient-looking room is the dining room, where a dramatic Renaissance-style chimneypiece of the time of Charles I, with black slate columns and coloured marble insets, is surrounded by wonderfully carved oak panelling – which in fact was brought here in the 1800s.

The family was unrepentantly Catholic, and on display is a linen shift said to have been worn by Mary Queen of Scots, 'the holy martyr' as a Latin inscription stitched on it says.

Churches, farm, stables, extensive gardens with lakeside and riverside walks (open as house), restaurant, shop.

Signposted on A435 Studley to Alcester road, 3 miles north of Alcester. Small parking fee for NT members.

Charlecote Park: an attractive Elizabethan manor house, completely remodelled inside in the 1830s

Croft Castle, Herefordshire

National Trust • £££ • Open mid-Apr to Sep, W-F, S & Su (also Jul and Aug, Tu), Oct, S & Su

A rather pleasing and graceful 18th-century Gothicisation of a late-medieval castle. Its Georgian elegance has recently been given extra polish as part of a programme of restoration and refurbishment.

This was the seat of the Croft family from at least the time of Hugh de Croft, who in 1243 was given a baronetcy after helping to save Prince Edward from the rebellious Simon de Montfort, but there was probably a castle on the site long before. Indeed, there is also a fine big prehistoric 'castle' – an iron age hill fort, known as Croft Ambrey – nearby, on a pleasant walk from the castle car park.

Unfortunately for the Crofts, they didn't manage to hang on to their estate. The family finances never recovered after the Civil War, when the castle was plundered by Irish mercenaries before it could even fall into Parliamentarian hands, and in the 1700s it was mortgaged, eventually being sold to the Davies family. In 1923 it was recovered when Sir James Croft – a soldier who died on active duty with the Commandos in 1941 – finally bought it back.

Ironically, then, the Crofts had little to do with the process by which the castle ended up in its present form. The walls and the basic structure – it consists of four ranges surrounding a courtyard, with a tower at each corner – are probably of the 1300s and 1400s, but the earliest timber in the castle dates to the 1660s, when it was rebuilt after its devastation in the Civil War by Herbert Croft, Bishop of Hereford, who had been one of King Charles I's royal chaplains. Bishop Croft probably also planted the splendid three-mile-long avenue of Spanish chestnut trees in the grounds.

The interiors, however, are almost entirely the work of later, non-Croft occupants. The superb plasterwork ceilings in the oak room and blue room are of the mid-1700s, while the restrained Georgian painted panelling in the drawing room is from later in the same century – as are the majority of the stylish pointy windows and much of the house's noted collection of Gothic furniture. It all fits together well as a comfy and not too showy whole, sprinkled with family portraits and heirlooms such as Bishop Croft's prayerbook and a copy of Johnson's dictionary annotated by Sir Herbert Croft.

Parkland walks (open daily, all year), gardens (open as house), tearoom, shop.

Signposted on B4362, off B4361 Leominster to Ludlow road, 5 miles north-west of Leominster.

Eastnor Castle, Herefordshire

Privately owned (HHA) • £££ • Open late Apr to Sep, Su, also Jul and Aug, M-F

A superb Norman-style castle built in 1810–24 for John, 2nd Baron (and later 1st Earl) Somers, who had inherited one fortune and married another, and designed by Robert Smirke, an architect who, at the relatively youthful age of 30 when work began, already had a reputation for getting difficult jobs done on time and to budget.

It was one of the first designs to take Gothic inspiration to the extreme by recreating the stark, almost industrial lines of a medieval castle as first built, rather than reproducing a softened, picturesque ruin – it anticipates by a few years Thomas Hopper's even bolder Norman castle, complete with keep, at Penrhyn in North Wales, built in 1820–45.

The interiors took a good deal longer to find their completed form, only really coming good after the 2nd Earl brought in AWN Pugin in 1847, after the designer finished his

Croft Castle: a plain, rectangular fortress of the 1300s and 1400s given a Gothic makeover in the 1700s

Eastnor Castle: a faux-Norman extravaganza of 1810–24 with superb interiors by Pugin

stint at the Houses of Parliament. Pugin worked with his usual team of top craftsmen – Herbert Minton for tiles, John Hardman of Birmingham for metalwork and stained glass, JD Crace for painted decoration, furniture and carpets – to produce some of his finest interiors.

Unfortunately, the castle went into steep decline after 1939, with most of the rooms locked up and unused: it was nearly demolished, but even that was too expensive an option. Fortunately, it has been completely restored in recent years, thanks to the efforts of the present owners, and now glows again with the rich colours of its Victorian heyday. It is a welcoming place to visit, with bedrooms that are still used for guests (often paying guests) contributing to the feel of a warm, lived-in house.

Gardens, grounds with lakeside walks (open as house), maze, children's play area, tearoom, shop.

Signposted on A438 Ledbury to Tewkesbury road, 3 miles east of Ledbury.

Hanbury Hall, Worcestershire

National Trust • £££ • Open Apr to Oct, M-W, S & Su

A handsome red-brick mansion of the William and Mary period, completed in 1701 and built for Thomas Vernon, a lawyer in the profitable Court of Chancery who amassed, by his own estimation, a fortune of some £112,000 in fees during 40 years of practice. By far its most notable feature is a superb set of wall-paintings on the staircase by Sir James Thornhill, completed in 1710.

For a long time only two rooms of the house were open, mainly so that visitors could see the murals, but a recent restoration, combined with the fortuitous reappearance of some of the original contents, has returned it to something like its state when built. It's still not quite as rounded an experience as some other houses, since Hanbury's chief role within the National Trust is to accommodate conferences, but there is enough of interest to make a visit worthwhile.

Particularly deserving of attention is the dining room, where the attractive ceiling paintings, again by Thornhill, betray the fact that the room has been enlarged by taking in a little entrance hall. On the fireplace wall hangs a portrait by Reynolds of Emma, only child and heir to Thomas Vernon II, whose mother forced her into a disastrous marriage to Henry Cecil, Earl of Exeter, in 1776: 23 years later she eloped with the local curate, William Sneyd.

The star of the show, however, is undoubtedly Thornhill's staircase. Such paintings were the height of fashion for self-respecting noblemen at the end of the 17th century, and the three leading exponents were Antonio Verrio, an Italian who had worked at the court of Louis XIV and brought the style to England, Louis Laguerre and Thornhill, whose most famous work is in the cupola at St Paul's Cathedral.

The classical scenes depicted in Thornhill's paintings are not without contemporary relevance. The figure of Mercury, falling from the ceiling, points to a portrait of Dr Sacheverell, a Tory clergyman prosecuted by the Whig government for preaching a sermon denouncing the war with France – a move that backfired when Sacheverell won popular support and the Queen eventually replaced her Whig ministers with Tories, making peace with France in 1713. As a Whig himself, Thomas Vernon must have seen Sacheverell as an evil influence, deserving of divine retribution.

Crown green bowling, gardens (both open as house), tearoom, shop.

Signposted on B4090 Droitwich to Alcester road, 5 miles east of Droitwich.

Hanbury Hall: a William and Mary house, finished in 1701, with superb murals by Sir James Thornhill

Lower Brockhampton, Hereford and Worcester

National Trust • ££ • Open Apr to Oct, W-F, S & Su

Surely the prettiest house in Britain, nestling in the rolling hills of one of England's least-discovered and most beautiful counties, in a sheltered valley where time almost seems to have stood still for 600 years, and surrounded by a moat where fish swim, ducks dabble and sky-blue damselflies dart.

It's also a rare and interesting example of the earliest type of English house, in which one very large room – the great hall – is of prime importance. In this one room the majority of the household ate, slept and passed whatever indoor leisure time they were lucky enough to have. A fire would have burned in a hearth in the centre of the floor, with a louvre above to let smoke out – the brick chimneys were added in the 1600s. A screens passage sheltered the hall from the doorway, with doors leading to the buttery and storerooms. Only the lord and his family had a private room – the great chamber or 'solar', on the first floor of the east wing – in which to take their ease and receive guests.

Lower Brockhampton was built at some time between 1380 and 1400 by John Domulton, who owned a great deal of land in the area. His descendants prospered but were never noteworthy, although one son of the family was cofferer to Queen Elizabeth and another was involved in the Gunpowder Plot. The valley was occupied in Saxon times and probably farmed long before (there are Roman forts nearby). Ideal for fruit trees, it was once one of the county's best apple-growing districts; in autumn, the trees by the house are heavy with damsons.

It doesn't take long to visit Lower Brockhampton, since there isn't that much of it to see: three small rooms, including a 17th-century parlour downstairs and a 'reconstructed' bedroom of the same era upstairs, and the great hall itself. But it is still a richly rewarding experience.

The thing to do here is to stand on the 'minstrels' gallery' – actually the remaining part of a floor inserted in the 1600s to provide upstairs bedrooms – and admire the skilful construction of the hall, all the work of local craftsmen. The great crucks – arches formed of two curved timbers – would collapse like a row of dominoes but for the beautiful 'cusped' windbraces.

Even rarer than the house is the tiny half-timbered gatehouse, said to have been built to celebrate a marriage in the 1480s, but probably 50 years more recent. It had to be rebuilt in 2000, and already the new cross-beams are sagging under the five-ton weight of the stone roof.

Estate walks in woodland and parkland (open all year), tearoom and shop, ruin of Norman chapel (next to the house).

Clearly signposted on A44 Leominster to Worcester road, 2 miles east of Bromyard.

Lower Brockhampton: its cottage-like looks conceal the size of the great hall (tucked away to the left of the picture, behind the lord's private 'solar block')

Packwood House: restored in the 1920s and 1930s in inauthentic fashion, but charming nonetheless

Packwood House, Warwickshire

National Trust • £££ • Open Mar to Oct, W-F, S & Su

Not the 16th- and 17th-century manor house it looks, but more a charming creation of the 1920s by a man named Graham Barton Ash. Ash was fascinated by old buildings (and by Shakespeare – he had plays performed in his garden every year and bought furniture that has links with the playwright), and 'restored' the ancient house in a manner he thought was authentic. He was unable to resist the temptation of adding a rather splendid new long gallery and great hall, both made up of timber and stonework recycled from other old buildings.

Ash's restorations never have the ring of authenticity, but the effect is of a comfy and welcoming home. And if it seems a little too tidy to conjure up the feel of a lived-in house, well, apparently it was no less ordered when Ash, a compulsive tidier, lived here.

One of the highlights is the yew garden, thought to have been planted in the 1660s, its conical trees grouped around a spiral mount.

Gardens known for herbaceous borders and yews (open as house), parkland walks (open all year), shop.

Signposted from A3400 Solihull to Stratford-upon-Avon road, on B4439 2 miles east of Hockley Heath.

Ragley Hall, Warwickshire

Privately owned (HHA) • £££
• Open Apr to Sep, Th-F, S & Su

It's good to see such a grand house still thriving as a family home, especially since Ragley – in common with so many large country houses – was used as a hospital during the Second World War and has had to be restored extensively since 1956.

Ragley, an early precursor of the Palladian style of architecture, was designed in 1680 by Robert Hooke, the scientist who gave his name to a law about the stretching of springs and invented an array of devices including the universal joint (used in motor cars) and the iris of a camera lens. As a city surveyor, Hooke had helped Sir Christopher Wren rebuild London after the Great Fire of 1666.

Peculiarly, though, its owners, the Hertfords, chose not to live at Ragley until the 1700s, when it was finally decorated and furnished. Spectacular interiors survive from that century, among them the great hall, with its effusive baroque plasterwork overseen by James Gibbs, who remodelled the house in the 1750s, and a series of rooms revamped in 1780 by James Wyatt, who also added the portico that gives the front of the house a more elegant appearance than the rear.

Wyatt's opulent red saloon and mauve rooms have not been touched since, and there is craftsmanship of the highest quality wherever you look, including woodcarvings by Grinling Gibbons in the library. Equally impressive is a modern addition, the striking *trompe l'oeil* mural on the south stair, painted by Graham Rust between 1969 and 1983.

Gardens, parkland, woodland walks, children's adventure playground and maze, carriage collection, tearooms, shop.

Signposted from the A435 and A422 Alcester to Worcester road 2 miles south-west of Alcester.

Ragley Hall: designed by the scientist Robert Hooke in 1680, before the great age of Palladian houses

Selly Manor, West Midlands

Local trust • ££ • Open all year, Tu-F, also Apr to Sep, S & Su

Not one but two ancient timber-framed buildings, both rescued from destruction in the early 1900s by the chocolate magnate George Cadbury, dismantled and moved from their original sites to be put up in the model village of Bournville, which the Cadburys built from 1895 to house their workers.

The smaller and older of the two is Minworth Greaves, a hall of about 1250 which would originally have had a typical open hearth in the centre. It was bought in 1911 and taken from its site just north of Birmingham, but not re-erected until the 1930s. The larger building, Selly Manor itself, came from about a mile away in 1912 and was opened as a museum in 1917. It is in three parts, the oldest of which dates from 1327 while the newest is Elizabethan. It has a typical medieval layout with a great hall, parlour and solar bedchamber; the kitchen is, most unusually, intact. Re-created Tudor-style gardens, with kitchen garden and orchard, surround the house.

Tudor-style gardens (open as house), shop.

Signposted off A4040 in Bournville, 4 miles south-west of Birmingham city centre.

Shugborough: an averagely grand house of the late 1700s, in a park with superbly grand follies

Shugborough, Staffordshire

National Trust and local council • £££ • Open Apr to Sep, Tu-F, S & Su

If Shugborough has a slight air of having fallen upon hard times, that's probably because it was so splendid in the first place. One of the greatest English country estates, it was the property of Thomas Anson, a man of more taste than wealth, whose younger brother, George, Admiral Lord Anson, secured the family fortunes in the 1740s with his pirated Spanish gold. From about 1750 Thomas was able to employ the architect Samuel Wyatt to remodel the house, fill it with fine paintings and porcelain commissioned from the likes of Reynolds and Wedgewood, and pepper the grounds with a wonderfully varied collection of follies designed by Thomas Wright of Durham and the great Greek revivalist James 'Athenian' Stuart.

Part of the house is still lived in by Thomas's descendant, the photographer Lord Lichfield, while the service quarters in the stable block have been restored and form the centrepiece of the Staffordshire County Museum.

Both the follies and the museum are vastly more entertaining than the house itself. The only truly impressive room is the immense red drawing room, completed by Wyatt in 1794, with a curving Adam-style ceiling by Joseph Rose the younger; the only really engaging room is the one in which objects and paintings associated with Admiral Lord Anson are displayed, including the largest surviving piece of HMS *Centurion*, the ship in which he sailed round the world in 1740–44 – one leg of its lion figurehead.

County museum, farm with rare breeds, gardens (all open as house), parkland with follies (open Apr to Oct, daily, Nov to mid-Dec, M-F & Su), tearoom, shop.

Signposted on A513 Stafford to Rugeley road, 6 miles east of Stafford.

Selly Manor: an attractive and interesting medieval timber-framed house, rebuilt here in 1911–16

Stokesay Castle, Shropshire

English Heritage • £££ • Open Apr to Oct daily, Nov to Mar W-F, S & Su

A most beautiful and fascinating fortified manor house of the late 1200s, which has survived remarkably unaltered thanks in part to its use as a farm for about 150 years, but also to the efforts of the Allcroft family, who bought it in 1869 and opened it to the public as early as 1908. Arguably the oldest intact and visitable house in Britain, it offers an extraordinary glimpse of the medieval way of life.

Standing close to the border between England and Wales, it dates from the first real period of peace in the area, following the conquest and subjugation of North Wales by Edward I between 1277 and 1284. Although parts of it are older, the majority of the manor house was built by a merchant named Lawrence of Ludlow, who bought the tenancy of the estate in 1281 for the price of a juvenile sparrowhawk. Lawrence's father, Nicholas, had made the family's fortune in the wool trade, often providing vast sums of silver to the Royal Mint; the son was even more successful, becoming the greatest wool merchant in England, at a time when wool was the nation's chief export.

Perhaps that was why Lawrence decided to build a country manor at a time when such places were the preserve of nobility and merchants almost always lived in towns. Although it looks castle-like – it was surrounded by a moat, now drained, and Lawrence took the trouble to obtain a licence to crenellate from Edward I in 1291 – Stokesay was in fact, by the standards of the time, a very grand and comfortable house.

At its centre is the great hall, in which life was lived communally by the majority of those who worked on the estate. It is a barn-like space, with a high cruck-beamed roof; no fireplace has ever been installed, and the original open hearth still sits in the middle of the floor.

To either side of the hall are private apartments of an unusual sophistication for the time. The apartment on the top floor of the north tower – this tower is perhaps half a century older than the rest of the castle – has the most wonderful windows in timber-framed additions that jut out over the tower's walls; there is also a very fine stone fireplace. On the first floor of the block on the south side of the hall is the solar, the lord's main living room, decorated with marvellously carved oak panelling of the early 1600s.

These three rooms alone make Stokesay worth visiting, but it is altogether a perfect place to soak up the atmosphere of the last 600 years. The guidebook has some excellent explanatory material, too.

Tearoom, shop.

Signposted on A49 Craven Arms to Ludlow road, 2 miles south of Craven Arms.

Stokesay Castle: a fortified manor house built in the late 1200s by Lawrence of Ludlow, the greatest wool merchant in Britain, and remarkably little altered

Sunnycroft, Shropshire

National Trust • £££ • Open Apr to Oct,
M & Su • Tours only

What makes Sunnycroft so
interesting is its very ordinariness.
There's no great art hanging on the
walls, no evidence of superb
craftsmen at work in its interiors.
Rather, it is a classic example of the
late Victorian suburban villa, with
modest pretensions to grandeur in
such details as its ornate but mass-
produced light fittings, originally
meant for gas and only converted
for electricity in 1947.

Built in 1880, extended in 1899
and lived in by three generations of
the same family until it was given to
the Trust in 1997, Sunnycroft is
unusual in that few houses of its
period and size have survived in
anything like their original state.
From the first room of the tour, the
billiard room, it is filled with echoes
of the restrictive, convention-bound
lives led by its Victorian occupants
– here the gentlemen would retire
after dinner, betting on a game of
pool with the help of the most
unusual scoreboard. The ladies,
meanwhile, repaired to the drawing
room overlooking the rose garden,
where vast quantities of embroidery
speak of gentler ways of whiling
away the hours.

Sunnycroft: pretensions to grandeur in a Victorian suburban villa, built in 1880 and extended in 1899

There is much evidence of the
house's former occupants, and many
intriguing details (the 'modesty light'
by the bedroom window; the unusual
fold-away grates in the upstairs
fireplaces). Don't expect grandeur,
but do expect a fascinating glimpse of
a past way of life.

Gardens (including conservatories,
pigsties, hen houses, orchards), stables,
coach-house and garage with vintage car.

Ten-minute walk, clearly signposted, from
the car park in Wrekin Road, Wellington.

Upton House, Warwickshire

National Trust • £££ • Open Apr to Oct,
M-W, S & Su

Not so much a house as an art
gallery in the countryside. Upton
was built in 1695 for the son of a
London merchant by the colourful
name of Sir Rushout Cullen, but had
been greatly modified over the
years. It was bought in 1927 by
Walter Samuel, second Viscount
Bearsted, the son of one of the
founders of the oil company Shell,
who spent the next two years
updating it as a comfortable family
home and a worthy showplace for
his considerable art collection.

Little remains of the original
interiors; instead, the architectural
highlight is Lady Bearsted's superb
Art Deco-flavoured bathroom, its
walls lined with aluminium foil. Her
ladyship's Chinese bedroom is also
being restored to its 1920s grandeur.

Worth seeing, certainly; but the
principal attraction is the superb art
collection, with beautiful works by
Holbein, Canaletto and many others,
and quantities of Sevres porcelain.

Extensive (but steep) gardens (including
kitchen garden and terraces with
mediterranean planting), shop, restaurant.

Signposted on A422 Stratford-upon-Avon
road, 7 miles north-west of Banbury.

Upton House: built in attractive, warm local stone in 1695 and greatly remodelled in the late 1920s

Wightwick Manor: beautiful imitation medieval timberwork, superb Arts and Crafts interiors

Wightwick Manor, West Midlands

National Trust • £££ • Open Mar to Dec, Tu & S, timed tickets, partial tours

It's hard to believe, when you wander round to the lawn at the rear and get a full view of the exterior, that this is actually a Victorian house. It looks like a genuine medieval half-timbered manor with a rather sensitive addition. In fact the 'newer' part – the bright-red brick apparently giving it away – is actually six years older.

Wightwick was built in 1887 for a wealthy Wolverhampton paint and varnish manufacturer, Theodore Mander, and his wife, Flora. Mander was a keen adherent of the Arts and Crafts movement, inspired by the ideas of John Ruskin and William Morris. He was also eager to include the latest technology and, having met Edison while on honeymoon in the United States, decided that his house would have electricity right from

the start – generated by an engine in a shed in the grounds – as well as central heating.

Mander employed the Cheshire architect Edward Ould, known for his half-timbered buildings and love of the medieval, then got him back again when his family started to fill the modestly sized house and he decided that some guest bedrooms would not go amiss. Ould went to town on the new extension, using timber for all the structural work (where the original had relied on brick) and adding details inspired by the North West's great medieval houses such as Little Moreton Hall in Cheshire and Speke Hall near Liverpool. The result is glorious, especially in the great parlour – a vast space like a medieval great hall, but laid out as a very cosy living room.

The Manders decorated and furnished their home in the Arts and Crafts style, with textiles and light fittings bought from William Morris's firm, stained

glass (and a superb Elizabethan-style frieze around the walls of the great parlour, featuring a very non-Elizabethan kangaroo) designed by the renowned Charles Kempe, ceramics by William De Morgan and paintings by a number of Pre-Raphaelite artists.

The acquisition of works by these artists and craftspeople has continued ever since, so that today the house is a living museum, the best place to see the furnishings and art of the period in context. Visiting arrangements are a little unusual, with a tour of the first few rooms and 'free-flow' access thereafter. The guidebook is worthwhile for the introduction by Anthea Mander Lahr, with its hints at a less than entirely warm and happy childhood in this now warm and cheery house.

Gardens (including fine rose garden), tearoom, pottery and shop.

Clearly signposted off A454 Bridgnorth road 3 miles west of Wolverhampton.

Witley Court, Worcestershire

English Heritage • ££ • Open Apr to Oct, daily, Nov to Mar, W-F, S & Su

The grandest of ruined houses, the remains of a spectacular Italianate villa rebuilt in the 1800s from an earlier house that had itself developed in several stages from a Jacobean original, with superb architecture by John Nash. It burned down in 1937 while the then owner, Sir Herbert Smith, a Kidderminster carpet manufacturer, was away.

The immense columned portico is outdone only by the graceful arches of the huge conservatory, which survived the fire but slowly decayed over the following 30 years as the estate failed to find a buyer. English Heritage is slowly restoring the parterre gardens to their former glory.

Sculpture park, grounds with lakeside and woodland walks, gardens with fountain and cascades, church, tearoom, shop.

Signposted on A443 Tenbury Wells to Worcester road, 2 miles south-east of Great Witley.

Witley Court, below: one of the most splendid houses of Victorian England, developed in Italianate style by John Nash in the early 1800s but burned down in 1937

See also…

The Ancient High House
Greengate Street, Stafford
Local council, free, open all year, M-F & S
Said to be the largest timber-framed town house in Britain, now a museum.

Benthall Hall
Broseley, Shropshire
National Trust, £££, open Apr to Sep, W & Su
Pleasant stone-built house of 1500s with classy garden.

Blakesley Hall
Yardley, Birmingham
Local council, free, open mid-Apr to Oct, Tu-F, S & Su
Timber-framed farmhouse of the late 1500s, recently restored with period furniture, displays explaining the customs of the times, exhibition of archeological finds. Also traces of Elizabethan wall paintings.

Broadway Tower
Broadway, Worcestershire
Privately owned, ££, open Apr to Oct daily, Nov to Mar, S & Su
Rather nice folly-like tower of the late 1790s on the Cotswold ridge, with exhibits on famous former occupants, including William Morris. Also animal park (separate charge).

Boscobel House
Boscobel, nr Albrighton, Shropshire
English Heritage, ££, Open Mar to Oct daily, Nov, W-F, S & Su, guided tours only
Jacobean hunting lodge used as hiding place for Catholic priests, where the future King Charles II hid from Parliamentary troops after the rout of his army at the Battle of Worcester on 3 September 1651. Original attics and hiding places.

The Commandery
Sidbury, Worcestershire
Local council, ££, open all year, daily
Complex of mainly timber-framed buildings of monastic origin that served as the Royalist HQ for the Battle of Worcester in 1651, with appropriate Civil War exhibits.

Croome Park
Severn Stoke, Worcestershire
National Trust, ££, open Apr to Oct, M, F, S & Su
Not a house, but Capability Brown's first complete landscape, with buildings largely by Robert Adam, currently being reconstructed.

Dudmaston
Quatt, nr Bridgnorth, Shropshire
National Trust, ££, open Apr to Sep, Tu-W & Su
House of late 1600s, still lived in.

Elgar Birthplace Museum
Lower Broadheath, Worcestershire
Privately owned by trust, £££, open Feb to Dec, daily
Country cottage where composer was born, with appropriate collections.

Farnborough Hall
Near Banbury, Warwickshire
National Trust, ££, open Apr to Sep, W, S
Stone-built house of mid-1700s with fine plasterwork, still lived in by Holbech family; grounds with temples, terrace walk, obelisk.

The Greyfriars, Worcester
Worcester
National Trust, ££, open Apr to Oct, W-F, S
Timber-framed house built in about 1480, next to a Franciscan friary. Panelled rooms, textiles, furniture, walled garden.

Harvington Hall
Near Kidderminster, Worcestershire
Privately owned (HHA), £££, open Apr to Sep, W & Su (also Mar and Oct, S & Su)
Red brick, moated Elizabethan manor house with earlier parts; some rooms have Elizabethan wall paintings.

Hellens
Much Marcle, Herefordshire
Privately owned (HHA), ££, open Easter to Sep, W, S, & Su, tours only
Fortified manor of 1292 on the site of a monastery, with Tudor, Stuart and Jacobean additions. Many old artefacts on display.

Honington Hall
Shipston-on-Stour, Warwickshire
Privately owned (HHA), ££, open Jun to Aug, W only, tours only
Tidy Carolinean mansion of 1680s in mellow brick with stone details, modified 1751, with excellent mid-Georgian plasterwork.

Langstone Court
Ross on Wye, Herefordshire
Privately owned, free, open mid-May to Aug, W & Th
House mostly of late 1600s but with older parts, fine plasterwork ceilings, wood panelling and staircases.

Boscobel House: a hunting lodge of the early 1600s, where the future Charles II hid in a tree in 1651

Little Malvern Court
Malvern, Worcestershire
Privately owned (HHA), £££, open mid-Apr to mid-Jul, W & Th
Former prior's hall of a Benedictine monastery with interesting oak-framed roof, forming part of Little Malvern church (also open).

Longner Hall
Uffington, Shrewsbury, Shropshire
Privately owned (HHA), £££, open Apr to Oct, Tu & Su, tours only
House of 1803 in Tudor gothic style by John Nash, park by Repton.

Lord Leycester Hospital
High Street, Warwick
Privately owned, ££, open all year, Tu-F, S & Su
Range of 1300s half-timbered buildings converted to almshouses in 1571, now homes for ex-servicemen. Guildhall, great hall, chapel and kitchen all still in use.

Mawley Hall
Cleobury Mortimer, Shropshire
Privately owned, open mid-Apr to mid-Jul, M, Th
Tall, elegant brick house of 1730 by Smith of Warwick, with magnificent plasterwork and extensive gardens.

Middleton Hall
Near Tamworth, Staffordshire
Privately owned, ££, open Apr to Sep, Su only
Hall of 1285 with various changes through to 1824, the former home of Tudor explorer Hugh Willoughby and 1600s naturalists Francis Willoughby and John Ray.

Moccas Court
Moccas, Herefordshire
Privately owned (HHA), ££, open Apr to Sep, Th only
House with 1700s Adam interiors and Capability Brown park.

Moseley Old Hall
Fordhouses, Staffordshire
National Trust, £££, open Apr to Oct, W, S & Sun, Nov and Dec, Su
Elizabethan house where Charles II stayed during his flight after the Battle of Worcester in 1651, with ugly Victorian remodelling.

Shipton Hall
Much Wenlock, Shropshire
Privately owned (HHA), £££, open Easter to Sep, Th
Pleasing Elizabethan house of about 1587, with Georgian additions.

Soho House
Handsworth, Birmingham
Local council, free, open mid-Apr to Oct, Tu-F, S & Su
Restored home of industrial pioneer Matthew Boulton from 1766 to 1809, with early hot-air heating system, period rooms, displays about Boulton and his inventions.

Stoneleigh Abbey
Kenilworth, Warwickshire
Privately owned, £££, open Easter to Oct, Tu, Th & Su, West Wing and stables only, tours only
House developed from medieval abbey, with medieval gatehouse, baroque West Wing, Regency stables.

Sufton Hall
Mordiford, Herefordshire
Privately owned (HHA), ££, open late May and mid-Aug, daily
Small Palladian mansion of 1788 by James Wyatt, set in park by Repton.

Wilderhope Manor
Longville, Shropshire
National Trust, ££, open Apr to Sep, W & Su, Oct to Mar, Su
Manor of 1586 used as youth hostel, with fine plaster ceilings.

Weston Park
Near Shifnal, Shropshire
Privately owned (HHA), £££, open May to Jun, S & Su, Jul to Aug, daily (except certain days in Aug)
Elegant red brick house of 1671 with many visitor attractions (pets' corner, deer park and miniature railway).

Whitmore Hall
Whitmore, Staffordshire
Privately owned (HHA), ££, open May to Aug, Tu-W
Elegant small Carolinian house incorporating earlier building, with rare Elizabethan stable block.

And...

Arbury Hall
Nuneaton, Warwickshire
Privately owned, ££, open Easter to Sep, Su & M of bank holidays only
Elizabethan and Tudor house gothicized in 1700s with fan vaults and filigree plaster. The novelist George Eliot was born on the estate.

Casterne Hall
Ilam, Staffordshire
Privately owned, ££, open Apr, M-F, tours only
Manor house in fine rural setting.

Chillington Hall
Codsall Wood, Staffordshire
Privately owned (HHA), £££, open Jul, Th & Su, Aug, W-F & Su, tours only
House of 1700s by Francis Smith of Warwick and John Soane, in park by Capability Brown.

Combermere Abbey
Whitchurch, Shropshire
Privately owned, ££, open only to groups by appt
Cistercian abbey remodelled as Gothic house in 1820.

Erasmus Darwin House
Lichfield, Staffordshire
Privately owned, £££, open all year, Th-F, S
Red brick Georgian home of the scientist, botanist, inventor and grandfather of Charles Darwin.

Ford Green Hall
Smallthorne, Staffordshire
Local council, ££, open all year, M-Th & Su
Home of the Ford family from the 1600s, now a museum with period furniture and artefacts, Tudor garden.

Hagley Hall
Hagley, Worcestershire
Privately owned (HHA), open Jan, Feb, Apr, May and Aug, certain days only, tours only
Elegant Palladian house of 1760 with fine Italian plasterwork (used mostly for conferences and events).

Hartlebury Castle
Near Kidderminster, Worcestershire
Privately owned, ££, open Feb to Nov, Tu-Th (museum also M, F, & Su)
Home of Bishops of Worcester, largely Georgian, with state rooms open. Also extensive local museum.

Madresfield Court
Malvern, Worcestershire
Privately owned, ££, open mid-Apr to Jul certain dates only, tours only
Elizabethan and Victorian house with medieval origins.

Morville Hall
Near Bridgnorth, Shropshire
National Trust, free, open by written appt only
Stone-built Elizabethan house modified in the 1700s.

Samuel Johnson Birthplace
Lichfield, Staffordshire
Local council, ££, open all year, daily
House where Johnson's father ran a bookshop, now a museum.

Sandon Hall
Sandon, Staffordshire
Privately owned, £££, open all year, daily, museum only, by appt only
Large neo-Jacobean house of Earls of Harrowby, built 1854, with family museum in some of the state rooms.

Walcot Hall
Lydbury North, Shropshire
Privately owned (HHA), ££, open two days in May and to groups by appt
The Georgian home of Lord Clive of India, remodelled in 1763.

Blakesley Hall: timber-framed farmhouse of the late 1500s swallowed up by Birmingham's suburbs

North West
Cheshire, Lancashire, Cumbria

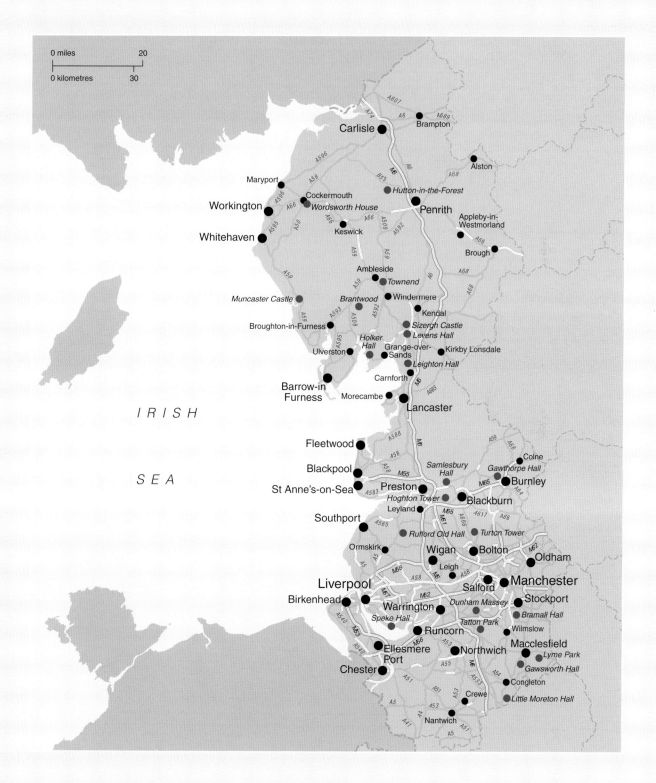

0 miles 20
0 kilometres 30

Carlisle
Brampton
Alston
Maryport
Hutton-in-the-Forest
Workington
Cockermouth
Wordsworth House
Penrith
Appleby-in-Westmorland
Whitehaven
Keswick
Brough
Ambleside
Townend
Muncaster Castle
Brantwood
Windermere
Kendal
Broughton-in-Furness
Sizergh Castle
Levens Hall
Holker Hall
Grange-over-Sands
Kirkby Lonsdale
Ulverston
Leighton Hall
Barrow-in Furness
Carnforth
Morecambe
Lancaster

IRISH

Fleetwood
Blackpool
Samlesbury Hall
Gawthorpe Hall
Colne
St Anne's-on-Sea
Preston
Burnley
SEA
Hoghton Tower
Blackburn
Leyland
Southport
Rufford Old Hall
Turton Tower
Ormskirk
Wigan
Bolton
Oldham
Leigh
Liverpool
Salford
Manchester
Birkenhead
Stockport
Warrington
Dunham Massey
Bramall Hall
Speke Hall
Tatton Park
Wilmslow
Runcorn
Macclesfield
Ellesmere Port
Northwich
Lyme Park
Gawsworth Hall
Chester
Congleton
Crewe
Little Moreton Hall
Nantwich

Bramhall Hall: superb Tudor timber-framed manor, the oldest parts dating back to as early as 1400, with barely distinguishable Victorian additions

Bramall Hall, Greater Manchester

Local council • £££ • Open Jan to Mar, S & Su, Apr to Sep, daily, Oct to Dec, Tu-F, S & Su

One of the finest of Cheshire's black-and-white half-timbered houses, much of it Tudor but with sympathetic Victorian additions. The oldest parts, at the centre of the house and in the south wing, were built between 1400 and 1450 (or in some cases possibly earlier); they include the great hall in the middle and the 'banqueting room' with solar above (the latter is now known as the 'ballroom').

This solar, now unfurnished, has the finest original features in the house: a gloriously carved oriel window overlooking the courtyard and faded but distinct wall-paintings of the early 1500s and early 1600s.

Other rooms mix original ceilings, fireplaces, panelling and furniture with Victorian copies in a rich blend that occasionally evokes the house's former occupants. Don't miss the sentimental-heroic paintings by the Victorian artist Schmalz.

Parkland with walks, shop, cafe.

Signposted on north side of Bramhall, near Stockport, off A5102 and A5143.

Brantwood, Cumbria

Privately owned • £££ • Open mid-Mar to mid-Nov daily, rest of year W-F, S & Su

The home of the artist-philosopher John Ruskin, one of the men whose ideas defined the Arts and Crafts movement, from 1872 until his death here in 1900. It has a beautiful setting, looking across a grassy field to Coniston Water, but it is undistinguished as a house, its interest lying in a few eccentricities – the little turret Ruskin had built on to his bedroom, with superb views of the lake and mountains – and in the furniture and paintings collected by the man himself.

The most original rooms are the dining room, designed by Ruskin, and his study, still looking much as it did in his day. A gallery room has a changing display of his paintings.

Extensive semi-wild gardens, estate walks, bookshop, craft shop, excellent cafe.

Signposted on minor road off B5285 north-east of Coniston village.

Brantwood: overlooking Coniston Water, the home of the artist John Ruskin from 1872 to 1900

Dunham Massey: not the most handsome of houses, but with a great deal to commend it nonetheless

Dunham Massey, Cheshire

National Trust • £££ • Open Apr to Oct, M-W, S & Su

Set in a beautiful park where deer wander up to the front door and with beautiful gardens beside it, this is a far from beautiful house – though full of interest. It's said to owe its utilitarian looks to the man who rebuilt it (from a Tudor and Jacobean original) in the 1730s, George Booth, 2nd Earl of Warrington, who was so affected by seeing his father weep 'from the greatness of his debts' that he devoted his life to practicalities, making a loveless marriage to secure his family's fortunes.

His grandson altered it again in 1789-90 in the hope of making the house look a little better, but it owes its current appearance to a wholesale restoration by the architect Joseph Compton Hall in 1905-8, when William Grey, 9th Earl of Stamford, inherited and brought the family back to Dunham. This makes the house an unusual mix of ancient and relatively modern, but Lord Stamford kept as much as he could of the old and set about buying back as much of the original contents – all sold off in the 1800s – as he could.

The result is a right old mixture of an interior in which an Edwardian saloon follows a late-17th-century (in style) great hall. Occasionally you trip over an astonishing object – such as the first known carving by Grinling Gibbons, a crucifixion scene, in the little upstairs library. Also a highlight are the kitchens and service rooms in a separate courtyard beside the house.

Superb plantsman's gardens (open Apr to Oct daily), deer park (open all year), Elizabethan water-powered sawmill (open as house), restaurant, shop.

Signposted off A556 and J7 of M56 near Bowden, south-west of Manchester.

Gawsworth Hall, Cheshire

Privately owned • ££ • Open mid-Apr to Sep, M-W & Su

A friendly little cottagey house, fundamentally a timber-framed Tudor manor but much altered over the years, including the demolition in about 1700 of most of the great hall and solar, which were about to fall down. Time has not stood still here, and it feels very much like a lived-in home – which it is. Visiting is rather like being invited in for a quick look round while the family is out shopping.

Wandering through the house, you make a haphazard series of discoveries – a piece of old timberwork here, a lovely fragment of Elizabethan plaster frieze there. Particularly pleasing are a number of Victorian Arts and Crafts and Gothic Revival items that chime nicely with the ancient setting, including bookcases designed by Pugin in the library and a superb set of four lights of stained glass by William Morris in the ambulatory beside the chapel.

There are some excellent stories, too, including a jester, a famous duel, the woman who may have been Shakespeare's Dark Lady and a mysterious skeleton found not in, but behind, a cupboard.

Small gardens and parkland walks, tearoom, open-air concerts.

Off the A536 Macclesfield to Congleton road 3 miles south of Macclesfield.

Gawsworth Hall: much Tudor work is still apparent, but the house has changed with the times, too

Gawthorpe Hall: Sir Charles Barry raised the tower and chimneys and added the openwork parapet

Gawthorpe Hall, Lancashire

National Trust and County Council
• £££ • Open Apr to Oct, Tu-Th, S & Su

The strikingly tall, vertical outline is enough to mark Gawthorpe out as the work of Robert Smythson, the great late-Elizabethan architect, designer of Hardwick Hall in Derbyshire and Wollaton Hall in Nottingham, though Smythson may have had little to do with it beyond sketching the front elevation. It's a typically bold and clever design, the central tower housing a stair and topped with a 'prospect room'. Only once inside do you realize that the hall is actually not nearly as large as it seems.

Gawthorpe is a combination of two things: a classic Jacobean house, with typical features such as elaborate plaster ceilings and a long gallery running the whole width of the second floor; and a further example of how comfortably the Victorian taste for the medieval sits with Elizabethan and Jacobean houses. Indeed, Gawthorpe was restored in 1850–2 by Sir Charles Barry, architect of the Houses of Parliament in London, with the aid of AWN Pugin and the decorator JD Crace. It is thought to be the only other building apart from Westminster on which Barry and Pugin worked together.

The hall was built between 1600 and 1605 by the Rev Lawrence Shuttleworth, whose family fortune had largely been made in the previous century by an ancestor who was a London lawyer and rose to become Chief Justice of Chester. Household account books survive for all but one of those years in which work on the house progressed, giving a detailed record of what happened when.

The basic structure was finished by June 1602, when the roof was laid and a piper was paid sixpence to help celebrate the 'Rearing day', but the work of the plasterers and joiners in fitting out the interior took until the end of 1605 and the house was not ready to be occupied – with beds, tables, benches and chests all made for it – until the end of 1606.

Barry's renovation involved keeping or repairing many of the original features, such as the glorious ceilings of the drawing room and long gallery, but he also had to destroy one whole room to make height for his entrance hall.

Several rooms on the first floor are used to display just a selection of items from the vast Rachel Kay-Shuttleworth collection of needlework, lace and costumes from around the world.

Gardens (open daily all year, free), shop and tearoom.

Signposted off A671 east of Padiham; watch carefully for turning to Hall.

Hoghton Tower, Lancashire

Privately owned • £££ • Open Jul to Sep, M-Th & Su, guided tours only

Looking dramatically castle-like as it perches, guarded by a wall and a battlemented gatehouse, on top of its hill at the end of a long, straight drive, Hoghton is actually an unusual variant on the Elizabethan fortified manor, sturdily built in 1560–5 in a squat, old-fashioned, no-frills style from local stone.

It's best known for two things: its links with William Shakespeare, who as a young man worked as a tutor here, and the knighting of Sir Loin of Beef by James I in 1617, when the king visited on his return from Scotland. That apart, it's dull.

The house is built as a rectangle of four wings around a courtyard. The tour visits first a series of largely Elizabethan bedrooms, then the Victorian ballroom, with its elegant pretend-Jacobean decoration, before descending the stairs to see the finest room of the house, the two-storey banqueting chamber. Visits end with a look at the Tudor well-house and the eerie basement tunnels that run under the house.

Doll's house collection, small gardens, tearoom, shop.

Signposted on A675 south-east of Hoghton, from J3 of M65 west of Blackburn.

Holker Hall: beautifully crafted Victorian work in the Elizabethan style, built following a fire in 1871

Holker Hall, Cumbria

Privately owned (HHA) • ££££ • Open Apr to Oct, M-F & Su

Of all the houses in Cumbria, this is the most developed as a tourist attraction, in the Beaulieu mould, with the Lakeland Motor Museum helping to draw the crowds. All the same it's an interesting house to look round, if expensive, with the highly regarded gardens adding an extra lure.

The house was rebuilt after a fire in 1871 in the grandest and most appealing Victorian look-back-to-the-past mode. It was described by the eminent architectural writer Pevsner as the 'outstanding work' of the Lancaster architects Paley and Austin, built from red sandstone 'in the Elizabethan style'. The design and craftsmanship throughout is of the highest quality (especially the 'Tudorbethan' chimneypiece in the dining room and the Jacobean-style staircase), the furnishing is comfortable and welcoming (the bedrooms are still used regularly) as well as grand, and the rooms feel light and airy.

There's no great art, but lots of fascinating and valuable objects, including an 18th-century rent table with a central well for the money and alphabetized drawers.

Motor museum (admission inclusive), gardens (open as house), shop, cafe.

Signposted on B5278, 5 miles west of Grange-over-Sands.

Hoghton Tower: a plain house of 1560–5 with four wings around a rectangular courtyard (through the arch)

Hutton-in-the-Forest, Cumbria

Privately owned (HHA) • £££ • Open mid-Apr to Sep, Th, F & Su, tours only (except Jul & Aug)

An attractive castle-like house consisting of four distinct parts: an early medieval 'pele tower'; a Jacobean wing containing a fine long gallery; a classically styled block of about 1680; and a Gothic tower designed in the 1830s by the prominent Victorian architect Anthony Salvin. The house is still lived in – by the Vane family, descendants of the man who employed the huntsman John Peel in the 1830s – and has a well-cared-for, welcoming atmosphere. The guided tour is a pleasure, too.

Inside, the different styles of the different periods are delightfully apparent, and this variety is the key to Hutton's appeal. The highlights include the long gallery – a rarity in the north of England, and a very graceful room – and the sensibly named big dining room at the base of Salvin's tower, a splendid piece of neo-gothic self-confidence softened a little by William Morris wallpaper and curtains.

Walled gardens and woodland walk with arboretum (open as house, also M-W), tearoom and shop.

Clearly signposted on B5305, 6 miles north-west of Penrith.

Hutton-in-the-Forest: an attractive blend of four elements, with Salvin's Victorian Gothic tower on the left

Leighton Hall, Lancashire

Privately owned (HHA) • £££ • Open May to Sep, Tu-F & Su, tours only

One of the most beautiful settings of any house in England, approached from a gently sloping road through parkland grazed by cows, with the Lake District fells providing a stunning backdrop. It's a quietly appealing little place, with a cosy, lived-in feel and plenty of amusing gothic details from its rebuilding in the early 1800s.

Leighton was bought in 1822 by Richard Gillow, grandson of the founder of the famous Lancaster furniture-makers, who spent the next three years rebuilding it in the gothic style, all pointy arches and delicate curves (seen at its best in the entrance hall). The house is still lived in by his descendants, and one of its most interesting features is the Gillow furniture.

Only a few rooms are shown, most pleasing of which are the interconnecting library and drawing room, both crumpled and comfortable and scattered with an intriguing collection of objects (including buttons inset with a lock of King James II's hair).

Gardens with maze, birds of prey (flown daily), tearoom.

Clearly signposted off A6 Carnforth to Kendal road, 3 miles north of Carnforth.

Leighton Hall: set against the superb backdrop of the Lake District fells, a small house remodelled by the Gillows in 1822–5, in the fashionable gothic style

Levens Hall, Cumbria

Privately owned (HHA) • £££ •
Open mid-Apr to mid-Oct, M-Th & Su

World famous for its gardens, and especially its lofty and exuberant yew topiary, Levens deserves to be just as well known as a historic house. It is fundamentally Elizabethan in character, although built around a fortified 'pele tower' of the late 1200s, and, perhaps because it is still lived in, has a warm and welcoming atmosphere.

This warmth is most evident in the bedrooms open to the public, still used as guest rooms, where such modern comforts as electric blankets and reading lamps coexist happily with Elizabethan fireplaces and handsomely carved panelling. Scattered around are dozens of interesting objects, such as the campaign bed used by the Duke of Wellington, ancient bowls (as in the lawn game) carved from the hard wood lignum vitae, iron grenades that once belonged to Bonnie Prince Charlie's army and, everywhere, lots of needlework, a particular interest of the family.

It's the downstairs rooms, however, that are particularly striking. Their Elizabethan layout and decoration is owed largely to James Bellingham, who inherited in about 1580 and set about turning Levens into a 'modern' home, in which the multi-purpose great hall was superseded by a separate dining room and drawing room.

The hall was still an important room, however, as the superb plasterwork attests. The frieze, created by Italian craftsmen, is filled with the coats of arms of the Bellingham family – now brightly painted, as they would have been originally, and outshone only by the Queen's arms, surrounded by delicate foliage, over the fireplace. Elsewhere on the frieze, naively depicted animals cavort gaily among trees.

The drawing room, with its Elizabethan plasterwork and panelling intact, is the highlight of the house – a large and airy room in spite of the heavy decoration. On display here are several of the treasures of Levens, including a cheerfully coloured portrait by Rubens of Anne of Hungary with her dog – he really wasn't very good at animals – and portraits by Sir Peter Lely of Colonel James Grahme, Privy Purse to King James II until his abdication in 1688, and his wife, Dorothy.

Colonel Grahme bought the house in 1688 from Alan Bellingham, apparently in settlement of Alan's gambling debts; a tradition holds that Levens was won on a turn of the ace of hearts, and indeed the lead downspouts on the front of the house are decorated with gilded hearts and James and Dorothy's initials.

Superb gardens with topiary garden of 1694 (open as house), steam engine collection with showman's engine (in steam Sundays), shop, tearoom.

Signposted on A6 Kendal to Lancaster road, 5 miles south of Kendal.

Levens Hall: started out as a 'pele tower' of the late 1200s, but developed in the 1580s into a pleasing Elizabethan house and retains many original features

Little Moreton Hall: the south wing, built in about 1570–80 and topped off by the lavishly glazed long gallery, which was probably added as an afterthought

Little Moreton Hall, Cheshire

National Trust • £££ • Open mid-Mar to Oct, W-F, S & Su (also Nov to late Dec, S & Su, free admission)

This exceptionally beautiful timber-framed manor house is in the top rank of Britain's historic buildings. Its particular charm lies not just in the liveliness of its timberwork – especially the crazy pattern of diagonal braces that covers the front – but also in the way it has been buckled and bowed over the years by the weight of the roof, a total of 200 tons of heavy gritstone tiles, and the lavishly glazed long gallery added as an afterthought at the top of the south wing.

The older parts, most notably the great hall, date from the 1480s, but the bulk of what you see today was built between 1559 and 1580 by William Moreton II and – after William's death in 1563, and in accordance with his will – by his son John. The Moretons were

wealthy landowners who profited from buying land cheaply after the Black Death struck in 1348 and at the dissolution of the monasteries from the 1530s onwards. Their income was largely from farming, but they also owned an iron mill and later a coal pit.

Clearly status was important to the Moretons – there is a record of a legal dispute between William's father, William I, and a neighbour over 'which of theym should sit highest in churche and foremost goe in procession' – and the display of prestige is a dominant theme in the rebuilding of Little Moreton that started in 1559 with the addition to the great hall and the neighbouring old parlour of two enormous bay windows (signed by 'Rychard Dale, carpeder'). Glass was still rare and hugely expensive; to use so much of it was a bold assertion of wealth.

Another change to the great hall, the insertion of an upper floor in the 1550s, is indicative of the way that an up-to-date house now ran. No longer was life lived communally in

the hall; instead there were private withdrawing and dining rooms for the lord, his family and guests. These rooms were richly decorated in a trendy Renaissance-influenced style, the most remarkable example of which is a superb set of wall-paintings in the parlour, their colours still glowing, found accidentally by an electrician in 1976.

There is no furniture in the house save one long table, one round table and a drawer-filled 'cubborde of boxes' (in which expensive spices were locked away), all of which have been here since at least 1601. The beauty of the house, however, is in the building itself. The highlight is the long gallery, where the wooden floor undulates like a rolling sea, but there is lots more of interest – not least the garderobe toilets overhanging the moat, with their original wooden seats.

Small, interesting gardens, tearoom, shop.

Signposted on A34 Congleton to Newcastle-under-Lyme road, 4 miles south-west of Congleton.

Lyme Park, Cheshire

National Trust and local council • £££
• Open Apr to Oct, M-Tu, F, S & Su

A frankly peculiar but frequently fascinating blend of styles and periods, with a dark, archaic and slightly crumbling feel that best suits the earlier parts of the house.

Lyme is essentially one of the grandest houses of the Elizabethan age, rebuilt in about 1570 from an earlier hunting lodge set in a park with a native herd of red deer. The estate was granted to the warlike Legh family by Richard II in 1398, in thanks for the deeds of an ancestor by marriage who had helped rescue the Black Prince at the Battle of Crecy in 1346.

The original house was built by Sir Piers Legh VII (all the heirs for hundreds of years were named either Piers or Peter), knighted in 1544 while taking part in Henry VIII's Scottish campaigns. But it was only finished by his grandson, Piers IX, in the early Jacobean period, and it was added to or remodelled many times after: in the 1660s and 1670s; in the 1720s and 1730s, when the Venetian architect Giacomo Leoni gave it a monumental classical facelift; and in the early 1800s, when it was restored and updated by Robert Wyatt.

The exterior, then, still features the Elizabethan frontispiece, a tall, charmingly naive concoction of classical elements from about 1570, under which visitors pass into Leoni's courtyard, which is thoroughly and austerely classical. A grand flight of steps leads up to the vast Palladian entrance hall, created by Leoni in what was the Elizabethan great hall, its lack of symmetry disguised by the cunning use of columns. A fascinating feature is a pair of hinged picture frames that fold back to cover openings into other rooms. Look for the portrait from 1591 of Peter Legh IX, builder of most of the older part of the hall.

The next few rooms are Lyme's finest: first the Jacobean drawing room, with superb strapwork plaster ceiling, arcaded panelling inlaid with holly and bog-oak, and immense chimneypiece bearing the arms of Queen Elizabeth; then the intriguing stag parlour, apparently just as old but in fact rebuilt in the early 1800s – in this room the local Jacobites met from the 1690s through to 1745.

There's a pleasing contrast in the dining room that follows, designed by Wyatt with Palladian proportions but using masses of carved woodwork to give a late-1600s feel. Equally impressive is the saloon, with a rococo ceiling embellished by Wyatt and limewood carvings by Grinling Gibbons. The rest of the house continues the jumble of styles, with some real eccentricities – a vastly oversized stone fireplace jammed haphazardly on top of the sagging wooden floor of the knight's bedroom – as well as some real successes (the glorious Jacobean long gallery). There is a notable collection of clocks in an exhibition room at the end.

Two hunting lodges (The Cage, open Apr to Oct, 2nd and 4th weekend of each month; Paddock Cottage, open 1st and 3rd weekend), extensive gardens (open as house, but also W & Th, and Nov to late-Dec, S & Su), parkland (open all year), restaurant, tearoom, shop.

Clearly signposted on A6 Stockport to Buxton road near Disley.

Lyme Park: a grand Elizabethan and Jacobean house, rebuilt in serious neoclassical style by the Venetian architect Giacomo Leoni in the 1730s

Muncaster Castle, Cumbria

Privately owned • £££ • Open early Mar to Oct, M-F, Su

A welcoming Victorian family home, developed from a defensive 'pele tower' of the 1300s but owing its present appearance mostly to the efforts of the architect Anthony Salvin in the 1820s. Muncaster has been owned by the Penningtons since 1208; in 1464 Sir John Pennington gave shelter to King Henry VI after the Battle of Hexham, and a beautiful glass drinking bowl in the great hall is said to have been left by the king, with the promise that as long as it remained whole, the Penningtons would live here. It still is; their descendants still do.

The only spectacular room is Salvin's octagonal galleried library, but it's a friendly house with enough of interest to make a visit well worthwhile, especially with the lovely gardens – and the owls!

Owl centre (birds flown daily), extensive gardens, woodland walks, tearoom, shop.

Clearly signposted on A595 Whitehaven to Barrow road, just south of Ravenglass.

Muncaster Castle: one old tower plus a beautifully balanced bit of Victorian gothickry by Anthony Salvin

Rufford Old Hall, Lancashire

National Trust • £££ • Open Apr to Oct, M-W, S & Su

There is a single room at Rufford that far outstrips the rest: it is the great hall of the original timber-framed manor, built in about 1530–50 by Sir Robert Hesketh, an illegitimate son who had managed to claim his wealthy family's estates and so had good reason to make a statement. It's a wonderful room, the beams of its lofty open roof decorated with carved angels (they may have come from a dismantled monastery), separated from the entrance by a unique movable screen with grotesquely carved finials. In this very hall a young Shakespeare may have performed; Sir Robert's son, Sir Thomas, kept a company of players which Will is said to have joined in 1581.

The rest of the house is just a bonus, then, but there is a good deal of interest here too. It consists of a brick wing of the 1660s and a small block of about 1724, the whole refurbished and extended in 1820–25. Its interiors have a cosy Victorian feel – especially in the drawing room, where the table is laid for tea – and are piled high with interesting items, including two Genoese cabinets (one is of the late 1600s) carved with tiny figures, and a beautiful set of watercolours of flowering plants painted in 1880–1904 by Ellen Stevens, an amateur botanist from Southampton. Don't miss, either, the manic clock in the study: it must tick four times a second.

Small but pleasant gardens, tearoom, shop.

Clearly signposted on A59 Preston to Skelmersdale road, in Rufford.

Rufford Old Hall: the 1662 wing on the left, and a glimpse of the 1724 block; the great hall is to its right

Samlesbury Hall, Lancashire

Privately owned • ££ • Open all year, Tu-F, Su

A somewhat odd visiting experience, since Samlesbury is preserved by a trust that saved it from demolition in the 1920s, but is made to earn its keep by acting as an antiques centre. It's a pretty timber-framed building, the oldest parts built in about 1325; three unfurnished rooms are simply open to wander through, while the rest is crammed with furniture and bric-a-brac and secondhand books.

The downstairs rooms are the parlour, converted in 1530 and with an Elizabethan feel; the great hall, with a minstrels' gallery added when the place was used as an inn in the early 1800s; and a chapel built on in 1420, with a rather splendid medieval gothic window said to have been taken from Whalley Abbey in 1530.

Tearoom, antiques and craft shops.

Signposted on A59 Preston to Clitheroe road, 4 miles north-west of Blackburn.

Samlesbury Hall: the older wing, glimpsed to the right, was built in about 1325, the rest added in 1420

Sizergh Castle, Cumbria

National Trust • £££ • Open Apr to Oct, M-Th & Su

The fascinating gardens and grounds and the wonderful setting on the edge of a slice of that rarest of upland habitats, limestone country, are in themselves a recipe for a good day out, but there is a good deal of interest inside the castle too.

Essentially it is a genuine medieval castle of about 1310–60, with wings added in the 1550s and a rebuilt central domestic range of 1773–4; but most of its interiors have a romanticized Victorian feel, created when the place was remodelled in the late 1890s by the colonial diplomat Sir Gerald Strickland. Sir Gerald rescued Sizergh by taking ownership from his debt-ridden cousin, Walter, who had already sold off many of its treasures.

The old tower – far larger than the usual pele tower found in Cumbria and the border counties – is structurally more or less as it was when it was built. On its second floor (originally the 'solar chamber', the private sleeping apartment of the lord and his family) are the castle's most remarkable rooms: first the 'banqueting hall', a theatrical Victorian use of the huge medieval space, and then the Elizabethan 'inlaid chamber', fitted out in the late 1570s and early 1580s with a superb ceiling and the beautiful inlaid panelling that gives the room its name. This panelling was sold to the V&A museum by Walter in 1891, along with the bed and stained glass, but was returned here in 1999.

Gardens and grounds (open as house), estate walks, tearoom, shop.

Clearly signposted off A591 Kendal to Grange road, 4 miles south of Kendal.

Sizergh Castle: the old tower, built in 1310–60 and structurally little altered since, is seen on the left

Speke Hall: one of the North West's two most splendid half-timbered manors, built from 1530 to 1600

Speke Hall, Merseyside

National Trust • £££ • Open Apr to Oct, W-F, S & Su, Nov to early Dec, S & Su

The second of the North West's two outstanding half-timbered manors (the other is Little Moreton Hall, above), Speke grew up in stages over the course of about 70 years, finally reaching its present shape not long after 1598, the date inscribed over the entrance in the north range.

The hall consists of four ranges grouped around a courtyard in which two ancient yew trees stand. There are traces of a cruck-beamed hall of the 1300s in the south-east corner, but really the oldest parts are the great hall in the south range, built (according to tree-ring dating of the timbers) in 1530, and the parlour next door, from 1531. Then the rest of the west range was added on to the parlour, and finally the north and east ranges were added by Edward Norris, who had inherited his father's considerable estates in 1568 and continued the building work his father had begun.

The fortunes of the unrepentantly Roman Catholic Norris family declined after William Norris IV, who inherited in 1606, was fined by the Star Chamber for striking a Protestant magistrate who had been checking up on his attendance at church. Thereafter little changed at Speke until its sale in 1795, in a greatly dilapidated state, to a local merchant, Richard Watt, who had made his fortune in the West Indies.

A partial restoration followed, but the interiors owe most of their present appearance to a major remodelling in the Arts and Crafts style in the 1850s. Not long after, in 1867, it was let to the 36-year-old manager of the Bibby shipping line, Frederick Leyland, the son of a Liverpool pie-shop owner who had worked his way up from the humble position of clerk. He ended up owning his own shipping line and gathering a considerable collection of Old Master paintings.

Leyland made his own changes to the interiors in an antiquarian style and some rooms, as a result, have an almost cottagey feel, with a scattering of interesting furniture. Far and away the finest of the interiors, however, is the great parlour, which retains its original ornate plaster ceiling of about 1612, in the foliage of which several birds are hidden, and the amazing carved overmantel of about 1567, on which carved figures show the story of the Norris family up to Edward Norris's time, including a prostrate, naked figure that seems to represent his brother, William III, killed at the Battle of Pinkie in 1547.

Gardens, woodland walks, restaurant, shop.

Clearly signposted on A561 Runcorn road, 5 miles east of Liverpool town centre.

Tatton Park, Cheshire

*National Trust and local council • £££ •
Open Apr to Sep, Tu-F, S & Su*

A very gracious-looking house in
the neo-classical style, begun in
1780 by Samuel Wyatt and
completed after his death in 1807
by his nephew, Lewis William
Wyatt, for the Tatton estate's owner,
William Egerton.

The interiors are almost stupidly
opulent in a garish, Victorian-tinged
manner, disguising the simple
elegance of the spaces created by
the two Wyatts. The house feels like
a museum, and is interesting more
for its outstanding collection of
Gillow furniture (over 200 pieces
commissioned especially for the
house) and its paintings than for its
own merits. Really it is little more
than a bonus in a visit to the estate
as a whole, which includes the
lovely brick-encased, timber-framed
Tudor Old Hall and the still-
working estate farm as well as the
superb gardens and the extensive
parkland (complete with two
different types of deer).

*Tudor Old Hall (open Apr to Sep, S & Su),
working farm (open as house, also in
winter, S & Su), extensive gardens (open
all year, Tu-F, S & Su), parkland (open
Apr to Sep daily, in winter Tu-F, S & Su),
children's play area, restaurant, shop.*

*Signposted on A5034 Knutsford to
Bowdon road, 4 miles north of Knutsford.*

Townend: a Cumbrian gentleman farmer's residence of the early 1600s, steeped in period atmosphere

Townend, Cumbria

*National Trust • ££ • Open Apr to Oct,
Tu-F & Su*

A gentleman farmer's residence of
the 1600s, notable not just because it
is built in the local style (or, as
architects put it, 'vernacular'), but
also because it is steeped in the
atmosphere of the period from the
moment you step through the door
into the kitchen – built in 1623–6,
although with a cast-iron range
replacing the original hearth.

The central hall is older than the
rest of the house, dating from the late
1500s. It still has the long oak table
of the 1600s at which the household
– family, servants and farmhands –

gathered for meals, so big that it was
almost certainly made in situ. It's just
one example of the oak furniture for
which Townend is noted.

The house was built, or extended,
by George Browne, whose marriage
in 1623 to Susannah Rawlinson of
Grizedale Hall not only brought him
up in the world but also gave him
money to spend. The property
remained in the family until 1943.
Don't miss the 'state' or guest
bedroom, where the bed, cradle and
linen chest are all inscribed with the
initials of the younger George and
his wife, Ellinor.

*Signposted on minor road off A591
Keswick road and A592 Penrith road,
3 miles north of Windermere.*

Tatton Park: the immense neo-classical mansion begun by Samuel Wyatt in 1780 was scaled down after the architect's death and completed by his nephew

Turton Tower, Lancashire

Local council • ££ • Open Mar to Oct, M-W, S & Su (also Apr to Sep, Th), Feb and Nov, Su

An odd but engaging little house, developed in haphazard fashion around a defensive 'pele tower' of about 1420 with the addition of two cruck-framed service wings on the north in the early 1500s, then three timber-framed pieces in the corner between the tower and the wings in about 1596. In 1835 it was bought and restored by the Kay family, keen antiquarians, who added a few flourishes of their own.

Its interest lies mainly in the glimpses of architectural details from all the various periods: the garderobe toilet tucked in at the back of the old tower, the beams of the cruck-framed wing, the 'mock Elizabethan' bedroom suite of the 1800s at the top of the house. Best of the furnished rooms are the dining room in the base of the tower and the lovely morning room, both Victorian recreations. A room in the top of the tower is used for art and craft exhibitions.

Small garden, tearoom, shop.

Signposted on B6391, off A666 Blackburn to Bolton road, 6 miles north of Bolton.

Wordsworth House: the poet's childhood home is an elegant Georgian townhouse remodelled in 1745

Wordsworth House, Cumbria

National Trust • £££ • Open Apr to Sep, M-F (also Jun to Aug, S)

The house in which the Lakeland poet William Wordsworth was born in 1770 is actually more interesting in its own right, as the Georgian townhouse of a well-to-do gentleman, which its complete restoration in 2004 should enhance.

The house was built in about 1690 and remodelled in 1745 for Joshua Lacock, High Sheriff of Cumberland, who sold it not long afterwards to Sir James Lowther. In 1766, Sir James installed the land agent who managed his estates, John Wordsworth, in the house, apparently allowing him to live here rent-free as part of his salary.

A few items of furniture that belonged to William, including a bookcase and the piano from his home at Rydal Mount, are scattered around the place, but really sit somewhat uncomfortably, since he never lived here as an adult. Far more appealing is the sense of the place as his childhood home, and a rather comfortable and elegant one at that; most of the decoration is unchanged.

Riverside gardens, tearoom, shop.

Signposted in Cockermouth town centre, off A66 and A595.

Turton Tower: the pele tower of about 1420 had large windows added in the restoration of 1835

See also...

Abbot Hall
Kendal, Cumbria
Privately owned, ££, open mid-Feb to late Dec, M-F & S
Elegant Georgian house of rusticated stone, used as art gallery with works by Romney, Ruskin and Turner.

Adlington Hall
Macclesfield, Cheshire
Privately owned (HHA), £££, open Jun to Aug, W only
Half-timbered manor house with great hall of 1480 to 1505 and elegant red brick additions of 1749–57, in Capability Brown landscaped park.

Arley Hall
Northwich, Cheshire
Privately owned (HHA), £££, open Easter to Sep, Tu & Su
Smart brick-built Tudor home in rather good grounds.

Astley Hall
Chorley, Lancashire
Local council, ££, open Easter to Oct, Tu-F, S & Su, Nov to Easter S & Su
Extraordinary looking house with huge windows, built in 1578 and modified in 1660s and 1825, now used as an art gallery.

Blackwell
Bowness on Windermere, Cumbria
Privately owned, £££, open mid-Feb to Dec, daily
Elegant Arts and Crafts house by Mackay Hugh Baillie Scott, finished in 1900, with unusual stained glass windows. Exhibitions of Arts and Crafts art and design.

Browsholme Hall
Clitheroe, Lancashire
Privately owned (HHA), £££, open early Jul and end Aug, Tu-F, S & Su
House of 1507 with collections of oak furniture and antiquities.

Capesthorne Hall
Macclesfield, Cheshire
Privately owned (HHA), £££, open Apr to Oct, W & Su
Elegant Jacobean-style hall built 1719–32 and remodelled by Salvin following a fire. Interesting grounds.

Dalemain
Penrith, Cumbria
Privately owned, £££, open Apr to mid-Oct, M-Th & Su
Impressive Georgian facade on top of medieval and Tudor manor.

Dorfold Hall
Acton, Nantwich, Cheshire
Privately owned (HHA), £££, open Apr to Oct, Tu only
Jacobean country house built 1616, still a family home.

20 Forthlin Road, Allerton
Liverpool
National Trust, ££, open Apr to Oct, W-F, S, also Nov and Dec, S, by tour from Speke Hall or Albert Dock only
A 1950s terrace house, the childhood home of Paul McCartney.

Hall i' th' Wood
Bolton, Lancashire
Local council, ££, open Apr to Oct, W-F, S & Su
Late medieval manor house with 1600s and 1700s furniture.

Hilltop
Near Sawrey, Ambleside, Cumbria
National Trust, £££, open Apr to Oct, M-W & Su
Small house of the 1600s in which Beatrix Potter lived and worked.

Mirehouse
Keswick, Cumbria
Privately owned (HHA), ££, open Apr to Oct, W & Su
'Solid, unpretentious' house of the 1600s set beside Bassenthwaite Lake, with Georgian interiors, literary links.

Peover Hall
Over Peover, Knutsford, Cheshire
Privately owned (HHA), ££, open Apr to Oct, M, tours only; stables and gardens also open Th
Elizabethan house of 1585 with fine Carolinean stables.

Rode Hall
Scholar Green, Cheshire
Privately owned (HHA), £££, open Apr to Sep, W only
Red brick house completed 1752, with later alterations, in Repton landscaped park, with fine gardens.

Rydal Mount
Ambleside, Cumbria
Privately owned (HHA), £££, open Mar to Oct, daily, Nov to Feb, M, W-F, S & Su
Small stone house where William Wordsworth lived with sister Dorothy from 1813 to his death in 1850.

Smithills Hall Museum
Bolton, Lancashire
Privately owned, ££, open Apr to Sep, Tu-F, S & Su
Manor house of 1300s with excellent Tudor panelling.

Tabley House
Knutsford, Cheshire
Privately owned, £££, open Apr to Oct, Th-F, S & Sun
Large Palladian mansion with the earliest known collection of English paintings in the state rooms.

Warton Old Rectory
Warton, Carnforth, Lancs
English Heritage, free, open any reasonable time
Rare medieval stone house with hall, chambers and 'domestic offices'.

And...

Derwent Island House
Derwentwater, Cumbria
National Trust, ££, open May to Sep, one day each month, tickets must be booked in advance
Italianate house of 1840s set on an island in the lake, but privately let and only parts open to visitors.

Martholme
Great Harwood, Lancashire
Privately owned, ££, open only to groups by appt
Part of medieval manor house with 1600s additions, Elizabethan gatehouse.

Towneley Hall
Burnley, Lancashire
Local council, free, open all year, M-F & Su
House of 1300s with later additions, used as art gallery, museum of local crafts and industry and natural history centre, with aquarium in the grounds.

Yorkshire

including Humberside

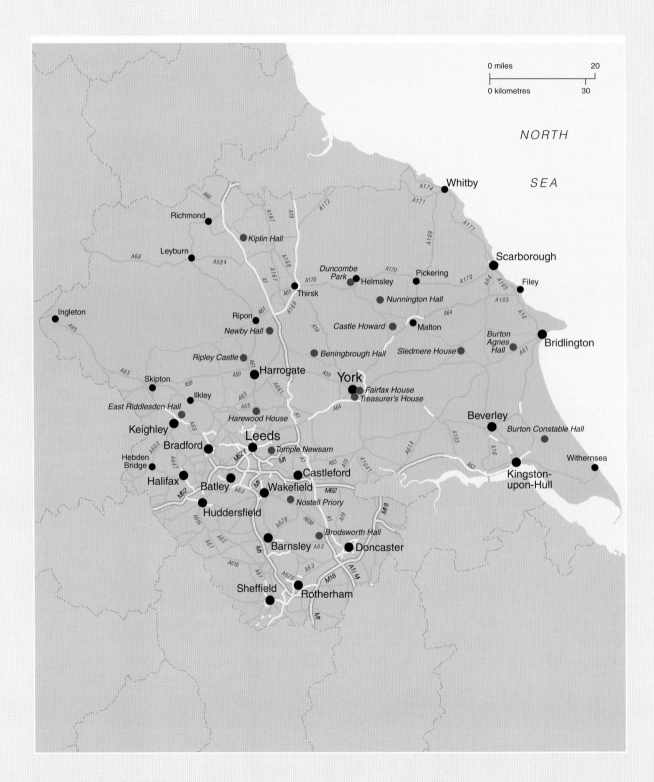

0 miles 20
0 kilometres 30

NORTH

SEA

Whitby

Richmond

Kiplin Hall

Leyburn

Scarborough

Duncombe
Park

Pickering

Filey

Helmsley

Thirsk

Nunnington Hall

Ripon

Newby Hall

Castle Howard

Malton

Burton
Agnes
Hall

Bridlington

Ripley Castle

Beningbrough Hall

Sledmere House

Harrogate

Skipton

York

Ilkley

Fairfax House

East Riddlesden Hall

Treasurer's House

Harewood House

Beverley

Keighley

Burton Constable Hall

Bradford

Leeds

Temple Newsam

Withernsea

Hebden
Bridge

Castleford

Kingston-
upon-Hull

Halifax

Batley

Wakefield

Huddersfield

Nostell Priory

Brodsworth Hall

Barnsley

Doncaster

Sheffield

Rotherham

172

Beningbrough Hall, North Yorkshire

National Trust • £££ • Open Apr to Oct, M-W, S & Su (also F in Jul and Aug)

Now more of an art gallery than a house, displaying pictures from the National Portrait Gallery in London. Beningbrough was long thought to have been designed by Sir John Vanbrugh and is a classic example of the baroque style – a plain, powerful shape, with lots of ornamentation.

It was completed in 1716 for John Bourchier, who had inherited the family estates in 1700, at the age of 16, and made a good marriage to a wealthy heiress, which enabled him to pull down an Elizabethan house and build anew, using ideas picked up on the Grand Tour.

The portraits are mostly from the period 1688 to 1760 and sit well in the context of the house. Some are displayed in themed exhibitions in the attic, but many are in the main rooms of the house downstairs, which are sparsely furnished but offer a wealth of extravagant baroque woodcarving and plaster. The house has an interesting layout, with a series of interior vistas provided by corridors and aligned doorways.

Extensive gardens and grounds (open as house), shop, restaurant.

Signposted on minor road from A19 York to Thirsk road, 8 miles north-west of York.

Beningbrough Hall: built in 1716, typically baroque in its simple shape, and now really an art gallery

Brodsworth Hall, South Yorkshire

English Heritage • £££ • Open Apr to Oct, Tu-F, S & Su

In theory, the interesting thing about Brodsworth, a fairly plain house built in the Italianate style in the 1860s, is that the decision has been made not to restore it, but to conserve it as it was was when its last owner, Sylvia Grant-Dalton, died in 1988. In practice, the interiors seem no more tattered and torn than many houses that are still lived in, and the approach is certainly not as appealing as that other well-known experiment in 'preserving it in all its faded glory', the National Trust's Calke Abbey in Derbyshire.

In particular, the upstairs is a little disappointing, with several rooms given over to museum-style exhibits and too few furnished bedrooms to give a real idea of a functioning house of the age. But the idea of keeping it in its existing state comes into its own in the bedroom she used, where the struggle to keep such a large house in repair is all too obvious. Equally evocative is a downstairs room once used by the builder of the house, Charles Sabine Augustus Thelusson, for his hobby of wood-turning.

These intimate touches apart, the main appeal lies in the grandly furnished reception rooms on the ground floor, redolent of the haphazardly opulent tastes of a very wealthy Victorian. Marble sculptures – most of them contemporary, Italian and a little sentimental – are scattered among imitation-marble (scagliola) pillars against backdrops of faded crimson silk and velvet.

Extensive formal gardens (open as house, also S & Su in rest of year), shop, tearoom.

Signposted from A635 Doncaster to Barnsley road, on B6422, 5 miles north-west of Doncaster.

Brodsworth Hall: a Victorian italianate villa, its interiors have changed little since the day it was built

Burton Agnes: this superb Elizabethan manor by Sir Robert Smythson is still a family home

Burton Agnes Hall, East Yorkshire

Privately owned (HHA) • £££ •
Open Apr to Oct, daily

The red brick Elizabethan manor is the most satisfying kind of English house, and this is one of the finest. It is also a thoroughly pleasant place: still a family home, and a welcoming place for families to visit, it has a satisfying blend of original features and later – even very modern – furnishing and artworks. There are some good Impressionist paintings (no major works, but some very enjoyable ones) as well as new artworks commissioned by the present owners. But above all, it is the original features that are truly striking.

Burton Agnes has an impeccable pedigree: it was built between 1601 and 1610 by Sir Robert Smythson, master mason to Queen Elizabeth I. It still has its original matching gatehouse (most such gatehouses were pulled down in later years, since their defensive qualities were scarcely needed even when they were built). The entrance front is handsomely symmetrical, with the front door tucked in at the side of one of the bays so that the balance is not disturbed. The entrance bay is decorated in carved stone, with three layers of columns representing the 'orders' of classical architecture, framing the arms of Sir Henry Griffiths, who built the mansion, and his wife, Elizabeth Throckmorton, with the royal arms above in deference to Queen Elizabeth.

Inside, a medieval-style screens passage gives access to the great hall, covered with extraordinary Elizabethan plasterwork and carvings in stone and wood – it's almost like a series of picture-books from which to tell stories. The Wise and Foolish Virgins above the fireplace are particularly entertaining, with nude figures frolicking happily above.

Next door in the red drawing-room there is more remarkable Elizabethan carving above the fireplace, but this time on the macabre theme of the Dance of Death. The ornate carved panelling is also Elizabethan, and is most unusual in being brightly painted and gilded – as it doubtless would have been. Other welcoming rooms follow, with some very pretty paintings, before visitors climb the grand staircase (again the original Elizabethan work) to the upstairs drawing room, which has an elegant 18th-century feel. A series of bedrooms follows, the highlight being the remarkable plaster ceiling of the Queen's state bedroom, in a honeysuckle design with stems looping out of the surface of the ceiling. The room is said to be haunted by the ghost of Anne, the youngest of Sir Henry's three daughters, whose head is buried inside the walls of the house.

At the top of the house is a beautiful long gallery, restored in the 1970s and again with a fine plaster ceiling. The room is used to display many of the house's most interesting works of art, and some of the most beautiful porcelain in the house is kept up here, too.

Award-winning gardens, with children's maze and games (open as house), shop, restaurant.

Signposted on A614 York to Bridlington road, 5 miles south-west of Bridlington.

Burton Constable Hall, East Yorkshire

Privately owned (HHA) • £££ • Open Easter to Oct, M-Th, S & Su

The imposing Elizabethan facade that looks so impressive as you drive up to the house belies an interior that has been greatly messed about with over the years. Despite the best efforts of the family who owned the house from the 1560s right up until 1992, and those of the charitable foundation that has taken over since, the inside of the house, though grand in scale, can seem musty and forlorn. It has a Victorian feel – often dark and grotesque, occasionally fascinatingly so. In parts a good dose of restoration would not go amiss.

The tone is set in the entrance hall, the original great hall, a vast room that would have been the heart of the Elizabethan house. Remodelled in the 1760s, with plasterwork that is powerful but not pleasing, it has the feel of a little-used public building rather than a home.

The finest three rooms are next. The dining room – also remodelled in the 1760s, and by the same architect, Timothy Lightoler – is entered through a disguised door, with a similar door diagonally opposite leading to the servants' passage and the kitchens. The neoclassical plasterwork on the theme of Bacchus, the Roman god of wine, is a little brutal, but the room has a graceful feel.

Beyond is the staircase hall, a spacious and airy room painted a cheery shade of yellow and with a striking cantilevered stair (again of the 1760s and by Lightoler). Comfortable sofas by the fire make this the only room in the house that is truly welcoming. Up the stairs is the long gallery of the late 1500s, very impressive, but without its original decoration: the Jacobean-style plasterwork frieze, with its amusing animals, is of the 1830s.

Next door are rooms containing the house's most unusual objects: a collection of scientific instruments and gadgetry, fascinating in a slightly grotesque way. Much of it was gathered by William Constable, the man responsible for remodelling the house in the 1700s. Among the collection is his electricity-making machine from the 1750s.

Next comes a series of bedrooms, liberally splashed with heavy, ugly Victorian furnishings, then the chapel, and finally there are several drawing rooms, garishly decorated and with no real sense of identity, although one has a fine collection of Chippendale furniture restored to its original bright colours.

Garden with orangery of the 1780s, parkland walks, shop, tearoom.

Clearly signposted on B1238, 7 miles north-east of Hull.

Burton Constable: behind the handsome Elizabethan facade is a peculiar mixture of later alterations

Burton Agnes Manor

English Heritage • Free • Open Apr to Oct, daily

Not much to look at, but certainly worth popping into if you're already visiting Burton Agnes Hall (above), this is a much-altered Norman dwelling, remarkable for its rarity and the fact that it survives at all. It stands just to one side of the Elizabethan building, looking extremely modest and plain by comparison. The outside of the old manor was encased in brick in the 1600s, so it hardly looks ancient, but as soon as you enter the vaulted undercroft – reminiscent of a church or abbey – its age becomes more apparent.

The narrow spiral stair leading to the upper floors is still intact and in use, and although the upper floors are much altered and are unfurnished except for a table, enough traces of the original layout remain to give an impression of how it might have been in its heyday as the hall of a local lord.

Directions as Burton Agnes Hall, above.

Burton Agnes Manor (left): a very rare surviving example of a Norman hall-house

Castle Howard, North Yorkshire

Privately owned (HHA) • £££ • Open mid-Feb to Oct, daily

Seen from one side, at least, this is one of the most splendid houses ever built, designed by Sir John Vanbrugh in 1699 for his friend Charles Howard, 3rd Earl of Carlisle. But the story is far more complex, for Vanbrugh's house was never completed.

After Carlisle's death in 1738, his heir, working with his architect brother-in-law, Sir Thomas Robinson, decided to finish the house in the newly fashionable Palladian style – a choice the 4th Earl came to regret. Not until 1801–11 was the decoration of the new wing finally finished, and even then there were further changes in the 1870s to try to make new match old a little better. Then a disastrous fire in November 1940 left the house a gutted, roofless shell. In all, it is extraordinary that Castle Howard survives.

There are two places where this bizarre history hardly matters: the south front, which, despite a slight lack of symmetry, looks much as Vanbrugh intended; and inside, where most of the work to restore the ground-floor state rooms is now done. Not all trace of the fire has been tidied away. In by far the most striking of Vanbrugh's rooms, the great hall – a church-like space 70ft high surrounded by soaring columns and topped by the central dome – there are great dents and scrapes in the marble floor, caused by collapsing debris, and the smoke and water damage to the painted decoration created by the Venetian artist Giovanni Pellegrini in 1709–1712 has been left unrestored.

If there is a sense of anti-climax in some of the rooms that follow, it is probably because they are not on the same epic scale. But there is consolation in the sumptuous decoration, beautiful furniture and porcelain and excellent paintings, including the very famous Holbein portrait of Henry VIII.

One room of Robinson's wing does impress: the long gallery, with a dome-topped octagon at its centre. The broad, long oak floorboards were once ship's decking, acquired from the navy in the early 1800s on the condition that they must be returned if the Napoleonic wars meant they were needed.

Formal gardens and rose garden, park with lake, fountains, woodland walks (open as house, but also most days in winter), restaurant, shops, superb follies on surrounding estate.

Signposted from A64 Malton to York road near Coneysthorpe, 4 miles west of Malton.

Duncombe Park, North Yorkshire

Privately owned (HHA) • £££ • Open late Apr to Oct, M-Th & Su, guided tours only

Set in acres of parkland where the ancient trees provide an important wildlife habitat, is another house that is fortunate to have survived, having been lovingly restored quite recently after years of use as a girls' school.

Its imposing exterior is still largely as designed by William Wakefield in about 1713 for an heir of the impossibly wealthy London banker

Castle Howard: the south front is still one of the most thrilling exteriors in Britain, even though Vanbrugh's original design of 1699 was never completed

Duncombe Park: the garden front, an unusual blend of baroque and Palladian elements

Sir Charles Duncombe. Wakefield may have had the help of Vanbrugh, who was working on Castle Howard at the time. The house is fundamentally baroque in style but, unusually, with a Palladian influence both inside and out: this is seen in the garden front, with its temple-like portico, and in the layout of the two principal rooms, the vast entrance hall and the saloon beyond.

A fire in 1879 gutted the main block and rebuilding was slow, so for the most part the interiors have a French-influenced Edwardian feel. This makes the tour, which visits six downstairs rooms and two bedrooms, a little disappointing, the promise of the astonishing entrance hall – soaring Corinthian pillars and baroque plasterwork – never quite fulfilled. But there are certainly compensations, not the least being that this is now a lived-in house again and new furniture and decoration sits comfortably alongside the old. The guidebook is essential, Lord Feversham's witty commentary bringing the house alive.

Terraced landscaped gardens of the 1740s and 1750s, parkland walks (open as house), tearoom, shop.

Signposted off A170 Helmsley to Thirsk road on west side of Helmsley.

East Riddlesden Hall, West Yorkshire

National Trust • ££ • Open Apr to Oct, Tu-W, S & Su (also M in Jul and Aug)

This squat, purposeful-looking house of dark local stone dates mostly from the 1640s, although to the right is the facade of a now-demolished wing of the 1690s, which incorporates earlier work, and between the two is a former great hall of the 1500s. Its shallow pointy gables, large mullioned windows and projecting porch are typical of houses in this area from this period – tentatively fancy touches on a largely practical building – but the rose window in the porch is an unusual flourish.

East Riddlesden was built by James Murgatroyd, the son of a local family who had made their fortune in milling and weaving, for his son, John. It spent most of its life as the centre of a farming estate – two barns survive, one now modernized, but the other in its original 17th-century state, with a beautiful oak roof – and this is reflected in the interiors, which have been considerably altered over the years, but are now furnished to give a good impression of the simple lives of a slightly-wealthier-than-average farming family in the mid-1600s.

The alterations mean that the original uses of many of the rooms isn't even certain. There are some good surviving decorative features, including especially fine ceilings and plasterwork friezes, but in the end it's the contents of the house that are its most engaging feature.

Only one piece of furniture was still in the house when it was given to the National Trust in 1934: it is a 'grain ark', a massive oak chest for storing wheat or oatmeal through the winter, keeping it dry and out of the reach of mice. It's just one of many objects that give a pleasing insight into the daily life of the period: tables covered with carpets, 'curfew' guards to keep the fires safe but lit overnight, all kinds of crockery and cutlery, strange cooking implements, drug jars for such odd preparations as oil of foxes or oil of scorpions – and much more besides.

A particular feature is a collection of embroidery from the late 1600s through to the late 1700s illustrative of the changing styles and materials. There are interesting later objects, too, including an unusual jug and several teapots made from a pewter-like alloy of tin, antimony and copper known as Britannia metal, popularized by a Sheffield manufacturer in the early 1800s.

Gardens and grounds (open as house), barn, tearoom, shop.

Signposted on B6265, off A650 Keighley to Bradford road just east of Keighley.

East Riddlesden Hall: a largely no-nonsense design of the 1640s, typical of the period and the area

Fairfax House, York

Privately owned • £££ • Open mid-Feb to early Jan, M-Th, S & Su (also F for guided tours only)

Restored by the York Civic Trust in 1984, Fairfax House is, by some margin, the most interesting example of a Georgian town house open to the public in Britain. Not only is it a splendid building in the first place – built from red brick in about 1740–45; possibly remodelled and certainly redecorated by the great architect John Carr of York in the early 1760s – but it is also furnished and equipped in loving detail with outstanding pieces of appropriate age, thanks in no small part to the lucky coincidence that one of the finest collections of Georgian furniture in private hands had just become available following the death of the philanthropist and chocolate manufacturer Noel Terry.

What's so good about it is that so many of the rooms are restored and furnished to reflect their original function – including bedrooms, which even in the most interesting of stately homes are seldom in anything like their original state. Even the kitchen has been lovingly recreated,

Kiplin Hall: built in about 1620 by Sir George Calvert, the founder of the American colony of Maryland

although not in the basement but in what was probably the rear parlour. Best of all is the dining room, where the table is laid with splendid silver, the forks turned prongs down so as not to catch in the gentlemen's ruffed cuffs.

The house was bought in 1759 by Viscount Fairfax, a Catholic nobleman from Gilling, some 20 miles from York. He was an educated man with an interest in architecture, and the interiors Carr created for him feature superb neoclassical plasterwork with a rococo tinge and woodwork of the highest quality.

Shop.

Signposted for pedestrians on Castlegate, York city centre.

Fairfax House (left): a glorious Georgian town house, remodelled by John Carr of York in about 1760–62

Kiplin Hall, North Yorkshire

Privately owned • £££ • Open May and Sep, Tu & Su, Jun to Aug, M-W & Su

A somewhat plain Jacobean manor built in red brick, retaining parts of its original layout – notably the long gallery running through the middle of the house, from front to back, on the first floor – but with extensive Victorian modifications. It is still lived in and has been restored as the Victorian mansion it ultimately became.

Kiplin was built in about 1620 by George Calvert, 1st Lord Baltimore, son of a local landowning Catholic family, who trained as a lawyer and went on to become Secretary of State to James I and eventually, in 1634, under Charles I, to found the colony of Maryland in America. The house was remodelled several times, ending in a vast expansion in gothic style in the early 1800s by Lord and Lady Tyrconnel and a gentle remodelling in about 1890.

The Victorian interiors are in a comfortable, pleasant gothic style, but nothing special.

Formal gardens, tearoom, shop.

On B6271 Northallerton to Scorton road, 6 miles north-west of Northallerton.

Harewood House: the south front was given a new Italianate look in the 1840s by Sir Charles Barry

Harewood House, West Yorkshire

Privately owned • £££ • Open Apr to Oct, daily (also S & Su in Nov and early Dec)

To describe Harewood as another masterpiece by John Carr of York (the house) and Robert Adam (the interiors) is not far off the mark, but is not quite the whole story. Built between 1759 and 1772 for Edwin Lascelles, the son of a prominent local family whose existing wealth was augmented by income from sugar plantations in Barbados, the house was remodelled in the 1840s for Henry, 3rd Earl of Harewood, and his wife, Louisa, who wanted more space for their 13 children and for entertaining.

The new work was done by Sir Charles Barry, who made the house's appearance less graceful and more monumental by adding an extra storey and redesigning the south front in a palatial Italianate style, with formal terraced gardens completing the picture (these have just recently been restored).

Some of Adam's interiors were destroyed in the process, but a gradual process of restoration that began in the 1930s has brought back much of the original scheme. Adam worked with his usual 'dream team' of top-class artists and craftspeople, so there are painted walls and ceilings by Angelica Kaufmann, Antonio Zucchi and Biagio Rebecca, plasterwork by Joseph Rose and William Collins, and furniture by local boy Thomas Chippendale. Lancelot 'Capability' Brown was employed to landscape the park between 1772 and 1781.

The quality of their work is matched by that of the collections acquired by the Earls of Harewood in the intervening years. Edwin's eldest son, Edward, was a patron of the arts and a friend of JMW Turner, and he laid the foundations of the English watercolour collections that occupy two rooms of the house, with views of Harewood painted by Turner and works by Girtin and Varley, among others. He also started the porcelain collections, and displays of Sevres and Crown Derby are now a prominent feature of Harewood.

The acquisition of artworks is still important today (as evidenced by the extraordinary Epstein statue in the entrance hall), which seems appropriate in a house that is eager to have a future as well as a past. And although it is one of the more tourist-attraction-like houses, well, at least it does it with a certain style and grace.

Terrace gardens, parkland with lakeside and woodland walks (open as house), old kitchens in basement of house, gallery, bird garden, restaurant, shop.

Clearly signposted on A61 Harrogate to Leeds road, 7 miles north of Leeds.

Newby Hall: to the left, Etty's main block of the 1690s; to the right, Robert Adam's sculpture gallery

Newby Hall, North Yorkshire

Privately owned (HHA) • £££ • Open Apr to Sep, Tu-F, S & Su

Wonderful gardens and excellent visitor facilities make Newby a good place for a family day out, and it's also one of the most entertaining houses to visit, the somewhat sober red brick baroque exterior of the 1690s belying a flamboyant interior remodelled by Robert Adam in the 1760s, with a couple of typically over-the-top Victorian additions.

The hall was built for Sir Edward Blackett, a local bigwig who had bought the estate in 1689, by John Etty, an assistant to Sir Christopher Wren, and is one of only a few Wren-influenced houses to survive. The main block has not changed much since, but new wings were added and many other alterations were made in the 1760s by William Weddell, whose family had bought the estate in 1748, and who made the house what it is today.

Weddell was a man of wealth and taste who made the Grand Tour in 1765–6, gathering an impressive collection of antique classical statues and commissioning a set of Gobelin tapestries, both of which he wanted to show off to full effect. He employed John Carr to build the new wings and Robert Adam to design the interiors, the most stunning of which is the statue gallery, opening onto the garden and with a beautiful top-lit rotunda at its centre. Weddell's statues are still here (most are of dubious provenance, but they are beautiful enough for it not to matter), standing serenely against Adam's arches and niches and delicately coloured plasterwork. It's one of his finest rooms.

Not all is still as Weddell left it. His heir – his cousin, Lord Grantham – changed Adam's dining room into a library and built a new dining room on the opposite side of the house, while the great-great-grandfather of the present owner added an ugly new wing to provide that great late-Victorian necessity, a billiard room. It might seem out of place among the elegant Georgian rooms, but it's still highly amusing, with a weighty baronial feel and lots of odd sporting gadgetry lying around.

The rest of the house offers a blend of superb Adam details and fine Chippendale furniture, nicely garnished with the occasional thoroughly eccentric collection – a wall-sized cabinet filled with chamber pots, for instance, or a bedroom decorated with nude engravings discovered in an attic. Don't miss the circular room, where the domed ceiling – painted with delicate classical scenes – gives a really odd acoustic effect.

Superb gardens (open as house) with children's adventure garden and miniature railway, restaurant, shop.

Clearly signposted on minor road from B6265 Ripon to Boroughbridge road, 2 miles south-east of Ripon.

Nostell Priory, West Yorkshire

National Trust • £££ • Open Apr to Oct, W-F, S & Su

An imposing house in a plain, massive Palladian style, lacking the grace and lightness of the Italian designs by which it was influenced. The interior is far more interesting, if not necessarily more welcoming, than the exterior. Sometimes a little dark and dingy, it has a largely unrestored feel despite several major restorations (one following a fire in 1980 that destroyed the breakfast room) and a complex history that makes it something of an essay in the different styles of different periods.

The house was built from 1735 for Sir Rowland Winn, 4th Baronet of Nostell, by James Paine, who worked at the house for most of the next 30 years. When Sir Rowland's son inherited in 1765, he brought in Robert Adam to finish the interiors. Adam also wanted to remodel the outside, adding four elegant pavilions at the corners and removing the ugly chimneys, but only one of his pavilions was built, to act as the family wing. Work stopped in 1785, on the death of the 5th Baronet, and some rooms were not decorated until 30 years later.

The result is an odd mixture, with some of Paine's rococo interiors surviving, often touched up by Adam; and much of Adam's work still in place, but alongside alterations made by Thomas Ward for Charles Winn, the nephew of the 6th baronet, who inherited from his uncle in 1817. The finest of Paine's rooms is the state dining room, with ceilings and mouldings in a florid and lively rococo style celebrating the abundance of nature and the worship of Bacchus.

Adam called in many of his usual collaborators, including the plasterer Joseph Rose and the painter Antonio Zucchi, and as is always the way in a house Adam has worked on, the highlights are the superb ceilings. However, probably the most striking contribution to survive is that of Thomas Chippendale, who created furniture especially for the house. Chippendale's influence is strongest in the state dressing room and state bedroom, where his green and gilt japanned chinoiserie furniture is matched by the hand-painted Chinese wallpaper he supplied.

Besides Chippendale's furniture and some excellent paintings, there are several objects of outstanding interest to be seen at Nostell Priory. One is the longcase clock with a wooden movement, made in 1717 by John Harrison, the son of the estate carpenter, who found fame as the creator of a clock accurate enough to measure longitude; another is the extraordinary doll's house made in about 1735 for the Winn family, with its original furniture, decoration and figures.

Grounds with lakeside walks, gardens (open as house, also in winter, S & Su), tearoom, shop.

Signposted on A638 Wakefield to Doncaster road, 5 miles south-east of Wakefield.

Nostell Priory: the exterior is too massive and plain to be pleasing, but the jumbled interiors have outstanding work by Robert Adam and Thomas Chippendale

Nunnington Hall: a picturesque manor of the early 1600s, restored and remodelled in the 1920s

Nunnington Hall, North Yorkshire

National Trust • £££ • Open Apr to Oct, M-W, S & Su (also Aug, Tu)

A pretty little stone-built manor of the 1600s, in a picturesque rural setting beside the little River Rye. Many of the rooms still have original features, retained during a sensitive remodelling in the 1920s by York architect Walter Brierley, who made Nunnington into a comfortable country house for Margaret Fife, a daughter of the Rutson family who had owned the estate since 1839, and her husband Colonel Ronald D'Arcy, a soldier and big-game hunter who had served in India and South Africa. His trophies line the walls of the entrance hall.

It's by no means a large house, and the highlights are mostly the surviving details from the 1680s. They include an unusual heraldic painted ceiling in a little closet off what was originally the main 'state' bedroom on the ground floor, and the rather wonderful wood panelling and ornamentation in the oak hall, thought to be the work of the master carpenter and architect John Etty. Equally pleasing are the panelled bedrooms, with intact woodwork from the 1630s.

An extra lure for visitors is a collection of scale models, on display in the attics, of rooms from various periods of English architecture, all decorated with miniature furniture and *objets d'art*, commissioned and collected from 1939 to 1970 by a London lady named Mrs Carlisle.

Pleasant walled gardens (open as house), tearooms, shop.

Signposted on minor road off B1257 Helmsley to Malton road, 5 miles south-east of Helmsley.

Ripley Castle, North Yorkshire

Privately owned (HHA) • £££ • Open all year, Tu, Th, S & Su (also Jun and Aug, daily)

Ripley has been the home of the Ingilby family since roughly the early 1300s, but the oldest part of the castle is the old tower, which dates from 1548–55. It's far from stately but it's very much a home, and its long and colourful history makes it a fascinating place to tour, if you forgive its eccentricities.

The more house-like parts of the castle date mainly from the 1780s, when Sir John Ripley found that the old fortified manor was too dilapidated to last much longer. They involve a pleasant set of drawing and dining rooms grouped around an entrance hall, but the decoration and furnishings are competent rather than thrilling and, although there are some interesting family stories along the way, the tour only really comes alive in the old tower.

Best of all are the tower's two upper rooms, dripping with Tudor plaster and panelling and scattered with evocative ancient objects.

Walled gardens, park with lakeside and woodland walks, tearoom, shop.

In Ripley, off A61 Harrogate to Ripon road, 4 miles north of Harrogate.

Ripley Castle: a fortified manor of the 1500s and earlier, remodelled as a comfortable house in the 1780s

Sledmere House: rebuilt after a disastrous fire in 1911, but retaining much of its 18th-century elan

Sledmere House, North Yorkshire

Privately owned (HHA) • £££ • Open May to Sep, Tu-F & Su

One of the most charming houses in Britain, Sledmere is a successful blend of work from three different periods: it was built in the 1750s, extended and remodelled in the 1780s and then rebuilt from scratch at around the time of the First World War, following a fire in 1911 that gutted the interiors and left it as nothing more than a shell.

The original house was the work of Richard Sykes, son of a wealthy merchant family from Leeds. He came into the estate through his wife, Mary Kirkby, who inherited when her brother died in 1748. Far more of an influence on the character of the house at the time of the fire, however, was Sykes's nephew, Christopher, whose father inherited the estate in 1761 and passed it on in 1776, seven years before his death. No doubt this early transfer of title was down to his recognition of Christopher's exceptional ability, since the young man had already proven himself by

introducing exemplary new agricultural practices to the estate, turning it from 'a bleak and barren tract of country' into 'one of the most productive and best cultivated districts in the County of York' (so says his memorial inscription, set up in 1840 at the village well). There's a splendid portrait of Sir Christopher and his wife in the dining room, along with Romney's polite letter asking for payment.

Sir Christopher engaged Capability Brown to landscape the park, then designed his own house, consulting both John Carr and Samuel Wyatt. Work started in the early 1780s, but in 1789 Sir Christopher met Joseph Rose, Robert Adam's plasterer, and the two men became firm friends. From then on, the design of most of the interiors – not just the ceilings – was entrusted to Rose.

The result was a series of elegant Adam-style rooms that were more or less unchanged until they were utterly destroyed in the 1911 fire. Fortunately, the then owner, the soldier, diplomat and orientalist Sir Mark Sykes, decided to employ

the York architect Walter Brierley to reconstruct much of the house as accurately as possible. They were even able to use the original moulds to reproduce Rose's plasterwork.

Brierley also had a free hand to make the restored house more comfortable, however, and added touches of his own more robust and less Adam-like classicism.

Put simply, the result is a house that just works. It's both a proper family home, with modern gadgets such as phones and fax machines sitting on desks, and a grand piece of architecture. Much of the furniture, saved from the fire, has been in the house since the 1780s. There are many highlights, including Rose's plasterwork in the music room and drawing room and the superb view of Capability Brown's park through the door in the south front, but the *piece de resistance* is the glorious gallery on the first floor, again with outstanding views of the park.

Chapel, church, walled gardens, parkland, restaurant, shop.

Clearly signposted on B1252 Malton to Driffield road, 7 miles south-east of Malton.

Temple Newsam: vast and splendid Jacobean mansion built in 1622–8 by wealthy businessman Sir Arthur Ingram, with interiors of many subsequent periods

Temple Newsam, Leeds

Local council • Free • Open Feb to Dec, Tu-F, S & Su

A vast, elegant Jacobean mansion in a classical, symmetrical style, based on an earlier house built in about 1500 by Thomas, Lord Darcy, a courtier, mercenary and ally of Cardinal Wolsey, who was beheaded in 1537 after taking part in the Pilgrimage of Grace. His estate was forfeited to the Crown and given by Henry VIII to his niece, the Countess of Lennox, whose sons Henry, Lord Darnley, the husband of Mary, Queen of Scots, and Lord Charles Stuart were born and brought up here – which inevitably led to the house being forfeited to Elizabeth I.

In 1622, the neglected estate was bought by the wealthy businessman and courtier Sir Arthur Ingram, who demolished three sides of the Tudor house and built two new wings, completing the new mansion in 1628.

The house retains a good deal of its Jacobean layout and feel, with the great hall still the most important room, but has been altered, updated and redecorated numerous times since. Its many rooms have a wealth of decoration in the styles of numerous periods, including some splendid rococo plasterwork of about 1740 and elegant fireplaces by William Kent in the long gallery.

Extensive parkland and gardens (open all year, daily), home farm with rare breeds (open as house), tearoom, shop.

Signposted on A63 Leeds to Garforth road, 4 miles east of Leeds.

Treasurer's House, York: built in the early 1600s, remodelled in Arts and Crafts style in 1897–1903

Treasurer's House, York

National Trust • £££ • Open Apr to Oct, M-Th, S & Su

A peculiar but friendly little house, fundamentally of the early 1600s but remodelled in 1897–1900 by Frank Green, the wealthy bachelor grandson of a Wakefield industrialist, who wanted an appropriate place in which to display his collections of art and furniture. One of the things that makes it so interesting is that Green's personality pervades the house, from the individual style of some of the rooms – he created a medieval-style great hall – to the notices specifying how servants and visitors to the house should behave ('All workmen are requested to wear slippers').

It's a warren of a place, with rooms in a variety of styles, but linked by the warm, Arts and Crafts feel and the subtle use of coloured paint. There's an array of excellent furniture, including not one but two splendid tester beds of about 1740, which came from Houghton Hall in Norfolk.

Small gardens, gallery, tearoom, shop.

Signposted for pedestrians in Minster Yard, York city centre.

See also...

Bolton Castle
Leyburn, North Yorkshire
Privately owned (HHA), £££, open all year, daily
Square courtyard castle of 1399 that has remained in use as a home, with many interesting original details.

Brockfield Hall
Warthill, near York
Privately owned (HHA), £££, open Aug, Tu-F, S & Su
Late Georgian house designed by Peter Atkinson, whose father was an assistant to John Carr of York, with cantilevered stair in oval hall. Features a most unusual collection – of walking sticks.

Fountains Hall
Ripon, North Yorkshire
National Trust, £££ (with admission to Fountains Abbey), open Feb to Oct, daily, Nov to Jan, M-Th, S & Su
Stone-built Elizabethan manor, but only two rooms are open. The real attractions here are the wonderful ruined abbey and nearby Studley Royal church and water gardens.

Lotherton Hall
Garforth, near Leeds
Local council, ££, open all year, Tu-F, S & Su
Handsome Victorian and Edwardian mansion built from dark stone in Georgian style, with interesting interiors and displays of 1800s and 1900s costume and decorative arts.

Norton Conyers
Ripon, North Yorkshire
Privately owned (HHA), £££, open mid-May to Sep, Su, also early Jul, daily
Manor of the late 1400s, updated in the early 1600s with Dutch gables, said to have inspired Thornfield Hall in Charlotte Bronte's *Jane Eyre*.

Scampston Hall
Malton, North Yorkshire
Privately owned (HHA), £££, open late May to early Jun, late Jul to early Aug, M-F & Su
House of 1600s remodelled in 1801, with fine Regency interiors.

Sion Hill Hall
Kirby Wiske, North Yorkshire
Privately owned (HHA), £££, open Jun to Aug, W only
Edwardian country house by local 'school of Lutyens' architect, Brierley. Also falconry centre.

Stockeld Park
Wetherby, West Yorkshire
Privately owned (HHA), £££, open mid-Apr to mid-Oct, Th, tours only
Stone Palladian villa completed in 1763, with fine cantilevered staircase.

Sutton Park
Sutton-on-the-Forest, York
Privately owned (HHA), £££, open May to Sep, W & Su
Georgian house with landscaped parkland, with 1700s furniture collection including items from Buckingham House (before it became Buckingham Palace).

And...

Aske Hall
Richmond, North Yorkshire
Privately owned, £££, open all year, only to groups by appt
Georgian house of 1763 with earlier pele tower, interiors in fascinating range of styles, Capability Brown landscaped grounds with follies.

Bramham Park
Wetherby, West Yorkshire
Privately owned (HHA), £££, open only to groups by appt

Elegant villa of 1700s, but the main attraction is the gardens (*open Apr to Sep, daily*).

Braithwaite Hall
Leyburn, North Yorkshire
National Trust, £, open only by arrangement with tenant
Remote stone farmhouse of 1600s.

Broughton Hall
Skipton, North Yorkshire
Privately owned, £££, open all year, only to groups by appt
Built in 1597, but extensively remodelled in very grand classical style in the 1700s and 1800s.

Hovingham Hall
Near York
Privately owned, £££, open Jun, M-F, S
Palladian house of about 1760 with oldest cricket ground in England.

Longley Old Hall
Huddersfield, West Yorkshire
Privately owned, £££, open Apr, May, Aug and Dec, on one S & Su only
Timber-framed manor of 1300s.

Maister House
Hull, E Yorks
National Trust, £, open all year, M-F
Merchant's residence of 1743, but only entrance hall and stairs open.

Moulton Hall
Richmond, North Yorkshire
National Trust, £, open only by arrangement with tenant
Stone manor of 1650.

Bolton Castle: wonderful castle of 1399, built to a square plan around a courtyard, partially ruined

Dunham Massey, Cheshire

North East

Tyne and Wear, County Durham, Northumberland

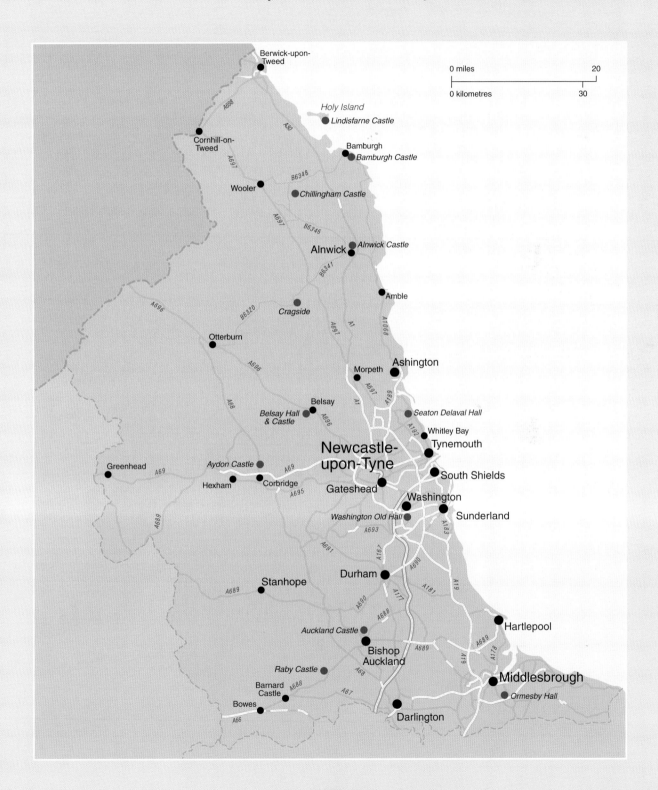

0 miles 20
0 kilometres 30

Berwick-upon-Tweed

A698

A1

Cornhill-on-Tweed

A697

Wooler

B6348

Holy Island

Lindisfarne Castle

Bamburgh
Bamburgh Castle

Chillingham Castle

B6346

A697

B6341

Alnwick
Alnwick Castle

Amble

A696

B6320

Cragside

A697

A1

A1068

Otterburn

A696

Morpeth

Ashington

A697

A189

Belsay
Belsay Hall & Castle

A68

A696

Seaton Delaval Hall

A192

Whitley Bay

Tynemouth

Greenhead

A69

Aydon Castle

A69

Newcastle-upon-Tyne

South Shields

Hexham

Corbridge

A695

Gateshead

Washington

A689

Washington Old Hall

Sunderland

A693

A183

A691

A167

A690

A181

A19

Stanhope

A689

Durham

A690

A688

A177

Auckland Castle

A689

A178

Hartlepool

A19

Bishop Auckland

Raby Castle

A68

A689

Middlesbrough

Barnard Castle

A688

A67

Ormesby Hall

Bowes

A66

Darlington

Alnwick Castle, Northumberland

Privately owned (HHA) • £££ • Open Apr to Oct, daily

Very few castles are still lived in as private residences – chiefly because, at the time of the Civil War, the Parliamentary forces were keen to destroy (or 'slight') any castle that might be held against them, but also because the inconveniences of a medieval castle led many owners to abandon them for something more modern and comfortable.

Indeed, the same happened at Alnwick, home of the powerful Percy family since 1309 when Henry Percy, trusted by Edward I to act as regent in his absence, bought the barony with the blessing of the king. Much of the fabric of the castle dates from this time, when Henry updated the curtain walls and towers and added extra towers to the shell-keep at the heart of the castle. By 1752, when the castle was painted by Canaletto, the Percy Dukes of Northumberland were living mostly at their London residences – the now-demolished Northumberland House and the beautiful Syon Park – and Alnwick was neglected and crumbling.

It was saved by an elaborate restoration in the gothic style, but this was swept away in the mid-1800s when Algernon, 4th Duke of Northumberland, employed the best possible architect for this sort of work, Anthony Salvin, to rebuild the castle in a more authentic style and transformed the interiors with the help of the Roman architect and archaeologist Luigi Canina, who was expert in the restoration of historic Italian villas and palaces. The result is an almost flawless combination of utterly correct medieval castle on the outside, and gloriously rich Italian palace within.

The ceilings designed by Canina and his assistant Giovanni Montiroli, who completed the work after Canina's death in 1856, are masterpieces in themselves, created by a specially established school of local carvers trained by a young Florentine master. That of the dining room is particularly pleasing, with trapdoors through which candelabra could be wound down to light the room.

Everywhere there is work of similar quality, from the Carrera marble fireplaces carved in Rome to the superb friezes and doorcases, and it is matched by equally notable furnishings and works of art – not least the paintings of the three Northumberland homes by Canaletto, but also portraits by Lely and Van Dyck and Italian works by such masters as Titian and Sebastian del Piombo.

Splendid though the keep's interiors are, it feels like a lived-in house, too, and is never po-faced – a Simpsons chess set sits proudly on a table in the drawing room.

Vast and ambitious new gardens (open all year, daily), military and archaeological museums, restaurant, shop.

Signposted on north side of Alnwick town centre, beside B6341.

Alnwick Castle: its walls and towers were restored by Anthony Salvin in the 1850s, and the keep's interior was transformed into a glorious Italian palace

Auckland Castle: the medieval home of the Prince Bishops of Durham, remodelled by Wyatt in the 1790s

Auckland Castle, County Durham

Privately owned by Church Commissioners (HHA) • £££ • Open Apr to Sep, M, Th & Su

The palatial country home since medieval times of the Prince Bishops of Durham, whose main base was at Durham Castle and who only officially gave up their power over the county in 1836. The castle, sensitively modified in the 1790s by the gothically minded architect James Wyatt, is now the bishop's official residence.

Only a few of the rooms created by Wyatt are visited and these are sparsely furnished with a somewhat institutional feel. Two highlights are Wyatt's immense throne room, with its clever tinted glass, and a priceless collection of paintings of Jacob and his twelve sons by the Spanish artist Francisco de Zurbaran which is currently in danger of being sold off.

These apart, the best reason for visiting is the rather lovely chapel, converted in the 1660s from a banqueting hall of the 1100s and full of interesting details, including beautiful stained glass windows.

Deer park with 18th-century deer house (free, open all year, daily).

Signposted off A689 (Crook road) on north side of Bishop Auckland.

Aydon Castle, Northumberland

English Heritage • ££ • Open Apr to Oct, daily

A fascinating fortified manor house of the late 1200s, which has survived in remarkably original condition and stands in a beautiful setting, on a rise in a loop of a small river, the Cor Burn, surrounded by woodland.

The manor, the earliest parts of which date from between 1296 and 1305, was originally built as an unfortified house in a time of rare peace in the border country; but as building work proceeded, the need to fortify it rapidly became obvious. Its defences were not, however, sufficient to prevent it from being sacked and burned by the Scots in 1315, or from being captured by English rebels two years later. The cost of repairs and new, better fortifications was eventually enough to bankrupt its builder, Robert de Reymes, a wealthy merchant from Suffolk.

The first part built was a chamber block, containing the solar, the lord's private apartment, on the first floor. Next came the hall block with, most unusually, a kitchen in the basement and the great hall on the first floor. Later a separate kitchen range was built.

The castle became a farmhouse in the 1600s, which it remained until 1966. The later alterations have since been stripped away, revealing the primitively beautiful original work in pale yellow stone.

Shop.

Signposted on minor road off B6321 or A68, 1 mile north of Corbridge.

Aydon Castle: a handsome fortified manor house of about 1300, built by Suffolk merchant Robert de Reymes

Bamburgh Castle, Northumberland

Privately owned (HHA) • £££ • Open Apr to Oct, daily

In a perfect coastal setting on a craggy rock beside a beautiful sandy beach, this is a genuine Norman castle on the site of an ancient stronghold of Northumbrian kings. It has twice been remodelled: first in the 1750s, when it was bequeathed to be used for charitable purposes and was put to use as a school; and again in baronial style from about 1890 to 1900, when Lord Armstrong bought it to convert into a home.

The square keep, possibly built by Henry II's masons, looks much as it always has – you can only visit a part of the basement – but the rest is in a Lutyens-like neo-castle style, echoed in the romantic medieval interiors – an appropriate setting for the collections of arms and armour spread throughout. Most striking of the rooms is the immense king's hall, with superb craftsmanship in its lofty false hammerbeam roof and delicate stained-glass window.

The castle no longer feels like a home, however, since it is now filled with museum-style displays and glass cabinets laden with trinkets.

Restaurant, shop.

Signposted off A1 Alnwick to Berwick-upon-Tweed road, on B1341 or B1342 in Bamburgh, 20 miles south of Berwick.

Bamburgh Castle: a Norman fortress restored as a mock-medieval home between about 1890 and 1900

Chillingham Castle, Northumberland

Privately owned • £££ • Open May to Sep, M-F & Su

There's nowhere quite like this place to visit, and a hugely enjoyable experience it is too: like a journey back through time to the medieval origins of the castle, enlivened all the way by the sharp observations and sheer enthusiasm of the present owner, who has been restoring it since the 1980s.

The castle was built in the 1340s by the Grey family, and has been altered and modified many times over the years, with the addition of Elizabethan facades and Georgian oval state rooms, culminating in a gentle remodelling in 1828 by Sir Jeffrey Wyattville. Abandoned in the 1930s, the castle was a roofless and largely floorless shell until the recent restoration began.

The interiors are mostly medieval in feel, but the aim seems to be to preserve anything of interest, no matter what period it belongs to. The result is a haphazard but comfortable blend, and huge fun.

Grounds with woodland walks, lake, Italian gardens (open as house), tearoom, craft shop.

Signposted on minor road from A697 or B6348, 6 miles south-east of Wooler.

Chillingham Castle: built in the 1340s by Sir Thomas Grey, the castle was revamped in 1828 by Sir Jeffrey Wyattville and restored from a ruin after 1980

Belsay Hall and Castle, Northumberland

English Heritage • £££ • Open all year, daily

Really rather a treat, with a whole jumble of fascinating sights on offer and, most unusually, open all year round. The famous Grade I-listed gardens, covering 30 acres, include fascinating landscaping with ravines and a quarry garden. There's a gentle stroll through the gardens to the castle, which is actually the ruin of a medieval tower-house and an attached Jacobean manor, both roofless now, but lived in until 1817. And then there's the hall, an extraordinary little house in the Greek revival style, designed by its owner, Sir Charles Monck, following a visit to the Temple of Theseus in Athens, and built in 1807–17.

Belsay was the home of the Middleton family continuously from the late 1300s, when the estate was returned to them, having been confiscated by the crown after an unfortunate episode that involved the kidnap of two cardinals, until 1962, when the contents of the hall were sold and the building was left to decay. It was rescued in the early 1980s, but only partially restored; some rotting floors were removed and the voids left to show the structure of the house.

So it's an oddity, in that it is shown empty and partially ruined, but the lack of furnishings makes it easier to appreciate the simple elegance of the design. The house is a 100-foot square in plan, with a single room, the pillared hall, occupying all three storeys at the centre, surrounded by columns and lit by a clerestory above. It's a serenely beautiful room. The other rooms have many an interesting architectural flourish, including simple marble fireplaces and pretty friezes of Greek honeysuckle pattern in the bedrooms.

Superb gardens, tearoom, shop.

Signposted off A696 Newcastle-upon-Tyne to Otterburn road north of Belsay village, 14 miles north-west of Newcastle.

Belsay Hall: a plain but quietly elegant house, built in the Greek revival style in the early 1800s

Belsay Castle: a fortified tower of the early 1400s with a Jacobean manor attached, now ruinous

Cragside, Northumberland

National Trust • £££ • Open Apr to Oct, Tu-F, S & Su

One of the most extraordinary houses in Britain, a Victorian country mansion that exhibits three of the finest qualities of its era: the romanticism and love of craftsmanship that gave rise to an outpouring of creativity in the Arts and Crafts movement, and the fascination with engineering that was a product of the still-recent Industrial Revolution. It stands in a most unusual setting, not among acres of gentle, spreading lawns but tucked in, as the name suggests, against a craggy rock and perched on the lip of a steep-sided glen, with rock gardens tumbling down the hillside to a stream below.

Its principal claim to fame is that this was the first house in the world to be lit by water-generated electricity, which is hardly surprising given the nature of its builder. William Armstrong – whose father, a prominent Newcastle merchant, became lord mayor of the thriving industrial city – started his career as a lawyer, but continued to indulge his childhood love of science and engineering. Hydraulics interested him above all else – 'William always had water on the brain,' said his family – and in 1844–5 he became the prime mover behind a series of engineering companies that first improved Newcastle's erratic water supply and then, exploiting the improved water pressure, began to build hydraulic cranes for the city's docks.

In 1847 he finally abandoned the law and set up WG Armstrong & Co to manufacture hydraulic cranes and other heavy engineering projects: it built the water-engines that power Tower Bridge in London. A move into the manufacture of artillery followed, and he was knighted in exchange for giving up his patents. By 1863, when he started to build the original smaller house at Cragside, Armstrong was 53 years old and more or less retired. By

Cragside: a remarkable Victorian mansion built in 1863–83, full of engineering and craftsmanship

now, however, his company was a thriving international business and, as its figurehead, he was obliged to entertain princes and envoys who came to Newcastle to order arms. In 1869, he employed the London architect Norman Shaw to rebuild Cragside in a grander mode.

Inevitably, an intriguing aspect of a visit here is the engineering: the mechanism for the still-working hydraulic lift in the basement; the simple turbine that drove the kitchen spit; and, in the library, the first lamps to use Joseph Swan's new filament lightbulbs, which were switched on by being stood in a dish of mercury. But it is also a beautiful house in its own right, conjuring up the spirit of its era with touches such as the William Morris stained glass set into the inglenook fireplace in the dining room, and the collection of contemporary paintings in the library.

A beauty of the visitor route is that it ends with a surprise at the top of the house, which is too good to spoil here. Suffice to say that it involves ten tons of Italian marble…

Thousand-acre forest gardens with walks and forest drive, rock gardens, terrace gardens with glasshouses (estate open Apr to Oct, Tu-Su, Nov to Dec, W-Su), restaurant, shop.

Signposted on B6341 Rothbury to Alnwick road, 1 mile north of Rothbury.

Lindisfarne Castle, Northumberland

National Trust • £££ • Open mid-Mar to Oct, M-Th, S & Su

The 'castle' is actually a small artillery fort built by Henry VIII to guard the coast, converted into a house in 1903 by Edwin Lutyens. Lutyens was still a young architect then, but had a growing reputation, thanks initially to a series of Arts and Crafts houses he had designed in Surrey – but also to the publicity he had received in a new interiors and lifestyle magazine, founded in 1897, called *Country Life*. It was for the magazine's publisher, Edward Hudson, that Lutyens remodelled the castle.

It's a delightful little place, its small rooms, restrained but beautifully crafted decoration and Edwardian home comforts making it a perfect holiday home; and the setting, at the tip of Holy Island, is absolutely perfect. Do note, however, that the island is reached by a causeway and cut off at high tide, so the exact times of opening depend on the tide.

Coastal walks, shop (in village).

Signposted on Holy Island, off A1 10 miles south of Berwick-upon-Tweed.

Lindisfarne Castle: an artillery fort of the 1500s, remodelled as a cosy house by Edwin Lutyens in 1903

Ormesby Hall, Middlesbrough

National Trust • £££ • Open Apr to Oct, Tu-Th & Su

A handsome mansion, designed in a plain local Palladian style by an unknown architect and completed in about 1743. It incorporates a Jacobean house with a doorway ornamented with the arms of the Pennyman family, who had owned the estate since 1601.

In 1770, Ormesby was inherited by Sir James Pennyman, the 6th Baronet, whose aunt had built the house. He managed to spend the entire family fortune in just eight years, earning himself the nickname 'Wicked Sir James' as a result; most of the money went on enlarging the estate and making the interiors of the house even more lavish, but no sooner was it finished to his satisfaction than he was obliged to hand the whole lot over to the bailiffs.

The interiors feature splendidly opulent rococo plasterwork and woodcarving by local craftsmen, with equally lavish decorations and furnishing in styles from Regency to Victorian. There's a good collection of family portraits, but little of outstanding quality to set the pulse racing.

More interesting is the Victorian kitchen, with scullery and game larder attached, and the laundry. But possibly the most pleasing part of all is the stable block, thought to be by John Carr of York, to which access is limited because it's full of police horses.

Extensive gardens (open as house), model railway exhibition, stable block used by Cleveland mounted police, tearoom, shop.

Signposted from A174 and A172, 3 miles south-east of Middlesbrough.

Ormesby Hall: completed in about 1743 in a plain Palladian style as a remodelling of a Jacobean house

Raby Castle, County Durham

Raby Castle: built in the late 1300s, remodelled twice in the 1700s and again in the 1840s

Privately owned (HHA) • £££ • Open May and Sep, W & Su, Jun to Aug, M-F & Su

In a part of the world dominated by its castles, this is another splendid example of a medieval fortress that is still lived in and has been updated over the years to create a grand and opulent home. Part of its beauty is that the castle is still so castle-like in appearance, so it's a delightful surprise to stroll through a gatehouse into a courtyard enclosed by severe stone walls, then pop through a door and find oneself in a series of elegantly proportioned and lavishly decorated rooms in a mixture of styles from 18th-century classical to unrestrained Victorian baronial.

Raby was built in the 1300s by the Nevills, one of the most powerful families of the North East, who owned it until 1569, when it was forfeited to the crown after their involvement in the Rising of the North. It was bought in 1626 by Sir Henry Vane the Elder, an important member of Charles I's government, whose descendants still live here today, the present owner being the 11th Lord Barnard.

The castle has been through three major phases of restoration and remodelling, each of which left the 14th-century structure largely unaltered and each under the aegis of a leading architect: in the mid-1700s by James Paine, in the 1770s by John Carr and in the 1840s by William Burn.

Burn's influence dominates, but of the two most spectacular rooms in the castle, only one is his work. It is the octagon drawing room, created in 1848 from an existing round room. Recently restored, it glows in jewel-like colours: its sumptuous curtains and wall-hangings of crimson and gold silk had to be either conserved or reproduced, but the astonishing gilded and painted ceiling was merely washed and now sparkles like new.

The other magnificent room is the cathedral-like entrance hall created by Carr in 1787 and aptly described as 'the first truly dramatic interior of the gothic revival'. Its immense doors and high vaulted ceiling meant that a carriage could be driven straight in to keep its occupants warm and dry. In one corner stands a beautiful marble statue, a female nude by American sculptor Hiram Powers.

Not all trace of the old castle's interiors has been lost. The visit ends with the medieval kitchen, a rare and remarkable survival, built in 1360, in use until 1954 and still in pretty much its original form.

Parkland and gardens, stable block with coaches, playground, restaurant, shop.

Signposted on A688 Bishop Auckland to Barnard Castle road, 2 miles north of Staindrop.

Seaton Delaval Hall, Northumberland

Privately owned • ££ • Open Jun to Sep, W & Su

Possibly the nation's most intriguing ruin, this is the shell of an elegant house built by Sir John Vanbrugh in 1718–28 and considered by some to be his masterpiece, destroyed by fire in about 1900 and left roofless for 50 years. It is a tribute to the public-spiritedness of the present owner, Lord Hastings, who lives in the west wing, that he has taken the trouble to have it partially restored, roofed and made safe for visitors to look round.

There is great fascination both in the effects of the fire, which left several statues in the lofty entrance hall as crumbling shadows of their former beauty, and in the structure of the building itself. Visitors can climb stairs with lovely, delicate iron railings to a first-floor gallery and descend into the slightly eerie vaulted basements. Displays include details of how the restoration took place and a collection, in the one decorated room, of documents and paintings associated with the house and its occupants.

Norman church, tearoom.

Signposted on A190 Seaton Delaval to Seaton road, 2 miles east of Seaton Delaval.

Seaton Delaval Hall: engaging ruin of a graceful house built in 1718–28 by Sir John Vanbrugh

Washington Old Hall, Tyne & Wear

National Trust • £££ • Open Apr to Oct, M-W & Su

This modest stone-built manor of the 1600s is chiefly notable as the home of George Washington's ancestors, and as such is more a shrine-cum-museum to one of the founding fathers of the United States than it is a historic house in its own right. None the less, it has several features of interest – not least the kitchen, incorporating parts of an earlier hall – and it evokes nicely the oak-panelled, oak-furnished feel of a typical gentry residence of the mid-1600s.

Jacobean gardens and nuttery, shop.

Signposted in Washington village, off A195 on north side of town centre.

Washington Old Hall: a small stone manor built in the 1600s from the remains of an earlier building

See also...

Bessie Surtees House
Newcastle-upon-Tyne
English Heritage, ££, open all year, M-F
A pair of handsome timber-framed town houses of the 1500s and 1600s.

Black Middens bastle house
Near Bellingham, Northumberland
English Heritage, free, open all year, at any reasonable time
Interesting and unusual fortified farmhouse of the 1500s, of a type found only in the Borders.

Cherryburn
Mickley, Northumberland
National Trust, ££, open Apr to Oct, M, Th-F, S & Su
Farm of 1800s with older cottage, the birthplace of Thomas Bewick, naturalist and wood-engraver. Craft demonstrations, farm animals.

Wallington, below: built in 1688 but much altered since, with a fine Palladian exterior

Chipchase Castle
Near Hexham, Northumberland
Privately owned (HHA), £££, open Jun, daily, tours only
Fortified pele tower of the 1300s with additions of 1620s and mid-1700s.

Crook Hall
Sidegate, Durham
Privately owned, ££, open Jun to Aug, M-F & Su, also May and Sep, Su
Small medieval hall attached to a later house, in rural setting on edge of Durham. The house is lived in and has interesting gardens.

George Stephenson's Birthplace
Wylam, Northumberland
National Trust, ££, open Apr to Oct Th, S & Su
Small stone tenement built for mining families in about 1760. Stephenson was born here in 1781.

Meldon Park
Morpeth, Northumberland
Privately owned (HHA), £££, open late May to late Jun, daily
Greek revival house of 1832.

Preston Tower
Chathill, Northumberland
Privately owned (HHA), ££, open daily, all year
Fortified pele tower built in 1392, attached to a later house, with two rooms furnished in contemporary style and local history displays.

Rokeby Park
Barnard Castle, Co Durham
Privately owned (HHA), ££, open May to Sep, M-Tu
Palladian country house completed in 1735.

Wallington
Cambo, Northumberland
National Trust, £££, open Apr to Oct, details to be confirmed
House of 1688 much developed over later generations, with Palladian exterior and magnificent rococo plasterwork. Recently reopened after major programme of repairs. Walled gardens and extensive grounds (*£££, open daily, all year*) laid out in the 1700s by Sir Walter Blackett with the help of Capability Brown.

Kedleston Hall, Derbyshire

Wales

Anglesey, Conwy, Denbighshire, Wrexham, Gwynedd, Ceredigion, Powys
and the counties of South Wales

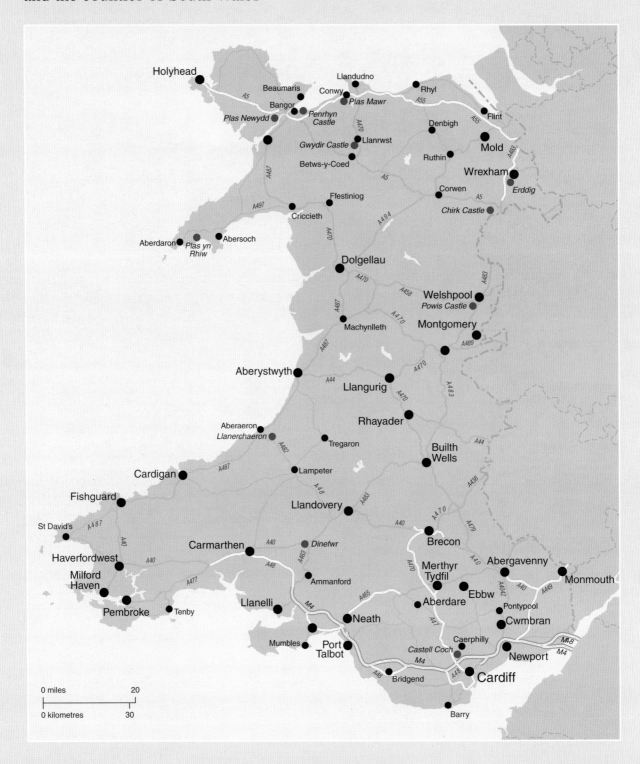

Castell Coch: built on the foundations of a castle of the late 1200s by William Burges in 1871–91 as a summer residence for the 3rd Marquess of Bute

Castell Coch, South Glamorgan

Cadw (Welsh Historic Monuments) • £££
• *Open all year, daily*

The most exuberant and fascinating of the Victorian gothic revival medieval-style castles, with touches of authenticity but, above all, a sense of the fairytale. It was built by the thoroughly eccentric William Burges in 1871–91 as a summer residence for John Patrick Crichton-Stuart, 3rd Marquess of Bute, the wealthiest man in Britain.

Lord Bute's father, John, 2nd Marquess of Bute, had inherited vast estates in South Wales from his grandfather, and had secured the family's fortunes by building the docks at Cardiff and turning it into a major port. On his coming of age in 1868, the 3rd Marquess enjoyed an annual income of more than £300,000. A keen medievalist and a great architectural enthusiast, he employed Burges to remodel the interiors of Cardiff Castle (from 1865) as well as to create Castell Coch; Burges set up craft workshops at Cardiff to make woodwork, stonework and furniture, and gathered together a team of craftsmen of exceptional ability – in particular, the decorative painters who transformed the interiors into the colourful pre-Raphaelite fantasies that Burges envisioned.

Bute and Burges's new castle was built on the foundations of the Red Castle, constructed in the late 1200s and early 1300s to guard the Taff river and ruined in the 1400s. It followed the ground plan of the old castle more or less exactly, consisting of one large tower – the keep – and two smaller ones, linked by a curtain wall. Many of the details show a keen eye for authenticity: Burges reconstructed a drawbridge, arrow slits, even the 'putlog holes' that medieval masons would have used to support wooden scaffolding while a castle's walls were built. He even recreated the dungeon. Only the tall, conical roofs are really fanciful.

Between the keep, which housed the family accommodation, and the kitchen tower, Burges built a long range, the entire upper floor of which is filled with the vast banqueting hall, sparsely furnished but beautifully decorated with painted walls and a splendid fireplace. There's a starkness, by contrast, to the interiors of the kitchen tower (with a dining room on the first floor) and well tower; but in the keep, which houses the drawing room on the first floor and Lady Bute's bedroom above, the carved and painted decoration of walls and ceilings is extraordinarily rich and really very beautiful.

Woodland walks, tearoom, shop.

Signposted on A470 Cardiff to Merthyr Tydfil road, 5 miles north-west of Cardiff.

Chirk Castle: a Marcher fortress built in 1310, with surprisingly graceful Adam-style interiors of the 1760s

Chirk Castle, Wrexham

National Trust • £££ • Open Apr to Oct, W-F, S & Su

A peculiar and fascinating blend of castle and stately home. On the outside, Chirk still looks very much like the Marcher fortress it started out as, completed in 1310 by Roger Mortimer; but it has been occupied continuously ever since and altered many times, ending up with graceful and comfortable interiors that reflect, more than any other period, the Adam-style neoclassical remodelling it received in the 1760s.

Chirk had already had a fairly chequered career when it was bought in 1595 by Sir Thomas Myddleton, whose family has lived here ever since. Sir Thomas built a new accommodation range on the north side, which would form the basis of the later state apartments. His son, another Sir Thomas, changed sides during the Civil War and so achieved the distinction of having his castle besieged and captured by both royalist and parliamentary forces, after which it had to be rebuilt.

Sir Thomas's grandson added the long gallery, with elegant if archaic Renaissance-style panelling, in the late 1600s; while in the 1760s and 1770s, the main rooms were given the graceful, pleasing neoclassical update that characterizes the house today. Pugin and Crace worked here in the 1840s, but many of their changes have been removed.

Extensive grounds, formal gardens (open as house), tearoom, shop.

Signposted on B4500, off A5 Wrexham to Oswestry road, 2 miles west of Chirk.

Dinefwr estate and Newton House, Carmarthenshire

National Trust • ££ • Open Apr to Oct, M, Th-F, S & Su

The house itself, built in 1660 and remodelled with a mildly gothic facade in Victorian times, is really not the main attraction at Dinefwr: the only reason to come is for the extensive estate, with fallow deer, a small herd of white cattle, a large array of walks and a ruined medieval castle. If that attracts you, Newton House is worth seeing while you're here; but it has lost much of its original decoration and is largely devoid of furniture.

Only the entrance hall and two downstairs rooms – a drawing room at the back and dining room at the front – are furnished, with a few items original to the house and some good Welsh landscape paintings of the 1600s. The upstairs rooms are given over to displays on the history of the house and estate, and a museum that reconstructs the house's role as a hospital during the Second World War.

Estate (open as house), tearoom.

Signposted on minor road off A40 Llandeilo to Carmarthen road, on west side of Llandeilo.

Newton House, Dinefwr: built in 1660, but given a mildly gothic exterior makeover in Victorian times

Erddig: built in 1683–93, with wings added in the 1720s and a fascinating blend of later redecoration

Erddig, Wrexham

National Trust • £££ • Open Apr to Oct, M-W, S & Su

Fascinatingly different, as a place to visit, from most houses, since it places a great emphasis on the role of the servants and estate workers. The house was built in 1683–93 for Joshua Edisbury, the son of a family of minor local gentry, who was going up in the world, shortly after his appointment as High Sheriff of Denbighshire; the work was overseen by a mason from Nantwich.

Edisbury's house was in the style popularized by Sir Roger Pratt in the 1660s (see Kingston Lacy, Dorset): tall and narrow, topped by a domed cupola, and laid out on the 'double pile' plan, with two sets of rooms back to back (as opposed to the single-room depth of most Elizabethan and Jacobean houses), and two sets of stairs (main and service) in the middle. The original house survives with its layout remarkably little altered, although new wings added to either side in 1721–4 now give it a long, low appearance.

Edisbury had overstretched himself and went bankrupt in the late 1690s, and in 1714 the house was bought by John Meller, who had grown rich as a barrister in London. Meller not only built the new wings, but also furnished the house in fashionably opulent style: a good deal of his furniture and decoration survives, along with, most interestingly, a sequence of rooms making up a 'state apartment', without which no great house of the time could be regarded as truly noteworthy.

The story of Erddig really starts, however, after it passed first to Meller's nephew, Simon Yorke, and then, in 1767, to Simon's son, Philip Yorke. Philip also came into an inheritance from his uncle, and so was able to employ the architect James Wyatt to remodel the house in the 1770s; but, more importantly, he took a paternal interest in the staff who ran the house and the estate, and in the 1780s began a tradition of having portraits painted of his servants, with a little verse added to record their character and achievements. The tradition carried on into the late 1800s, although with photographs rather than oils.

This remarkable record has led the National Trust to take an approach to showing Erddig that is quite different from most houses. Visits start in the service courtyard, where the stables still house horses and, once a week, carpenters work in the joiners' workshop, and a baker in the bakery. The house itself is entered not by the front door, but through the kitchens and servants' quarters, where the Yorkes' pictures of their servants and the gently humorous accounts of their characters and their daily responsibilities are on display in the corridor and the servants' hall. This makes Erddig a wonderfully rewarding place to look round – a house to be read, like a book, not just admired.

Park with woodland walks, gardens (open as house, also Nov and Dec, S & Su), stables, workshops, restaurant, shop.

Signposted on minor road off A525 Wrexham to Whitchurch road and A483/ A5152 Wrexham to Oswestry road, 2 miles south-west of Wrexham.

Gwydir Castle, Gwynedd

Privately owned (HHA) • ££ • Open Mar to Oct, daily

A surprising little treat, tucked away in the hills of Snowdonia, this is a semi-fortified Tudor manor house, consisting of a low wing that contains the original great hall, and a solar tower with the lord's private reception rooms. It was built in about 1500 by Meredith ap Ieuan ap Robert (whose varied career – he went twice to Rome and served as a military commander in France – gives an insight into the far from isolated life of a nobleman of the time) and was completed in the mid-1500s by his son, John, using a great deal of stonework from the dissolved abbey at Maenan.

The castle was burned down in 1922 and insensitively restored in the 1940s, but is now being carefully re-restored by its present owners, who live here. Most remarkable of

Llanerchaeron: an attractive little house built in 1794–6 by John Nash, at the heart of an unspoiled estate

its interiors is a Renaissance dining room of the 1640s, brought back from America where it had been kept in boxes since 1921.

Interesting historic gardens.

Signposted on B5106 Llanrwst to Betwys-y-Coed road, 1 mile south-west of Llanrwst.

Llanerchaeron, Ceredigion

National Trust • £££ • Open Apr to Oct, W-F, S & Su

A charming little house, built in 1794–6 and the most complete example of the early 'picturesque' work of the architect John Nash, best known for such dramatic later creations as the Brighton Pavilion and for laying out Regent's Park and most of London between there and St James's Park. In addition, the house stands at the centre of a typical minor gentry estate of the late 1700s, virtually unaltered: the home farm, with its stables and threshing barns, is still working; while the service courtyard contains the dairy, laundry, brewhouse and salting rooms, all equipped as they were when in use.

The kitchens and service wing are far more interesting than the house itself, the interiors of which are decorated and furnished in a comfortable mix of late Georgian and Victorian styles. There is, however, an interesting collection of Georgian glass and 'treen' (wooden dishes and utensils).

Estate and parkland with extensive walks (open all year, daily), organic farm, walled gardens (open as house), tearoom.

Signposted on A482 Aberaeron to Lampeter road, 3 miles east of Aberaeron.

Gwydir Castle: the solar tower was built between about 1500 and 1560 by two generations of owners

Penrhyn Castle: the most impressive of the late Georgian and early Victorian pretend-castles, built in 1820–45 by Thomas Hopper for the Pennant family

Penrhyn Castle, Gwynedd

National Trust • £££ • Open Apr to Oct, M, W-F, S & Su

The most impressive and dramatic of Victorian gothic revival castles, built on the scale and in the style of a Norman fortress, complete with curtain wall, gatehouse and towers (in one of which an ice house is cunningly concealed). It was built in 1820–45 by Thomas Hopper for the Pennant family, who had made their considerable fortune through sugar plantations in Jamaica and slate mines in North Wales.

This fortune was secured by Richard Pennant, who inherited his father's West Indian plantations and estate in North Wales in 1781, and set about applying the profits of one to improving the other. One of his first acts was to call in the leases on the Penrhyn slate quarries and set about maximising their income; in which he was helped greatly by close connections with the Wyatt family of Staffordshire, whose architect sons James and Samuel he supplied with slate and employed on creating new buildings for the estate, most of which are now gone.

Such was the success of his enterprises over the course of almost 30 years that Pennant was credited with transforming the whole of Caernarfonshire from a 'wild, barren and uncultivated' place to an area 'covered with handsome villas, neat cottages, rich meadows and well-cultivated fields'. On his death in 1808, his estate passed to his cousin, George Hay Dawkins, who in about 1819 engaged Hopper to build the castle.

Almost exclusively, local men and materials were used: oak from the estates was carved for interior detailing and made into neo-Norman furniture by the estate carpenters; limestone from Anglesey was, although not easy to work, used with great skill by local masons to build the walls. The quality throughout is extraordinary, and perfectly complements Hopper's extraordinary vision.

The most impressive of the rooms is the cathedral-like grand hall; the most lavishly finished is the grand staircase, where the stonework is richly carved. But the whole place is remarkable, both on the large scale and in the intensity of detail – from the slate bed in one of the family bedrooms in the keep, to the gorgeous textiles in the ebony room.

Parkland with walks, walled gardens (open as house), industrial railway museum, model railway exhibition, doll museum, tearoom, shop.

Signposted on A5122 Bangor to Betwys-y-Coed road, 1 mile east of Bangor.

Plas Mawr, Conwy

*Cadw (Welsh National Heritage) • £££ •
Open Apr to Oct, Tu-F, S & Su*

Described with considerable justification as the best-preserved Elizabethan town house in Britain, Plas Mawr is an exceptionally interesting place to visit. It was built in stages between 1576 and 1585 by Robert Wynn, the third son of John Wynn ap Meredith of Gwydir Castle, Llanrwst (see above), who had served in the households of Sir Walter Stonor, Lieutenant of the Tower of London, and Sir Philip Hoby, rewarded by Henry VIII for his bravery at the siege of Boulogne in 1544 and one of the leaders of the king's military ventures in Scotland later the same year. Robert almost certainly took part in both campaigns and later probably travelled throughout Europe with Sir Philip, but by the 1560s he was concentrating on his business interests back home, which included a share in a ship bringing wine from La Rochelle to the port at Conwy.

The oldest part of Robert's house is the range at the back, built in 1576–9 as an extension to an existing house on the site and containing a kitchen and brewhouse, a parlour, two main bedrooms on the first floor, and servants' accommodation above. In 1580 he demolished the old house and built a new wing containing a great hall, and a central block joining the new wing to the old one, with the great chamber – the main private reception room – on the first floor. The original front door was in the side-street, Jugler's Lane (now called Crown Lane); but in 1585 Robert bought the patch of land between his house and the High Street and added a grand gatehouse to form a new formal entrance, with a courtyard behind, from where a door led into the great hall.

Despite the house having slipped into decline in the 1700s and 1800s, with parts used as a courthouse and others subdivided as homes for

Plas Mawr, Conwy: the gatehouse added in 1585 to the house built in 1576–80 by Robert Wynn

poor families, the essential layout remains pretty much unaltered and a great deal of the original decoration survives. By far the most striking decorative detail is in the plasterwork, which survives on ceilings and walls throughout the house. It is at its most elaborate in the parlour and two bedchambers of the older north range, where it is dated 1577; it incorporates a number of finely detailed heraldic emblems of local families, including the severed head of an Englishman, the badge of the Griffiths family.

What makes a visit so rewarding, however, is that the rooms have been furnished and equipped to reflect their original function. It's good to see how the servants' quarters would have been furnished – not too uncomfortable, actually – and it's particularly pleasing to peer into a little alcove in one of the bedrooms and find a 'close stool' toilet.

There are also museum displays in the first-floor chambers above the hall, which give a fascinating insight into the everyday details of Elizabethan life.

Signposted for pedestrians in High Street, Conwy town centre.

Plas Newydd, Anglesey

National Trust • £££ • Open Apr to Oct, M-W, S & Su

The setting, among gently sloping lawns overlooking the Menai Straits, is glorious; the house itself less so, although it does have its moments. Somewhat plain in appearance, it finally reached its present state in the early 1800s, having gone through a number of mildly gothic additions and rebuildings since Sir Nicholas Bayly added two towers to an ancient hall-house.

Inside, its most interesting features are the gothic and neoclassical interiors created in 1793–8 by James Wyatt and Joseph Potter of Lichfield for Henry Bayly, 1st Earl of Uxbridge, whose distinguished military career in Portugal is reflected in the cavalry museum in the house. Most remarkable of all, however, is the wonderful mural in the dining room painted by the artist Rex Whistler in 1936–7, and another small museum reflects Whistler's life and works.

Estate with walks, gardens (open as house), boat trips, restaurant, shop.

Signposted off A4080 Menai Bridge to Llangeinwen road, 2 miles south-west of Llanfairpwll.

Plas yn Rhiw: a tiny manor house of the 1600s and early 1800s, restored by three sisters after 1938

Plas yn Rhiw, Gwynedd

National Trust • £££ • Open Apr to Sep, M, Th-F, S & Su (also mid-May to Sep, W, Oct, S & Su)

A tiny little manor house rescued from ruin by three sisters in the late 1930s, with an Arts and Crafts sensibility about it, but more the feel, in both its form and its furnishings, of a traditional cottage. Parts of it date back to the 1600s, but much is Georgian; the whole was sensitively restored by the architect and conservationist Sir Clough Williams-Ellis.

The house is notable mainly for the way it reflects the lives and the conservationist instincts of its owners, the Keating sisters, and for its superb setting on a hillside overlooking Cardigan Bay.

Gardens, shop.

Signposted on minor road off A499 and B4413, 16 miles south-west of Pwllheli.

Plas Newydd: a rather plain and mildly gothic house completed in 1793–8 by James Wyatt and Joseph Potter for the cavalry commander Lord Uxbridge

Powis Castle: built by the Prince of Powys in the late 1200s, with notable interiors from the 1580s, the late 1600s and early 1700s, and the early 1900s

Powis Castle, Powys

National Trust • £££ • Open Apr to Oct, W-F, S & Su (also Jul to Aug, Tu)

Some of the most remarkable interiors in Britain are to be found inside this much-altered medieval castle, built in the late 1100s by Owain Cyfeiliog, Prince of Powys. They consist, essentially, of the work of three eras, but all three hang together beautifully to form a surprisingly cohesive whole.

The castle was bought from Owen's descendants in 1578 by Sir Edward Herbert, a younger son of William Herbert, Earl of Pembroke, of Wilton in Wiltshire. He made considerable changes to the castle, of which only his long gallery survives, with splendid Renaissance-style woodwork and a superb plaster ceiling. In 1667 it was inherited by William Herbert, 1st Marquess of Powis, who in the course of 30 years transformed the interiors into a baroque palace, notable chiefly for the grand stair, with its outstanding painted ceiling by Antonio Verrio, and the state bedroom, which imitates the full formal splendour of the French court, with the bed set in an alcove and barred to unwelcome guests by a balustrade. The transformation was continued by his son William, who commissioned Verrio's pupil, Gerard Lancsroon, to produce extraordinary painted walls and ceilings on the stair and in the blue drawing room and library.

Last, but of course not least, the castle was inherited in 1891 by George, 4th Earl of Powis, who removed some later alterations and replaced them in artfully authentic Jacobean style, creating the plaster ceiling (based on one at Aston Hall, Birmingham) and wood panelling of the oak room.

The extraordinary blend of these different but equally lavish and equally archaic styles in the rooms on the first floor of the castle, together with the splendid views through the windows over the world-famous gardens (also laid out by the 1st Marquess) and out across the countryside, makes a visit to Powis highly rewarding. There are some splendid paintings and furniture, too; among the highlights are the illuminated book of hours of the 1400s in the gateway room, and a jewel-like miniature of Edward Herbert, from the early 1600s, in the library.

One more owner of the castle deserves a mention: in 1801, it was inherited by Edward Clive, the son of Clive of India, whose collection of Indian artefacts is on display in a Victorian wing built to house a ballroom and billiards room.

World-famous gardens (open as house), restaurant, shop.

Signposted on A458 Welshpool to Newtown road, 1 mile south of Welshpool.

See also...

Aberconwy House
Castle Street, Conwy
*National Trust, ££, open Apr to Oct,
M, W-F, S & Su*
Small stone and half-timbered
medieval merchant's house of 1300s.

Bodelwyddan Castle
Bodelwyddan, Denbighshire
*Privately owned, £££, open Easter
to Sep, daily, Oct to Easter, Tu-Th,
S & Su*
Fine gothic castle-style house of the
early 1800s, the Welsh home of the
National Portrait Gallery, with period
furniture from the V&A and statues
from the Royal Academy of Arts.

Bodrhyddan Hall
Rhuddlan, Clwyd
*Privately owned (HHA), £££, open
Jun to Sep, Tu, Th, tours only*
House of 1600s, the home of the
Conwy family, remodelled in 1875
by William Andrew Nesfield.

Cardiff Castle
Cardiff
Local council, £££, open all year, daily
Norman castle with wonderful
Victorian mock-medieval interiors by
William Burges.

Llancaiach Fawr Manor
Nelson, Treharris
*Local council, £££, open Mar to Oct,
daily, Nov to Feb, Tu–F, S & Su*
Fortified manor of 1530 with Stuart
additions; costumed guides.

Margam Castle
Port Talbot, Glamorgan
*Local council, £, open Apr to Oct,
daily, Nov to Mar, W-F, S & Su*
Vast country house by Thomas Hopper
in cathedral gothic style, now being
restored after fire. Access to staircase
hall only (but well worth seeing).

Fonmon Castle
Barry, Glamorgan
*Privately owned (HHA), £££, open
Apr to Sep, Tu-W*
Medieval castle still in use as home,
much altered, with fine interiors in
various styles, extensive gardens.

Penarth Fawr
Criccieth, Gwynedd
*Privately owned, ££, open mid-Mar
to mid-Oct, daily*
Interesting small timber-framed,
stone-clad hall house of about 1450.

Penhow Castle
Newport, Gwent
*Privately owned (HHA), ££, open
Easter to Sep, W-F, S & Sun, Oct to
Easter, W and occasional Su*
Early medieval castle with great hall of
1400s, restored Norman bedchamber.

Penyclawdd Court
Llanfihangel Crucorney, Gwent
*Privately owned (HHA), ££, open
Easter to Oct, Th-F, S & Su*
Medieval manor house with additions
of the 1600s.

Picton Castle
Haverfordwest, Pembrokeshire
Privately owned (HHA), £££, open
Apr to Sep, Tu-F, S & Su, tours only
Castle of 1200s greatly modified in
1750s and 1790s to become a
Georgian mansion. Fine gardens.

St Fagans Castle
Near Cardiff
*Local council, free, open all year,
daily*
House of 1500s, set in the remains of
a castle of the 1200s, now home to
the Museum of Welsh Life.

Trebinshwn
Near Brecon, Powys
*Privately owned, £, open Easter to
Aug, M-Tu*
Medium-sized manor house of the
1500s, rebuilt in 1780, with fine
courtyard and walled garden.

Tredegar House
Newport, Gwent
*Local council (HHA), £££, open
Easter to Sep, W-F, S & Su, tours only*
Large and impressive mansion, of
older origins but greatly enlarged in
the late 1600s, in classical style, for
the Margam family. Sumptuously
decorated state rooms, servants'
offices, kitchens, stables, orangery
and restored formal gardens.

Tudor Merchant's House, Tenby
Tenby, Pembrokeshire
*National Trust, ££, open Apr to Oct,
M-Tu, Th-F, S & Su*
Interesting little house of late 1400s
reflecting life in the medieval port.

And...

Bryn Bras Castle
Llanrug, Caernarfon, Clwyd
*Privately owned, ££, open only to
groups by appt*
Romantic neo-Romanesque house of
1830s attributed to Thomas Hopper;
walks with superb views of Snowdon.

Cochwillan Old Hall
Near Bangor, Gwynedd
Privately owned, ££, by appt only
Medieval hall house of about 1450,
restored from use as a barn in 1970s.

*Picton Castle, left: a castle of the 1200s with
additions and interiors of the 1750s and 1790s*

Northern Ireland

Counties Down, Antrim, Londonderry, Tyrone, Fermanagh and Armagh

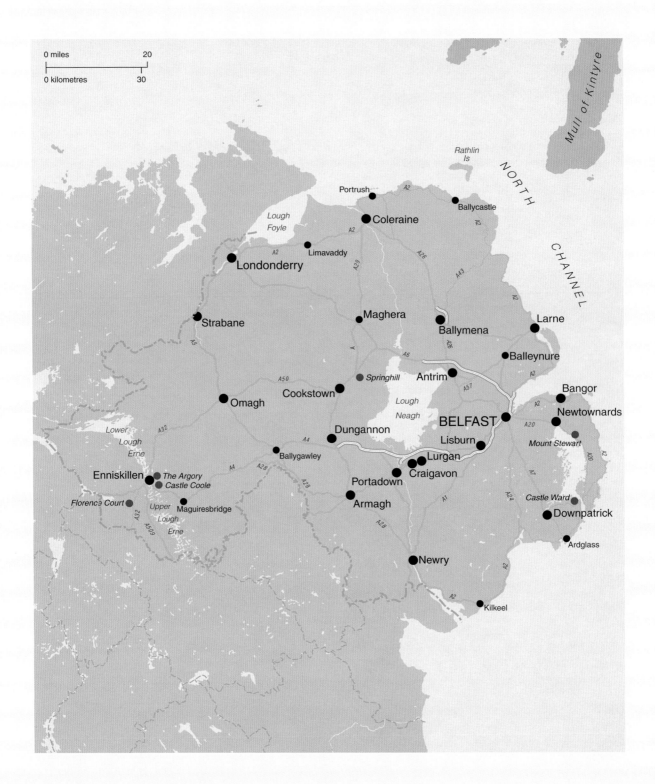

0 miles 20

0 kilometres 30

Mull of Kintyre

NORTH CHANNEL

Rathlin Is

Portrush
Coleraine
Ballycastle

Lough Foyle

Limavaddy
Londonderry

Strabane

Maghera

Ballymena

Larne

Balleynure

Springhill
Antrim

Bangor

Cookstown

Omagh

Lough Neagh

BELFAST

Newtownards

Mount Stewart

Dungannon

Lisburn

Ballygawley

Lurgan
Craigavon

Lower Lough Erne

Enniskillen
The Argory
Castle Coole

Portadown

Armagh

Castle Ward

Florence Court
Maguiresbridge

Upper Lough Erne

Downpatrick

Ardglass

Newry

Kilkeel

A2

A2

A26

A43

A2

A2

A20

A5

A50

A

A6

A26

A57

A2

A20

A7

A2

A32

A4

A28

A28

A4

A32

A509

A1

A24

A2

A2

The Argory: completed in 1824, rebuilt in 1834 and a fine example of a Victorian gentleman's residence

The Argory, Co Tyrone

National Trust • £££ • Open Jun to Aug, daily, also mid-Mar to May and Sep, S & Su, guided tours only

An odd-looking house of the early 1820s, standing as an unusually complete and convincing example of the country home of a reasonably well-heeled Victorian gentleman, unchanged since 1900 and with its original contents largely intact.

Its origins are pretty odd, too: it was built as the result of a will by which the landowning Joshua McGeough, on his death in 1817, left his estates to his second son, Walter, and his three sisters, stipulating that Walter could not live at the family home at Drumsill as long as two of his sisters remained unmarried.

Since all three died as wealthy spinsters, Walter's early decision to build a new house on the family's lands at Derrycaw, overlooking the Blackwater River, has to be admired for its prescience. With two

daughters and five sons from his two marriages, Walter decided by 1834 to extend the house, moving the main entrance to the west front, where his architects added a strange-looking pseudo-classical portico. After Walter's death in 1866, The Argory was inherited by his second son, Ralph, who achieved the rank of Captain in the army and changed his surname to Shelton. Ralph rebuilt the house on a slightly smaller scale following a fire in 1898, and it is his personality that has left the greatest stamp on The Argory.

Ralph brought acetylene gas to the house, but electricity did not reach it until 1983, and no electric lights have ever been installed. This is typical of the feeling of authenticity throughout the house, which, although never especially large or grand, has a lived-in feel and is cluttered with objects that reflect the daily lives of its occupants. More than with most houses, and especially thanks to the lively tales told by the tour guides,

a visit here is like stepping a hundred years back into the past.

Captain Shelton, whose family motto *Nemo me impune lacessit* (No one provokes me with impunity) may be familiar from the milled edges of pound coins, was one of the few male survivors of a shipwreck off South Africa in 1852; on the wall of the central corridor hangs a print of an artist's re-creation of the sinking ship, drawn from the Captain's own sketches. Even more redolent of family life in the house, however, is a set of scales nearby, with which visitors were weighed on arrival, to make sure they gained a few pounds while enjoying the house's hospitality. Possibly the rarest and most valuable item in the house is a vast barrel organ installed in 1822; it is still played once a month for visitors.

Grounds with walks, gardens (open all year, daily), tearoom, shop.

Signposted on minor road 4 miles from Moy, off junction 13 or 14 of M1.

Castle Coole,
Co Fermanagh

National Trust • £££ • Open Jun to Aug, M, W-F, S & Su, also Jul and Aug, Tu, mid-Mar to May and Sep, S & Su, guided tours only

Quite simply the finest of Northern Ireland's historic houses, this is a superb neoclassical mansion, built between 1790 and 1797 for the 1st Earl of Belmore by James Wyatt and considered to be one of that prolific architect's finest creations, even though Wyatt himself never so much as visited the site, and his extravagant and costly interiors were never completed.

Palatial and temple-like rather than homely and welcoming, it simply oozes quality, from the graceful proportions of the exterior, faced with Portland stone brought by boat from Dorset, to the stunning scale and wonderful details of the interior. Only three rooms are anything like Wyatt would have envisaged them, however: the lofty and noble entrance hall, largely bare of furnishings; the glorious staircase hall, with a beautiful top-lit lobby at its head graced by delicately conceived cast-iron stoves; and the saloon, with a ceiling by the plasterer Joseph Rose. Rose and the sculptor Joseph Westmacott, who carved many of the chimneypieces, fabricated decorative details in London ready to be shipped over.

As early as 1793 Belmore had been keen on making economies, asking Rose to provide a plainer and less costly design for the ceiling of the staircase hall, but by 1798 the money had pretty much run out and on the 1st Earl's death in 1802 the house was still not complete. Rather than abandon it altogether, his son, the 2nd Earl, decided to finish and furnish it in an appropriately grand manner, employing the Dublin upholsterer and interior decorator John Preston to complete the job between 1807 and 1822. The sumptuous, exuberant Regency style that he chose was fashionable at the time, and sits well enough in Wyatt's more restrained and austere rooms.

Preston's work is at its most pleasing in the state bedroom, with furnishings in the richest crimson, which was fitted out, according to family legend, in the hope of attracting a visit from King George IV, who in the event never came. Also far more Preston's creation than Wyatt's is the drawing room, with its gilded Grecian couches.

In the end, however, it is Wyatt's commitment to quality that made the house what it is: don't miss the marvellous curved mahogany doors of the saloon, hung on pivots, not hinges, because of their weight.

Extensive landscaped parkland with long walks, stables, ice house, servants' tunnel, tearoom, shop.

Signposted off A4 Enniskillen to Belfast road, 2 miles south-east of Enniskillen.

Castle Coole: a superb neoclassical mansion begun by James Wyatt for the 1st Earl of Belmore in 1790–97, but only finally furnished some 30 years later

Castle Ward: built in the 1760s, with this facade in a neoclassical style and the other in trendy gothic

Castle Ward, Co Down

National Trust • £££ • Open mid-Apr to Aug, M, W-F, S & Su, also Jul and Aug, Tu, mid-Mar to mid-Apr and Sep to Oct, S & Su, guided tours only

Set in possibly the most fascinating estate in Britain – on the shores of the wildlife-rich Strangford Lough, with two ruined castles (or, to be more accurate, tower houses), landscaped grounds, an ornamental lake and a temple folly of about 1750 – Castle Ward is also a fascinating house.

It was built in the 1760s by Bernard Ward, descended from a family of English settlers who had bought the estate in 1570. His political career was rewarded with the title of Baron Bangor in 1770 and that of Viscount in 1781, and during his lifetime he vastly increased the size of his family's landholdings both here and elsewhere in County Down. It is thought that the unusual design of the house owes a great deal to an architectural pattern-book by

Abraham Swan entitled *Collections of Designs*, published in 1757, a copy of which can still be found on the shelves in the library; but, more importantly, the story goes that it owes even more to a dispute between Ward and his wife, Lady Anne, over what style their new house should adopt. Whatever the truth, Castle Ward is unique in having one side, both inside and out, built in a neoclassical style, while the other is in Strawberry Hill gothic.

One room from each side of the house stands out in particular. On the gothic side, which on the whole is the more interesting, it is the boudoir, undoubtedly a feminine room both in its decoration and its use. It has the most extraordinary fan-vaulted ceiling, thought to have been copied from Henry VII's chapel in Westminster Abbey, which gives the room a tent-like cosiness.

On the classical side of the house, meanwhile, the room that stands out is the entrance hall. Here the large, austere and mostly

empty space is enlivened by fanciful rococo-style plasterwork, not actually original to the room but carried out in a hurry in 1827. It features garlands hung with objects modelled realistically and in high relief; in fact, some of the objects – such as a violin – are not modelled at all, but are the real thing dipped in plaster and stuck up to finish the job quickly.

The excellent guided tours point out this and many other quirks and, although the remainder of the house is not exactly overflowing with spectacular features, make for a thoroughly interesting visit by highlighting the many objects from daily family life that still litter the place.

Extensive grounds and parkland with two ruined castles (open all year, daily), wildlife centre (open as house), stables, corn mill, sawmill, lead mine, laundry, tearoom, shop.

Signposted on A25 Downpatrick to Strangford village road, 7 miles north-east of Downpatrick.

Florence Court: built mostly in the 1760s, finished in 1771 and noted for its superb rococo plasterwork

Florence Court, Co Fermanagh

National Trust • £££ • Open Jun to Aug, daily, also mid-Mar to May and Sep, S & Su, guided tours only

A tall, slightly unwieldy, not altogether handsome house flanked by colonnades with pavilions at their ends, Florence Court was built by three generations of the Cole family, powerful landowners descended from Plantation incomers who had lived at Enniskillen Castle and effectively ruled the town and surrounding country. The bulk of the house was built in the 1750s and 1760s by John Cole, Lord Mount Florence, and its most notable feature is the vigorous rococo plasterwork he commissioned from unknown craftsmen, said to be the finest in Ireland. Some of it was lost in a huge fire in 1955, but fortunately much survives.

The grounds were laid out and the house begun by Lord Mount Florence's father, Sir John Cole, who named the estate after his wife, Florence Bourchier Wrey; while the last phase of building was completed in about 1771 by his son, the 1st Earl, who also swept away his grandfather's formal gardens and replaced them with parkland laid out by the landscape gardener William King.

The last member of the family to make an impact was the 3rd Earl, a noted amateur scientist who turned the south pavilion into a museum in which to display his collection of fossil fish. After the collection was sold to the British Museum in 1883, the pavilion became a billiard room. The 3rd Earl also laid out the pleasure grounds and built a sawmill, an ice house and a picturesque thatched summer house, all of which survive.

Inside, the bold and lively plasterwork easily steals the show, particularly in the formal and restrained entrance hall, and in the dining room, where the ceiling was saved from the fire of 1955 when holes were drilled in it to let the water from the firemen's hoses escape: some of these holes have been left unblocked as mementoes. That apart, the main interest lies in the Irish furniture, the family portraits and memorabilia, and the powerful evocation of local history.

Grounds with extensive walks (open all year, daily), sawmill, walled garden, restaurant, shop.

Signposted off A32 Enniskillen to Swanlinbar road, 8 miles south-west of Enniskillen.

Mount Stewart, Co Down

National Trust • £££ • Open May to Sep, M, W-F, S & Su, also Jul and Aug, Tu, mid-Mar to Apr and Oct, S & Su, guided tours only

The home of the Londonderry family from the early 1700s, most famous nowadays for its wonderful gardens, laid out largely in the 1920s by Edith, Lady Londonderry, the wife of the 7th Marquess, and nominated as a world heritage site. The house itself is a neoclassical affair on a pleasingly grand scale, built in the late 1700s by an unknown architect and much altered over the years. What makes it particularly enjoyable to visit is that it is still lived in and feels very much like a family home, with vibrant modern paint colours giving a warmth to its echoing marble halls.

The most notable of its occupants was Lord Castlereagh, the 2nd Marquess of Londonderry, whose part in the Act of Union between Ireland and England in 1801 made him unpopular in his native country, but who also played a vital role, as Foreign Secretary, in arranging the coalition of European countries that opposed Napoleon in 1813–14. He presided, too, over the Congress of

Vienna in 1815, which brought the Napoleonic wars to an end: among the house's most surprising treasures, shown in the dining room, are 22 chairs on which the major delegates at the Congress sat.

History does not play as strong a part in the house's appeal, however, as its comfortable air of continuing use. Among the most pleasing of its rooms are the light and sunny drawing room where Lady Edith planned the gardens, and a bedroom named Rome – all the bedrooms were romantically named after European cities – where more vibrant and cheerful paintwork is apparent.

Among the many treats on offer in the gardens and grounds is the Temple of the Winds, a wonderful banqueting house in authentic neoclassical style built in 1785 by the Greek revival architect James 'Athenian' Stuart.

Lakeside gardens with walks (open all year, daily), formal gardens (open Apr to Sep daily, Mar and Oct to Dec, S & Su), Temple of the Winds (open Apr to Oct, S & Su), restaurant, shop.

Signposted on A20 Newtownards to Portaferry road, 15 miles south of Belfast.

Mount Stewart, below: a grand but welcoming neoclassical house with wonderful gardens

Springhill: an intimate little house, built in the late 1600s, with flanking bays added in the 1760s

Springhill, Co Londonderry

National Trust • £££ • Open Jul and Aug, daily, also mid-Mar to Jun and Sep, S & Su, guided tours only

Smaller and older than the rest of the houses covered in this section, Springhill has an intimacy and a feeling of age that the others lack. It also has at least one remarkable ghost story, as well as many interesting and tragic family tales, which make the guided tour lively and intriguing even when the house itself is a little dull.

It was built in the late 1600s by William Conyngham, known to his family as 'Good-Will', the son of a family of Scottish Presbyterians who had come to Ireland in the first wave of the Plantations and had become considerable landowners. In 1680 he married Ann Upton, and part of their marriage contract stipulated that he must build 'a convenient dwelling-house of lime and stone, two stories high, with necessary office houses, gardens and orchards'. This he did, on an estate that until then had been largely forest.

His house was a blend of old and new styles, with a traditional Irish layout of a central hall and a projecting stair-tower at the back, but with a modern symmetrical facade and flanked by two pavilions – to house servants and estate workers – finished with curving Dutch gables.

The layout of the house was altered a number of times: first in the 1760s by William Conyngham, the son of Good-Will's nephew, George, who added the single-storey wings with bays on either side, and then in 1820 when a new dining room was added.

The most pleasing of the rooms are the oldest, including the entrance hall and its flanking library and gun room, but in truth the house and its contents are not half so interesting as the characters who lived here. There are tales of wasteful bachelor heirs, a mad brother named Clotworthy, a wife who hacked her husband's furniture to pieces, a suicide in the blue room, a lady who saved herself from a fire in a London house by jumping onto railings and lost a leg as a result – and that's before you even get to the ghost story.

Estate with extensive walks, walled gardens, costume collection (all open as house), tearoom, shop.

Signposted on B18 Moneymore to Coagh road, 1 mile east of Moneymore.

See also…

Ardress House & Farmyard
Portadown, County Armagh
National Trust, ££, open mid-Mar to May and Sep, S & Su, Jun to Aug, M, W-F, S & Su, tours only
Farmhouse of 1600s with elegant additions in 1700s by owner-architect George Ensor. Robert Adam-style drawing-room, fine furniture and pictures. Display of antique farming implements, gardens, riverside walks.

Derrymore House
Bessbrook, Newry, County Armagh
National Trust, ££, open May to Aug, S only
Elegant thatched cottage of late 1700s, with walks in picturesque parkland.

Hezlett House
Castlerock, Coleraine, County Londonderry
National Trust, £££, open mid-Mar to May and Sep, S & Su, Jun to Aug, M, W-F, S & Su, tours only
Thatched house of 1600s with 1800s furnishings and interestingly constructed roof, a rare survival of a pre-1700s Irish house.

Mussenden Temple
Castlerock, Coleraine, County Londonderry
National Trust, £ (parking fee), open Mar to May and Sep to Oct, S & Su, Jun to Aug, daily
Bizarre temple-style banqueting house surviving from house built in late 1700s by Frederick Hervey, Earl of Bristol and Bishop of Derry, set on headland on spectacular coastline.

Holkham Hall, Norfolk

Southern Scotland

Dumfries and Galloway, Ayrshire,
Borders, Lothian, Edinburgh, Glasgow

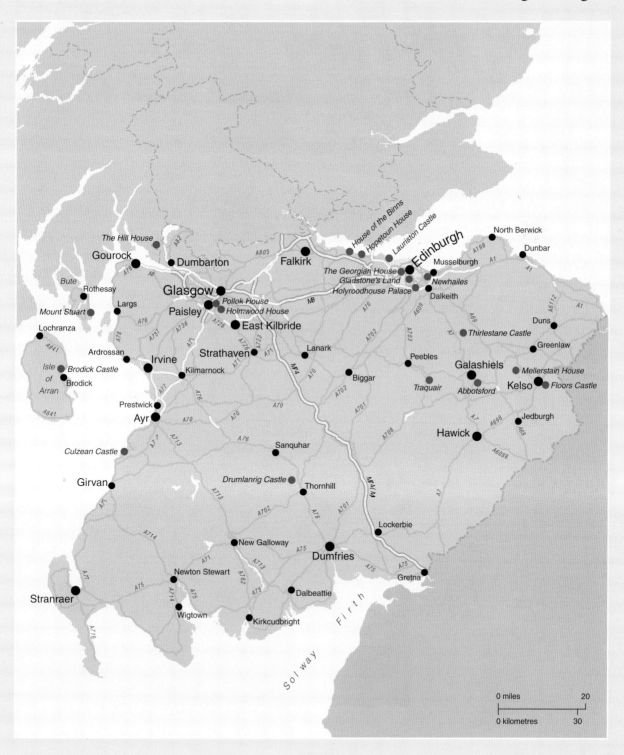

The Hill House
Gourock
Dumbarton
Falkirk
House of the Binns
Hopetoun House
Lauriston Castle
Edinburgh
North Berwick
Dunbar
Bute
Rothesay
Glasgow
The Georgian House
Gladstone's Land
Holyroodhouse Palace
Musselburgh
Newhailes
Dalkeith
Largs
Paisley
Pollok House
Holmwood House
Mount Stuart
East Kilbride
A6112
Lochranza
Duns
Ardrossan
Strathaven
Thirlestane Castle
Greenlaw
Irvine
Lanark
Peebles
Galashiels
Mellerstain House
Isle
Brodick Castle
of
Brodick
Kilmarnock
Biggar
Traquair
Abbotsford
Kelso
Floors Castle
Arran
Prestwick
Jedburgh
Ayr
Hawick
Culzean Castle
Girvan
Sanquhar
Drumlanrig Castle
Thornhill
Lockerbie
New Galloway
Stranraer
Newton Stewart
Dumfries
Gretna
Dalbeattie
Wigtown
Kirkcudbright
Solway
Firth

0 miles   20
0 kilometres   30

215

Abbotsford: built by Sir Walter Scott between 1818 and 1824 following the success of his Waverley novels

Abbotsford, Roxburghshire

Privately owned (HHA) • £££ • Open mid-Mar to Oct, daily

The house built by Sir Walter Scott, lawyer and part-time writer, in the early 1800s, when his fluctuating fortunes were on the up, and where he wrote the Waverley novels that brought him international repute. It's in exactly the sort of romantic Scots baronial style you would expect, with darkly gothic interiors and vast quantities of objects relating to the author's life and times.

Scott and his wife lived in Edinburgh (in a house which he was forced to sell after a crisis in his finances in 1826), but in 1804 he rented a house six miles from here to be nearer to his work as Sheriff-depute of Selkirkshire. In 1811, with his tenancy nearing its end, he bought the 100-acre estate and moved into the existing farmhouse. By 1818, with the success of *Waverley*, he was able to expand it; and in 1822 the old farm was pulled down to make way for a new main block, completed in 1824.

Inside, it's little altered since Scott's times. The spirit of his books pervades the house – dark, almost eerie in places, wood-panelled, littered with ancient weapons and all manner of strange objects, such as a toadstone amulet to ward off fairies. Among Scott's many personal possessions on show is the desk at which he wrote.

Gardens, tearoom, shop.

Signposted on B7060, off A6091 Galashiels to Melrose road, 2 miles east of Galashiels.

Brodick Castle, Isle of Arran

National Trust for Scotland • £££ • Open Apr to Oct, daily

Although it is based on an ancient tower, with modifications of the late 1500s and a gun battery added by Cromwellian troops in the mid-1600s, Brodick as it appears today is essentially a Victorian creation, built in the 1840s by James Gillespie Graham, one of the architects of Edinburgh New Town, for the 10th Duke of Hamilton, who installed his newly married eldest son here.

The Duke himself was married to Susan Euphemia, daughter of the wealthy eccentric William Beckford; Beckford's death in 1844 probably provided the money to rebuild Brodick, and its greatest claim to fame is that it houses the largest collection of Beckford's possessions to be found anywhere.

It's a comfortable house, if not a spectacular one, but its wonderful setting in gardens at the foot of Arran's highest mountain with lovely sea views makes it special.

Country park (open all year, daily), extensive gardens (open as house), restaurant, shop.

Signposted on A841 2 miles north of Brodick village and ferry terminal.

Brodick Castle: a Victorian creation in a superb setting, it has interesting links with William Beckford

Culzean Castle: built between 1776 and 1792 by Robert Adam for the 10th Earl of Cassilis, but both men died in 1792, leaving their work unfinished

Culzean Castle, Ayrshire

National Trust for Scotland • £££ •
Open Apr to Oct, daily

One of the most enjoyable houses to visit, as much for the superb clifftop setting with sea views out to the Isle of Arran as for the wonderful structure, a blend of the medieval and the classical created by Robert Adam in stages between 1776 and 1792 for David Kennedy, the 10th Earl of Cassilis.

Although it is almost impossible to believe, there is an ancient castle at the core of the house: it was an L-plan tower house, to which Adam added flanking wings with tall, thin towers at the corners in the first stage of his rebuilding. The library, designed by Adam as an 'eating room', with curved apsidal ends added to make its proportions more elegant, occupies the ground floor of the old tower.

A fascinating series of plans in the guidebook shows how Adam's proposals developed as his client became more ambitious about what he wanted, wishing to expand the castle towards the sea to make the most of the views. So it was that two of Adam's most remarkable rooms were created: the astonishing oval staircase, so beautiful and graceful that it seems like an integral part of the house, although Adam had to fit it in a space between the old tower and a separate range on the seaward side; and the round drawing room, originally called the saloon, on the first floor of the seaward range. As the name suggests, it is perfectly circular, and its tall, closely spaced windows give remarkable views.

When the Earl died in 1792, he had amassed debts of £60,000; Adam died the same year, and his work at Culzean was left unfinished. This, together with alterations to some rooms in the 1870s, meant the full glory of Adam's ideas was never realized; but there is certainly enough to make a visit a treat.

Particularly pleasing are the kitchens, set off to one side on the ground floor of the seaward range, with windows looking out over the water so that the kitchen staff could enjoy the same superb views as their masters.

Country park with extensive walks (open all year, daily), visitor centre (open as house, also Nov to Mar, S & Su), gardens, estate buildings, ice house, gas house, swan pond, restaurant, tearoom, shops.

Signposted on A719 Ayr to Turnberry road, 12 miles south of Ayr.

Drumlanrig Castle: a remarkable Renaissance residence built in 1679–91 by the Duke of Queensberry

Drumlanrig Castle, Dumfriesshire

Privately owned (HHA) • £££ • Open mid-Apr to early Sep, M-F & Su

A handsome and interesting building, with a castle-like form but with graceful Renaissance symmetry and detailing, constructed around an earlier castle in 1679–91 by William Douglas, 1st Duke of Queensberry, and still lived in by his ancestors, the Montagu Douglas Scott family. It has a slightly worn but welcoming atmosphere and the interiors, laid out in the typical manner of the period, with state apartments, have an ancient feel.

The most remarkable aspect of the house is the extraordinary quantity of fine paintings and furniture, and objects with great historical resonance, that have found their way here over the years. There are pictures by Rembrandt, Holbein and Da Vinci, woodcarving by Grinling Gibbons, Napoleon's despatch box and, in the room in which he slept in 1745, Bonnie Prince Charlie's moneybox, sash, rings and camp kettle.

Country park with cycle routes and walks, gardens, adventure woodland (all open mid-Apr to Sep, daily) tearoom, shop.

Signposted on A76 Dumfries to Kilmarnock road, 18 miles north of Dumfries.

Floors Castle, Roxburghshire

Privately owned (HHA) • £££ • Open Apr to Oct, daily

A vast, palatial and attractive mock-castle. Although the original conversion from an earlier tower was carried out for the 1st Duke of Roxburghe in the 1720s by William Adam, the leading architect of his day, Floors owes its external appearance largely to the Edinburgh architect William Playfair, who remodelled it in picturesque style in 1837–47.

Inside, however, its dominant influence is even later. Following the marriage of the 8th Duke to May Goelet, a beautiful young American heiress, many of the principal rooms were redesigned by the firm of Lenygons, which had established a reputation for creating authentic period interiors on both sides of the Atlantic. Duchess May brought with her a great deal of French furniture and a richly varied art collection, of which the greatest treasure was a set of Brussels tapestries: the drawing room was redesigned around them and they, cut to fit, around it.

Grounds with woodland and riverside walks, walled gardens, adventure playground (all open as house), restaurant, tearoom, shop.

Signposted on A6089 Kelso to Lauder road, 1 mile north of Kelso.

Floors Castle: remodelled in picturesque style by William Playfair for the 6th Duke of Roxburghe in 1837–47, with interiors dating largely from the 1930s

The Georgian House: Number 7 Charlotte Square, with an exterior designed by Robert Adam in 1791

The Georgian House, Edinburgh

National Trust for Scotland • £££ •
Open Mar to late Dec, daily

Number 7 Charlotte Square is more than just a typical Georgian town house, since the square was designed in 1791 by Robert Adam, brought in by the city fathers to add an extra touch of class to their new town development. However, Adam died the following year and other architects had a hand in turning design into reality; the square was not finally completed until 1820, although No 7 was first occupied in 1796.

By the 1760s, the crowded tenements of the old town on the castle rock had begun to seem beneath the dignity of the prosperous city, so a decision was taken to build a new town alongside. The competition to design its layout was won in 1766 by a young architect called James Craig, whose proposal featured two squares, St Andrews Square and Charlotte Square, linked by the broad avenues of George Street, Princes Street and Queen Street.

The last stage of the project, Charlotte Square was occupied by lawyers, doctors, bankers and merchants. The first occupant of No 7 was John Lamont, a landowner from Argyllshire; it was later owned by a widow and then, from 1845, by a distinguished lawyer.

It has now been restored as a typical town house of the early 1800s, when the average family had four children and five or six servants. Not all the rooms are open, so there's no glimpse of the nursery and servants' quarters on the top floor, but the reception rooms on the ground and first floors are furnished in appropriate style, and the service quarters in the basement are also shown, though not appropriately equipped.

In Charlotte Square, central Edinburgh.

Gladstone's Land, Edinburgh

National Trust for Scotland • £££ •
Open Apr to Oct, daily

This remarkable and surprising building, completed in 1620, is typical of the tall, narrow tenements of Old Edinburgh, with their cramped apartments in which even the wealthy lived. Often an apartment consisted of a single room, so the comparatively spacious set of four little rooms on the first floor of Gladstone's Land was clearly the home of someone very well-off: in fact, it was lived in by a merchant named Thomas Gledstanes and his wife, Bessie, who bought it in 1617 and extended the front by 23 feet into the street.

The most evocative room is the tiny kitchen, with a fold-away bed to make best use of the space and no oven, so that all 'baking' was done on a griddle; but most impressive is the painted chamber at the front, with superb decoration on its walls and on the beams of its ceiling, and with a splendid bed of the early 1600s.

Signposted at 477B Lawnmarket, in the centre of Edinburgh's old town.

Gladstone's Land: a remarkable tenement modified in 1620 and inhabited by a wealthy merchant

The Hill House: created in 1901–3 by Charles Rennie Mackintosh for the publisher Walter Blackie

The Hill House, Argyll

National Trust for Scotland • £££ • Open Apr to Oct, daily

A unique, fascinating and at times inspirational house, built in 1901–3 by the Glasgow designer and architect Charles Rennie Mackintosh for the publisher Walter Blackie, his wife Anna and their four children (five by the time the house was ready).

Mackintosh is such a well-known name these days, with such a loyal band of followers, that it comes as something of a surprise to discover that the early promise of his career was never fulfilled. He began to earn a reputation in the mid-1890s, when in his late twenties, and designed a number of important public buildings in Glasgow between 1894 and 1904. He was 33 when he designed the Hill House. But thereafter he failed to establish a practice of his own, and he never designed another major building.

At the Hill House, the client was specific about what he wanted, explaining that he disliked red-tiled roofs 'in the West of Scotland with its frequently murky sky'. Mackintosh created for him something like a modernist version of a traditional Scottish tower house, all plain slabs and angles, but with a grey slate roof, harled exterior and round stair-tower topped by a conical roof.

Inside, the house retains most of the decorative details and furniture designed for it by Mackintosh and his wife, Margaret Macdonald. The decoration displays all the qualities typical of Mackintosh – stylized designs, flat colours, simple, geometrical shapes – and shows traces of all the styles that influenced him – Arts and Crafts, art nouveau, Japanese, abstract modernism.

This is not, however, a place that will appeal only to existing fans of Mackintosh's style. There are two particularly interesting things about it: first, that it was designed to be

an artistic whole, the decoration tying it together into a single statement (and yet each room also has an individual character); and second, that it is very much a modern house, sufficiently comfortable, well-designed and practical that even the most demanding of families could move in tomorrow, with such modern touches as built-in wardrobes and – not common even as late as 1903 – electric lights and electric fires.

In addition, then, to artistic treats such as Margaret's gesso panel of Sleeping Beauty in the drawing room and Mackintosh's lights and furniture, there are interior design tips to be picked up in the cosy bathroom and beautifully laid out main bedroom. Don't miss, either, the plates painted with lovely images of birds by one of the Blackie girls.

Gardens, tearoom, shop.

Signposted off B832, between A82 and A814, 2 miles north of Helensburgh.

Holmwood House, Glasgow

National Trust for Scotland • £££ • Open Apr to Oct, daily

Very like the Hill House (left) in that it is an eloquent expression of the vision of one man – in this case Alexander 'Greek' Thomson, the most accomplished exponent of the Greek revival style of the mid-1800s. It was built in 1857 – a year after Thomson had set up a joint practice with his brother, George – for James Couper, the joint owner, with his brother, of the Millholm papermills, which stood on the banks of the River Cart just below the house.

Thomson was at his most prolific when Holmwood was built, creating dozens of buildings for the thriving Victorian industrial city of Glasgow – churches, warehouses, tenements and terraces as well as suburban villas for prosperous merchants and industrialists. At the time he lived in Hutchesontown, near the Gorbals, where the insanitary conditions of the city centre were tragically close

to home – four of his children died of cholera between 1854 and 1857.

Today, Holmwood's setting leaves something to be desired, in a slightly run-down part of the city, but the grounds are an oasis of calm and the gardens are not only thriving but also made to work for a living, with freshly picked vegetables often on sale.

The exterior of the house, with its large areas of glass, plain, blocky interpretations of Greek shapes and unusual lantern at the top, is surprisingly modern in feel. The interiors are equally idiosyncratic, but their true glory is only starting to become apparent as the painted decoration with which Thomson covered them – often with his own hand, and usually with stencils he himself had cut – is slowly and painstakingly stripped of many layers of paint and wallpaper, and gradually restored. Thomson designed furniture for the house, too, but what happened to it is largely unknown.

Thomson had an eclectic range of influences – not just Greek, but also Egyptian, Assyrian, Moorish and

Hindu – and this becomes apparent immediately, both in the entrance hall, with its remarkable omega-shaped marble fireplace, and in the first room in which restoration has been completed, the staircase hall. The glowing colours and eccentric variety of patterns are extraordinary, but it all hangs together. The lantern cupola that lights the stairs is wonderfully detailed, with figures of chimeras supporting it and delicate Greek patterns adorning it.

The only other room that currently gives a real impression of the house's original splendour is the dining room, where the frieze, hand-painted on paper and depicting scenes from Homer's *Iliad,* has recently been uncovered and restored. The doors, like something from an Egyptian temple, are simply amazing.

Holmwood will be a fascinating place to come back to over the years, as more is discovered and the restoration slowly proceeds.

Grounds, kitchen garden, tearoom, shop.

Signposted off B767 Clarkston road in Cathcart, south-east Glasgow.

Holmwood House: a picturesque suburban villa built in 1857–8 for papermill-owner James Couper, possibly the finest work of Alexander 'Greek' Thomson

Holyroodhouse Palace: built in the 1560s for Mary, Queen of Scots, whose apartments are unaltered

Holyroodhouse Palace, Edinburgh

Royal Palaces • £££ • Open all year, daily (closed on certain dates, usually in May and Jun, for royal events), guided tours obligatory in Nov to Mar

The Queen's official residence in Scotland is a Renaissance palace built in the 1560s after the abbey on the site (its ruined church can still be visited) was dissolved. The only part to retain its original decoration is the apartment in the west tower used by Mary, Queen of Scots, where her husband Lord Darnley murdered her secretary, Rizzio, although the 'uncleanable' bloodstain is now no longer refreshed annually.

The state apartments have been greatly altered and, though sumptuously decorated, are, after all, public spaces and have a hotel-like tidiness. The main interest is in the paintings from the royal art collections, including 89 of the 110 portraits of real and imaginary Kings of Scotland painted by Jacob de Wet in 1684–6.

Queen's Gallery (separate admission), abbey ruin, gardens, tearoom, shop.

On edge of Holyrood Park, at eastern end of Royal Mile, central Edinburgh.

Hopetoun House, West Lothian

Privately owned (HHA) • £££ • Open Apr to Sep, daily

A peculiar house, of astonishing scale and grandeur but with few real treats to offer. It was built in 1699–1707 by Sir William Bruce, the leading Scottish architect of his day, for Charles Hope, later the 1st Earl of Hopetoun; and rebuilt from 1721 by the successor to Bruce's title, William Adam. After Adam's death in 1748, the decoration was completed by his son John, whose work was finally done by 1767.

The older part of the house, designed by Bruce, has a vastly more ancient feel; most interesting of its rooms is the unusual staircase with its twisting stair, richly carved wood panelling and, up above, a cupola with wonderful painted decoration by an unknown hand. The suite of rooms designed by the Adams is on a far grander scale, with ornate rococo plasterwork and furniture, the latter by the noted maker James Cullen. But none of it is as enjoyable as the climb up a service stair to the roof, from where the views are excellent.

Parkland with woodland walks, gardens (both open as house), tearoom, shop.

Signposted off A904 South Queensferry to Bo'ness road, 12 miles west of Edinburgh.

Hopetoun House: built on an epic scale for the Earl of Hopetoun by Sir William Bruce in 1699–1707 and remodelled by William Adam and sons in 1721–67

House of the Binns, West Lothian

National Trust for Scotland • £££ • Open Jun to Sep, M-Th, S & Su, guided tours only

Originally a castle-like house built in 1612–30 by Thomas Dalyell, an Edinburgh butter merchant who made his fortune after he accompanied James VI to London to take the English throne in 1603. Still lived in by the Dalyells and now the home of respected politician Tam Dalyell, it's a welcoming and warm place – literally warm, since the fire in the entrance hall blazes merrily in all but the hottest weather – and the tour is equally friendly, but the house has no special merit beyond the story of how it has grown and changed over the years under its different owners.

Most famous of these owners was General Tam Dalyell, whose exploits include escaping from the Tower of London after he was imprisoned for fighting on the side of the royalists in 1650. After that he spent 10 years in Russia, training the Tsar's armies, marrying and becoming a Russian nobleman. Best of the house's features are some fine plasterwork ceilings added in about 1630, ready for a visit by Charles I.

Parkland with walks (open all year, daily).

Signposted on A904 South Queensferry to Bo'ness road, 15 miles west of Edinburgh.

The House of the Binns: built in 1612–30 by Thomas Dalyell, a merchant, and altered greatly since

Lauriston Castle, Edinburgh

Local council • £££ • Open Apr to Oct, M-Th, S & Su, guided tours only

Set in a park in an Edinburgh suburb, Lauriston is, surprisingly, an extraordinarily interesting place to visit. A tower of the 1500s that, being conveniently close to the city, was continually lived in and updated over the years, it was eventually converted into a very comfortable dwelling between 1903 and 1919 by its then owner, William Robert Reid. Although it is chiefly Edwardian in character – not a period that lends itself readily to fascinating interiors – what makes it so absorbing is the story told by its contents of the character and nature of its owner.

William, who lived here with his wife, Margaret, and her bachelor brother, was the owner of the prestigious cabinet-making firm of Morison and Co. The firm came to specialize in creating interiors for luxury trains, a business for which it built an international reputation, and as a result William travelled throughout Europe and often entertained European visitors. Perhaps the room that reflects him best is the library, a long, narrow room with a railway-carriage-like air to it, carpeted with the same hard-wearing fabric used in trains.

Above all, though, William was fascinated by examples of the skills and cleverness of good craftsmen, and the house is filled with objects that he bought because he admired them. For example, he had a superb collection of bow-fronted cabinets and commodes, some of which curve in two directions. Not everything he collected was expensive: the 'wool mosaics' in the hall were cheap and mass-produced, but again the way they were made was unusual.

Gardens with views over Firth of Forth.

Signposted off A90 in Lauriston, near Cramond, north-west Edinburgh.

Lauriston Castle: an Edwardian conversion of a tower of the 1500s, with a fascinating collection of objects

Mellerstain: begun by William Adam in 1725 for George Baillie, and completed in 1770–8 by Robert Adam in typically elegant style for another George Baillie

Mellerstain House, Berwickshire

Privately owned (HHA) • £££ • Open May to Sep, M, W-F, S & Su, Oct, S & Su

One of the most wonderful houses in Scotland, thanks to the input of the superlative Robert Adam, and with a marvellously romantic story attached, too.

The estate of Mellerstain was given by Charles I in 1642 to George Baillie, the son of a prosperous Edinburgh merchant. George's son, Robert, who inherited in about 1646, was imprisoned in 1676 after an attempt to rescue his brother from jail. While he was incarcerated in the Edinburgh Tollbooth, his friend Sir Patrick Hume, later Earl of Marchmont, sent his 12-year-old daughter Grisell on a dangerous mission to get a message to Robert, which the plucky young lady was able to do. In 1684, both Robert and Sir Patrick,

who as Covenanters were in conflict with the government, were forced to flee abroad and had their estates confiscated; but after the accession of William III in 1688 their estates were returned and they came home. In 1691, Robert's son, George Baillie, married Grisell. Her portrait at about the age of 60, painted by Maria Varelst, hangs in the front hall; it is a remarkable picture, full of life and spirit.

In 1725, work started on a new house for George and his wife, designed by William Adam; but for some reason it seems that only the two wings were completed, and that between them an older house was left standing. In 1759 George's grandson, another George, inherited and between 1770 and 1778 he employed Robert Adam to finish what the architect's father had begun. The house has not been altered since.

From the outside, it doesn't look much like a Robert Adam house – although that may be because of

the client's preferences, or perhaps to blend in with the earlier work, and the internal layout is typically Adam. But there is no mistaking the decorative details: the ceiling of the library, dated 1770, with roundels painted by Antonio Zucci and still in its original shades of pale green, Wedgewood blue and sand, has a reputation as one of Adam's outstanding creations.

As ever, Adam was adept at solving tricky problems and paid attention to the smallest detail: both qualities are obvious in the staircase hall, where the graceful stairs are squeezed into a narrow space and the polished wooden handrail is so gracefully shaped and beautifully finished that it's worth coming here just to run your hand along it.

Extensive gardens and grounds (open as house), tearoom, shop.

Signposted on minor road off A6089 and B6397, 6 miles north-east of Kelso.

Mount Stuart, Isle of Bute

Privately owned (HHA) • £££ • Open May to Aug, M, W, F, S & Su

Possibly the most extraordinary house ever built in Britain, created for the equally extraordinary John Patrick Crichton-Stuart, 3rd Marquess of Bute, from 1878 and occupied from 1886, but still unfinished on the Marquess's death in 1900. It was the first house in Scotland lit by electricity, and the first in the world with an indoor swimming pool.

Designed by the leading Scottish architect of the time, Sir Robert Rowand Anderson, who had worked in London with Sir George Gilbert Scott (architect of the Midland Hotel at St Pancras) and had restored many Scottish churches and cathedrals, it is a gothic extravaganza, but with French and Italian influences rather than British ones. At its heart is a vast, cathedral-like hall ringed with marble pillars which must be one of the most impressive rooms ever built for a private home.

The 3rd Marquess's father had inherited, through his first wife, vast estates in Cardiff and South Wales and had secured the family's fortunes by developing those estates, building the docks at Cardiff and so turning the city into a major port. By the time he came of age in 1868, the 3rd Marquess was thought to be the richest man in Britain. Architecture was one of his chief passions: with the wayward gothic genius William Burges he built the medieval fantasy of Castell Coch, near Cardiff, and restored Cardiff Castle in similarly over-the-top fashion.

The interiors of Mount Stuart were the responsibility of Burges's assistant at Cardiff, William Frame, who coordinated the activities of many superb craftsmen and artists who had also worked at Cardiff: the decorative painter and stained-glass artist Horatio Walter Lonsdale, the sculptor Thomas Nicholl, the painter Charles Campbell. Their astonishing work is what makes the house so fascinating to visit.

Although a little more work was carried out, by the 1920s the house was abandoned and put up for sale, on the condition it was demolished. Happily, however, it survived, and in the 1980s John Bute, 6th Marquess, set about restoring and completing it, employing a new generation of artists and craftspeople to give it fresh creative input: the results are wonderfully fresh, yet in keeping with the original work.

Besides its superb decoration, the house also has a splendid collection of art, much of it gathered in the late 1700s by the 3rd Earl of Bute, patron of the arts and sciences and Prime Minister from 1762 to 1763. Portraits in the dining room by Gainsborough, Reynolds and Ramsay were all commissioned by him.

Extensive grounds with walks, gardens (all open as house), visitor centre, adventure playground, restaurant, shop.

Signposted on A844, 5 miles south of Rothesay ferry terminal.

Mount Stuart: one of the most splendid and extraordinary houses in Britain, built in 1878–1900 for the wealthiest man in Britain, the 3rd Marquess of Bute

Newhailes, Edinburgh

*National Trust for Scotland • £££ •
Open Apr to Sep, M, Th-F, S & Su, Oct,
S & Su, guided tours only – admission by
timed ticket, booking advised*

Not an especially large house – its broad facade makes it seem bigger, but it is only one room deep – nor particularly distinguished, Newhailes appeals mostly because it has been little altered over the past two centuries. It has a gentle air of daily wear and tear – not decay so much as a comfortable settling in – that has been left untouched since its acquisition by the Trust in 1996, except for the careful repair and conservation of anything that might be dangerous. So the iron handrail of the front steps has been made safe, but its timeworn beauty has been retained.

The house was built in 1686 by the architect James Smith as his own home, but he sold it in 1702 when his debts and large family made it impractical. In 1709 it was bought by Sir David Dalrymple, who made some changes, as did his son, Sir James, and grandson, David, Lord Hailes. Hailes was a key figure in the Scottish Enlightenment,

Newhailes: built in 1686, bought by the Dalrymples in 1709 and little changed in the past 200 years

and Dr Johnson is said to have called his library 'the most learned room in Europe'.

The huge library is easily the most impressive room, but the interest lies in the house's unaltered state and the stories it tells – and not just of the family, either; the walk through the servants' tunnel is especially evocative.

Estate and gardens (open all year, daily), restaurant, shop.

Signposted on A6095, off A1 on west side of Musselburgh.

Pollok House, Glasgow

*National Trust for Scotland • £££ •
Open all year, daily*

The Maxwells had lived on their estates here for centuries, building several castles, until in the 1740s Sir John Maxwell felt the need for a more modern and fashionable home. Designed by an unknown architect, it is a tall and slightly austere structure, its rustic stone giving it a castle-like severity, but inside it was enlivened by flowing rococo plasterwork, thought to be by the Clayton family, much of which survives.

The house was left unaltered until the 1890s, when Sir John Stirling Maxwell decided to update it to the standards required for late Victorian entertaining. He added a new entrance hall and kitchen block, but appreciated the Georgian interiors and fitted them out with appropriate Chippendale furniture.

The plasterwork apart, the chief appeal today is in the superb art collection that the last Sir John brought to the house, in particular a wonderful and famous El Greco, *Lady in a Fur Wrap*, and intriguing pictures by William Blake.

Country park, Burrell Collection of art (separate admission), restaurant, shop.

Signposted from junctions 1 & 2 of M77, 3 miles south of Glasgow city centre.

Pollok House: built in the 1740s by Sir John Maxwell and updated in the early 1900s, with fine plasterwork

Thirlestane Castle, Berwickshire

Privately owned (HHA) • £££ • Open May to mid-Oct, M-F & Su

From the front, the square-towered wings of the 1800s give Thirlestane a wide, leadenly fairytale look – but from the garden side you can see the original long, tall keep built in the late 1500s by John Maitland, Lord Chancellor to James VI of Scotland, James I of England.

The keep did not stay unaltered for long. In the 1670s it was remodelled in palatial style by the first great Scottish architect, Sir William Bruce, for the 2nd Earl (and later Duke) of Lauderdale, who fought on the Royalist side in the Civil War, spent nine years in the Tower of London and became a leading member of Charles II's government after the restoration.

Inside, its 1670s splendour is still seen in the outstanding plasterwork of the ceilings. Furnishings are in a lavish Victorian style, and there are many excellent portraits.

Craft and country museums, gardens (open as house), tearoom, shop.

Signposted on A68 Edinburgh to Jedburgh road at Lauder, 28 miles south of Edinburgh.

Thirlestane Castle: built in the late 1500s, revamped in palatial style in the 1670s, with Victorian additions

Traquair, Lothian

Privately owned (HHA) • £££ • Open mid-Apr to Oct, daily

Sometimes said to be the oldest inhabited house in Scotland, this is a wonderfully haphazard, ancient and welcoming place. Its fascination lies not only in the way it has developed over the years – and in details such as the decorations applied, later covered over and eventually revealed again – but also in the many characters associated with the house, and the unusual objects that have found their way here.

The oldest part is a tower of the 1100s, on the first floor of which is a bedroom used by Mary, Queen of Scots and furnished with a bed (brought from elsewhere) in which she once slept. At the top of the same tower, in an extension of the 1300s, are traces of a superb mural of 1530, one of the earliest of its kind in Scotland. The room is now used as a museum, with Mary's rosary and crucifix on show.

The Stuart family, who acquired Traquair in 1491 and still live here, was Catholic from the 1650s, and one of the most evocative parts of the house is the priest's room in which the resident chaplain lived in hiding, with a secret altar and a hidden stair, which visitors can explore if they wish.

The drawing room on the first floor of an extension built in the 1500s has traces of the original elaborate painted decoration on the beams, but, typically for this ever-changing house, was done out in classical style in the mid-1700s; while the main dining room is, again typically, a Victorian creation in a wing of the 1600s – one of two 'modern' wings that flank the house.

Grounds and gardens (open as house), working brewery, craft shops, tearoom.

Signposted on B709, off A72 Peebles to Galashiels road at Innerleithen.

Traquair: a pleasingly ancient house, based on a tower of the 1100s with modifications through to the 1600s

See also…

Arniston House
Gorebridge, Midlothian
Privately owned (HHA), £££, open Apr and Jun, Tu-W, Jul to Sep, M-F & Su, tours only
Nice William Adam mansion begun in 1726 with fine plasterwork.

Ayton Castle
Ayton, Eyemouth, Berwickshire
Privately owned (HHA), ££, open mid-May to mid-Sep, S & Su
Pleasing Scots baronial castle-style house of red sandstone built in 1846, designed by James Gillespie Graham.

Bachelors' Club
Sandgate Street, Tarbolton
National Trust for Scotland, ££, open Apr to Sep, M-Tu, F, S & Su
Thatched house of 1600s where Robert Burns and friends formed a debating society in 1780.

Blairquhan Castle
Maybole, Ayrshire
Privately owned (HHA), £££, open mid-Jul to mid-Aug, daily
House of 1821–4 with original Regency furniture, in large grounds.

Bowhill House
Selkirk
Privately owned (HHA), £££, open Jul, daily
House of 1812 with restored Victorian kitchen, garden, landscaped grounds.

Burns Cottage
Alloway, Ayrshire
Privately owned, ££, open all year, daily
Thatched cottage in which the poet Robert was born in 1759, with museum in adjacent building.

Carlyle's House
Ecclefechan, Dumfries and Galloway
National Trust for Scotland, ££, open May to Sep, M, Th-F, S & Su
House in which Thomas Carlyle was born in 1795, early 1800s furnishing.

Dalmeny House
South Queensferry, Edinburgh
Privately owned (HHA), £££, open Jul and Aug, M-Tu & Su, tours only
Gothicky, castle-like house of the 1700s in unspoilt parkland on the outskirts of the capital, the family home of the Earls of Rosebery, with outstanding collection of 1700s French furniture.

Ferniehirst Castle
Jedburgh, Roxburghshire
Privately owned, ££, open Jul, Tu-F, S & Su
Stone castle of 1500s kept in use as family home and restored in 1980s.

Gosford House
Longniddry, East Lothian
Privately owned (HHA), £££, open late Jun to Jul, W-F, S & Su
Robert Adam house plus wing built in 1890, with spendid marble hall.

Kelburn
Fairlie, Largs, Ayrshire
Privately owned (HHA), ££, open Jul, Aug, early Sep, daily
Developed castle, home to Earls of Glasgow; also countryside centre.

Lennoxlove Castle
Haddington, East Lothian
Privately owned (HHA), £££, open Apr to Oct, W-Th, S & Su, tours only
Medieval tower house with 1600s and 1700s additions, strong links with Mary, Queen of Scots.

Manderston
Duns, Berwickshire
Privately owned (HHA), £££, open mid-May to Sep, Th & Su
Grand house rebuilt 1903–5 with Adam-style interiors, interesting service rooms, dairy, stables.

Newliston
Kirkliston, West Lothian
Privately owned (HHA), £, open May to early Jun, W-F, S & Su
Late Robert Adam house with costume display, landscaped grounds.

Paxton House
Near Berwick-upon-Tweed
Privately owned (HHA), £££, open Apr to Oct, daily, tours only
Country house of 1758–62 by John and James Adam, with picture gallery of 1814 acting as 'partner gallery' of National Galleries of Scotland.

The Tenement House
Buccleuch Street, Glasgow
National Trust for Scotland, free, open Mar to Oct, daily
Tenement flat built in 1892, kept as 'time capsule' of early 20th century.

Lennoxlove Castle: a medieval tower house that has strong associations with Mary, Queen of Scots

Eastern Scotland
Perthshire, Fife, Grampian Highlands (including Aberdeenshire)

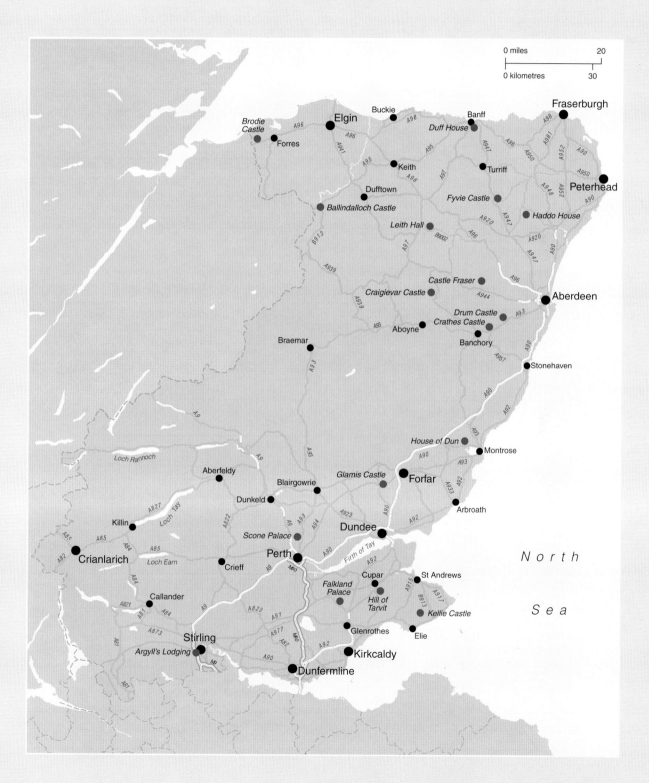

0 miles 20
0 kilometres 30

Fraserburgh

Buckie

Banff

Brodie
Castle

Elgin

Duff House

A96

A96

Forres

A941

A98

A98

A981

A952

A90

Peterhead

A95

A95

Keith

A947

Turriff

A950

A948

A950

A96

Dufftown

A97

Fyvie Castle

A920

Haddo House

Ballindalloch Castle

Leith Hall

B9002

A96

A947

A920

B913

A97

A939

Castle Fraser

A960

Craigievar Castle

A944

A96

Aberdeen

A939

Drum Castle

A93

Braemar

A93

Aboyne

Crathes Castle

Banchory

A93

Stonehaven

A957

A90

A92

House of Dun

A935

Montrose

Loch Rannoch

A90

A93

A926

Aberfeldy

Blairgowrie

Glamis Castle

Forfar

A933

Dunkeld

A827

A832

A93

A923

A90

Arbroath

Killin

Loch Tay

A94

Dundee

A92

North

Scone Palace

A9

Firth of Tay

Crianlarich

A85

A84

A85

Loch Earn

Perth

A90

A92

Sea

A82

Crieff

A9

Cupar

St Andrews

A915

Callander

A823

Falkland
Palace

Hill of
Tarvit

A917

B913

A821

A81

A84

A9

A91

Kellie Castle

A873

A977

A82

Glenrothes

Elie

Stirling

A90

A92

Argyll's Lodging

M9

Kirkcaldy

A91

Dunfermline

229

Argyll's Lodging, Stirling

Historic Scotland • £££ • Open all year, daily

A rare and fascinating example of the town house of a wealthy nobleman of the 1600s, used when in attendance on the king at the royal castle of Stirling. It was developed from an 'L-plan' tower house of the late 1500s; first in the 1630s by Sir William Alexander, Secretary of State to James VI and I from 1626; then in the 1670s by Archibald Campbell, 9th Earl of Argyll, from whom it gets its name.

The interiors have been restored and furnished with modern replicas in accordance with inventories of 1680 and 1682. Although these furnishings inevitably have a slightly artificial, theatrical quality, they do serve to give an impression of what the house was like and how the rooms were used, and bring to life intimate details such as the toilet arrangements, provided by a 'close stool' in the corner.

Nearby is the splendid ruin of the Earl of Mar's house of about 1570.

Shop.

On Upper Castlehill Wynd, just below the castle, in central Stirling.

Argyll's Lodging: a remarkable town house of the 1630s and 1670s, once the home of the Earl of Argyll

Ballindalloch Castle, Banffshire

Privately owned (HHA) • £££ • Open Easter to Sep, M-F & Su

A surprisingly cosy, cottage-like castle, developed from a 'Z-plan' tower house built in about 1546 and the home of the Macpherson-Grants ever since. A wing was added in 1770 by General James Grant, who fought in the American War of Independence, and the whole was renovated in 1850 by the architect

Thomas MacKenzie, whose changes include a weird but appealing vaulted ceiling in the entrance hall.

Where the interiors are not Victorian, they are unashamedly modern; but the place has such a pleasing, lived-in feel that this hardly matters. Its greatest treasures are the fine collection of Spanish paintings of the 1600s – and the old teddy bears in the nursery.

Gardens, tearoom, shop.

On A95 Elgin to Grantown-on-Spey road, 22 miles south of Elgin.

Ballindalloch Castle: a cosy, comfortable, almost cottage-like castle, based on a 'Z-plan' tower house of 1546, expanded in 1770 and remodelled in 1850

Brodie Castle, Moray

National Trust for Scotland • £££ • Open Apr to Sep, M-Th & Su (also Apr, Jul, Aug, F & S)

The friendliest and most pleasant of the many lived-in castles of the region to have been 'improved' in the 1800s, marked out from the rest by an excellent art collection with a particular emphasis on works by 20th-century artists. Fundamentally it is a 'Z-plan' tower house of the late 1500s, its tall central block having square towers at opposite corners to form the 'Z'. Extensions were added in the early 1800s and further improvements made not long after, but these have not swamped the original tower house.

The Brodies have lived on this site for more than 800 years, and in the castle for more than 400. Built in the 1560s by Alexander, 12th Laird of Brodie, it was probably started before he forfeited his lands to the Crown for his involvement in the Earl of Huntly's rebellion against Mary, Queen of Scots in 1562; but it was certainly finished

Brodie Castle: built in the 1560s, enlarged in the 1630s and 1820s, and with a splendid art collection

not long after his estates were restored to him in 1566, since the date 1567 appears on the caphouse at the top of the south-west tower.

An extra wing was built in the early 1600s by Alexander, the 13th Laird, who inherited in 1632 at the age of 15. The wonderfully extravagant and naive strapwork plaster ceiling of what is now the blue sitting room – originally the Laird's private room – carries his initials and those of his wife, Elizabeth Innes, who died in 1640, five years after they were married.

Alexander was closely involved with the political events of those turbulent times, travelling to The Hague and Breda with the Scottish government delegations that negotiated with Charles II over his return in 1651, and summoned by Cromwell in 1653 to talk about a possible union with England.

Little changed at the castle until 1824 when William, 22nd Laird, commissioned William Burn to enlarge it greatly. The plan was abandoned when only partly completed, and William had to sell

the contents of the house to pay for even that. Luckily he married a wealthy heiress, Elizabeth Baillie, in 1838 and was able to engage the York architect William Wylson to remodel Burn's extension and create the entrance hall and library.

Today, its restored interiors are richly decorated and furnished, but always comfortable and welcoming. The excellent art collection is the house's outstanding feature, with a changing display of 20th century pictures joining many earlier works – 17th-century Dutch paintings, English watercolours of the 1800s, works by the Scottish Colourists. Some of the fine family portraits, among them works by Ramsay and Romney, have stories to tell, too: Lady Margaret Duff, depicted by John Downman, eloped with the 21st Laird, James, in 1767 but died tragically in a fire in 1786.

Grounds with woodland walks, gardens (open all year, daily), Victorian dairy, tearoom, shop.

Signposted on A96 Nairn to Elgin road, 5 miles west of Forres.

Castle Fraser, Aberdeenshire

*National Trust for Scotland • £££ •
Open Apr to Sep, M-Tu, F, S & Su (Jul and
Aug, daily)*

The largest and most elaborate of all
Scotland's 'Z-plan' tower houses,
and one of the last, begun in 1575 by
Michael Fraser, the 6th Laird, and
completed by his son, Andrew, in
1636. At its heart is an older hall
which may already have been
standing in 1454 when the Frasers –
a family of Norman origin, whose
emblem, a strawberry, is a pun on the
French word *fraise* – were granted
the lands here by King James II, who
was looking to settle loyal supporters
in the area after taking over the
powerful Earldom of Mar.

Both outside and in, it seems
almost unchanged since it was built,
thanks to a careful restoration in
the 1920s. The furnishings are
largely Victorian (although the
dining room was painted in its
present colours as recently as
1977), but the main interest is in
the fabric of the ancient building.
The climb to the top of the round
tower is particularly worthwhile.

Many of the Frasers led colourful
lives, reminders of which are
abundant: notably the wheelchair
of Charles Mackenzie Fraser, who
lost a leg fighting with Wellington
in Spain in 1812.

*Grounds with walks, walled gardens
(open as house), tearoom, shop.*

*Signposted on minor road off A944 Aberdeen
to Alford road, 16 miles west of Aberdeen.*

Craigievar Castle: a wonderful tower house built in 1610–26 by a wealthy merchant, William Forbes

Craigievar Castle, Aberdeenshire

*National Trust for Scotland • £££ •
Open Apr to Sep, M-Tu, F, S & Su,
guided tours only*

Like Castle Fraser, this is one of
the last of the tower houses, built
between 1610 and 1626 – but so
pleasing in its form, and designed
with such sophistication and
delicacy, that it seems almost like
an affectionate pastiche, as if
deliberately archaic, anticipating
the Scots baronial style that would
become popular two centuries later.

Indeed, it owes its survival in
such a largely unaltered state to the
early recognition of its qualities by
the Aberdeen architect John Smith,
brought in by Sir John Forbes to
assess its condition in 1824. Smith
recommended vital repairs and also
enlarged some windows, but from
this time its fame as a beautiful and
interesting old building seems to
have spread. The Forbes family
used it only as a summer residence,
in which role its cramped quarters
weren't too much of a problem.

Castle Fraser: one of the last castles, built between 1575 and 1636 by Michael Fraser and his son, Andrew

It was built by William Forbes, an Edinburgh-born merchant who made a fortune trading with the Baltic and earned the nickname 'Danzig Willie'. Its outstanding feature is its moulded plaster ceilings, a decorative technique made fashionable in Scotland after the royal apartments at Edinburgh Castle were remodelled for the visit in 1617 of King James VI and I.

Equally rare and interesting are the Jacobean carved woodwork in the hall, in the same Renaissance style as the plasterwork, and the screens passage. Some of the furniture in the hall may be original, too. The last major changes were made in the early 1700s, with baroque additions such as wooden panelling in several rooms, and the acquisition of a quantity of fashionable furniture. After that, little changed.

The appeal is not just in the old decoration and furnishing, however. From its time as a Victorian holiday home, Craigievar has a lived-in and loved feel, and offers glimpses – such as the servants' quarters in the cramped attics – of daily life in those upstairs, downstairs days.

Grounds with walks (open all year, daily).

Signposted on A980 Alford to Banchory road, 6 miles south of Alford.

Crathes Castle, Aberdeenshire

National Trust for Scotland • £££ • Open Apr to Oct, daily

Another of the region's splendid tower house castles. Although, like most of the others, it was lived in and modified over the past four centuries, the difference with Crathes is that its interest lies exclusively in the original decoration and furnishings that survive.

The Burnett family who built it were descendants of Alexander Burnard, who in the early 1300s was rewarded for his loyalty to Robert the Bruce when he was granted an estate at Banchory and made Royal Forester of the king's newly declared Forest of Drum. Alexander set up home on an artificial island (a crannog) on the Loch of Leys; an ivory horn called the Horn of Leys, which hangs in the castle, is said to have been the badge of office given to him by the king.

The family was still living on the loch in 1543 when Alexander Burnett married Janet Hamilton, who owned large quantities of church land. With Janet's money, Alexander was able to start building the castle as their new home. Work started in 1553, but Alexander died in 1574,

and his son and grandson followed within the next four years, so it was left to his great-grandson, another Alexander, and his wife, Katherine Gordon, to finish it, which they did in 1596. The arms of both Alexander and Janet and Alexander and Katherine are set over the door.

The outstanding feature of Crathes is the colourful painted decoration of its beamed ceilings, dating from the late 1500s and early 1600s. It survives in many rooms, each with a different theme: the nine nobles in one room, the nine muses and seven virtues in another. Not as attractive, but equally interesting, is the oak panelled ceiling of the long gallery.

No less extraordinary is the original furniture that survives: a bed dated 1594 and carved with holly leaves, the Horn of Leys and boars' heads, all symbols of Alexander's and Katherine's families; and two armchairs carved with their initials. The later furniture scattered around the place scarcely seems to matter by comparison, although a fine William Morris tapestry seems very much at home.

Grounds with walks, extensive gardens (open all year, daily), restaurant, shop.

Signposted on A93 Banchory to Aberdeen road, 3 miles east of Banchory.

Crathes Castle: built between 1553 and 1596 and completed by Alexander Burnett and his wife Katherine, some of whose furniture and decoration survives

Drum Castle, Aberdeenshire

National Trust for Scotland • £££ •
Open Apr to Sep, daily

Very different from most remodelled tower houses, in that the ancient keep – one of the three oldest in Scotland, dating from the 1100s – was simply abandoned in the early 1600s and a new, Jacobean house built on the side of it. Although the new house was not quite as modern and elegant as it now looks on the garden side, with large windows and a Georgian doorway added in the late 1700s, it was certainly very different from the archaic tower houses then being built at Craigievar and Castle Fraser.

The new house was the work of Alexander Irvine, 9th Laird of Drum, known as 'Little Breeches' because he followed the European fashion of doublet and hose, and his wife, Marion Douglas, whose initials appear on the Renaissance-style dormer windows. The heir of a family that had lived at Drum since the time of Robert the Bruce, Alexander was wealthy enough to lend money to King James VI, served as Sheriff of Aberdeen and was a philanthropist who founded a scholarship at Aberdeen University and established benefactions for the poor; his wife built a hospital.

The Irvines were, unusually for this area, Catholics and Royalists who fought on the King's side in the Civil War and supported the Jacobite risings of 1715 and 1745, and were often impoverished. This changed somewhat under the 18th Laird, another Alexander, who lived a quiet life and was Master of Drum for 83 years, until his death in 1844. His grandson, Alexander Forbes Irvine, recovered land lost in tougher times and improved the estate. With his wife, Anna, a noted amateur artist, he employed the architect David Bryce to make improvements in keeping with the Jacobean house.

The most striking change was the conversion of the first floor of the old keep into a library, its barrel-vaulted ceiling newly decorated with the coats of arms of the Irvines and the families they had intermarried with, the Forbes and Keiths. Apart from this impressive room, the house is mostly a pleasant but uninspiring mix of Georgian and Victorian, notable more for family heirlooms – such as paintings by Anna Forbes Irvine – than for its furnishing and decoration.

Extensive grounds with woodland walks (open all year, daily), walled gardens with historic roses, tearoom, shop.

Signposted on minor road off A93 Banchory to Aberdeen road, 10 miles west of Aberdeen.

Duff House, Aberdeenshire

Local council, Historic Scotland and National Galleries of Scotland • ££ •
Open all year, Th-F, S & Su

Architecturally one of the most interesting houses in Scotland, designed in a wholeheartedly baroque style by William Adam in the 1730s. It was meant to have

Drum Castle: the ancient tower, built in the 1100s, was abandoned for a new Jacobean house, completed in 1619, with Georgian and Victorian alterations

*Duff House: the finest baroque exterior in
Scotland, designed in 1735 by William Adam*

two vast, sweeping wings, but the
architect fell out with his client,
William Duff, 1st Earl of Fife, an
exceptionally wealthy businessman
and politician, and the wings were
never completed. Instead a separate
kitchen block was built, now gone.

In the early 1800s the 4th Earl,
who had fought under Wellington
in the Peninsular War, achieved a
reputation as a patron of the arts
and gave lavish parties among the
fine paintings and furnishings of
Duff House, so it seems appropriate
that the house is now an art gallery,
displaying paintings from the
national collections chosen to fit
the style and period of the house.

Some of the splendid interiors
are furnished in the style of the
mid-1700s and retain their original
feel, with fine plasterwork and
decoration, most impressive of all
being the great drawing room,
furnished with a set of chairs
designed by Robert Adam and
made by Chippendale.

Grounds with walks, tearoom, shop.

*Signposted off A97 Banff to Huntly road
on south-west side of Banff.*

Falkland Palace, Fife

*National Trust for Scotland • £££ • Open
Mar to Oct, daily*

This graceful and fascinating
building was a royal hunting
palace, almost a holiday home for
the Kings of Scotland. It was begun
in 1453–63 by James II and
enlarged in 1500–13 by James IV,
but achieved its ultimate size and
sophistication under James V
between 1536 and 1541. By the
latter date, it had become the finest
Renaissance building in Britain.

The palace was used by Mary,
Queen of Scots and James VI and I,
and was visited by Charles I and,
before his defeats in England in
1651, Charles II, but after the Civil
War it slowly decayed – although it
is still, even now, Crown property –
and a Hereditary Keeper continued
to be appointed.

In 1887 the office went to the
3rd Marquess of Bute, who besides
being astonishingly wealthy was
also an architectural enthusiast: he
built two of the most remarkable
houses of late Victorian times,
Mount Stuart on the Isle of Bute
and Castell Coch in South Wales.
Lord Bute restored much of the
palace and in 1946 his grandson,
Major Michael Crichton Stuart,
made it his home and employed a
leading garden designer, Percy Crane,
to revitalize the gardens.

As Lord Bute's creation, it is one
of those rare houses where the
'new' work is as pleasing as the old.
Much of the palace was a shell,
needing floors as well as a roof, but
the craftsmanship and antiquarian
spirit of the interiors
of the replacement rooms in the
gatehouse, known as the Keeper's
quarters, makes them as interesting
as the one room in which much
original work survives, the chapel
royal. Here the painted ceiling and
trompe l'oeil frieze added for the
visit of Charles I in 1633 survive.

Equally satisfying, although
totally artificial, are the king's and
queen's bedrooms. The former was
reconstructed in 1952 to look just
as James V's bedroom might have
done, in a room wrongly identified
by Lord Bute as the king's, with a
bed from the time of James VI. The
latter was decorated and furnished
in 1987, in the full knowledge that
it was in the wrong room, in a style
appropriate to the time of Mary,
Queen of Scots, although the bed
was made in 1889 for Lord Bute.

*Restored 'real tennis' court of 1539,
the oldest in the world, gardens, shop.*

*In centre of Falkland, off A912, 11 miles
north of Kirkcaldy.*

Falkland Palace: the restored south range of a splendid Renaissance palace built by James V in 1536–41

Fyvie Castle: wonderful Scots baronial creation of about 1592 by Alexander Seton, Lord Chancellor of Scotland, revamped as a sumptuous Edwardian house

Fyvie Castle, Aberdeenshire

National Trust for Scotland • £££ • Open Apr to Sep, M-Tu, F, S & Su (Jul and Aug, daily)

One of the biggest and most extravagant of the original 'Scots baronial' castles of the late 1500s and early 1600s, Fyvie passed through the hands of many wealthy owners who enlarged it and enhanced it, culminating in the late 1800s and early 1900s with its purchase by a wealthy industrialist descended from one of its first owners, who turned it into one of the most remarkable houses of the Edwardian era.

Fyvie was a royal possession until 1391, when King Robert III gave it to Sir Henry Preston in exchange for the English knight Ralph de Percy, captured at the Battle of Otterburn in 1388, whose ransom would be a small fortune. Thereafter it passed by marriage to the Meldrum family, who in 1596 sold it to Alexander Seton, a leading lawyer and political adviser to James VI, later Chancellor of Scotland, who rebuilt it in the wonderfully exuberant style that it retains today. An extra tower was added to Seton's three in the late 1700s by the Hon William Gordon of Fyvie, a general under, and loyal servant to, George III; a fifth tower was added in 1890 by Alexander Leith, who bought the castle in 1889, having made a vast fortune in the steel industry in America. His mother, Mary Forbes, was a descendant of Sir Henry Preston.

Inside, the only survival from Seton's day is the superbly broad spiral stair. The decoration spans many centuries, but is dominated by the sumptuous Edwardian interiors added by Alexander Leith. These are at their most impressive in the new rooms of Leith's tower, at the top of which is a room so unrestrained that it's enough to make you laugh out loud: the gallery, used for entertaining, has a huge self-playing pipe organ crammed in under the barrel vault of its roof.

Excellent paintings in the house include portraits by Gainsborough and Romney and the finest collection of Raeburns outside the Scottish National Gallery.

Extensive grounds with lochside walks, walled gardens, racquets court, bird hide, restored earth closet, tearoom, shop.

Signposted on A947 Turriff to Oldmeldrum road at Fyvie, 8 miles south of Turriff.

Glamis Castle, Perthshire

Privately owned (HHA) • £££ • Open Apr to Oct, daily, guided tours only

The birthplace of Elizabeth Bowes-Lyon, wife of King George VI and mother of the present Queen, this has been the home of the Lyon family since 1372, when Sir John Lyon was made Thane of Glamis by King Robert II. The tall 'L-plan' tower at its centre was started by his son,

Haddo House: designed in 1732 by William Adam for the 2nd Earl of Aberdeen, extensively remodelled and decorated in 'Adam revival' style in the 1880s

Patrick, in about 1435 and finished in 1484, and the castle achieved its present form in about 1679.

The interiors, with fine plaster ceilings of the 1620s, are largely Victorian in character and piled high with family memorabilia.

Park, Italian gardens, restaurant, shop.

Off A94 Perth to Forfar road in Glamis village, 12 miles north of Dundee.

Glamis Castle, below: a wonderful concoction based on an 'L-plan' tower of the late 1400s

Haddo House, Aberdeenshire

National Trust for Scotland • £££ • Open Jun, M, F, S & Su, Jul and Aug, daily, guided tours only

The most elegant of the region's large houses, designed in 1732 by William Adam for William Gordon, 2nd Earl of Aberdeen, a Jacobite sympathizer who managed to sit out the 1715 uprising without getting involved, no doubt fearing the financial consequences: he was described in a family history written by a descendant as 'ambitious, financially accumulative and a thumping snob', and is known to have squeezed his tenants for everything he could get.

Very little remains, however, of the house as it was created by Adam for the 2nd Earl, since it was comprehensively refurbished in the 1880s by John Campbell Gordon, 7th Earl of Aberdeen, and his wife, Ishbel, who on first seeing the house after her husband inherited in 1870 described it as 'horrible'. The main rooms were remodelled – quite successfully, it has to be said, especially in the case of the light and airy morning room, to which a large bay window was added –

and the house was decorated and furnished in the 'Adam revival' style by the fashionable London firm of Wright and Mansfield.

The 'horrible' house had been good enough, however, for the 7th Earl's grandfather, George, 4th Earl of Aberdeen, Prime Minister from 1852 to 1855, and was good enough for Queen Victoria, who visited in 1857. The bedroom in which she stayed is the only upstairs room shown to visitors. George was a remarkable character who began from nothing, his impoverished, widowed mother having died when he was 12, leaving him and his five younger brothers and one sister penniless.

The house, which is still lived in, has a welcoming feel acquired in the 20th century, since when all its owners have been involved in the arts – photographs on a table in the drawing room recall many of the well-known guests. Finest of all its rooms is the chapel designed in 1881 by G.E. Street, the last work he produced.

Country park (local council, open all year, daily), gardens (open all year, daily), tearoom, shop.

Signposted on minor road off B9170 and B999, 4 miles north of Pitmedden.

Hill of Tarvit, Fife

National Trust for Scotland • £££ • Open Apr to Sep, daily, Oct, S & Su

The inside of this attractive little house is not at all what you would expect, having seen the outside. Indeed, the outside isn't quite what it seems, either. There was originally a small Jacobean manor on this site, called Wemyss Hall, built in 1696 by the renowned Scottish architect Sir William Bruce. It was bought in 1906 by Frederick Sharp, a Dundee financier whose father had made a fortune from jute, supplying sackcloth for sandbags to both sides in the American Civil War. Sharp pulled down the old house, keeping only the Victorian service wing at the back (which presumably had been designed in keeping with the Jacobean house).

Sharp himself had made his money through venture capital and the railways: he was a director of the London, Midland and Scottish. A keen golfer, he bought a country estate convenient for St Andrews and wanted to build a house that would be a suitable setting for his art collection, most of which is still on view in the house. He employed the architect Robert Lorimer, who came up with a most unusual creation: a house described in the guidebook as 'like a series of jewel caskets', with each room in a completely different style.

The result is both comfortable and very pleasing. The spacious hall, used as a sitting-room, has a Jacobean feel, with lots of wood panelling and Renaissance-style arches leading to the staircase; it is hung with Flemish tapestries of the 1500s and scattered with interesting Chinese porcelain and bronzes. The drawing room is, by contrast, in a French style of the 1700s, a suitably delicate backdrop to Sharp's Louis XV and XVI furniture.

The library is essentially Scottish, with fascinating portraits by Raeburn and Ramsay, while the dining room is Palladian, to suit Sharp's Georgian furniture. Just as interesting are the well-preserved servery, pantry and kitchen, and there is a fine display of Chinese porcelain upstairs.

Grounds with walks, gardens (open all year, daily), tower house of 1500s (open as house), Edwardian laundry, tearoom, shop.

Signposted on A916, 2 miles south of Cupar.

House of Dun, Angus

National Trust for Scotland • £££ • Open Apr to Sep, M-Tu, F, S & Su (Jul and Aug, daily), guided tours obligatory in quiet periods

This fascinating house is the best surviving example of the work of the architect William Adam, designed in 1730 for David Erskine, a judge of the Scottish Court of Session, whose family had lived on this site overlooking the Montrose Basin since 1375. The new house replaced an old tower house not far away, of which only an arch survives.

The exterior, at least, is not exclusively Adam's work, since Erskine first consulted his friend the Earl of Mar, an architectural enthusiast, who influenced the original design and encouraged more ornamentation in the final revision. It's a most unusual exterior, the entrance front adorned not with the temple-like portico of later Palladian houses, but with a version of a classical triumphal arch.

Inside, the layout is typically Adam and on a pattern that would influence many later architects,

Hill of Tarvit: a very original mansion built in 1906 by Robert Lorimer for financier Frederick Sharp

House of Dun: a splendid William Adam design of 1730 for a well-to-do lawyer, David Erskine

with an entrance hall (with stairs) and saloon running through the centre of the house, and family and state apartments on either side. Typical of him, too, was the placing of the library on the first floor, where it would be quieter, in traditional Scottish fashion.

The house was finished in about 1742–3, when the superb plasterwork by Joseph Enzor was added. This is at its finest in the saloon, where its depictions in high relief of gods and weaponry are filled with subtle Jacobite allusions.

The interiors were remodelled in about 1840, however, and the furnishing and decoration date largely from this time. Outside, the service courtyard with game larder, gamekeeper's room, hen house and potting shed is also fascinating.

Estate with walks, bird reserve with walks and hides, gardens and woodland garden, weaver's workshop, tearoom, shop.

Signposted on A935 Montrose to Brechin road, 3 miles west of Montrose.

Kellie Castle, Fife

National Trust for Scotland • £££ •
Open Jun to Sep, daily

An interesting castle-cum-mansion, made up of one old tower, one newer tower and a block linking the two. The old tower was built in the 1400s, but not much is known of its origins; the newer, almost modern in its simplicity, was completed in 1573 by Lawrence, 4th Lord Oliphant, a wealthy nobleman who was on the council of Mary, Queen of Scots. He gave the castle and estate as dower to his wife, the Lady Margaret Hay, whose initials are carved on the south face.

The new tower stood about 50 feet away from the old one, and nothing is known about what buildings may have stood between the two: but in about 1600 they were linked by a mansion block and a third tower was built by the 5th Lord Oliphant, who in 1613 was forced to sell his new house. It was bought by Sir Thomas Erskine, a childhood friend of King James VI who saved the king's life during the Gowrie conspiracy of 1600.

His grandson Alexander, the 3rd Earl, fought with Charles II at the Battle of Worcester in 1651 and had to flee abroad for a time; his arms appear with those of his first wife on the plasterwork ceiling of the dining room, and with those of his second wife on the even finer ceilings of the great hall and the earl's room. But after the death of the 7th Earl in 1797, the castle was neglected, lived in for a time by a coal prospector and used as a barn by the home farm.

In 1878 it was leased and restored by James Allan Lorimer, a professor at Edinburgh University, who lived here with his wife and six children – one of his sons being Robert, who grew up to become one of Scotland's foremost architects.

Today, the castle is a little sparsely furnished but has many interesting original features and, perhaps more importantly, a spacious, welcoming feel – the air, almost, of a holiday home – which, like the furnishing, reflects the period of the Lorimers' occupation.

Organic walled garden with old-fashioned roses, summerhouse, tearoom, shop.

Signposted on B9171 Drumeldrie to Crail road, 3 miles north-west of Pittenweem.

Kellie Castle: towers of the 1400s and 1573 linked by a mansion of the 1600s, rescued in the 1870s

Leith Hall, Aberdeenshire

National Trust for Scotland • £££ • Open May to Sep, M-Tu, F, S & Su, guided tours only

A handsome little house, the oldest parts of which were built in 1650 by James Leith, son of a family of shipping merchants from Aberdeen, Leith Hall developed in stages over many years. It started as a main block of three storeys with a lower wing and a stable block at its sides, forming three sides of a courtyard; the fourth side was blocked by a wall with a gateway. In 1756–97, the lower wing was enlarged and the stable block rebuilt as kitchens; between 1797 and 1868 this kitchen block was replaced by a new south wing that matched the original house in size; and in the late 1800s a billiards room was built over the old gateway.

The interiors are comfortable, occasionally a little pretentious but never very spectacular, the nicest room being the oval drawing room built in 1797; but what makes a visit interesting is the long and complicated history of the Leith (later Leith-Hay) family, many of whom were military men. Rooms on the top floor are dedicated to a family military museum, full of

Leith Hall: a modest mansion built in 1650 by James Leith and developed greatly in the 1700s and 1800s

objects that bring these characters to life, including the huge stockings of the seven-foot-tall Andrew Hay, a loyal follower of Bonnie Prince Charlie, and the writing case he was given by the Prince on the eve of the Battle of Culloden.

Estate with woodland walks, large gardens, collection of Pictish stones (open all year, daily), ice house, 18th-century stables, tearoom, shop.

Signposted on B9002 Huntly to Kennethmont road, 1 mile west of Kennethmont.

Scone Palace, Perthshire

Privately owned (HHA) • £££ • Open Apr to Oct, daily

Originally the bishop's house and accommodation ranges of the Augustinian Abbey of Scone, standing at the traditional crowning-place of Scottish kings. The abbey was burned down by a mob at the reformation in 1559, and the remaining buildings given by King James VI and I in 1604 to Sir David Murray, his Cup-bearer (depicted in that role in a nice contemporary portrait that hangs in an ante-room), whose descendants, the Earls of Mansfield, have lived here ever since.

The palace was remodelled in a tidy and appropriate gothic castle style in 1802 by William Atkinson, a pupil of James Wyatt. Its interiors, with some splendid gothic touches, have been carefully restored and are almost too tidy and neat – a little hotel-like. There are outstanding collections of ivory figures and porcelain (Meissen, Sevres, Derby, Chelsea, Worcester and more).

Extensive grounds and gardens with maze, Moot Hill chapel, tearoom, shops.

Signposted on A93 Perth to Blairgowrie road, 3 miles north of Perth.

Scone Palace: the former accommodation ranges of Scone Abbey, remodelled in gothic style in 1802

See also...

Alloa Tower
Alloa, Clackmannanshire
National Trust for Scotland, ££, open Apr to Oct, daily
Largest tower in Scotland, built in the 1300s by the Earls of Mar with unusual alterations of the early 1700s. With furniture of various periods.

Balmoral Castle
Near Ballater, Aberdeenshire
Her Majesty the Queen, £££, open mid-Apr to Jul, daily
The Royal family's holiday home, bought by Prince Albert in 1852. Only the grounds and gardens and an exhibition in the ballroom are open.

Blair Castle
Pitlochry, Perthshire
Privately owned, £££, open Apr to Oct, daily
One of the grandest of Scots baronial castles and the most High Victorian in feel, with ornate interiors and lots of armour everywhere.

Culross Palace
Culross, Fife
National Trust for Scotland, £££, open Easter to Sep, daily
Fine Renaissance palace of 1567–1611 with much original painted decoration.

Stirling Castle: severe-looking fortress, hiding great hall of about 1500 and Renaissance palace of 1540s

Drummuir Castle
Near Keith, Banffshire
Privately owned, ££, open Sep, daily (also two weekends in Aug), tours only
Victorian gothic castle-style house of 1842 with tall lantern tower.

Lickleyhead Castle
Near Insch, Aberdeenshire
Privately owned, free, open Jun to late Sep, Tu, S
Tower of about 1450 remodelled in baronial style in 1629.

Monzie Castle
Crieff, Perthshire
Privately owned (HHA), ££, open mid-May to mid-Jun, daily
House of 1791 rebuilt and furnished after fire in 1908 by the architect Sir Robert Lorimer.

The Pineapple House
Near Airth, Falkirk
National Trust for Scotland and Landmark Trust, free, open all year, daily (grounds only)
Surely the most eccentric building in Britain, built in 1761 as a garden retreat, in the shape of a pineapple. It is now used as a holiday cottage, so the public can only view it from the gardens (or rent it).

Provost Skene's House
Guest Row, Aberdeen
Local council, ££, open all year, daily
'Burgh' town house of 1500s with plasterwork ceilings of 1600s, plus Georgian and Edwardian interiors.

Stirling Castle
Stirling
Historic Scotland, £££, open all year, daily
Royal castle and palace of the kings of Scotland, with splendid great hall of about 1500, recently restored to its full glory, and Renaissance-style palace of about 1540.

Blair Castle: an extravagant Victorian Scots baronial transformation of a castle of the 1200s

Scottish Highlands and Islands
Highlands, West Highlands, Skye, Western Isles and Orkney

The Black House, Isle of Lewis

Historic Scotland • ££ • Open all year, M-F, S

A very far cry from the stately homes of the wealthy that make up the bulk of this book, but a place that nobody who visits Britain's remote north-western coast should leave without seeing. Typical of the sort of dwelling lived in by the island crofters and smallholders until very recently, the Black House looks like something out of the ancient past – indeed, there are ruined neolithic houses over 5,000 years old that are very similar in their layout – but in fact this one was built in the 19th century and lived in until 1964.

It consists of a kitchen and bedroom, to the left of the entrance, and a byre to the right, where cows could be kept, with a small barn attached at the back. A peat fire burns on the open hearth in the centre of the kitchen floor; a pot hangs over it on a chain; in the bedroom are three small box beds. It's wonderfully evocative of a life not long gone, but certainly gone.

Signposted off A858 in Arnol village, 16 miles north-west of Stornoway.

The Black House, Arnol: a typical crofter's dwelling on an ancient pattern, in use up until the 1960s

Castle of Mey, Caithness

Privately owned • £££ • Open late May to Jul and mid-Aug to mid-Oct, Tu-F, S & Su

Delightfully, the Castle of Mey is exactly what you would expect of the private home of Queen Elizabeth the Queen Mother, who died in 2001. It has something of the haphazard air of a holiday cottage, with a random assortment of comfortable furniture and lots of very unpretentious knick-knacks cluttering the place up; and though it is, after all, a castle, and certainly has its regal moments, it is far less formal than it might be. And yes, it will appeal to non-royalists too.

The castle is a tower house on a Z-plan (that is, with a central block and projecting towers on diagonally opposite corners) built in 1566–72 by George, 4th Earl of Caithness and lived in by his son William, the 1st Lord of Mey. It was bought by the Queen Mother in 1952, shortly after the death of her husband, King George VI. The views over the sea to Orkney are superb.

Greatly modernized, the castle has no particular architectural or historical distinction beyond its famous owner. But it does contain many items of significance from her life, including a superb model of the first *Queen Elizabeth*, which she launched, and paintings by Prince Philip and Prince Charles. More engaging, however, are the personal touches: the sprinkling of stuffed toys that were a running joke with her equerries, and even jigsaws of the royal yacht, *Britannia*.

Gardens, shop.

On A836 Thurso to John O'Groats road, just east of Mey village.

The Castle of Mey: a tower house of 1566-72, the private home of Queen Elizabeth, the Queen Mother

Cawdor Castle: an ancient tower of about 1380, with courtyard dwelling ranges improved in about 1700

Cawdor Castle, Nairn

Privately owned (HHA) • £££ • Open May to mid-Oct, daily

One of the most enjoyable to visit of all the lived-in Scottish castles, and also one of the most picturesque, having avoided the massive expansions and alterations that afflicted – and sometimes enhanced – so many in Victorian times, when 'Scots baronial' was at its trendiest. Cawdor is on a far smaller and more comfortable scale, and the severe old defensive tower at its centre still dominates.

The tower was probably built in the late 1300s, and was, most unusually and for no known reason, built around a living holly tree, which can still be seen in the vaulted basement; it must have died straight away through lack of light, and has been dated to about 1372.

The castle was the home of the local bigwigs, the Thanes of Cawdor, until the last thane died and his young daughter was kidnapped by the Earl of Argyll. In 1510, aged 12, she was married to the earl's younger son, Sir John Campbell, from whom is descended the family that still lives here today.

Improvements were made to the castle from the 1670s to 1702 by Sir Hugh Campbell, whose nephew was the architect Colen Campbell. Sir Hugh improved the old hall by the tower and developed the courtyard ranges in a tidy, up-to-date style with restrained classical touches. After his death in 1716, the family quit Scotland for about 100 years and the castle was left alone.

Further extensions were built in the late 1800s, but these blended in sympathetically, and the result is a house that looks ancient and, except for the tower, all of a piece. Inside, its furnishing and decoration is a happy blend of everything that has pitched up at the place over the years, but clearly assembled with a discerning eye. The castle is lived in and has been sensitively modernized to become almost too comfortable and friendly for its ancient walls.

A visit is made particularly enjoyable by the the drily witty tone of the guidebook and accompanying room notes, written by the 6th Earl of Cawdor, and by the eclectic scope of the art collection, from ancient family portraits to modern Japanese sculpture. Among the finest older pieces is a set of Flemish tapestries shipped over from the Low Countries by Sir Hugh in the late 1600s.

Extensive gardens, tearoom, shop.

Signposted on B9090, off A96 5 miles south-west of Nairn.

Duart Castle, Isle of Mull

Privately owned (HHA) • £££ • Open Apr, M-F & Su, May to early Oct, daily

Not the formidable stronghold it first appears, but in fact a sensitive and comfortable restoration in the same Arts and Crafts tradition that inspired Sir Edwin Lutyens (who did a similar job at Lindisfarne Castle in Northumberland), completed in 1912 by the Scottish architect Sir John Burnet for Colonel Sir Fitzroy Maclean, who had bought the ancient, ruined seat of his clan in 1911.

Duart has possibly the most attractive setting of any house in Britain, perched on a rock beside the Sound of Mull with views up Loch Linnhe to the mountains of the Highlands; Ben Nevis can easily be seen on a clear day. To make the most of this view, with shipping drifting idly past, Burnet added a wonderfully simple gallery on the seaward side of the house, known as the sea room. It's well worth spending a few minutes here, especially if the weather is a little too rough for the even finer views

from the wall walk on the roof of the keep to be properly appreciated.

The oldest parts of the castle date from about 1360, but it was denied to the Macleans after the clan fought for the Jacobite cause in the 1680s, and was garrisoned by English troops, slowly decaying, until it was finally abandoned in 1751.

The restoration is consistently plain and unpretentious, making the most of the original stonework and other features of the building. Only a few rooms are open to visitors, and those are mostly in the keep and clearly set aside as public spaces – the topmost room, for example, is devoted to a small clan museum – so the feeling of visiting a lived-in house is not what it might be.

But there are personal touches, too: the chintzy decoration of the state bedroom was carried out for Sir Charles Maclean and his wife, when they spent their honeymoon here during the Second World War.

Tearoom, shop.

On minor road off A849, 3 miles south-east of Craignure ferry terminal.

Duart Castle, below: in ruins from 1751, but restored as a comfortable house after 1911

Dunrobin Castle: extended and given its fairytale appearance by Sir Charles Barry in the late 1800s

Dunrobin Castle, Sutherland

Privately owned (HHA) • £££ • Open Apr to mid-Oct, daily

It looks like a French chateau crossed with a Disney fairytale castle – so much so that it is almost comical – but Dunrobin is actually a genuinely ancient castle. It was added to and modified in stages over three centuries, achieving something like its present form in the late 1800s, when it was rebuilt by the architect of the Houses of Parliament, Sir Charles Barry, for the 2nd Duke of Sutherland, whose father amassed immense wealth through investments in industry and made himself hated for the speed and ferocity of the 'clearances' by which he turfed thousands of people off the land. Unfortunately, a fire in 1915 destroyed parts of Barry's castle, and it was rebuilt in a somewhat debased form.

Easily the most fascinating of its interiors are the palatial rooms created by Barry and remodelled after the fire by Sir Robert Lorimer. Most have an early 17th-century feel, with fine pseudo-Jacobean plaster ceilings and friezes, but the scale and the richness of the furnishing is typically Victorian, particularly in Lorimer's drawing room, where the furniture is French – largely Louis XV – and well suited to the *faux-chateau* exterior.

There are some superb portraits, by artists such as Ramsay, Romney and Reynolds; it is particularly fascinating to compare the Reynolds portrait of Elizabeth, Duchess-Countess of Sutherland with another by John Hoppner.

Formal gardens, falconry displays, museum of Pictish carved stones, tearoom, shop.

Signposted on A9 Inverness to Thurso road, 1 mile north of Golspie, 50 miles north of Inverness.

Eilean Donan Castle: a tower of the late 1300s, restored as a comfortable home in 1911–32

Eilean Donan Castle, Wester Ross

Privately owned • ££ • Open Mar to Nov, daily

One of Scotland's most picturesque and most photographed castles, sitting on a small island near the shore of Loch Duich, and reached by a stone bridge. Like Duart Castle on Mull (above), it was restored as a house in the early 20th century, having been in ruins for years.

The castle, the oldest parts of which date from the late 1300s, was being held by Spanish troops as part of a minor Jacobite uprising in 1719, when three British frigates sailed up the sea loch and pounded it into submission with cannon fire. It was left abandoned and crumbling until 1911, when Lieutenant-Colonel John MacRae-Gilstrap, a descendant of the MacRae family who had owned it since the early 1500s, bought it to restore.

An accurate restoration was thought to be impossible, because no records of the original layout survived; but in 1932, within weeks of the the rebuilding being finished, a full and detailed set of drawings from about 1700 was discovered.

The castle is smaller than it looks and consists of just two blocks: the keep or tower, and a smaller accommodation block on the other side of the walled courtyard.

The rooms on show are principally in the keep, plus the 1930s kitchens, where much of the original equipment is intact and the preparations for a big dinner have been reconstructed.

The lowest room in the keep, a sort of informal living room, is thought to have originally been a billet for off-duty soldiers. Its main feature is a superb stone barrel-vaulted roof. Upstairs is a dining room (called, in pretentiously baronial style, the banqueting hall), heated by a vast baronial fireplace. The ceiling has wooden beams brought from America. All manner of Jacobite memorabilia is on display, including a lock of Bonnie Prince Charlie's hair.

Most pleasing of all, however, are the small but comfortable bedrooms at the top of the house, cosily equipped with the comforts of the 1930s, which make you wish you were a guest for the weekend.

Restaurant, shop.

On A87 Invergarry to Kyle of Lochalsh road, 8 miles east of Kyle of Lochalsh.

Inverary Castle, Argyll

Privately owned (HHA) • £££ • Open Apr to May and Oct, M-Th, S & Su, Jun to Aug daily

A very odd-looking house, its round, conical-roofed towers and pointy arched windows giving it a strong flavour of Strawberry Hill gothic with a hint of French chateau, while the square, battlemented, medieval-style towers of the top-lit armoury hall at its centre make it look as though someone's dropped a church on it. Built between 1745 and 1790 for the Dukes of Argyll, who still live here, it was designed by Roger Morris, who worked with Vanbrugh and helped Lord Pembroke create the Palladian bridge at Wilton in Wiltshire, with interiors by Robert Mylne, later surveyor at St Paul's Cathedral and the designer of Blackfriars Bridge.

The interiors are more successful than the exterior. Particularly splendid is the state dining room, with a wonderful Adam-style ceiling decorated by the French painters Girard and Guinand. Their only surviving work in Britain is

Inverary Castle: an unusual gothic creation of 1745–90 by Roger Morris, with some Adam-style interiors

See also...

Balfour Castle
Shapinsay, Orkney
Privately owned, £££, open mid-May to mid-Sep, Su only, tours only
Superb Victorian castle-style house built in 1846–50 by David Bryce, the leading Scots baronial architect, for David Balfour; still lived in by the Balfour family. Wonderful island setting; entrance fee includes ferry trip from Mainland of Orkney and afternoon tea.

Dunvegan Castle
Dunvegan, Isle of Skye
Privately owned, £££, open all year, daily
Rather plain Scots baronial rebuilding, in the 1800s, of an ancient castle. The interiors aren't exciting, but there are a few unusual and interesting items on show, including a thank-you letter written by Dr Johnson after he stayed. Attractive gardens.

here: that in the equally French-influenced tapestry drawing room, for which the ceiling actually was designed by Robert Adam, is just as fine. None of the other rooms, save perhaps the dramatic armoury hall, can match the delicate splendour of these two.

Gardens, restaurant, shop.

Signposted on A83 Tarbet to Inverary road, just west of Inverary.

Torosay Castle, Isle of Mull

Privately owned (HHA) • £££ • Open Apr to Oct, daily

A Victorian mansion completed in 1858 by the Edinburgh architect David Bryce, the leading exponent of the the Scots baronial style, for John Campbell, the owner of a sugar-importing business, whose father had bought the land here, including an existing Georgian house, from the Duke of Argyll. Campbell's family were greatly pleased with the house, but his fortunes went downhill during the American Civil War and in 1865 he was forced to sell to Arbuthnot Charles Guthrie, the son of a merchant banker from Fife, whose descendants still live here today.

The superb gardens, laid out by Sir Robert Lorimer in about 1900, are actually more of an attraction than the house, but it's worth a look inside while you're here. The principal rooms are comfortable but ordinary, but the displays of family memorabilia in the Viking and archive rooms are fascinating.

Extensive gardens (open all year, daily), tearoom, shop.

Signposted on A849 2 miles south of Craignure ferry terminal.

Torosay Castle: a mansion of 1858 designed by David Bryce, leading exponent of the Scots baronial style

Index of house names

Main entries in normal type; *'See also' entries in italic*